Buddhist Poetry and Colonialism

Buddhist Poetry and Colonialism

Alagiyavanna and the Portuguese in Sri Lanka

STEPHEN C. BERKWITZ

OXFORD
UNIVERSITY PRESS

OXFORD
UNIVERSITY PRESS

Oxford University Press is a department of the University of Oxford.
It furthers the University's objective of excellence in research, scholarship,
and education by publishing worldwide.

Oxford New York
Auckland Cape Town Dar es Salaam Hong Kong Karachi
Kuala Lumpur Madrid Melbourne Mexico City Nairobi
New Delhi Shanghai Taipei Toronto

With offices in
Argentina Austria Brazil Chile Czech Republic France Greece
Guatemala Hungary Italy Japan Poland Portugal Singapore
South Korea Switzerland Thailand Turkey Ukraine Vietnam

Published in the United States of America by
Oxford University Press
198 Madison Avenue, New York, NY 10016

Library of Congress Cataloging-in-Publication Data
Berkwitz, Stephen C., 1969–
Buddhist poetry and colonialism : Alagiyavanna and the Portuguese
in Sri Lanka / Stephen C. Berkwitz.
pages cm
Includes bibliographical references and index.
ISBN 978–0–19–993578–9 (pbk. : alk. paper) – ISBN 978–0–19–993576–5
(hardcover : alk. paper)
1. Buddhism—Sri Lanka—History—16th century. 2. Buddhism –
Sri Lanka—History—17th century. 3. Buddhism and culture—Sri Lanka.
4. Portugal—Colonies—Asia—Religion. 5. Alagiyavanna Mukaveti,
16th cent.—Criticism and interpretation. 6. Buddhist poetry, Sinhalese—
History and criticism. I. Title.
BQ372.B47 2013
294.3095493—dc23
2012022334

ISBN 978–0–19–993578–9

Dedicated with love to Imali, Rashmi, and Anjuli, who played crucial supporting roles in the formation of this book

Contents

Preface

EARLY IN 1996, while searching bookstores in the Maradana neighborhood of Colombo, I walked into Ratna Book Publishers and asked the clerk if there were any old Sinhala books. The man disappeared into the back and emerged a few minutes later with an old copy of *Kusa Jātaka Kāvyaya* by Alagiyavanna Mukaveṭi. I bought it without knowing much about it and stored it away with the other texts that I was collecting as a graduate student in Sri Lanka. Around ten years later, when I decided to choose a new book project, I turned back to that old book bought by chance and began to sketch out an idea for a monograph on the poetry of Alagiyavanna. In the intervening decade, I had completed a book on Sinhala Buddhist *vaṃsas* and became somewhat more familiar with the outlines of Sinhala literature. I had learned that Alagiyavanna was a notable Sinhala poet, and that he had written several works near the end of the so-called classical period of Sinhala literature. Further, he converted to Catholicism late in life and worked under the Portuguese colonialists, giving him an exceptionally interesting life story.

This book also has its own, distinctive history. Being the product of research and writing conducted in Sri Lanka, Portugal, the United States, and Germany, it has developed in ways that I could have never foreseen back when I started this work in 2005, much less in 1996 and that fateful visit to a Colombo bookshop. *Buddhist Poetry and Colonialism* is an attempt to understand the relationships between literature, culture, and history in an eventful period in early modern Buddhist history. As such, I found it necessary to study Sinhala Buddhist poetry (*kavi*) and the history of Portuguese colonialism in Asia so that I could begin to draw some conclusions about the significance of Alagiyavanna's life and work. I learned to read and interpret the *eḷu* poetic form of Sinhala writing, which is substantially different from both prose writing and colloquial speech.

I also began to take classes in the Portuguese language in order to consult sources that in some ways were in dialogue with Alagiyavanna's writings. The ambitiousness of this approach has always been evident to me, but I persisted in these efforts in the hope of contributing something of value to the study of Buddhist literature and history in sixteenth- and early seventeenth-century Sri Lanka.

A number of different organizations supplied me with crucial institutional support to pursue the research and writing of this book. The US-Sri Lanka Fulbright Association awarded me a Senior Fulbright Fellowship from the US State Department to read and translate Alagiyavanna's poetic works in Sri Lanka. Missouri State University awarded me a sabbatical to write first drafts of several chapters and, later, a Summer Faculty Fellowship to collect and read Portuguese materials in Lisbon. The Käte Hamburger Kolleg in Ruhr-Universität Bochum provided me the time and resources of a Visiting Research Fellowship courtesy of the German Federal Ministry of Education and Research to finish the manuscript. In Sri Lanka, the University of Colombo served as my host institution for my Fulbright research. The libraries at the Royal Asiatic Society of Sri Lanka and the University of Peradeniya supplied with me important resources for my research. Likewise, in Portugal, the Centro da História de Além-Mar at the Universidade Nova de Lisboa and the Biblioteca Nacional de Portugal assisted me in my efforts to locate and read some valuable sources about the Portuguese in Sri Lanka.

All along, I have incurred many debts from people who have given me valuable assistance and advice related to this project. I am fortunate to have consulted regularly with P. B. Meegaskumbura, Wimal Wijeratne, and Charles Halliesy about Sinhala poetry and Alagiyavanna's works, and they generously shared with me their considerable knowledge of these subjects. Several scholars consented to read a chapter or two of my manuscript, offering their valuable feedback on my arguments and sources. I thus gratefully acknowledge the insightful comments of Ananda Abeysekara, Jorge Flores, Jack Llewellyn, Eric Nelson, Alan Strathern, Ashley Thompson, and Kevin Trainor on my text. Several MA students in my seminar on South Asian poetry at Missouri State University read through two draft chapters and gave helpful feedback. I also wish to thank the anonymous referees who read through the entire manuscript, offering important and relevant advice. These individuals all helped substantially to improve this book, although I am, of course, solely responsible for any errors or other shortcomings herein.

Many others assisted my research by suggesting resources, sharing ideas, and providing me with materials for the book. I am particularly grateful to Herbert Kumar Alagiyawanna, a living descendent of the poet, who shared his knowledge of his ancestor, introduced me to other relatives, and took me around to visit the family's ancestral lands in Sri Lanka. P. B. Meegaskumbura, Rohini Paranavitana, and Sandamale Wijenayake provided me with critically important sources for my research on Alagiyavanna. C. R. de Silva, W. S. Karunatillake, Ranjini Obeyesekere, K. D. Paranavitana, Asanga Tilakaratne, and Nira Wickremasinghe contributed important insights on Sri Lankan literature and history from which I have benefited greatly. Similarly, Steven Collins, Christoph Emmrich, Sherry Harlacher, Elizabeth Harris, and Ulrike Roesler shared helpful ideas on Buddhism that I have incorporated into the book. My work in Portugal and in the Portuguese language was facilitated by the generous assistance of Zoltán Biedermann, Jorge Flores, Malu Hayes, Christopher Larkosh, Timothy Walker, and Ângela Barreto Xavier. I also wish to thank Jane Terry for making a fine map of Sri Lanka and South India specifically for this book.

I wish to thank Cynthia Read at Oxford University Press for her interest and support for a book project that eludes simple categorization. Her encouragement and advocacy on my behalf are greatly appreciated. I am also grateful to Marcela Maxfield, Molly Morrison, and Maria Pucci for their efforts in ushering this book through the production process to publication. It is no exaggeration to say that I could not have finished this book without their help.

I presented papers related to this work in several different academic venues, all of which gave me the chance to test out my ideas prior to publication. These include invited talks given at the Oxford Centre for Buddhist Studies, the Symposium on the Seethawaka Kingdom, University of Pennsylvania, Arizona State University, University of Massachusetts-Dartmouth, and the Postgraduate Institute of Pali and Buddhist Studies. I also delivered papers on Alagiyavanna's works at the Association for Asian Studies Annual Meeting in 2010, the 35th Annual Conference on South Asia at the University of Wisconsin-Madison in 2006, and the XIVth Conference of the International Association of Buddhist Studies in 2005.

I am deeply gratified by the interest and assistance that so many people have given to this work. The years of research and writing involved in *Buddhist Poetry and Colonialism* have been challenging and time consuming, but the contributions of teachers and colleagues mentioned above have made this work possible and extremely satisfying. Finally, I must also acknowledge the invaluable support of my family and friends, especially Imali, Rashmi, and Anjuli for their patience and encouragement with my work on a daily basis.

Finally, I should note that all translations of Sinhala, Pali, and Portuguese are mine unless otherwise noted in the text or the endnotes. I have endeavored to include the original transliterated verses of poetic quatrains in the endnotes for those who wish to check my translations. I have followed the conventional usage of inserting diacritical marks with the exception of not marking the half-nasal *m* in Sinhala, as this mark is unique to the language and generally available only in specialized font packages that are difficult to use and create headaches in the publication process. In addition, for stylistic reasons but not for a lack of respect, I have chosen to leave out the honorific title of "Venerable" in the names of monks.

Timeline

1467 Death of King Parākramabāhu VI, ending unified Sri Lankan kingdom centered in Koṭṭe

1498 Vasco da Gama arrives in India

1499 Portuguese King Manuel I declares himself "Lord of Navigation, Conquest, and Commerce of Ethiopia, Arabia, Persia, and India"

1506 Dom Lourenço de Almeida lands a Portuguese ship in Colombo

1510 Portuguese establish the headquarters for Estado da Índia in Goa

1518 Portuguese construct a fort in Colombo

1521 King Vijayabāhu VI of Koṭṭe assassinated, his three sons divide and rule regional kingdoms of Koṭṭe, Sītāvaka, and Rayigama

1540 Foundation of the Society of Jesus under Ignatius Loyola in Europe

1541 King Bhuvanekabāhu of Koṭṭe sends golden image of grandson Dharmapāla to Lisbon, where he is recognized as the heir to the kingdom

1543 João de Vila de Conde arrived and launched mission in Ceilão with fellow Franciscans

1551 King Bhuvanekabāhu killed and succeeded by young grandson Dharmapāla

1552 Alagiyavanna Mukaveṭi born in Hissälla

1557 Dharmapāla converts to Catholicism, is renamed Dom João Dharmapāla, and transfers temple lands to Franciscan friars

1562 Māyādunnē's son Tikiri Banḍāra (later Rājasiṃha I) leads Sītāvaka army to defeat Portuguese-led force at Mulleriyāva

1567 Council of Goa announces policy to restrict practice of non-Christian religions in *Estado da Índia*

1579–81 Tikiri Banḍāra leads siege on Portuguese fort in Colombo

1580	Union of Portuguese and Spanish crowns under King Philip II of Spain; Dharmapāla bequeaths his kingdom to Portuguese crown
1581	Māyādunnē dies; his son Rājasiṃha I assumes throne in Sītāvaka
1582	Rājasiṃha I attacks and subdues kingdom of Kandy
1587–88	Rājasiṃha I undertakes last siege of Colombo fort but fails to expel Portuguese
1591	Portuguese dethrone the king of Jaffnapatnam, assume control over northern region
1593	Death of Rājasiṃha I
1594	Koṭṭe Kingdom under Dharmapāla and Portuguese annex Sītāvaka kingdom
1594	Dom Jerónimo de Azevedo begins a long tenure as captain-general of Ceilão
1597	Dom João Dharmapāla dies; Portuguese assume direct control over Koṭṭe kingdom
1602	Jesuits arrive in Ceilão; Dutch ship anchors in Batticaloa
1603	Portuguese assault on Kandy is repelled
1604	Death of King Vimaladharmasūriya followed by succession quarrel in Kandy
1612	Alagiyavanna converts to Catholicism; De Azevedo leaves Colombo to become viceroy in Goa
1613	Work on Portuguese land register (*tombo*) commences with assistance of Alagiyavanna
1616–19	Large-scale Sinhala revolts against Portuguese rule
1618	Alagiyavanna petitions king of Portugal to have his lands and title restored to him; Dom Constantino de Sá de Noronha arrives as new captain-general in Ceilão
1619	Sá de Noronha and Portuguese-led force defeat Sinhala rebellion led by António Barreto
1622	Last mention of Alagiyavanna in a written source
1630	Portuguese army routed by Kandyan force at Randenivala and Sá de Noronha is killed
1656	Portuguese fort in Colombo surrenders to Dutch forces
1658	Last Portuguese presence expelled from Ceilão by the Dutch

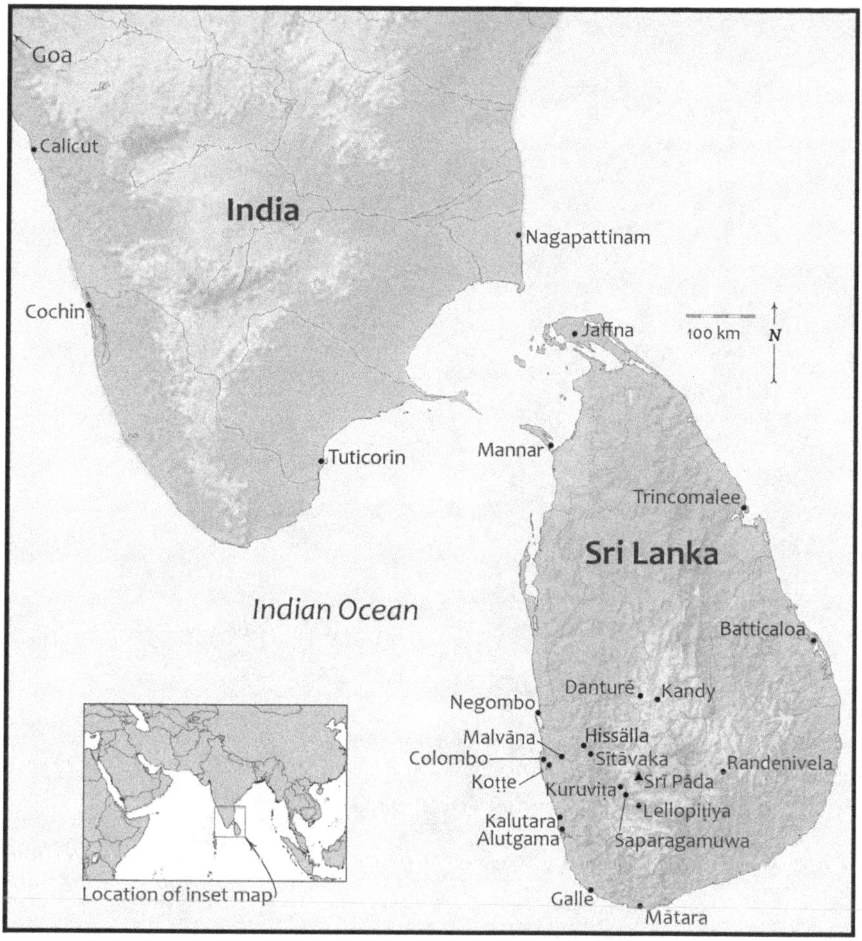

Map of Sri Lanka and South India in the Sixteenth and Seventeenth Centuries

Buddhist Poetry and Colonialism

I

Buddhist Literary Culture in Early Modern Ceilão

THE DECADES AROUND the turn of the seventeenth century were a turbulent but critical period for the Buddhist religion in Sri Lanka. Often spoken of as a dark age for Sinhala Buddhism and culture, it was marked by the expansion of Portuguese colonialism in the island. This was arguably the first time in history that a predominantly Buddhist society came under colonial control. The violence of this era, reflected in the many battles fought and religious sites destroyed, has largely pushed aside any sustained examination of how Buddhists in Sri Lanka reacted to the monumental changes ushered in by Portuguese colonial, military, and missionary agents.[1] At the same time, the focus on political history in early modern Ceilão (the term used for Sri Lanka by the Portuguese) has often overshadowed research on the history of Buddhist literature during this era. The present volume seeks to address these gaps by focusing on the literary works of a poet named Alagiyavanna Mukaveṭi (1552–ca.1625?), who composed poetry in the Sinhala language from around 1580 to 1620. Little known outside Sri Lanka, he stands as a remarkable figure who wrote poetry and served under both Sinhala and Portuguese rulers. From what little evidence of his life that survives through his poetry, scant archival materials, and oral histories, he appears as a privileged yet complicated individual. Alagiyavanna lived and worked at the point at which traditional Sinhala culture and Portuguese power encountered each other and competed for ascendancy. As such, Alagiyavanna's work is among the best surviving indices for understanding the effects of colonialism on Buddhism and Sinhala culture during the incipient stages of this momentous historical encounter between Asia and Europe.

The interests and approach of this book are somewhat unconventional for the study of Buddhism. Whereas many works in Buddhist studies focus on the Buddha or on monks, Alagiyavanna was a layman whose adherence to Buddhism would eventually be undermined by his conversion to Catholicism. Few people would think to look to him as an authoritative voice on the Buddhist religion. Further, while many scholars of Buddhism focus on its ancient history or, increasingly, its modern formulations, this book directs attention to what historians often call the early modern period in South Asian Buddhism. Research on Alagiyavanna and his works raises a host of interesting questions about how Buddhism is expressed as a system of practice and defined as an object of knowledge. This book aims to shed light on various aspects of the Buddhist religion that are often overlooked, including a consideration of how Buddhism was expressed and transformed by the historical encounters between local and foreign agents in the sixteenth and seventeenth centuries. Alagiyavanna's poetry offers a valuable perspective with which to understand how the religion began to undergo significant changes through contacts with European colonialists. Following Sanjay Subrahmanyam, who dates the early modern epoch between roughly 1350 and 1750, we can take stock in how the history of Buddhism in this period begins to be a "connected history," wherein Buddhist agents interact in increasing intensity with Portuguese Christians.[2] In other words, the history of Buddhism in early modern Sri Lanka is a history shaped by and through the interactions that Buddhists such as Alagiyavanna had with various colonial actors. To see Buddhism as a tradition that is imagined and discursively constructed through encounters with another religion and culture invites us to reinterpret the boundaries of the religion as more permeable and less essential than what is often assumed.

Related to the issue of how Buddhism was fashioned in early modernity, how poetry worked to transform and redefine Buddhist identity around the turn of the seventeenth century in Sri Lanka will also be considered. Alagiyavanna's writings speak directly to important shifts that took place in the ways that one expressed oneself as a devotee of the Buddha. His early poems maintained a fidelity to traditional religious understandings of devotion and authority that permeated Sinhala literature from at least the medieval period. Yet, as the Portuguese expanded and assumed control over much of lowland Sri Lanka, Alagiyavanna's ways of defining Buddhist identity became more assertive, exclusive, and self-conscious. Although his works address contemporary Buddhist practice only sporadically, his treatment of literary expressions of Buddhism yields insights into how Sinhala Buddhists could change their conceptions of religious identity during a period of intensified contact with European power. The contacts that Alagiyavanna and others like him had with the Portuguese spurred new ways of thinking about what it meant to be a devotee of the Buddha.

This book will also consider the role of poetry in the development of Buddhist literature and tradition. Canonical discourses, philosophical treatises, and biographical narratives comprise the subjects of most scholarly studies and translations. Buddhist poetry, however, is a literary form that has received comparatively less scholarly attention and is in need of more attention and analysis. Poetry's aesthetic and formal requirements often make such works difficult to read and interpret. It is also possible (although not advisable) to see such characteristics as largely secular or technical in nature and thus only marginally important to the understanding of the religion. However, poetry is an important medium for expressing Buddhist truths and values. In the case of Sinhala Buddhist poetry, the composition of verse works in accordance with recognizable meters and figures of speech drew on Indic poetic models for a literary genre that could effect change in the world. Well-written poems could in theory generate particular sentiments and emotional responses in an audience, conditioning different ways of thinking and acting in the world. The aesthetically rich verses of classical Indic poetry—*kāvya* in Sanskrit—could evoke valued aesthetic experiences, affirm distinctions of social status and connoisseurship, and enhance the power and majesty of the subjects of its composition.[3] Although it is far from clear that all of the presumptions about Sanskrit court poetry in classical India were recognized and influential in early modern Sri Lanka, it is important to note that the Buddhist poetry of Alagiyavanna could still be viewed as a cultural tool to influence and change the world through the skillful use of literature.

Alagiyavanna's works succeeded in both sustaining older literary norms and revising certain presuppositions about the roles that poetry may serve in Sinhala society. Aspects of his works are quite conventional and formulaic, betraying their dependence on numerous other works of Sinhala poetry. Where Alagiyavanna's works appear derivative, we may infer that he wished to honor local poetic traditions and demonstrate his skill in writing in this same manner. At the same time, other aspects of his works strike out in new directions. Over time he sought to simplify and popularize the genre of Sinhala poetry in order to edify and appeal to a broader audience of Sinhala speakers than could be found in the royal courts, which formed the original settings for much ancient Indic poetry.

As such, we see in Alagiyavanna's works evidence of a certain historical transformation in the interests and characteristics of Sinhala Buddhist literature, a transformation that coincided with the development of colonial power in the island.

Alagiyavanna recognized how poetry could be a performance of power, which is to say that its particular expressions could be used to influence the ways that people think, feel, and act in the world. As a capacity possessed or claimed by various persons and institutions, power here is not equivalent to force but rather evokes what Michel Foucault describes as the ability to act upon the actions of others.[4] Thus, when Alagiyavanna praises specific rulers or speaks eloquently about royal and religious ideals, the poet is engaging in transactions of power, seeking to compel action and influence events without the threat of violence or force. His poetry reflects a mode of literary composition that enables its subjects and its author to be presented in ideal terms as agents who can effect real, desired changes in the world. Significantly, in Alagiyavanna's works, poetry is an aesthetically rich, discursive form that generates effects through the articulation of language and ideas through the forms and contents of its verses. This power of poetry could be used to enhance, influence, and even contest the power wielded by kings, gods, and colonial rulers. Possessing a poet's skills to manipulate language and make reality conform to an ideal vision, Alagiyavanna appears to have used poetry as an instrument of power, enabling him to wield some degree of influence over the turbulent world in which he lived.

Furthermore, the historical relations between Buddhism and colonialism are examined. This particular subject has emerged with some frequency in recent years, as scholars have sought to find ways to explain the distinctive forms of the religion in modernity. Working in the wake of postcolonial theory, some scholars of Buddhist studies have likewise sought to assess the impact of colonial power on the study and practice of the religion in various Asian contexts. One notable example of such research is the 1995 volume *Curators of the Buddha: The Study of Buddhism under Colonialism.*[5] This path-breaking text examines colonialism as a determinative factor in the development of Buddhist studies as a modern academic field. Focused on nineteenth- and twentieth-century colonial formations, the book is limited both in its historical scope and by its emphasis on Euro-American interpretations of the religion. Our inquiry into Alagiyavanna's poetry expands upon earlier research by considering the earliest era of colonialism in Asia and, specifically, Asian Buddhist responses. As a field of inquiry, postcolonialism urges us to listen to the voices of the colonized and to avoid complicity in colonial endeavors to disempower the "native" by accepting hegemonic European discourses about the world as authoritative. Thus, it is imperative to go beyond a critique of colonial discourses. We must also study the discourses of colonized peoples who were subject to imperial and colonial authorities.

Alagiyavanna, the early modern poet, magistrate, and civil servant, is precisely the kind of native voice that has long eluded scholars of colonial history. His poetic writings and the few references to him found in other sources depict several possible responses to the imposition of colonial power in Asia. Moreover, his appearance near the beginning of a period of more than five hundred years of European presence in Sri Lanka allows us to view the impact of colonialism on Sinhala Buddhist culture differently from the perspectives found in other works. When speaking of Buddhist responses to colonialism, many scholars cite the phenomenon of "Protestant Buddhism." First used in 1970 by the esteemed Sinhala anthropologist Gananath Obeyesekere, the concept of Protestant Buddhism was meant to signify a new form of Buddhism that arose in the late nineteenth and twentieth centuries in Sri Lanka as a protest against British colonial rule and the activities of Protestant missionaries in the island. At the same time, it was marked by the tendency among urban, well-educated Sinhala Buddhists to adopt some of the main characteristics of Protestant Christianity into a revitalized form of modern Buddhism. Influenced by the Victorian-ethical ideas of British educators and missionaries, these Buddhists reinterpreted their religion along similar lines, stressing rational and egalitarian values whereby individual Buddhists are encouraged to permeate their lives with their religion while making Buddhism permeate their whole society through public expressions of Buddhist symbols and faith.[6] The interpretive utility of Protestant Buddhism has led many other scholars to employ the concept and seek to trace its historical development.[7]

Yet others have found some of the implications of Protestant Buddhism to be misleading and inaccurate. John Clifford Holt has articulated a cogent critique of the term, claiming that what was once a heuristic category has become reified into a historical phenomenon. He points out several differences between modern Sinhala Buddhism and Protestant Christianity, for example, in the former's emphasis on ritual activities, public holidays, and the adoption of certain monastic practices by laypeople.[8] Such a critique served notice that scholars should be careful not to presume that Protestant

Buddhism was little more than the historical offshoot of Protestant Christianity. In addition, Anne Blackburn has critiqued the presumption that certain features of modern Sinhala Buddhism (i.e., Protestant Buddhism) have their origin in its encounter with British colonialists and missionaries in the nineteenth century. Responding to those who equate the focus on the Pāli Canon with the imitation of Protestant Christianity's privileging of the Bible over other written works, Blackburn argues that Sinhala monks in the eighteenth century came to stress the study of Pāli and canonical texts from the Canon before Western Orientalists did, in large part to create a curriculum that would allow a particular monastic order to gain prestige and authority.[9] In a subsequent book, Blackburn argues that the work of Sinhala Buddhists such as Hikkaḍuvē Sumaṅgala (1827–1911) during the British colonial period could proceed according to indigenous forms of knowledge, associations, and logic relatively free of colonial influence.[10] In this way, she contests the notion of a profound shift in Sinhala Buddhist practice and thought resulting from colonial encounters with the British. In a similar fashion, Elizabeth Harris has argued that Western Orientalists and missionaries who are often credited with driving religious change in nineteenth-century Sri Lanka actually depended on instructions from Sinhala Buddhists. She also asserts that the origins of Protestant Buddhism ought to be pushed back to the eighteenth century when some leading Buddhist monks responded to a Dutch questionnaire by articulating an image of Buddhism that privileged philosophy, reason, and ethics.[11]

The various critiques of Protestant Buddhism are united in their attempts to correct the flawed assumptions in a theory that posits Sinhala Buddhists imitated British missionaries and Orientalist scholars by making Buddhism into a rational, doctrinally based religion, whereby individual laypeople are charged with attaining nirvana by their own efforts. These critiques are helpful in redressing the view that Sinhala Buddhists merely emulated British Protestants, which suggests that cultural mimesis is the only available response to colonial power. The study of Alagiyavanna's poetry, however, suggests a more varied and complicated picture of a range of responses ranging from resisting to accommodating colonialism. His multiple responses belie the presumption that colonized peoples maintained fixed identities and reacted in singular, consistent ways to the colonial experience. Alagiyavanna's case further demonstrates that one should not downplay the impact of European colonialism on Asian societies merely to reassert the agency of those who were colonized.

Moreover, the fact that Alagiyavanna's writings were composed more than two centuries earlier than the works of Sinhala Buddhists who began to protest the representations of their religion by British Protestants suggests that there is a need to extend the history of the encounters between Buddhists and European colonialists further back in time. Prior to the periods of Dutch and British colonialism in Sri Lanka, Alagiyavanna's is one of the earliest Buddhist voices to react to the intrusive presence of European colonialism in a Buddhist society. Significantly, his response to colonialism does not depend on quasi-Protestant notions of scripturalism, laicization, or the purification of the religion. An examination of his poetic works provides a clearer understanding of the early effects of colonialism on Sinhala Buddhist culture and the first steps toward the transformation of Buddhist literature and identity in modernity.

Alagiyavanna Mukaveṭi and His Works

Although Alagiyavanna's career in early modern Sri Lanka corresponds directly to several key issues in the historical development of Buddhism vis-à-vis European colonialism, our knowledge of the author is scant. He is listed as the author of four Sinhala poetic works from the period, and research suggests that he probably wrote a fifth. His name also appears in a few Portuguese language sources from the period, which serve as testimony to his continued importance under colonial rule. Moreover, there are extensive oral traditions preserved in folk literature and among his living descendents who share the Alagiyavanna name in Sri Lanka. Yet a detailed and historically reliable account of this man who lived during the second half of the sixteenth century and the first quarter of the seventeenth century remains elusive. He was born in 1552 in Hissälla near Sabaragamuwa (or Saparagamuwa, modern-day Ratnapura) to a scholarly pandit named Dharmadhvaja; he wrote several poetic works beginning in 1582 extolling King Rājasiṃha I; he received a few villages granted to him by his royal patron; he converted to Catholicism and took the baptismal name *Dom Jerónimo* around 1612; he worked for the Portuguese as a clerk (*mohottiar*) and later as an assistant in compiling the *tombo* or land registry; and he petitioned King Philip III of Portugal around 1618 requesting that his lands and title be restored to him. Reasonable estimates of his death range from about 1622 to 1625. However, aside from Alagiyavanna's works, there are few contemporary Sinhala texts from this period with which to construct a clear history of this poet and his milieu.

Contemporary scholarly interests in material culture and "everyday life" could lead one to disregard the writings of an elite court poet from the sixteenth and seventeenth centuries. Gregory Schopen has argued in regard to the primacy given to textual sources in Buddhist studies that scholars often fail to acknowledge that texts convey ideal notions rather than historical realities and that they "may not even have been known to the vast majority of practicing Buddhists."[12] To the degree that scholars of Buddhism have overestimated the historical value of texts and neglected other sources such as archaeological remains, Schopen offers an important corrective to the field. However, to dismiss the historical significance of written texts for being elite and inaccessible to most people is to ignore the fact that they often contained influential ideas and representations that affected people's worlds or that the normative visions of texts reveal something of how people thought, if not actually acted.[13] Thus, leaving aside the fact that there are few other extant historical sources in Sinhala from this period with which to reconstruct "what really happened" then and there, Alagiyavanna's texts yield insights into how religion, culture, and power were viewed and expressed. His poetry is significant for the interpretations and normative ideals it transmits, as well as for the fact that it bestowed him with a measure of fame and influence in a turbulent period of intercultural encounters and colonial expansion.

Alagiyavanna's poetry is a carefully constructed discourse that could both reflect and alter the world from which it emerged. This dynamic view of what literary texts could accomplish in early modern culture may complement more traditional historical research that seeks to ascertain what really happened in the past. As a scholar of Buddhist literature, I am less interested in actual historical verities than in the portrayal of religious and cultural ideals through literary texts that were composed and circulated precisely to cause certain effects and make a difference in the world.[14] Alagiyavanna's poetry may be historically significant not because it paints a clear and accurate picture of early modern Sri Lanka but because its aesthetics and rhetoric signal for us how he negotiated and responded to some early events in the European colonization of Buddhist Asia. We will see how Alagiyavanna expressed his views, ambitions, and designs through his poetry, expressions that reveal insights into the period's profound shifts in religious identity, textual culture, and political authority. To this end, two complementary methods of reading his works will be utilized: 1) reading them as individual works that contain cohesive messages and interests, and 2) reading them alongside one another as texts that collectively reflect distinct phases in the author's career and in the historical development of Sinhala Buddhist poetry. The study of Alagiyavanna and his works illustrate profound shifts in how Sinhala literature was conceived and used in the sixteenth and seventeenth centuries. At the same time, this study focuses attention on the transformations of what is now called "Buddhism," enabling an investigation of the initial impact of colonialism and Christian missions on how the religion of the Buddha was practiced and conceived.

Alagiyavanna increasingly turned to moralistic discourse in order to render Buddhism into an object of knowledge and to contest the colonial intervention into Sri Lankan society. When Portuguese-sponsored rulers and clerics began to command authority over lowland Sri Lanka around the turn of the seventeenth century, the style and aims of Alagiyavanna's poetry changed markedly. His work began to emphasize a more moralistic, self-conscious identification with the Buddha's teachings as a discernible tradition that can and should be distinguished from other religions and rival claims about truth made by Europeans. Then, in the last decade of his life, Alagiyavanna converted to Catholicism and entered into administrative service under the Portuguese on the island. What appears to be his last verse work mixes older poetic conventions with newer political realities, adapting Sinhala poetry to access and augment the power of Portuguese authorities. Although his poetic writings might not reveal much about actual historical events, they remain "real" in the sense that they comprise representations that were relational, local, and historically contingent.[15] Their historical worth lies in their expressions of the values, interests, and imaginative operations that Alagiyavanna drew on to compose poetry in response to the world in which he lived, a world susceptible to dramatic change yet still changeable through the efforts of a skilled poet like him.

Accordingly, any analysis of Alagiyavanna's works ought to give attention to the various, shifting contexts in which they were produced, circulated, read, and interpreted. This makes it necessary to consider Alagiyavanna's specific institutional and political location when he authored a particular text. His poetic works took on different styles and aesthetic sentiments whether he was serving a Sinhala king or a Portuguese captain-general and whether the Buddhist religion was in ascendancy or in decline. Although there was a Portuguese colonial presence in Sri Lanka throughout Alagiyavanna's entire life, the strength of this presence varied considerably. As such, there is no single, straightforward "colonial context" that could be used to explain Alagiyavanna's works. Such a fact reminds us that colonialism is not a singular phenomenon that impacts local culture in a coherent or uniform manner. The power of the Portuguese in early modern Sri Lanka waxed and waned during Alagiyavanna's life, a fact mirrored in the form and content of his poetic works. Thus, the link between Alagiyavanna's texts and the varying contexts in which they emerged can be used as the means to probe not only what his texts may have meant but also as the means to understand and reengage those same historical contexts with more clarity.[16]

In addition, the interpretive demands made by relating text and context lead to an evaluation of Alagiyavanna as a poet. Under the influence of romanticism—the set of cultural and ideological formations that came to prominence during the late eighteenth and early nineteenth centuries in western Europe—poetry came to be associated with the author's "feelings" and "imagination."[17] Once poets began to free themselves of the constraints of some of the older poetic conventions of meter and rhyme, they were able, so the theory goes, to make their poems more personally expressive of their inner lives. However, romantic interpretations of poetry do little to help us read and understand the early modern Buddhist poetry of Alagiyavanna. Leaving aside the problems in positing the existence of a pure inner life that remains untouched by the external world, it will be clear that we really do not learn that much about Alagiyavanna's personality from his poetic works. As an author, Alagiyavanna borrowed liberally from the established poetic conventions and genres of Sinhala literature from previous centuries. Rather than revealing his own, unique feelings and imagination, his works exalt him as a poet of learning and excellence in the manner of great Sinhala poets such as Toṭagāmuve Śrī Rāhula from the fifteenth century.[18]

Alagiyavanna the author initially appears as a poet both trained and skilled in composing Sinhala verse in accordance with longstanding poetic conventions. Although modern literary criticism sometimes derides the conventional and formulaic style of classical Sinhala poetry, Alagiyavanna understood himself to be a great poet who enhances and improves on the material the he borrowed from earlier works. His self-praise as an author is not based on his creativity or originality, but rather it depends largely on his ability to compose works that adhere to accepted poetic norms while still exceeding the quality of the works that precede his own. His first work, titled *Sävul Sandēśaya* (*The Cock's Message*), imitates the popular Sinhala genre of messenger poetry wherein a bird is given a message and sent along a particular path through the countryside of Sri Lanka to deliver it. This text borrows liberally from older Sinhala works while expressing aesthetically rich descriptions of landscapes and women, along with abundant praise for King Rājasiṃha I. *Sävul Sandēśaya* is thus the unmistakable product of a poet situated in a royal court. *Dahamsoňḍa Kava* (*Poem of King Dhammasoṇḍa*), his next work, combines richly descriptive verses with the narrative account of one of the Bodhisattva's previous lives—a popular, conventional subject of classical Sinhala verse. Subsequently, Alagiyavanna composed his longest work, *Kusa Jātaka Kāvya* (*Poem of the Birth-Story of King Kusa*), in which he devotes comparatively less attention to aesthetic figures of speech and places more emphasis on the narrative illustrating moral lessons from the Bodhisattva's career. Later, after the death of Rājasiṃha I and the fall of the Sītāvaka kingdom, Alagiyavanna composed a distinctive work called *Subhāṣitaya* (*Well-Spoken Words*) that consists of didactic verses offering moral advice and a defense of the Buddha's religion. Finally, Alagiyavanna also likely composed *Kustantīnu Haṭana* (*The War of Constantino*) to honor the early military achievements of the Portuguese captain-general Constantino de Sá de Noronha, who quelled local rebellions and reinforced Portuguese colonial rule in Sri Lanka between 1619 and 1629.

There is general agreement that Alagiyavanna composed the preceding five works, each of which will be explored in detail in subsequent chapters.[19] Collectively, these texts represent the diverse aims and features of Buddhist poetry in an era that may be said to mark the end of the Sinhala culture-power formation based in royal courts and expressed predominantly through aesthetically rich poetic compositions. The term *culture-power formation*, borrowed from Sheldon Pollock, is here meant to signify how cultural forms such as poetry were deemed integral to the expression and conception of power among rulers and other elites in premodern Sri Lanka. Thus, at the beginning of Alagiyavanna's career, the idea that poetry had the power to effect change in the world was traditional and taken for granted. Near the end of his career, however, he began to abandon the traditional poetic concerns with aesthetic conventions, court culture, and classical forms in favor of a more simplified poetic style. As such, Alagiyavanna's transformation of Sinhala poetry marks a later stage in what Sheldon Pollock calls the "vernacularization" of literature.[20] This is the stage at which vernacular poetry began to shed its affinities with Sanskrit *kāvya* and instead sought new avenues to influence contemporary political and social formations. However, in order to grasp the significance of these shifts in literature, the forms and features of Sinhala poetry before Alagiyavanna must be recounted.

The Development of Sinhala Literary Culture

The poetry of Alagiyavanna was composed and circulated in the context of a Sinhala literary culture that privileged two imports from the Indian subcontinent—the Buddhist religion and the aesthetic conventions of Sanskrit literature. Following the introduction and establishment of Buddhist monks around the third century BCE, Buddhist texts, practices, and institutions enjoyed a dominant position in the island up to the beginning of Alagiyavanna's poetic career. Meanwhile, Buddhist narratives and sentiments, often transmitted in Pāli texts, pervaded Sinhala writing throughout this same period.[21] Alagiyavanna thus inherited the poetic conventions that lay and monastic authors bequeathed classical Sinhala literature from as early as the fifth century CE. However, the bulk of literary writing in the Sinhala language begins around the tenth century with the composition of the *Siyabaslakara* (*Poetics of One's Own Language*), which was a Sinhala translation and adaptation of Daṇḍin's classical Sanskrit work on poetics called *Kāvyadarśa*. The *Siyabaslakara* shows authors how to avoid literary faults (*doṣa*) and compose fine poetic works in the prestigious, translocal tradition of classical Sanskrit poetry. The adoption of Sanskrit norms and forms into Sinhala literature, however, involved efforts to superpose local Sinhala literary features on their Sanskrit paradigms. Charles Hallisey has argued that Sinhala literary culture from the tenth to fifteenth centuries self-consciously adapted what counted as literature in Sanskrit but, at the same time, purposefully distanced itself by rejecting Sanskrit loanwords and incorporating the nasalized *ä* vowel and the half-nasal consonants, which are phonemes that are not found in Sanskrit or practically any other South Asian language.[22] The effective result of this ambivalent posture was that a new form of poetry arose in the second millennium in Sri Lanka, one that was distinctive for its use of language and subject, yet derivative in its reliance on the poetic conventions and the prestige associated with Sanskrit literary compositions.

This development of a new literary culture that privileged literary forms of the vernacular language of Sinhala would have profound ramifications on Sinhala authors, including Alagiyavanna, from the twelfth century onward. Pollock uses the term *literary culture* to refer to the dynamic practices by which languages and literatures are produced in conjunction with each other as discrete objects within a particular sphere of political power.[23] In Sri Lanka, the composition of poetry deemed excellent according to accepted poetic conventions was a practice intimately linked more to royal courts than Buddhist monasteries. The more that Sinhala authors endeavored to craft poetry reflecting the cosmopolitan vision of the aesthetic qualities and efficacy of Sanskrit works, albeit in the local Sinhala poetic dialect of *eḷu*, the more their works deviated from the traditional norms of monastic Buddhist morality, such as restrictions against immodesty and the indulgence of sensual pleasures.[24]

The development of Sinhala poetry (*kavi*) emerged in the second millennium reflecting the social location and aesthetic imagination of Sanskrit poetic creations. If Sinhala poems aspired to a kind of timeless, formal beauty that could give rise to certain aesthetic effects long after they are written, such a cultural presumption exposed the elite sociopolitical environments in which such goals could be expressed and pursued. Pollock refers to the interaction of *kāvya* (poetry) and *rājya* (kingship) as the site where culture and power met and worked to constitute each other in premodern South Asia.[25] Poets were intimately involved in promoting and enhancing the power of kings and nobles by composing verses that celebrated them as elite connoisseurs who could grasp and take pleasure in such literary works. Although early formulators of theories of poetry tended to assert that only the Sanskrit language (as well as two other closely related idioms of Prakrit and Apabhraṃśa) could suffice for the composition of *kāvya*, later authors writing around the turn of the second millennium expanded this requirement to include various literary versions of vernacular languages including Sinhala. This development, which occurs at roughly the same time across numerous linguistic communities in South Asia, gave rise to what Pollock has called "cosmopolitan vernaculars." Of particular interest is the effort made by vernacular languages such as Sinhala to adopt the cosmopolitan vision and features of Sanskrit literary culture in order to invest their local literatures with the power and prestige associated with Sanskrit.[26]

This was the case with Sinhala *kavi* between the tenth and fifteenth centuries. Employing a vision of literature that can transcend time and place, extending its literary power outward without perceptible constraints, Sinhala *kavi* was used to create a local literary culture that imagined itself as utilizing a language equal to Sanskrit in terms of power and beauty.[27] Sinhala prose works were also written with increasing frequency and artistry beginning around the twelfth century in Sri Lanka. Some Sinhala prose narratives even adopted an embellished descriptive style and an awareness of the aesthetic power of texts from Sanskrit poetics.[28] However, Sinhala poetry more clearly evoked the norms and models of Sanskrit literature than prose works did. Significant changes seen in particular examples of Sinhala *kavi* notwithstanding, this form of writing is distinctive for the stability and unity of the Sinhala form of *eḷu* used in its expressions.[29] Sinhala *kavi*'s steadfast use of a smaller, restricted alphabet and of Sinhala derivations of Sanskrit loanwords resulted in a form of poetry that privileged convention and conservatism. In this literary culture, a premium was placed on rehearsing older literary models and following the patterns of usage established by earlier poets.[30]

Given the limited variations in structure and meter, there is a great deal of stylistic coherence among the Sinhala poetic works from the tenth to the fifteenth centuries in Sri Lanka. In addition to the *Siyabaslakara*, other treatises written to standardize and improve Sinhala literature, such as the grammar *Sidatsaṅgarāva* (*Compilation of Methods*), the lexicon of *eḷu* words called *Piyummala* (*Garland of Lotuses*), and the work on meter called *Eḷu Sandäs Lakuṇa* (*Marks of Sinhala Prosody*), began to appear around the twelfth and thirteenth centuries. These works offered a curriculum for aspiring poets to learn how to compose aesthetically excellent works in a language artificially created and specifically employed for poetic composition. Sinhala poetry, like other South Asian forms, was composed primarily for royal courts. Poets were thus involved in transactions of power and fame, using their works to augment each in their service to kings and nobles. Not coincidentally, poetic works composed up to the fifteenth century tended to celebrate what Hallisey has called an "ethos of complexity and difficulty," wherein linguistic comprehension was somewhat circumscribed by the deliberate usage of complicated forms of syntax, meter, and lexicon.[31] Written for learned connoisseurs of poetry, Sinhala *kavi* was largely a product that emulated the broader, cosmopolitan interests and values of palace courts.

The close, ongoing association of Sinhala *kavi* with court culture contributed a sense of stylistic conservatism and inflated self-importance to the poets of the tenth through the fifteenth centuries. Again, in imitation of the cosmopolitan horizons of Sanskrit literature, Sinhala *kavi* traditionally reflected a strong familiarity (either real or imagined) with the royal court (*sabhā*) where the king presided over recitals of poetry in the company of not only courtiers, ministers, princes, and other high-born listeners but also scholars (*paṇḍitas*), poets, singers, dancers, and others present to entertain and elucidate the cultural displays at the court.[32] In such settings, poetry was used to express royal power, for kings often appeared in such poems and were the primary patrons and connoisseurs for *kavi*. The culture of poetry had become instantiated with the trappings of power in Sri Lanka and elsewhere in South Asia. Its value as a literary form was measured according to the exact criteria established by scientific treatises (*śāstras*) that laid out a sense of the proper method of expressing and enjoying poetry.[33] Once again, this development is seen by Hallisey and Pollock as a sign of efforts in the tenth through the fifteenth centuries to give rise to a more localized literary culture that could express in written vernacular forms the aspirations of more regionalized political domains. Culture and power became mutually constitutive since it was in the realm of cultural expressions and connoisseurship that institutions of power could signal their prestige, while those same sociopolitical elites were the chief patrons and, at times, authors of poetry.

In Sri Lanka, the era coinciding with the fifteenth-century kingdom located at Koṭṭe in southwestern Sri Lanka is generally seen as the high-point of Sinhala poetic expression. It was during this period that the poetic works of Śrī Rāhula, Vīdāgama Maitreya, and other learned authors came to dominate Sinhala literary culture. Many of these works continued to draw on the norms and models provided by Sanskrit poetics. Some of the most renowned examples of the *mahākāvya* (court epic), *praśasti* (panegyrics), and *sandēśa* (messenger poems) poetic genres appear at the time when King Parākramabāhu VI ruled supreme in the island from 1410 to 1467. This king, who is eulogized in the poem *Pärakumbā Sirita* (*Account of Parākramabāhu VI*), is recalled as a powerful ruler and a keen patron and connoisseur of literature. Many renowned works of poetry, such as *Kāvyaśēkhara* (*Crown of Poetry*), *Säḷahiṇi Sandēśaya* (*The Mynah's Message*), *Parevi Sandēśaya* (*The Dove's Message*), *Pärakumbā Sirita*, *Lōväḍa Sañgarāva* (*Treatise on the Welfare of the World*), *Kōkila Sandēśaya* (*The Cuckoo's Message*), *Guttila Kāvya* (*Poem of the Bodhisattva Guttila*), *Girā Sandēśaya* (*The Parrot's Message*), *Haṃsa Sandēśaya* (*The Swan's Message*), and *Kavlakuṇumiṇimaldama* (*Garland of Jewels of the Features of Poetry*), were all composed under the political stability and patronage of learning in the Koṭṭe kingdom.

Yet when Alagiyavanna began his literary career in the late sixteenth century, the vitality and support of poetry were waning. He found a place at King Rājasiṃha I's court at Sītāvaka, but this ruler was seemingly more intent on fighting battles against the Portuguese and the Kandyans than he was in promoting a literary culture in the royal court. The divided, warring kingdoms within Sri Lanka gave rise to narrower, more localized visions of kingship, visions that were consistent with images of power in vernacular literature across South Asia after the tenth century.[34] One would not expect a poet like Alagiyavanna to repeatedly praise Rājasiṃha I if there was not any benefit or advantage in doing so. Yet Alagiyavanna's poetry appears near the end of what Pollock calls the "vernacular millennium," and thus it yields insights into how one vernacular literary culture would eventually drift away from the ideals of sovereignty and aesthetics adopted from Sanskrit literature. Under the authorial guidance of Alagiyavanna and later Sinhala authors, Sinhala literary culture would come to express new images of power focused more on moral excellence than on royal sovereignty and poetic connoisseurship. Aesthetics begin to serve new purposes in Alagiyavanna's later *kavi* works. His audiences are expected not only to delight in his poetry's aesthetic features, but they are also urged to develop an ethical awareness in regard to their own religious commitments and the moral effects of their deeds. Clearly, the rise of colonial power in Sri Lanka and the concomitant decline of local, autonomous kings paved the way for Sinhala authors to utilize the generative capacities of literature in different ways.

Portuguese Colonialism in Ceilão

An important aspect of Alagiyavanna's poetry is the shifting fortunes and locations of political power during his career. He began composing poetry in the setting of the Sinhala court of King Rājasiṃha I but likely ended his career under the rule of the Portuguese captain-general Constantino de Sá de Noronha. Given that the presence of colonial authorities, soldiers, and missionaries had a substantial impact on the society in which Alagiyavanna lived, it is necessary to rehearse briefly the history of Portuguese power in sixteenth- and seventeenth-century Sri Lanka.[35] This historical outline helps to frame how Alagiyavanna understood and utilized the power of poetry to negotiate other forms of power—both Sinhala and Portuguese—in the island.

The island of Ceilão never became the focal point of the Portuguese maritime empire in Asia. But between the arrival of Dom Lourenço de Almeida at the port of Colombo in 1506 and the final expulsion of the Portuguese from the island in 1658 by the Dutch, the Portuguese came to see the island as a profitable and strategically important land that could bolster their hold over seaborne trade in the Indian Ocean. Early Portuguese descriptions of the island included references to commodities of trade as well as to the value of the strip of water separating the island from India's southern tip for navigation.[36] Nevertheless, the Portuguese waited until 1518 to construct their first fort near the port of Colombo, several miles from the king's capital in Koṭṭe. There is little indication of any Portuguese intention to gain administrative control over Sri Lanka in the first decades of the sixteenth century. Their interests instead remained chiefly mercantile, as they sought to expand their commercial empire in the East by gaining access to the island's cinnamon, gems, pearls, elephants, and ivory in the form of tribute given by local kings.

Soon, however, the Portuguese became embroiled in a series of power struggles between various regional kings in the island. Following the assassination of King Vijayabāhu VI in 1521, his three sons divided the lands of the kingdom among themselves with the eldest prince, Bhuvanekabāhu, proclaimed the new emperor of Koṭṭe, while his younger brothers Pararājasiṃha and Māyādunnē were named as kings of the lands of Rayigama and Sītāvaka, respectively. Bhuvanekabāhu's relationship with the Portuguese became strained at times, not the least because of the stories that circulated about their misdeeds and violations of custom in his kingdom, but he became increasingly reliant on Portuguese assistance when his younger brother Māyādunnē sought to expand his authority.[37] Māyādunnē regularly sought out assistance from the Muslim ruler in Calicut on the Malabar Coast, and Bhuvanekabāhu tried to counter his younger brother's moves by appealing for aid from the Portuguese in Colombo and Goa. The battles fought between the armies that the two brothers commanded had a destabilizing effect on the southwestern region of the island, but they did not result in any dramatic shift in power as Māyādunnē's periodic territorial gains were subsequently reclaimed by Portuguese-led troops. What stands out from this period of history is the fact that Bhuvanekabāhu sought out vassalage to Lisbon in the expectation that by paying tribute to the Portuguese king, he would receive the assistance of foreign troops that would allow him to stabilize his rule.[38] Although his control over the Portuguese troops failed to meet his expectations, the Portuguese became increasingly involved in the political affairs of the island.

Portuguese religious interests in Sri Lanka were augmented in 1545 by the arrival of four Franciscan friars led by João de Villa de Conde.

Bhuvanekabāhu had invited King Dom João III to dispatch some Catholic missionaries to his island in the hope of winning more consideration from Lisbon for his requests. However, de Conde interpreted this to mean that the Koṭṭe king intended to convert, an act that Bhuvanekabāhu consistently refused. The king granted the Franciscans permission to construct churches and preach in his kingdom, offering them an income and decreeing that Christians would henceforth be exempt from the *marāla*, or "death duty," which obliged other subjects to part with a large proportion of their wealth at death.[39]

In time, other economic advantages were given to Christian missions and their converts, including the redistribution of lands owned by Buddhist and Hindu temples to the Catholic orders and the preferential assignment of offices to Christian converts. While these practices, which were started by Bhuvanekabāhu and continued by his successor, Dharmapāla, caused considerable resentment among Buddhists, the more aggressive policies of destroying temples and condemning Buddhist practices only deepened people's anger. Portuguese sources from the sixteenth and seventeenth centuries record the European's low esteem for the Buddhist religion. Therein one finds Sinhala Buddhists described as, among other things, "heathens" who are "deceived by the devils" and who collectively lack humility and gratitude before God, while their monks prefer vice to the discovery of the truth.[40] Although the missionaries achieved some success in converting local Buddhists and Hindus to Catholicism in lands under Portuguese control, their efforts were repeatedly obstructed by Sinhala rebellions and the abusive conduct of Portuguese Catholics in the island. It seems likely that their number of converts were no more than around 10 percent of the island's population.[41]

In the meantime, King Bhuvanekabāhu moved to secure the succession of his grandson Dharmapala to the throne in Koṭṭe. This was accomplished, much to Māyādunnē's chagrin, when Bhuvenekabāhu sent a gold statue of his grandson to Lisbon in 1541, whereupon the Portuguese king ceremoniously conferred his eventual succession. However, relations between Bhuvanekabāhu and the Portuguese were often strained throughout the 1540s due to continuing demands for his conversion and the assistance that the Portuguese were supplying Jayavīra, the king of Kandy in the central highlands. The jockeying for power among Bhuvanekabāhu, Māyādunnē, and Jayavīra led to various battles between the three kingdoms, with the Portuguese usually giving most of their support to the king in Koṭṭe, who supplied them with the tribute and trading privileges they coveted.

Yet with a young prince in line to succeed to the throne, the Portuguese eventually killed Bhuvanekabāhu in 1551. Māyādunnē, ignoring the agreement that the deceased king had secured with the Portuguese, proclaimed himself king of Koṭṭe and advanced toward the coastal kingdom. However, the Portuguese and the Koṭṭe nobility threw their support to the young prince Dharmapāla, appointing his father and Bhuvanekabāhu's son-in-law, Vīdiyē Baṇḍāra, as regent. The turmoil that once again engulfed Sri Lanka led the viceroy in Goa, Dom Alfonso de Noronha, to sail to Sri Lanka with a fleet carrying three thousand Portuguese soldiers. De Noronha's influence was hardly conducive to stabilizing the situation in the island. Although Ceilão was treated as part of the Portuguese *Estado da Índia*, de Noronha's excursion was marked by widespread plunder and the destruction of temples and villages. Rumors of Dharmapāla's imminent conversion to Catholicism and the destruction of the Buddhist temple at Koṭṭe caused larger number of Sinhalas to desert Koṭṭe for Sītāvaka. De Noronha left the island with much of the Koṭṭe king's treasure, but the conditions for more warfare and unrest remained as ripe as ever.

Thus, by the time Alagiyavanna was born in 1552, the island was already marked by internal division and frequent warfare. Many modern Sinhala scholars refer to the so-called Sītāvaka Period as a "dark age" during which the brutality of war overshadowed almost all forms of literary expression, except for Alagiyavanna's *kavi*. The movements of large number of troops between Colombo and Sītāvaka and between Sītāvaka and Kandy caused considerable destruction and hardships for the population. With the seizure of temple lands and with so many resources channeled to supporting warfare, there was less support available to the Sangha. Furthermore, the official Portuguese policy adopted in Goa after 1567 was to demolish all "heathen temples" in Portuguese-controlled territory; to expel all non-Christian priests, teachers, and holy men; and to seize and destroy the sacred books of all religions other than Christianity.[42] Even though Portuguese colonial power was more or less confined to the environs around Koṭṭe and Colombo, the overall conditions in the island disrupted monastic scholarship, and there are no extant literary works authored by Buddhist monks from this period.

In actuality, Portuguese power during the mid-sixteenth century was curtailed by the relatively small number of troops afforded to the island by the authorities in Goa. Due to the small population of Portugal and the far-flung reaches of its maritime empire, the Portuguese colonizers and traders were constantly on the move, seeking to protect and expand their mercantile interests across Asia, around Africa, and to Brazil.[43] Therefore, Portuguese troops in Sri Lanka had to be supplemented by large numbers of native Sinhala *lascarins*, soldiers who were enlisted to fight alongside the Portuguese. There were more occasions to do so when Vīdiyē Baṇḍāra led an anti-Portuguese and anti-Christian rebellion in the coastal regions south of Koṭṭe in the early 1550s. Portuguese concessions made to Māyādunnē caused the latter to turn against Baṇḍāra, leading to the defeat of the rebel regent. But the treaty between Koṭṭe and Sītāvaka soon fell apart, leading to a resumption of warfare not long after the young king Dharmapāla announced his conversion to Catholicism in 1557, which was followed by his confiscation of all temple lands in his kingdom and their bestowal to the Franciscans.[44] An uprising led by a group of monks was put down, and thirty monks were executed for their roles, further alienating Dharmapāla (now Dom João) from all but his Christian subjects.

Meanwhile, Māyādunnē's son Tikiri Baṇḍāra, called Rājasiṃha (Lion of Kings) after leading the army that defeated Vīdiyē Baṇḍāra, was given control of the Sītāvaka forces. He commanded a decisive victory over a substantial army of Portuguese and *lascarin* soldiers at Mulleriyāva in 1562. The Portuguese's command over the Koṭṭe kingdom had diminished substantially, and the forces of Sītāvaka conducted destructive raids into their territories. In 1565, over Dom João's objections, the Portuguese abandoned the capital at Koṭṭe and concentrated their beleaguered forces in Colombo. The loss of territory actually benefited the Portuguese forces, since they were then freed from defending Koṭṭe and able to conduct raids of their own in the villages under Sītāvaka control. In the 1570s, the Portuguese conducted raids along coastal cities and destroyed numerous temples at Kelaniya, Negombo, Alutgama, and elsewhere. The Sītāvaka forces led by Rājasiṃha occasionally turned their attention to their opponents in Kandy, whose kingdom was led by Karaliyaddē Baṇḍāra, a Christian convert, who sought Portuguese assistance in gaining independence for the hill kingdom. Unable to conquer a combined Kandyan and Portuguese force in the mountainous upcountry and distracted by other Portuguese forces who continued to sack coastal villages by sea, Rājasiṃha withdrew and, in 1579, marched a formidable attacking force of about 25,000 soldiers and a large corps of elephants toward the Portuguese fort in Colombo. The siege of the Colombo fort lasted until 1581, and it likely would have succeeded had it not been for the ability of the Portuguese to use their command of the sea to replenish their supplies of food and fighting men. Also in 1581, an aged Māyādunnē formally handed the throne over to his son Rājasiṃha and died. Shortly thereafter, Alagiyavanna began his service to the Sītāvaka court.

It appears that Rājasiṃha I was both respected and feared. His determination to expel the Portuguese from Sri Lanka led him to raise additional sieges on their base in Colombo. Later, Rājasiṃha also successfully defeated the Kandyan king, capturing Kandy and acquiring important resources in his battles against the Portuguese. Thus while Alagiyavanna was composing and reciting his first poem, *Sävul Sandēśaya,* a largely eulogistic work celebrating the virtues of Rājasiṃha and the city of Sītāvaka, his king continued to devise ways to defeat the Portuguese. Rājasiṃha's success in war notwithstanding, there are signs that a number of his own subjects began to turn against him. Whether it was due to his policy of higher taxes and continual warfare or to his patronage of Hindu institutions, Rājasiṃha made enemies who were bold enough to try to poison him.[45] When this failed, the king exacted his revenge, executing those suspected of conspiring against him, including a number of Buddhist monks. Rājasiṃha's last major siege on Colombo lasted between May 1587 and February 1588, a contest in which he again gained the upper hand against the beleaguered Portuguese and local inhabitants, but he failed to prevent supplies from India from reaching the seaside fort. Accounts of this epic battle have been preserved by Portuguese historians who recorded the series of ultimately unsuccessful attempts of the tens of thousands of Sinhala soldiers to breach the defenses of the Portuguese fort.[46] Rājasiṃha eventually withdrew back to Sītāvaka without having accomplished his aim. A revolt in Kandy could not be quelled, and others in some areas under Rājasiṃha's rule tried to follow suit. Meanwhile, Konappu Baṇḍāra in Kandy reneged on his conversion to Catholicism and took control of the Kandyan kingdom under the name Vimaladharmasūriya. This Buddhist king broke off relations with the Portuguese but still sought independence from Sītāvaka.

In 1593, King Rājasiṃha died from an accidental wound caused by a bamboo splinter in his foot, and the resultant contest for control over the kingdom led to the disintegration of its power within a few years. What Alagiyavanna did or where he went during this time is not known with certainty, but after the desertion of two leaders of the Sītāvaka forces, the Koṭṭe kingdom under Dom João Dharmapāla annexed Sītāvaka in 1594. In the same year, the arrival of a skilled and combative captain-general named Dom Jerónimo de Azevedo helped the Portuguese to turn these events in their favor. Azevedo consolidated Portuguese authority over the Koṭṭe kingdom. Following the defeat suffered at Danturē in a failed Portuguese attempt to conquer Kandy, periodic revolts broke out throughout the lands under their control. In response, Azevedo had a number of forts constructed between the coast and Kandy to strengthen Portuguese authority. Periodic battles between the Portuguese and strengthened Kandyan forces devastated many villages and disrupted cultivation in the lands between Colombo and Kandy. The destruction suffered was magnified by the Portuguese adoption of a scorched-earth policy as a means of terrorizing the local inhabitants into submission.[47] Azevedo gained a vicious reputation for cruelty shown toward rebels and those suspected of supporting them, as he was condemned even by Portuguese writers for his harshness in acts alleged to include feeding men to crocodiles, forcing mothers to pound their children to death, and piercing babies in the air with spears.[48]

In 1597, King Dom João died, and according to documents signed in 1580 and 1583 in which the Sinhala king bequeathed his kingdom to the king of Portugal and his heirs, the island was now formally claimed by the Portuguese. Although the legitimacy of the bequest and the Portuguese claim of ownership could easily be questioned, it is clear that the Portuguese had by this time forsaken their previous policy of operating through client rulers such as Bhuvanekabāhu and Dharmapāla (Dom João) in favor of assuming direct colonial control over the island.[49] Azevedo's desire to conquer Kandy remained strong, even though the Portuguese found it exceedingly difficult to overcome Vimaladharmasūriya's forces and the mountainous terrain of Kandy. In 1603, he adopted a policy of conducting periodic raids on the lands surrounding Kandy and attempted to enforce a blockade on goods traveling in and out of Kandy, although this effort was never fully successful. Vimaladharmasūriya died in 1604, and his death sparked a succession quarrel in Kandy. However, limited resources at Azevedo's disposal prevented him from launching another campaign, and he was forced to suspend military operations between 1605 and 1607.

Azevedo also moved on the religious front and allowed Jesuit, Augustinian, and Dominican missionaries to enter the island over the objections of the Franciscans who had enjoyed a monopoly over ecclesiastical missions and resources in the island. The Jesuits entered in 1602 and moved quickly to engage in the work of conversion and religious education. Azevedo had a house built for the Jesuits at his own expense and publicly showed his support for these priests, some of whom began to learn Sinhala to be able "to minister to the people of the country and to convert the infidels."[50] The close association between Catholic missionaries and Portuguese rulers in general allowed the project of converting the populace to accelerate, but it also meant that periodic rebellions could target not only Portuguese forts and stockades but churches and churchmen as well. Those who wished to remain in the good graces of the Portuguese colonialists often chose conversion as a path to do so. It appears that sometime in late 1611 or 1612, Alagiyavanna underwent a baptism ceremony and converted to Christianity, adopting the name Dom Jerónimo Alagiyavanna after the influential Portuguese captain-general Azevedo.[51]

Around the same time of Alagiyavanna's conversion, the Portuguese colonialists were instituting new offices to strengthen their control of the island. In addition to the post of captain-general created in 1594 for Azevedo as the chief administrative authority in Ceilão, a new financial superintendent—the *vedor da fazenda*—was appointed in 1608 who became responsible for drawing up a record of property and making an inventory of receipts for the *Estado da Índia*.[52] The surveying of lands now under Portuguese control and the assessment of their value became important priorities for the colonial effort. Antão Vaz Freire was appointed to become the *vedor* who would compile the *tombo*, or land register, which was completed in 1615. There is evidence in the *tombo* about Alagiyavanna, as he was one of the local officials employed in its compilation of information about the villages, the names of grantees, and the incomes they generate.[53] Elsewhere, a Dutch document records an event at which Alagiyavanna and three other Sri Lankans who assisted in the work on the *tombo* were made to swear an oath to confirm the truthfulness of their contributions to the revenue record.[54] The completion of the *tombo* signaled a more concerted effort on the part of the Portuguese to recoup some of their considerable expenditures in the island.

After Azevedo was appointed to the position of viceroy in Goa, a series of less effective Portuguese captain-generals of Ceylon held office. Serious concerns emerged over negotiations the king of Kandy had with the Dutch, who were keen to assist in expelling the Portuguese and gaining some of the more profitable commercial trade that had been developed in the island. This problem for the Portuguese was compounded by two large-scale revolts in parts of their territory. Initially supported by King Senarath of Kandy, one revolt from 1616 to1617 was led by a man falsely claiming to be Nikapiṭiyē Baṇḍāra, the grandson of King Rājasiṃha of Sītāvaka, while the other one lasted from 1617 to1620 under the leadership of a former Sinhala convert named António Barreto (Kuruviṭa Rāla).[55]

These rebellions proved to be major distractions to the Portuguese, who eventually had to forge alliances with Kandy to subdue them. The captain-general Dom Nuno Alvares Pereira distrusted the Sinhala leaders under Portuguese rule and increased the enmity of the ordinary public by refusing to discipline his subordinates involved in corruption and criminal behavior.[56] Significantly, it was this same captain-general who deprived Alagiyavanna of his title and some of his lands. This loss of status and wealth led Alagiyavanna to petition the king of Portugal in 1618, after Pereira had been recalled from Ceilão, in order to have what previously belonged to him restored.[57]

In 1618 a new, more able captain-general was sent to Ceilão. Dom Constantino de Sá de Noronha, the recipient of much praise in Portuguese chronicles as well as in the *Konstantīnu Haṭana*, arrived in the island and set out to quell the rebellion in the lowlands. His efforts were largely successful, and under his leadership the Portuguese also gained control over the Jaffna kingdom and began a project to construct and reinforce forts along the coastline. De Sá also adopted a more conciliatory approach to the Sinhalas under his authority, seeking to win the confidence of the chieftains who led the *lascarin* troops and offering a more just treatment of the native population.[58] De Sá was recalled to Goa in a move by the Portuguese governor of India to appoint his son to the post of captain-general, but he returned to serve a second stint after the latter proved ineffective. De Sá then governed in Ceilão up to 1630, when, after hostilities with Kandy resumed, he was killed in a battle with Kandyan forces at Randenivala.

From this point on, Portuguese colonial power in Sri Lanka began to diminish fairly rapidly. In 1635 Senarath's youngest son succeeded him in Kandy as King Rājasiṃha II, and he resolved to drive the Portuguese out of the island. The renewed communications between Kandy and the Dutch roused the suspicions of the Portuguese. The captain-general Diego de Mello de Castro advocated launching a preventative strike on Kandy to block any possible designs that the Dutch had on the island. De Mello's forces took Kandy, which had been strategically abandoned in 1638. After burning the capital, some of de Mello's mercenaries deserted to the Kandyan side, and he decided to retreat to safer ground in Colombo. However, the Portuguese army was surrounded and completely routed by the Kandyans at the Battle of Gannoruva. The remaining Portuguese in the maritime areas thereafter had to contend with an alliance between Rājasiṃha II and the Dutch that was forged to expel the Portuguese from the island and win concessions for Dutch traders. In 1656, the Colombo fort fell to a Dutch siege, and the last Portuguese presence on the island was removed in 1658 when Jaffna also fell.

Conceptualizing Religious Identity

One of the more salient effects of the Portuguese presence on Alagiyavanna's poetry is found in the various ways that the poet envisioned religious identity. Just as Portuguese power was variously expressed and unevenly felt at different times and places in Sri Lanka, so, too, did Alagiyavanna articulate differing conceptions of religious identity in his works. His early poetry expressed a more pluralistic vision that combined ritual practices and religious symbolism found in Buddhist *pansala*s (monasteries) as well as Hindu *kovil*s (temples). Then, over time, he began to emphasize moralistic instruction and greater reverence for the Three Jewels of the Buddha, his Dharma (or teaching), and the Sangha (or community of monastic disciples of the Buddha). Finally, near the end of his career, he converted formally to Catholicism and appears to have composed a work that expresses a hybrid vision of Christian devotion wedded to Buddhist conceptions of ethics and exemplary beings.

The multiple conceptions of religious identity that he held and presented in his poetry speak to the varying responses that he gave to Portuguese colonialism in the island. Focusing on the concept of identity rather than on a notion of agency allows us to sidestep the circular and somewhat unfruitful debate over the degree to which natives could act free of colonial influence.[59] The development of Alagiyavanna's poetry over time clearly reflects his responses to dramatic changes in Sinhala society that resulted from the extension of Portuguese colonial power in the late sixteenth and early seventeenth centuries. Yet it would be an exaggeration to claim that his work was entirely determined by this historical encounter, effectively obscuring any and all indigenous conceptions he held in regard to the Buddhist religion and Sinhala literary culture.

This book contends that Portuguese colonialism had a measurable impact on Sri Lankan Buddhism. Alagiyavanna's works show us that the disruption of Buddhist kingship and its traditional support of poets and monks led to transformations in, among other things, the ways that religious identity was conceived and poetry was expressed. Such changes in the conceptions and expressions of Buddhism provide a measure with which to theorize the impact of colonialism on the religion in early modernity. Such an impact was not unique, unilateral, or fully determinative, as there were other forces at play, and the Portuguese were transformed by their encounters with Sinhalas too.[60] But it would be a mistake to dismiss or overlook the effects of the Portuguese presence on Buddhists such as Alagiyavanna altogether. The identity of Buddhism as a religious system and the Buddhist identity of the author are significant sites on which to focus this analysis.

In seeking to uncover more about the composition of poetry and the representation of religion in early modern Sri Lanka, this book will avoid treating Buddhism as a discrete entity with certain timeless qualities passed down by the historical Buddha and preserved, more or less pristinely, up to this day. This view, which endures in some scholarly and popular books, encourages attempts to rediscover what is supposedly essential and timeless about Buddhism in the midst of its historical accretions. Instead, Buddhism is more accurately represented as a loosely bounded set of discourses and practices that are variously expressed according to the needs and interests of people in different times and places. There is no Buddhism to be found that is not already expressed within and contingent on particular spatial-temporal settings. The discursive formation of Buddhism—how it comes to be defined, differentiated, and understood—as a set of linguistic markers that can be applied to particular ideas, practices, and objects requires us to admit it always appears as a historically conditioned phenomenon.[61]

As one consequence of this position, it is necessary to state that while Alagiyavanna's works speak to the diverse body of Buddhist texts with wide-ranging interests and concerns that were composed or used in Sri Lanka, his poetic texts are not examples of *Theravāda* Buddhist literature per se. Although Theravāda is a recognizable and widespread label today for the form of Buddhism practiced in Sri Lanka, it was neither commonly used in the premodern period nor was it a part of the self-consciousness of Buddhists.[62] Alagiyavanna employs a notion akin to Buddhism in one of his works, but he nowhere speaks of Theravāda. His vision of Buddhism was not dependent on monastic views or canonical texts, nor was he concerned with establishing the authenticity or truth of one form of the tradition as opposed to others (e.g., Mahāyāna). The term *Theravāda,* although used to describe the normative ordination lineages for Buddhist monks in Sri Lanka, was not used to describe the wider community of Buddhists in Sri Lanka until around the twentieth century.[63] The endeavor to reconstruct how Alagiyavanna represented Buddhism around the turn of the seventeenth century requires refraining from attributing modern views of Buddhism to him.[64] Alagiyavanna had different interests and ideas in mind, and he was responding to a different set of historical events and circumstances.

Judging by Alagiyavanna's poetry, it appears that he did not always maintain a fixed sense of Buddhist identity. Early on, in *Sävul Sandēśaya*, he depicted religious identity in terms of a pluralistic combination of ritual practices and symbols taken from Buddhist and Hindu traditions. This dynamic enactment of religious identity, wherein one could worship the Buddha and deities in various locations while participating in rituals led by different kinds of religious specialists, was quite common in Sri Lanka in the medieval period. The assimilation of Hindu influences in Sinhala Buddhist culture, as seen in the rise of the construction of *kovils* and the worship of Purāṇic deities such as Viṣṇu and Śiva, the appearance of Hindu mythology in Sinhala literature, and the presence of Brahmins in royal courts, followed the waves of migrations into the island of Hindus from Tamil Nadu between the tenth and thirteenth centuries and from Kerala in the thirteenth and fourteenth centuries.[65] Although the increased vitality of Hindu religious elements occasionally provoked some resistance and backlash from Sinhala Buddhist monks—such as Vīdāgama Maitreya, who ridiculed Hindu deities in one of his texts—there is clear evidence of the widespread integration of Hindu practice and symbols in fifteenth-century Sri Lanka.

Although Alagiyavanna began writing poetry that expressed this more fluid sense of religious identity, the intensified spread of Portuguese authority and Christian missionaries led him to change his conception of religious identity in his later works. Over time, he appears to have developed and expressed a much clearer and exclusive sense of what it means to be a Buddhist. His *Subhāṣitaya*, in particular, contains the articulation of a Buddhist identity that emphasizes adherence to the Buddha's teaching and disparages other religious views and practices. While others before him at times expressed similar defenses of the Buddha's teaching as a superior and effective religious path, he went further in articulating a notion of Buddhism as a religious system among others but superior to all of them. This sharpened sense of religious identity would soon be replaced, however, following Alagiyavanna's conversion and his attempt to use Sinhala poetry to praise the Portuguese authorities and their Holy Trinity. However, even his embrace of Catholicism did not result in the complete rejection of his Buddhist background. Instead, one finds in *Kustantīnu Haṭana* a hybrid religious identity that combined and integrated certain Christian and Buddhist notions.

When looking at Alagiyavanna's sense of religious identity then, we are led to conclude that his conceptions of religious devotion and practice were subject to change and revision. The construction of Buddhist identity in premodern Sri Lanka was surely a contested process, with different ideas about what counts for Buddhism espoused by monks and others who sought to define the tradition. The case of Alagiyavanna stands out, however, since he represents a single individual who fashioned distinctly different notions of religious identity at different periods throughout his life. He serves as a clear reminder that religious identity could be a dynamic and fluid concept and that heterogeneity rather than uniformity was likely the norm when it came to being Buddhist.[66] This condition, wherein religious identity is continually subject to being revised and disputed, may thus have been typical, but it also must have only been intensified during periods of dramatic social and political change. The fashioning of new conceptions of religious identity may then be one of the primary effects of a colonial presence in a largely Buddhist society like Sri Lanka around the seventeenth century.

The Plan of the Book

Keeping this theory and history in mind, the present study of early modern Sinhala Buddhist poetry will proceed by examining in detail five works attributed to Alagiyavanna Mukaveṭi in more or less chronological order. Each of these works consists of multiple quatrains composed in the *eḷu* dialect of classical Sinhala poetry. Where appropriate, comparisons are made to other works of Sinhala Buddhist or Indic poetry to indicate places where Alagiyavanna shows signs of emulating the works of other authors. Aesthetic conventions and religious concerns are also noted to show that even though both features remained important to his works throughout his career, important shifts in emphasis between the aesthetic and the religious help us to understand something about corresponding shifts within the broader political and cultural contexts in which he wrote. Although the subjects and the visions of power expressed in his works could vary—sometimes dramatically—his poetry consistently attempts to influence and fashion particular forms of power in political and religious spheres. Buddhist poetry, in this sense, was employed as a cultural tool to transform and revive religious identity while wielding some influence over various royal and colonial powers. The mixed fortunes of Sinhala Buddhism in the sixteenth and seventeenth centuries can be detected between the lines of Alagiyavanna's poetry, and it is through these works that we begin to see how local individuals negotiated the changes introduced by the onset of European colonialism in Buddhist Asia.

The second chapter focuses on Alagiyavanna's earliest work, the *Sävul Sandēśaya,* which comprises his most conventional (some might say derivative) text. Drawing from established Indic and Sinhala works linked with the *sandēśa* genre of message poetry, this work relates how a bird is sent across the countryside in the Sītāvaka kingdom to deliver a message to the god Sumana and asks him to protect the dispensation (*sāsana*) of the Buddha (i.e., the teachings and institutions founded by the Buddha), King Rājasiṃha I, the royal ministers and army, along with the beings of the world in general. An examination of *Sävul Sandēśaya* invites us to consider the traditional Sinhala culture-power formation that was fashioned by poets and kings in the centuries prior to Alagiyavanna's time in Sri Lanka. This work, written at the height of Rājasiṃha I's power, is a model of the vernacularization of Sinhala literary culture and the regional efforts to create literature to imitate and compete with the prestigious, cosmopolitan language of Sanskrit.[67] The poem's concern with rich aesthetic descriptions and conventions, along with its resemblance to the praise poetry of Sanskrit *praśasti* texts, renders Alagiyavanna's first work into a paradigmatic example of the form and aims expressed in classical Sinhala poetry.

Chapter 3 includes a close study of Alagiyavanna's *Dahamsoňḍa Kava,* a text that has occasionally been attributed to the poet's father but is more persuasively identified as the second major work that he wrote while serving under King Rājasiṃha I in Sītāvaka. This poetic work evokes aspects of the richly descriptive style of older Sinhala *kavi,* but it focuses more on praise for the Buddha's Dharma and the characteristics of a righteous king. Read next to *Sävul Sandēśaya,* the poet in *Dahamsoňḍa Kava* begins to move away from the ethos of court poetry and its celebration of royal majesty and poetic embellishments. Although there are elements of aesthetically rich poetry in this work, it also introduces verses of ethical reflection and esteem for what the Buddha taught.

Chapter 4 explores Alagiyavanna's longest work, the *Kusa Jātaka Kāvya,* which appears to have been begun in the context of the Sītāvaka court but was finished several years after its downfall. Like his previous work, *Kusa Jātaka Kāvya* relates a poetic account of one of the Bodhisattva's previous lives, and thus it serves in part to extol the greatness of the being who went on to become the Buddha. A distinguishing mark of this work is its relative disinterest in inserting purely descriptive verses full of aesthetic conventions and poetic sentiments. Instead, *Kusa Jātaka Kāvya* devotes more attention to the content of the story and its sequence of events. The privileging of the narrative and the comparatively more accessible style in which this work was composed are indications that Alagiyavanna resolved to write for a more popular, broad-based audience than before. Rather than celebrating the greatness of kings, this work considers issues of love and power critically in the context of the Bodhisattva's story. It focuses more on timeless ideals rather than on historical instantiations of kingship.

The fifth chapter examines Alagiyavanna's *Subhāṣitaya,* a shorter verse work comprised of moral admonitions without a narrative structure. Emulating and adapting material from the vast body of gnomic *subhāṣita* literature from throughout the Indic world, Alagiyavanna composed a work that, in part, acknowledges the existence of rival religious systems and critiques the wicked kings and heretics associated with such traditions. Alagiyavanna thus utilizes poetry to teach people about virtue and wickedness. It is also in *Subhāṣitaya* that Alagiyavanna begins to articulate a self-reflexive sense of Buddhist identity in opposition to traditions that have rejected this identity. The marked shift away from poetry as an exercise in aesthetics toward poetry as a medium for religious debate and ethical instruction is highlighted here.

Kustantīnu Haṭana is discussed in the sixth chapter. Scholars disagree whether this work was actually composed by Alagiyavanna, although the evidence seems strong enough to attribute it to his hand. This poem is distinctive for being a Sinhala work written in praise of the Portuguese captain-general Constantino de Sá de Noronha and the Catholic religion to which he and his countrymen subscribed. Despite these innovations, many aspects of *Kustantīnu Haṭana* are conventional, and the work evokes features of the classical courtly style of Sinhala *kavi,* albeit with less aesthetic flourishes. Sá de Noronha becomes celebrated in poetic fashion much like great Sinhala Buddhist kings in earlier works, and the local landscape as traversed by him and his army is portrayed in vivid detail like the descriptions found in *sandēśa* poetry. Evidently the work of a Sinhala convert to Catholicism, *Kustantīnu Haṭana* introduces a hybrid form of religious identity and practice wherein Christian piety and notions of the divine are reimagined through Buddhist and other Indic terms and imagery. The distinctive features of this work go a long way in shedding light on religious and cultural conversion in early modern Asia.

The concluding chapter takes up the uses of Buddhist poetry in colonial Sri Lanka. Alagiyavanna's works served as tools for negotiating different spheres of power and conceptions of identity that jockeyed for supremacy in sixteenth- and seventeenth-century Sri Lanka. Whether working as a court poet under a Sinhala king or as a clerk in a colonial regime, Alagiyavanna employed his skills toward carving out a space within which he could function and achieve his aims within the competing structures of power at the time. This study of Alagiyavanna will allow us to see how Sinhala poetry could do more than just express conventional aesthetic sentiments in a vernacular language. His works illustrate attempts to speak persuasively and authoritatively through literature in order to influence how power is envisioned and religion is practiced. Alagiyavanna composed works that expanded the boundaries of what Sinhala poetry could accomplish and to whom it could speak. His works provide us with more insights into how the onset of colonial power effected marked changes in Buddhist culture and religious identity in early modernity.

2

The Aesthetics of Power and The Cock's Message

ALAGIYAVANNA MUKAVEṬI COMPOSED *Sävul Sandēśaya* (*The Cock's Message*) in the early 1580s, a time when King Rājasiṃha I enjoyed unsurpassed dominion and caused great anguish for the Portuguese. This work comprising 207 quatrains in the *sivupada* style reveals how poetry and power were envisioned to interrelate at this time. Sheldon Pollock, in writing on Sanskrit literature as the dominant mode of cultural and political expression in premodern South Asia, utilizes the terms *kāvya* ("poetry") and *rājya* ("kingship") to discuss how literary cultures were traditionally the products of specific polities that aspired to command extensive authority over land and people.[1] In Sri Lanka and other parts of South Asia, the work of poetry was therefore often engaged and exhibited in royal courts. Kings gave patronage to poets, while poets eulogized kings in verse. More specifically, the symmetry of this relationship provided poets with fame and wealth from their association with kings, while kings could depend on poets for friendship and to establish their properly regal identity, spreading and securing their fame.[2]

The development of poetic genres in South Asia was typically based on the prestige language of Sanskrit. Buddhist works in Pāli verse are likely as old as any other form of Buddhist literature preserved in Sri Lanka, a fact to which the *Dhammapada, Theragātha, Therīgātha,* and *Sutta Nipata* attest.[3] Although these canonical works appear in verse form, they exhibit characteristics that are distinct from Sanskrit *kāvya* and may be seen as possessing a different genealogy. While poetical in form, these mnemonic Pali works lack the "literariness" of *kāvya* works, which were composed through the technology of writing with a reflexive awareness of textuality.[4] Likely the oldest, extant example of *kāvya* that originated in Sri Lanka was the sixth-century *Jānakīharaṇa* (*The Theft of Sītā*), which was composed as a Sanskrit *mahākāvya* by an author known as Kumāradāsa. Tradition holds that this poet was King Kumāra Dhātusena, who ascended the throne in Sri Lanka around 515 CE.[5] The renown of this work is exhibited by the attention it received in India centuries after its original composition.[6]

The development of Sinhala poetry also occurred in proximity to kings and courts in later centuries. The oldest extant poetic works in Sinhala, the *Muvadevdāvata* (*Account of the Makhādeva Jātaka*) and the *Sasadāvata* (*Account of the Sasa Jātaka*)—both likely dating from around the eleventh or twelfth centuries, retell *jātaka* stories of the Bodhisattva's former lives in the ornate style of Sanskrit *kāvya*. In the former, a king is extolled for his virtue, while in the latter work the poet praises Queen Līlāvatī and her royal minister as his patrons.[7] Later, King Parākramabāhu II, taking the story of King Kusa as his subject, composed *Kavsiḷumiṇa* (*Crest-Gem of Poetry*) in the *eḷu* style of literary Sinhala in the thirteenth century. This work set the standard for subsequent poetic writing in Sinhala.[8] Fashioned in accordance with the literary norms of the Sanskrit *mahākāvya*, *Kavsiḷumiṇa* staked a claim for the ability to compose poetry in Sinhala that could still be recognized for its beauty and conformity to classical Sanskrit conventions.

In the fifteenth century, numerous Sinhala poetic works were composed and recited as practices in cultural refinement and in the eulogistic praise of kings. The rise of powerful kings in the kingdom of Koṭṭe in the southwest of the island set the stage for this era of Sinhala poetry. As Pollock has argued for India, the ideas of *kāvya* and *rājya* were also mutually constitutive in premodern Sri Lanka, whereby expressions of royal power were articulated in aesthetic practices of poetry. Thus, while kings such as Parākramabāhu VI (r. 1411–1467) governed the greater part of the island, poets such as Toṭagamuve Śrī Rāhula composed impressive works such as the *mahākāvya* called *Kāvyaśēkhara* (*Crown of Poetry*). The fifteenth century was also the period when works conforming to older Sanskrit *praśasti* (i.e., eulogistic) and *sandeśa* ("messenger poems") formats became increasingly popular. It was a literary world described by Charles Hallisey as "preeminently a court culture" that participated in a "political economy whose ideal world was a unified hierarchy of wealth, power, status, value, and culture."[9] In this same world, poetry and power were intimately interconnected and mutually generative.

Such is the case with the *Pärakumbā Sirita*, a Sinhala *praśasti* poem traditionally—but wrongly—attributed to the renowned Śrī Rāhula. This poem assigned to the panegyric category of *praśasti* poetry contains a eulogy of the great king of Koṭṭe, replete with meters suitable for instrumentation and dancing in court performances, as well as a tendency to resort to slightly modified Sanskrit borrowings for more pleasurable and distinctive sounds.[10] Like other vernacular *praśasti* works, the *Pärakumbā Sirita* relies heavily on its Sanskrit prototype in terms of content and form. It eulogizes the ruling king, provides a fixed genealogical succession, and catalogues the kingly traits of the dynasty to which the king is said to belong.[11] As the earliest extant and complete *praśasti* work in Sinhala, the *Pärakumbā Sirita* helped to inaugurate a new method of relating culture and power in premodern Sri Lanka. Closely related to the broader genre of *kāvya* in terms of its ornate qualities and its proximity to royal courts, the function of Sanskrit *praśasti* works was to communicate some vision of power and fame to the world.[12] At the same time, the *praśasti* poets who eulogize the king also claim some measure of skill and fame for themselves.

Sinhala literary culture in the fifteenth century also promoted the *sandeśa*, or "messenger," poem. At times closely related to *praśasti* works in terms of their eulogistic qualities, the *sandeśas* belong more specifically to a distinctive genre of verse works modeled loosely on Kālidāsa's *Meghadūta* (*Cloud-Messenger*) poem. Kālidāsa's classic work, in which a *yakṣa* petitions a cloud to carry a message of love to his wife from whom he has been separated, helps to frame the broader context for the composition of *sandeśa* poems throughout the Indic world. There is ample evidence of *sandeśa* works composed in Sanskrit and Tamil that dwell on the love and longing of a separated couple for whom the delivery of a message—often by a bird, a bee, or some other natural phenomenon—promises to ease the grief of separation.[13] The existence of such works throughout South India and Sri Lanka remind us of the fact that local literary cultures such as those involving Sinhala, Tamil, Telugu, and Malayalam were informed by and connected with one another.[14]

However, when Sinhala poets began composing *sandēśas* in Sinhala verse, probably around the thirteenth century, they discarded the theme of love and grief in separation. Instead, most of the early Sinhala *sandēśas* narrate a story in which a bird is sent to deliver a message to a deity or a similarly virtuous figure and invoke blessings of protection and prosperity for the king. The importance of regal figures in these works invites the insertion of eulogistic verses, further reinforcing the close ties between culture and power in premodern Sinhala society. Yet these poems still trace a clear and identifiable route along the countryside, utilizing local geographical knowledge to provide a familiar and attractive setting. Thus, prior to the sixteenth century, we find swans (*tisara* / *haṃsa*), a peacock (*mayūra*), a dove (*parevi*), a starling (*säḷahiṇi*), a parrot (*girā*), and a cuckoo (*kōkila*) all enlisted by Sinhala poets to carry messages that augment the fame and power of kings in specific Sri Lankan polities. Power, it must be noted, was not restricted to the political authority of kings at this time. It also reflected the cultural and religious power of monastic authors who often studied and resided at one of several *piriveṇas* or Buddhist monastic colleges known for their scholastic and literary activities.[15]

However, when Alagiyavanna Mukaveṭi emerges as a self-proclaimed "lord of poetry" (*kavindraya*) in the late sixteenth century, the Sinhala literary culture that he modeled and evoked was under stress. Frequent warfare in the island's lowlands took its toll on the lay support of Buddhist monastic institutions, making it increasingly difficult for monks to engage in educational and literary pursuits. Portuguese policies on religion, although at times erratically enforced, called for demolishing heathen temples, expelling non-Christian priests, and favoring converts in competition for public offices and remunerative posts.[16] Although Portuguese power was at this time generally restricted to the coastal regions of the west and south, their influence over the Koṭṭe kingdom led to the dissolution of many *piriveṇas* and the diminution of Sinhala verse works celebrating royal power and aesthetic pursuits. Over the approximately ninety years of the so-called Sītāvaka Period (1530–1620), there are only a handful of literary works that survive from that era.[17] The dearth of works from this period intimates both the reduction in scholarly activity and the difficulty in producing and preserving texts.

Alagiyavanna was the son of a renowned scholar named Dharmadhvaja, and thus he received a strong education in letters and languages in the village of Hisälla, close to the inland capital of Sītāvaka. He purportedly learned the academic sciences from his father, receiving training in grammar, prosody, and the literary languages of Sanskrit, Pāli, Sinhala, and Tamil.[18] Pandit Dharmadhvaja is credited with writing a manual on the interpretation of dreams called *Svapnamālaya*, having compiled material from Sanskrit, Pāli, Tamil, and earlier Sinhala sources.[19] Alagiyavanna's training made him a suitable candidate to find a place at the king's court. It has also been suggested that since his father served in the Sītāvaka court under Māyādunnē, Alagiyavanna was able to secure a position as a *mukaveṭi* in the court of Rājasiṃha I (r. 1578–1593).[20] The office of a *mukaveṭi* is perhaps best translated as a "magistrate." Modern scholarship often glosses the term as a "royal secretary" (*lēkam*), one who is responsible for writing down the orders of the king.[21] However, a fifteenth-century description of the *mukaveṭi* from the *Haṃsa Sandēśaya* illustrates that this office had broader responsibilities:

> On one side there are the palace *mukaveṭis*,
> Whose minds lack unwholesome, bad qualities, who avoid false speech,
> And who speak cleverly in all situations,
> Knowing with certainty the explanations of legal proceedings.[22]

It is in this respect that we can posit that Alagiyavanna functioned more like a magistrate who was empowered to hear and pass judgments on minor legal cases on behalf of the king, who acted as the supreme judge of the land. As a magistrate who enjoyed more power than an ordinary secretary, Alagiyavanna had the responsibility of solving legal disputes over lands, as well as recording births, deaths, and land revenues.[23]

Aside from being a palace official, Alagiyavanna evidently was also a poet of some regard. His early poetic works written in the 1580s exhibit the unmistakable traces of the courtly poetic tradition of previous generations. His occupation and his outlook were at this time profoundly shaped by his location in the court of Rājasiṃha I. Between around 1582 and 1585 when he composed his earliest extant work—*Sävul Sandēśaya*—his patron king was at the apex of his power, having driven the Portuguese out of Koṭṭe and having laid siege to their fort in Colombo from 1579 to 1581. Although Rājasiṃha I did not succeed in expelling the Portuguese from the island, he isolated their influence while setting out to bring much of the island's southern territory under his control. In 1582, Rājasiṃha I attacked and subdued the rival mountain kingdom of Kandy, effectively asserting his authority over the upcountry as well. The king's skillful command of large numbers of troops and war elephants put the Portuguese and Kandyans back on their heels. So Alagiyavanna, who served the king's court as both magistrate and poet, found it fitting to praise this powerful king in ways that adhered closely to the recognized poetic conventions of Sinhala *sandeśas*.

Sävul Sandēśaya tells the story of a cock sent to carry a message from Sītāvaka to the god Saman at his shrine in the city of Saparagamuva (modern-day Ratnapura) in the southern hills of the island. In authoring a *sandeśa* poem, Alagiyavanna was clearly modeling his work after the bird messenger poems that proliferated in the Koṭṭe kingdom in the previous century. The 207 quatrains (*sivupada*) in this work contain various meters, most of which contain the distinctive *eḷisama* rhyming scheme of Sinhala poetry wherein the final phoneme in each line of a quatrain is alike. This text is arguably his most ornate work, with lengthy sections that describe the king, cities, forests, and women in a highly embellished fashion. Alagiyavanna's *Sävul Sandēśaya* is highly derivative of the many *sandeśa* poems that appeared earlier—a fact that modern critics often denounce.[24] However, it is worth recalling that originality was not highly valued in the literary culture of premodern Sri Lanka. This work emulated and sought to improve on the older *sandeśa* works. *Sävul Sandēśaya* also portrays a consistency with the poetic ideals and political imagination of medieval Sinhala culture, which is a testament to the fairly marginal status of the Portuguese at the time.

Chief among the purposes of Sinhala court poetry was to eulogize the king and his court in the manner of Sanskrit *praśasti* poems. Pollock reminds us that in ancient India the Sanskrit *praśasti* reflected the purposeful joining of culture and power, wherein political selfhood was expressed in terms of aesthetic connoisseurship.[25] The fame of a king such as Rājasiṃha I was in theory established and confirmed in poetry written in a highly ornate and literary style. The *Sävul Sandēśaya* was clearly written to extol and to procure divine blessings for Rājasiṃha I. The effusive and extravagant praise offered to the king is characteristic of Sinhala *sandeśas* and their celebration of both aesthetic and political power. Alagiyavanna's work excels in this regard, devoting thirty-nine verses—more than the other *sandeśas* that preceded his own work—to describe in flowery terms the majesty, prowess, and virtues of Rājasiṃha I.[26] There was for Alagiyavanna perhaps no better way to build his reputation and receive patronage than to celebrate the king in aesthetically rich Sinhala verse as poets such as Śrī Rāhula did for King Parākramabāhu VI.

Before the poet lavishes his royal patron with praise, he first employs the cock to carry his message, and he dutifully describes the beauty of Sītāvaka in an idealized manner through the bird's eyes. He flatters the cock in the first lines, saying, "May you live long, O' noble lord of cocks," before praising his rubylike crest and pearl-like wings.[27] These lines appear in the alliterative, rhyming style of *vṛttagandhi* prose, a contrivance used to distinguish certain eulogistic statements within the work. The narrator begins by addressing the cock as "friend" (*saki*) to establish a bond between them and to persuade the bird to set off on his journey.[28]

> Friend, who is like a ray of light that has adorned the sky of friendship, and who is like a large, flapping gem-pendant, I shall recite that message [for the god Saman] subsequently. But now, as I send you off, adorn your ears with the gem earrings of praise for this city, which is the essence of splendor and which possesses all riches.[29]

At this point the poet begins a series of verses praising the city of Sītāvaka, its wealth, and its inhabitants. As the capital of King Rājasiṃha's realm, Sītāvaka was the site of the court in which Alagiyavanna served. He lauds the city in the characteristically overstated manner of ornate court poetry.

> My friend, may you understand that the decorated city of Sītāvaka,
> Which provides your protection, showing great splendor at all times,
> Is like a peerless mother to the entire world,
> With whitish glory shining like the luminous moon.
> The high, solid ramparts that shine with crystal rays,
> Equal to the dazzling light of the moon that extends throughout all directions,
> Are like the coils of Ananta, the Lord of Cobras, laid all around,
> As the milky ocean of this city shines with the Nārāyaṇa of the king.[30]

Such extensive praise borrows from stock imagery and ideas found in *kāvya* throughout South Asia. The supposed radiance of the capital is compared to the moon, while its walls are said to be beautiful and strong, akin to the coils of Ananta, on whom the god Viṣṇu—here, Rājasiṃha I—dwells. The city's magnificence mirrors that of the king who resides there, and thus the poet's praise of Sītāvaka also counts as praise for him.

From here the poet continues to describe and praise—note even the Sinhala word *varṇanā* means both "description" (*vistaraya*) and "praise" (*stuti*)—embellishing the city and its inhabitants in richly descriptive terms.[31] These verses testify to the poet's idealization of the close relationship between culture and power that was likewise the hallmark of *kāvya* and *praśasti* works throughout Indic civilization. It is important to note just how idyllic this description must have been. Rājasiṃha's power was impressive, but the frequent and extended military campaigns on which he embarked would have drained away much of the kingdom's available wealth. The city of Sītāvaka, which had been sacked by the Portuguese at least twice before Rājasiṃha acceded to the throne, was unlikely to have matched the imaginative vision of the poet.[32]

Instead, Alagiyavanna describes Sītāvaka with the stock images available to him in other Sinhala poetic works. For example, verse 15 of *Sävul Sandēśaya* cites a story from Hindu mythology to compare the appearance of the city's wealth to the size and luminosity of the ocean:

> This excellent city that is overspread with rays from the great heaps,
> Of costly pearls and gems shining in the large marketplace,
> Exhibited to all persons the appearance of the ocean,
> Whose water Agasti thence brought with cupped hands and drunk.[33]

The story of the sage Agasti drinking the ocean dry to reveal the gems stored within also appears in *Kavsiḷumiṇa*: "Because of the diffusion of the heaps of rays that shone from the numerous attractive jewels, [the city] exceeded the ocean whose waters were drunk by the sage."[34] The same image of the ancient Hindu sage drinking the waters of the ocean to reveal the *asuras*, but in the process also revealing marvelous gems appears in several other Sinhala *sandēśas*. The fifteenth-century *Säḷalihiṇi Sandeśaya*, for example, employs this image:

> Friend, look there at the dazzling lamps on the main road,
> Like the delightful multitude of gems that appeared at the time,
> The sage Agasti took into the lotus of his hand,
> The nectar of the deep, mass of water that filled the great ocean.[35]

The *Tisara Sandeśaya*, which also precedes Alagiyavanna's work, references the story of Agasti drinking up the ocean's waters: "In the past when one named Agasti, who was born from a water pot, took [the water] with his palm and dried up the seven oceans."[36] The repeated use of select images from Hindu mythology, common throughout most Sinhala *sandēśas*, illustrates the shared poetic imagery and conventions in this genre.

The readiness with which Alagiyavanna appropriates the poetry of earlier authors does not signal a lack of imagination on his part, but rather it shows a desire to be recognized as a great poet whose verse recalls and excels the *kavi* of renowned poets from earlier times. The poet's reliance on *kavi* to shape a world and to fashion a public image of himself in the process was an inherently conservative enterprise, one that drew on a plethora of older models ranging from ancient India to fifteenth-century Koṭṭe.[37] While describing the beauty of the city, Alagiyavanna follows established conventions to describe the beauty of those who inhabit it.

> There the elephants in rut, while looking at the splendid faces of the beautiful, adorned women,
> Who have entered the window terraces of the spotless mansions of gems,
> Thinking they are beautiful, fully blossomed lotuses,
> Extend their trunks and wander about with puzzled minds.[38]

Aside from the fact that no one would welcome elephants in rut wandering through a city, given their unpredictable and violent natures when they prepare to mate, this unreal description is again borrowed from another poetic work. In its ornate description of a city, *Tisara Sandeśa* similarly states:

> When elephants intoxicated with rut, seeing the beautiful faces of the delicate women,
> Who have entered upon the window terraces of sapphire mansions,
> Stretch out their trunks in wonder at those fully blossomed lotuses,
> It is like the great Rāhu who journeyed about to seize the moon.[39]

It is more important for Alagiyavanna to fashion an image of Sītāvaka that coheres with the literary visions of other cities than it is to portray a realistic picture of the city as such. The poem's description of the city must be beautiful and delightful. In the logic of *kāvya*, the poet may make the city appear more beautiful since well-crafted words of poetry were recognized as a profoundly generative force that could transform the world.[40]

In Praise of the Court

While Alagiyavanna sought to create a delightful, idealized world by using the aesthetic tools and tropes of literature available to him, this same world was also pervaded and enriched by symbols of power. So the city, which is so dazzling that its splendor is said to fool the prostitutes into ruefully mistaking night for day, must also be home to a large and impressive royal court.[41] Similar to Sanskrit *kāvya* (and earlier Sinhala *sandeśas*), the royal court was the primary location for the production and enjoyment of this work.[42] The genre presupposed a body of elites who commanded social power and the aesthetic skills to appreciate poetry. In particular, the *Sävul Sandēśaya* richly describes the royal princes, the kings of neighboring countries, Brahmins uttering blessings, ministers, poets, and generals, all fulfilling their prescribed roles and paying homage to the king. It is this description of the court that serves to aggrandize the power and fame of the king, who appears here as the foremost among elites and deserving of their veneration.

> The kings of various countries, making offerings and tributes,
> Presenting appropriate silken cloths, camphor, musk, and sandalwood,
> In the manner of rivers and streams that flow into the ocean,
> Stand well and offer the lotuses of their hands to the tops of their heads.[43]

This verse makes clear that the kings of all other lands submit to the power and authority of Rājasiṃha I. As the recipient of tribute from others, the king at Sītāvaka is established by the poem as the most powerful king. His court, meanwhile, is depicted as the site for elaborate displays of obeisance.

The Sītāvaka court is also the site for poets and magistrates—people like Alagiyavanna—to appear before the king and participate in these rituals of power. Such persons may also be recipients of praise, and thus Alagiyavanna engages in a conspicuous attempt to fashion himself as an invaluable member of the king's court. He does not overtly identify himself with these figures, but there is really no need for him to do so, since he describes himself at the end of the poem as a *mukaveṭi* who is learned in the art of poetry. The inclusion of both magistrates and poets in the idealized description of the royal court highlights the centrality of rule-based knowledge and verbal skills to the fusion of culture and power in early modern Sri Lanka.

> The collection of magistrates (*mukaveṭi*) who cause the world to flourish,
> Who have understood with their acute knowledge,
> The extent of the water in the great ocean along with the entire earth,
> Remain like the light of the full moon in the Milky Ocean of the court.[44]

Thus, like the rays of the full moon that cause the ocean's waters to rise, the palace magistrates similarly cause the kingdom to grow and prosper. Meanwhile, poets, too, have an important role to play in this idealized court.

> Great poets who know prosody, poetic embellishments, and grammar, which delight,
> Having a deep acquaintance with Sanskrit, Pāli, Sinhala and Tamil,
> Composing verses of praise while employing sweet meanings,
> Recite them continually in the assembly of the King.[45]

This verse depicts the figure of a poet in sixteenth-century Sri Lanka. A poet was ideally trained in the classical spheres of literary knowledge, multilingual and versed in the works of numerous genres and tongues, and able (if not expected) to recite his work before a king. Such an image, patterned after Alagiyavanna himself, was the norm in earlier poetic works and treatises on poetry.[46]

The verses describing and praising the members of the court are of course also designed to glorify the king. It is King Rājasiṃha I who presides over this assembly, and he emerges as the central figure throughout nearly the first half of the poem. In the idyllic world created by the poet, the king appears as an extraordinary being whose virtues and talents are unmatched. One of the first quatrains extolling the king summarizes some of the main features that recur continually throughout the eulogistic stanzas dedicated to the poet's patron and protector:

> Having limitless fame akin to the pure, white moon and a string of pearls,
> And who remains as fitting in the noble lineage of King Manu,

Like the lion who splits open the rutting elephants of enemy kings,
The noble King Rājasiṃha is triumphant in this excellent city.[47]

The king's fame is a central theme of the panegyric. For centuries throughout South Asia, poets lauded and contributed to the fame of the kings who were, or were expected to become, their patrons. A particularly rich bardic tradition was present in Tamil-speaking South India in the classical, pre-*bhakti* period of the first half of the first millennium CE. Tamil poetry was at this time essentially bardic in nature and divisible into the erotic, inward genre of *akam* poems and the heroic, outward genre of *puram* poems, both of which were collected into the so-called *caṅkam* anthologies and preserved.[48] These works are notable for celebrating the deeds and qualities of ancient kings. Sanskrit *praśasti* poems were similarly devoted to generating the fame of kings—as evidenced in their genealogies, generosity, and the power they commanded over others.[49]

Although panegyric verse works in Sinhala appear much later than their Tamil and Sanskrit counterparts, the *Sävul Sandēśaya* shows how they typically were directed toward the same purposes of celebrating and enhancing the fame of a king. Sinhala *kavi* transcended its everyday, vernacular status by availing itself to the highly affected poetic dialect of *eḷu*, thus describing and praising kings, cities, and courts in a version of the language reserved for poetic expression. Pollock reminds us, however, not to mistake poetic, aesthetic discourse for a sphere of concern outside the political. When *praśasti* works, in written or epigraphical form, drew on Sanskrit *kāvya*'s "rich repertoire of formal and rhetorical devices," they did so to create and preserve the fame of the king.[50] Sinhala *kavi* in the fifteenth and sixteenth centuries aspired to similar ends, and thus we find Alagiyavanna drawing direct correspondences between objects of divine creation and the features of the king:

Leaving aside the shining moon, ambrosia, and the wish-fulfilling gem and tree,
That arose when Viṣṇu stirred the Milky Ocean,
Considering his gentle face, speech, mind, and hands together,
It is as if this renowned lord was created by the Great Brahmā.[51]

Drawing on conventional descriptions from Sanskrit *kāvya* and Hindu mythology, Alagiyavanna portrays Rājasiṃha in a superlative way, as a person bestowed with exceptional beauty, eloquence, intellect, and generosity. He forgoes providing specific evidence for these claims—for example, describing how the king actually appears or citing specific events of pleasing speech or extensive benevolence—and instead relies on the rhetorical power of poetic tropes and language to make his case. In the context of the Sītāvaka court, this would certainly be enough.

Alagiyavanna's praise for his king was thus conventional by design. It was well understood that poets established the reputation of kings and their verses would in theory supply the ruler with seemingly eternal fame. To the extent that poetic works from earlier generations survived in the minds and words of Alagiyavanna's contemporaries, it was eminently reasonable to model his own verses after the bards that preceded him.

> The great abundance of fame of this Lord of Men, who is foremost in the whole world,
> And who appears like the multicolored gem on top of the crown of the Solar Dynasty,
> Displayed the appearance of the white parasol above the head of Brahmā,
> Covering the extent of the world with the shining staff of the celestial river.[52]

This description of Rājasiṃha's fame draws on various kingly and divine images to fashion a depiction of royal glory that is without equal.[53] Alagiyavanna's eulogistic verse also has the merit of recalling a couplet from *Kavsiḷumiṇa*:

> His fame remained like the splendor of the white parasol above the head of Brahmā,
> Covering the extent of the world with the shining staff of the heavenly river.[54]

Alagiyavanna's use of a verse extolling the fame of King Kusa in *Kavsiḷumiṇa* is creative and appropriate given the fact that he uses a description of the Bodhisattva from an exemplary Sinhala verse work to extol his king. Such poetic phrasings embellish the reputation of king and poet at the same time. The former is cast as deserving of extensive praise, while the latter is shown to be uniquely capable of doing so.

Elsewhere *Sävul Sandēśaya* confers the qualities of aesthetic excellence on the king and the poet in a more straightforward manner. As Pollock notes for premodern India, kingly virtuosity was defined in Sanskrit aesthetic treatises by showing the king to be centrally involved as a critic and a connoisseur in all of the entertainments held at the court.[55] This means that the king, as the living symbol of the interdependence of culture and power, must excel in both aesthetic as well as martial pursuits. His identity and reputation demanded that he should be both connoisseur and conqueror.

> This Lord of Men who is famous throughout the eight directions
> and the crown of the Solar Dynasty,
> Knowing how to handle the eighteen types of weapons, defeated
> and scattered his foes,
> He has come to know the meaning of the eighteen *Purāṇas* by
> heart,
> And has learned the languages of the eighteen countries like his
> own language.[56]

Here we are told that Rājasiṃha displays mastery over the realms of both war and learning.[57] He is lauded for his ability to overcome his enemies, but he is also attributed with the knowledge of numerous languages. The significance of being multilingual rests in the king's associated capacity to consult and recognize the treatises composed in many different tongues. His ear and his taste are thus presumed to be more refined, allowing him to appreciate *kāvya*.

It then follows that because of Rājasiṃha's capacity for aesthetic enjoyment, he requires the service of great poets who can recite verses that will delight and edify the king's court. In a setting in which power and fame are esteemed, modesty was not a virtue of poets. The final verse of the *Sävul Sandēśaya* shows Alagiyavanna bestowing himself with praise.

> The very fine pandit named Alagivan Mukaveṭi,
> Who dove into the deep ocean of poetry and drama in Sanskrit and
> Pāli,
> Who, like a lion, destroyed the elephants of poets who are his foes,
> Composed the *Cock's Message* with a sweet poetic sentiment.[58]

Modern readers would likely react first and foremost to the seeming arrogance in the poet's self-description in this verse.[59] More striking, however, is the obvious move to conflate kingly and poetic qualities. We have already seen praise for King Rājasiṃha I whereupon he is said to be "like the lion who splits open the rutting elephants of enemy kings."[60] Such an image fits Rājasiṃha, whose name translates as "Lion of Kings." When Alagiyavanna describes himself as a lion who slays other poet-elephants, he similarly casts his craft in terms of royal power. Hallisey points out that between the tenth and fifteenth centuries the accomplishments and abilities of Sinhala authors were commonly spoken of in terms of kingship, including the famed Pāli commentator Buddhaghosa who was said in the twelfth-century *Jātaka-aṭuvāgäṭapadaya* to have been able to destroy his opponents as if bursting open the frontal globes of elephants.[61] Likewise, Alagiyavanna fashioned an identity for himself based on the duality of culture and power. If kings were held to be like poets, then the reverse would be true as well.

But *Sävul Sandēśaya* does not paint a picture of cultured aesthetes engaged solely in leisurely forms of entertainment. Alagiyavanna's work repeatedly suggests instead that life at the Sītāvaka court was also connected with warfare. The military might attributed to Rājasiṃha I would obviously color a large part of the eulogistic praise used to portray his fame. Consequently, we find verses extolling the king's skill with his sword and bow, his horsemanship, and his control of his elephant (vv. 59–65). But there are other subtle signs that Rājasiṃha I's reign is characterized by frequent conflict with enemy forces. When Alagiyavanna writes "When the moon of this Lord is moving across the sky of this Sri Lanka, dispelling the thick darkness of enemies who are without limit" he indicates not only something about the beauty and attractiveness of Rājasiṃha I but also that this king is continually engaged in fighting hostile foes.[62] These lines appear to recall the numerous times that Rājasiṃha led armies into battle against the Portuguese and the Kandyans. In addition, the description of "the great army that destroys and conquers the enemy armies" remaining along the roads of Sītāvaka is suggestive of a city that was always on guard.[63]

Notwithstanding the poetic embellishments in the many references to warfare in this work, the reader comes away with the distinct impression that the idealized world of Rājasiṃha I was not free from threats or danger. Alagiyavanna never identifies exactly who these enemies are. It stands to reason that this would have been both unnecessary and inappropriate for the genre, since naming them would effectively introduce into the poem clear rivals to the king's power and authority. The enemies of this powerful king never rise to a level of significance that they require naming. It is preferable for the poet to speak of the king and his battles in abstract, conventional ways. Thus, for example, he mentions several times the trope of the grieving wives of enemy kings who were felled by the powerful and heroic Rājasiṃha.

> When the thunderbolt of the illustrious sword's edge continually strikes,
> The mountain peaks of the enemy kings from the great rain-cloud of this Lord's hand,
> The row of cranes of the pearl necklaces in the hands of their wives fall to the ground,
> When the great thunder of his fame spreads out in all directions.[64]

By depicting the women's jewelry falling to the ground, Alagiyavanna borrows a conventional poetic trope for demonstrating the grief of separation that women are said to feel when they must go on without their lovers. *Pärakumbā Sirita* contains a remarkably similar verse to praise King Parākramabāhu VI, albeit with the convention comparing women's breasts to swans rather than the image of a flock of birds frightened by a thunderclap.

> When the clouds of the edge of the sword, which whirls in the skilled hand
> Of the Lord of Lanka, continually rise in the west,
> The lotus sprouts of pearl necklaces fall from the swans of the breasts,
> Of the soft bosoms of the women of the enemy kings.[65]

To speak in this way of the grieving wives of one's slain enemies allowed poets like Alagiyavanna to incorporate poetic tropes about women into verses extolling the prowess of kings.[66] Their greatness defies specification—as this would suggest their feats were atypical for them—and instead demands the use of poetic conventions that would cast their fame in universal terms.

The themes of warfare and conflict, expressed as they are in classical poetic forms, are suggestive of the time when Alagiyavanna composed his first major work. In the context of an era marked by a Portuguese colonial presence, the obvious commitment Alagiyavanna makes to sustain classical poetic norms and conventions in *Sävul Sandēśaya* mirrors the martial attempts to keep the Portuguese at bay. In this sense, too, Alagiyavanna represents himself as a partner in the generation and extension of the power of the Sinhala king. Phrased differently, in the world of poetry, the centrality of the king is matched, or at least approached, by the poet. David Shulman speaks of the *kāvya* poet in the Tamil milieu as preeminently proud of his poetic achievement, as the work "reflects his linguistic skills, his command of a heavily conventionalized imagery and stock of conceits, and his general erudition, and which, moreover, is usually the source of his livelihood."[67] The ideal Sinhala *kavi* poet, a cocreator in the king's dominion that extended out from his court, was expected to exhibit a measure of pride as well.

Poetic Complexity and Aesthetic Excellence

Throughout *Sävul Sandēśaya* Alagiyavanna claims for himself the aesthetic skill and generative power that was celebrated in the poetry of medieval Sri Lanka. He identifies himself with the twin formation of culture and power, and the self-referential basis of his statements is unmistakable. The poet praises himself on several occasions when he rhetorically asks who can describe the beauty and majesty of the subjects of his poems. This move is subtle and clever since, at first glance, it seems to entail the rejection of one's own ability to describe something in verse. In several instances in his *Sävul Sandēśaya*, Alagiyavanna rhetorically asks if anyone short of a great god could describe and praise the virtues of something that he then goes on to describe and praise. For instance, while describing Sītāvaka, he writes:

> Who else except for Ananta or Śakra could praise or observe,
> The endless splendor in this city, which is filled with great riches,
> Where there always dwells an infinitely capable Great Army,
> Endowed with strong, powerful arms like Viṣṇu and Skandakumar?[68]

The answer, of course, is Alagiyavanna, since he is the one to praise the beauty of the city in his work. Even if he is not able to praise and describe Sītāvaka as well as a god, the fact that he makes the effort while displaying an impressive command of language and prosody suggests that his power of aesthetic expression approaches that of the gods themselves. Near the end of *Sävul Sandēśaya*, Alagiyavanna reminds us of his poetic skill when it comes to describing and praising the god Sumana, who is the recipient of the message carried by the cock.

What other erudite one, except for all these gods,
Such as Brahmā, Skandakumar, Brahāspati, Gaṇeṣa, and Ananta,
Is able to describe the splendor of the shining body of the majestic
god Sumana,
Which is like collyrium for the eyes of all gods and men?[69]

Again, the answer to this question is Alagiyavanna. He claims the capacity to describe Sumana in the preceding fourteen verses, in which he extols the god's appearance in detail from head to foot. Although his words seem to deny the possibility of description, they end up confirming the poet's tremendous power of aesthetic expression. It is only a poet like him who has the erudition and the linguistic skills to describe properly things of great beauty. He is the one who may create new worlds and experiences through his use of language. His command over lexicon, meter, and figures of speech allow him to sustain the culture-power formation that had long defined the courtly tradition in Sinhala culture.

Proficiency in *eḷu*, the artificial language of Sinhala poetry, was an important qualification required for composing and appreciating classical Sinhala *kavi*. The marked diglossia that characterizes the distinct differences between the Sinhala language as spoken and the version that is written has been ably discussed in linguistic research.[70] In general, literary Sinhala employs a more elaborate syntax, lexicon, and morphology, wherein verbs are inflected by number and person. Nevertheless, even with often lengthy sentences and "Sanskritized" forms of words, the Sinhala prose of the twelfth to fourteenth centuries retained a higher degree of accessibility than the Sinhala poetry of the tenth to fifteenth centuries had. The literary culture of *eḷu* poetry instead celebrated what Hallisey calls "an ethos of complexity and difficulty" that made it less accessible to most Sinhala speakers.[71] Poets and the connoisseurs of poetry made up a distinguished group in late medieval Sri Lanka. They utilized their aesthetic sensibilities as a measure of distinction, whereby their cultivated taste for poetry united them as a cultural elite and separated them from all others who were unable to produce or enjoy such works.[72] One's association with the royal court entitled one to a measure of social standing and privilege that few others in early modern Sinhala society could rival. Typically those who excelled in the arts of culture and war found a place in the courts of the Sinhala kings.

Aside from the cock-messenger, the only figures that appear in Alagiyavanna's *Sävul Sandēśaya* are members of the court, leading religious figures, divine beings, and beautiful women. The poem recognizes and celebrates a rather small, select population in the late sixteenth century. The beings encountered by the cock—and, by extension, the audience of the work—are an elite and exceptional lot, those belonging to and participating in the distinctive world evoked by Sinhala *kavi*. Full participation in this world required refined aesthetic skills. One must have some command over culture, an ability that entitles one to power and fame. This characteristic was made more exclusive by practices of difficulty, which in turn generated the power and prestige so prized by Sinhala literary culture.[73]

Among the practices of difficulty available to a poet like Alagiyavanna was the use of the language of *eḷu*. Despite some claims that hold *eḷu* to be the original form of the Sinhala language, it is more likely the case that it developed as a vernacular medium for producing poetry modeled after, yet distinct from, Sanskrit *kāvya*.[74] By creating a new vocabulary based on an abbreviated alphabet, Sinhala poets used new sounds to allude to familiar concepts borrowed from Buddhist thought and Sanskrit and Tamil literature. For example, the word for "Buddha" became *budu*, for "Dharma" became *daham*, *alaṅkara* became *lakara*, *puṇya* became *piṅ*, *śrī* became *siri*, and so forth. Consonant clusters were broken up, while aspirated consonants and the palatal and labial *s* were dropped. Although not every familiar word was transformed into a new poetic equivalent, many words did undergo substantial change for inclusion in Sinhala verse. The creation of a new poetic lexicon thus required a specialized linguistic knowledge that was the product of education in the sciences of literature (*śāstras*) and exposure to this literary genre.

Other practices of difficulty included the metrical and phonetic rhyming schemes used in the composition of Sinhala poetic works. The *sivupada* form of Sinhala poetry, on which Alagiyavanna based his verse works, dictated the use of certain meters and a structure in which the final phonemes of each line of verse are alike. These requirements meant that some words were given unusual accents by lengthening vowels that are normally short. Other words are often broken up to fit the meters and rhymes used in a particular verse. The voicing of certain words could then become elongated, making a given word possibly appear as two words to the uninitiated ear. For example, in verse 134 of *Sävul Sandēśaya*, the internal rhyme scheme involves a pause after an *-l* and a final *-a* in the first words of each line: *nil... kaṭa; nil .... gala; bäl... maṭa; pil ... äsa*. But in the first line, the second pause involves a break in the word *kaṭaroḷu*, which is a type of flower. In the third line, the verbal noun *bälmaṭa*, which appears in the dative ending, is also broken up to preserve the internal rhyme scheme. In this way, the writing and recitation of words in *eḷu* poetry can result in atypical usages, which makes the language of poetry more varied and complex than in ordinary usage.

The metrical and phonetic requirements of Sinhala *kavi* also frequently led to a looser, more complicated syntax to allow the poet to preserve the meter and rhyme of the verse. By ignoring the fixed word order of phrases found in Sinhala prose writing, Sinhala poets employed greater discretion in their arrangement of words, often separating adjectives from the nouns they modify and creating uncertainty over the referents for particular phrases and descriptions.[75] To illustrate this point, we may examine verse 120 from *Sävul Sandēśaya*, where the sun is described poetically:

> Friend, take a look at the sun with desire, as it wraps,
> Its yellow cloth of the dawn's rays around the sage of the eastern mountain,
> With shining fibres of rays like a solid gold broom that sweeps clean,
> The large heap of rubbish of the thick darkness in the courtyard of the world.[76]

The actual word order of the Sinhala verse is even more complicated than the English translation. Three modern editions of this work each provide a slightly different gloss to this verse, suggesting differences in the way that the word order should be read.[77] Different listeners or readers may then understand select verses differently. My translation of the verse renders the original Sinhala syntax in the following pattern (in which each number corresponds to the actual order of the Sinhala words):

5	9	8	6	7	11	12	10
22	28	27	25	26	24	23	
20	21	17	18	19	16		
1	15	14	13	3	2	4	

In order to understand the verse as it is read or recited, one must make numerous choices in regard to which word modifies another and which phrase more naturally follows another.[78] Practiced composers and connoisseurs of Sinhala *kavi* could be expected to make the necessary operations to understand such verses readily. For the rest of us, comprehension is a more challenging and time-consuming activity.

A poet's skill could be displayed in a great variety of ways. In *Sävul Sandēśaya*, Alagiyavanna occasionally goes to great lengths to demonstrate his poetic virtuosity. As such, another practice of difficulty found in *Sävul Sandēśaya* involves the use of double meanings to create patterns or ambiguity or even to allow a single verse to be interpreted in two wholly different ways. The skillful use of homonyms creates opportunities to generate linguistic complexity and aesthetic admiration. An example of this is seen in verse 151, in which Alagiyavanna reiterates the last word in one line as the first word of the following line, although with different meanings in each case. Thus, *dana* means "people" in one instance and "wealth" in the next, *nana* means "various" first and then the deity "Ananta," *vina* refers to "Ganeṣa" and then "except."[79] The repetition of words carrying multiple meanings requires skill in both composition and comprehension.

A more elaborate demonstration of the work's difficulty in composition is illustrated in verse 138, which can be read in two entirely different ways. It can be read as an ornate description of a city (*pura*) or a forest (*vana*), juxtaposing two different spheres of existence within a single quatrain.

> O' tawny-crested cock, look at the great splendor of the excellent city of the forest (*vana*),
> With sounds of birds spreading through the creepers and very expansive trees,
> Such as *sal* trees, *pil* trees, and *dorala* trees, endowed with buds and flowers in full bloom,
> And decorated with *nika* trees, *varana* trees, bees, and creepers.

Alternatively, the same Sinhala verse may be taken to describe an actual city, rather than a metaphorical one:

> O' tawny-crested cock, look at the great splendor and color (*vana*) of the excellent city,

With stalls and halls having open doors with gems, pearls, flowers, and coral,
With banners at intervals along the main road, overspread with the sounds of instruments and women,
And decorated with horses, elephants, kings, and royal ladies.[80]

Given that this verse is located within a section of the work that describes the jungle at Kuruviṭa, the former reading is more likely within the context of the narrative. However, the fact that the verse could be interpreted in an entirely different fashion signals an attempt by Alagiyavanna to display his mastery over the language of poetry. Both the poet and his audience may delight in the aesthetics of the verse and in the knowledge that they recognize its twin meanings. Displayed here and elsewhere in *Sävul Sandēśaya,* Alagiyavanna's literary skills endowed him with the elite status as a member of the court and, not coincidentally, as the recipient of several village lands given to him by the king.[81] Alagiyavanna's command of the literary arts enhanced his personal wealth and power as a landowner at a time when Portuguese power in the island had ebbed and did not obstruct either literary or martial expressions of Sinhala power.

Religious Pluralism, Religious Practice

The strong, timely validation that Alagiyavanna's *Sävul Sandēśaya* gives to the traditional culture-power formation in premodern Sinhala society is not the only noteworthy feature of the work. Along with the emphases given to aesthetic excellence and courtly life, this work also illustrates the prevalence of pluralistic religious forms and identity in late sixteenth-century Sri Lanka. Importantly, Buddhist thought and practice are not the primary concerns of this work. *Sävul Sandēśaya* nevertheless depicts a world where religious identity and practice appear unfixed and difficult to circumscribe in a clear and definitive way. In contrast to modern Sri Lankan Buddhism in which arguments over what is and is not legitimately Buddhist remains a central preoccupation in people's lives, Alagiyavanna's first work remains indifferent to such concerns.[82] Distinctions between Buddhist and Hindu practices are blurred, and there are no instances in which the poet articulates a concept comparable to Buddhism as a distinct system of religious thought and practice.

Instead, the religious landscape of *Sävul Sandēśaya* mirrors in many ways the pluralistic vision of religious practice found in the literature of fifteenth-century Koṭṭe. In this vision, Buddhists were encouraged to worship a pantheon of gods, mostly bequeathed to them from Hindu texts and rituals, for this-worldly blessings such as health, security, and prosperity. Veneration of the Buddha, Dharma, and Sangha was also to be expected, since these practices helped to ensure good rebirths and progress toward nirvana. This privileging of the Buddha and his dispensation (*sāsana*) over all other superhuman beings allows for the incorporation of various deities into the Sinhala Buddhist system. As Richard Gombrich and Gananath Obeyesekere have shown, while only the way of the Buddha is thought to be able to solve the miseries of worldly existence, various other deities—Viṣṇu, Pattinī, Saman, Kataragama (Skandakumar), Huniyam, Kālī, and so forth—have risen to prominence now and then to receive the worship of Buddhists seeking assistance with their worldly needs and wants.[83] Although there are signs of increased criticism of Buddhists worshipping Hindu deities, deity shrines are still found located in many Buddhist temples in modern Sri Lanka.[84]

By most accounts, during the fifteenth century when Koṭṭe was the seat of the Sinhala throne, the worship of Hindu deities by Sinhala Buddhists was a common phenomenon. Martin Wickremasinghe, the influential Sinhala literary critic from the first half of the twentieth century, wrote of the Koṭṭe Period as a time when "the beliefs and forms of worship of the folk religion also crept into Buddhism" and also when the "Bodhisatvas [sic] of the Mahayanic faith as well as several gods of Hinduism such as Viṣṇu and Vibhīṣana entered the Buddhist vihāra and took their permanent abode there."[85] In Wickremasinghe's view, the *sandeśa* poems of Śrī Rāhula and others were mainly contrived borrowings from Sanskrit literature, which similarly articulated devotional expressions to various deities. Although a handful of authors such as Vīdāgama Maitreya challenged contemporary beliefs and practices associated with deities, most Buddhists continued to worship nominally Hindu gods at this time.[86] Buddhist temples and *piriveṇa*s appear to have been vibrant and well-endowed under the patronage of Koṭṭe kings. Throughout the island, however, the growing influence of Hinduism on popular religion meant that Buddhist and Hindu temples often stood side by side and attracted the same pilgrims.[87]

Within this environment, the distinction between Buddhist and Hindu practices was blurred. Alagiyavanna's *Sävul Sandēśaya* serves as a testimony to the popularity and normality of a syncretic religious culture that kings such as Rājasiṃha I worked to sustain under their rules.

The high status given to Hindu deities is shown by the numerous times Rājasiṃha I is praised in reference to them.

> When the glory of this king, who has the power of Viṣṇu and
> Skandakumar,
> Spreads to the ends of all directions, shining like the fire at the end
> of an eon,
> Iśvara, while wondering if it is a row of evening clouds,
> Becomes tired of dancing, not knowing when to stop.[88]

Verses such as this show how easily Hindu deities were incorporated into royal imagery and literary forms in Alagiyavanna's work, as they often were in fifteenth-century Sinhala poetry. Hindu deities functioned both as symbols of kingship and as poetic tropes. By choosing to compare his king to such gods as Viṣṇu, Rāma, and Skandakumar, Alagiyavanna was singling the king—and the gods—out for praise. Further, by continually evoking Hindu imagery in his verses, the poet drew on some of the defining features of Sanskrit *kāvya* to endow his work with qualities of literary excellence.

Alagiyavanna's *Sävul Sandēśaya*, however, goes beyond simply employing Hindu imagery for aesthetic purposes. This work exhibits a form of religiosity that combines Buddhist and Hindu practices into a coherent whole. As the poet maps out the journey of the cock from the king's court in Sītāvaka to the shrine of the god Saman in Saparagamuva, he instructs him to stop and worship at several Buddhist and Hindu sites, just like the pilgrims of his time would have been expected to do. In these sections, the bird messenger appears as a humanlike devotee who is coached in his worship by the author. At the shrine of the god Bhairava (the wrathful form of Śiva), the cock is instructed to gaze on the dancing offered up to the god, admire the paintings of scenes from Rāma's victory over Rāvana and the battle of the *Mahābhārata*, purify his hands and body, and pay homage to the goddess Umā. The work includes a description of devout worship of the goddess at this Hindu temple, which was located close to the palace in Sītāvaka, in the *sähäli* form of ten lines containing rhymed and unrhymed *gī* verse.

> Paying homage, while giving rise to affection in your heart,
> To noble Umā, who is endowed with the highest qualities,
> Who is the delight of the King of the Himalaya Mountain, which is
> noble, high, and large,

Who does not stray from the meaning of his words every day,
And who remains close to the faultless Iśvara always,
Renowned in the Three Worlds with the three appearances she assumes in the three periods,
Shining with the one-hundred leaves of her well-decorated, resplendent feet,
With the petals of her red fingers and the pistil of her divine crown, which is venerated,
And who gives excellent boons unceasingly to limitless, noble gods,
Such as Brahmā, Viṣṇu, Iśvara, and Śakra, and then taking your leave.[89]

Here the poet praises the Śaivite goddess Umā solely for the sake of devotion. She does not appear here to glorify the king. While the narrator guides the cock through the ritual ablutions and veneration in this section, we see a glimpse of how visitors to this shrine were expected to show their devotion to the goddess.[90] This account represents how textual description in *Sävul Sandēśaya* can easily shade over to prescription, as the narrator's instructions to the cock messenger also appear as enjoinders to the audience of the work. At times, the cock is imagined as partly human, and thus the narrator's injunctions may also be directed to speak to other humans who visit this and other sites mentioned therein.

After the cock is told to depart from the Bhairava *kovil* in Sītāvaka, he is to proceed along the prescribed path, taking the readers and listeners along with him in an imagined journey toward the southern hill city of Saparagamuva. The work describes the road traveled by the cock, mentioning rest houses, guard posts, and other route markers along the way. Soon after the cock must journey to the Delgamuwa Temple in Kuruviṭa and engage in forms of Buddhist veneration. The seamless transition from worshiping Hindu deities to Buddhist objects of veneration is instructive. There is no indication from the work that the cock was doing anything unusual or improper by worshiping at both Hindu and Buddhist sites. Instead, he is simply observing his ritual obligations at shrines comprising a pluralistic religious landscape.

As the sun sets at Delgamuwa, the cock is instructed to take up flowers in his "hands" and offer them to the gods "with happiness and great devotion in mind."[91] Once again, the cock stands in for the work's ideal reader or listener, a person whose hands are suitable for making offerings to images of the gods that are housed at the temple. Yet when the dawn comes, the cock's next task is to worship the Buddha's Tooth Relic, which had been kept at Delgamuwa, away from the Portuguese in Koṭṭe, at this time.[92]

> Pay homage with devotion, my friend, to the venerable Tooth Relic,
> Which is like the moon decorating the sky of the mouth of the Best of Sages,
> Whose resplendent lotuslike feet, being worshiped, always shine,
> With the rays of the crest-gems on the crowns of *brahmās*, gods, humans, and *nāgas*.[93]

In this verse and in many others, Alagiyavanna draws on stock poetic images and expressions to embellish the scenes of worship. The cock is told to venerate the Tooth Relic just as the myriad of other beings regularly does. As a potent symbol of Sinhala Buddhist kingship from at least the eleventh century, possession of the Tooth Relic was recognized as a prerequisite for justifying one's claim to the throne, and the relic acquired central importance in the performance of political functions.[94] The bird's stop at Delgamuwa allows the author to reassert the symbolic authority of both the Buddha over the next world and the Sinhala king over the present world.

Before leaving the Delgamuwa temple, the cock must perform a complete set of devotional activities to honor the Buddha. Then, as now, all sizeable Buddhist temples in Sri Lanka possessed a relic shrine, a *bodhi* tree, and an image of the Buddha to which offerings (*pūja*) may be made by devotees.[95] The narrator again reminds the cock about what he must venerate before proceeding with his journey.

> Friend, remaining serenely joyful through the three moments of thought, pay homage with devotion,
> To the image of the Buddha fashioned with the renowned noble marks [of a Great Being],
> The relic shrine made to enshrine the Tooth of the Lord of Sages,
> And the large Bodhi Tree, which is like an expansive rain cloud.[96]

Here again the *Sävul Sandēśaya* reads like a ritual handbook, telling one where to go and what to do when one gets there. In sum, the cock is led through a basic outline of Buddhist devotional practice to be performed at a *vihāra* (monastery).

Many of these same directions are repeated in the instructions for the cock to visit and venerate the temple's chief monk. Alagiyavanna borrows again from Śrī Rāhula's *Säḷalihiṇi Sandēśaya* when he writes about Mihiňdulakara Thera, saying the "pearl-necklace of his fame adorns the necks of poets."[97] In a testament to *Sävul Sandēśaya*'s expansive vision of Buddhist identity, even this monk is said to know not only the canonical Three Baskets of Buddhist scripture but also the arts of poetry (*kav*), drama (*naḷu*), prosody (*saňda*), and poetic embellishment (*lakara*).[98] In the Sinhala literary culture of the tenth to fifteenth centuries, to find such expertise in the figure of a Buddhist monk was not unusual. Śrī Rāhula's fame, for example, was based in part on his literary skills, although there were dissenting voices that criticized monastic involvement in the arts of poetry and drama. The layman Alagiyavanna, however, seems to have given little notice to the alleged disputes between Śrī Rāhula and his followers on the one hand and Vīdāgama Maitreya and his supporters on the other.[99] The two monks mentioned by name in the *Sävul Sandēśaya*—Mihiňdulakara at Delgamuwa and Dahaṁlakara at Saparagamuwa—are praised for being great poets, further evidence of the centrality of cultural pursuits in the expression of power in Alagiyavanna's world.

Even in the midst of *Sävul Sandēśaya*'s most formulaic verses that are devoted to literary expressions of skill and power, Alagiyavanna does not fail to direct the cock in religious observances. After admiring the lovely female bathers of Saparagamuwa, the cock is sent to venerate the Buddha at the local monastery. In a manner much like the veneration performed at Delgamuwa, the work describes the ritualized performance of *pūja* toward the relic shrine, Buddha images (reclining and sitting), and *bodhi* tree at this sacred site. The cock is instructed to venerate these various relics of the Buddha. The work thus invites the cock and the audience to recall the virtues of the "King of Sages," who "preached the unfathomable Dharma," "delights the world," and "defeated the rough and greedy Mara."[100] When he reaches the *bodhi* tree, we are told that "in order to obtain the prosperity of heaven" one should "bow down with devotion to the very tall *bodhi* tree."[101] Directing the practice of venerating Buddhist shrines, the author also finds it fitting to emphasize the benefits in doing so.

A lengthy *sähäli* verse dedicated to praising Dahaṁlakara, chief monk at the Saparagamuwa temple, follows the circuit of devotional displays that the cock must make. Again, the bird is directed to bow down before this monk and recognize the greatness that the poet attributes to him. We are told that the monk's "sweet, limitless verses" contain gems of meaning about the Dharma.[102] Further, the monk is said to exhibit great glory from his moral virtues and unblemished behavior, while residing like the "full moon surrounded by the stars" of other monks who likewise excel in disciplined conduct. If, as historians suggest, praiseworthy Buddhist monks were scarce during the Sītāvaka period, *Sävul Sandēśaya* still suggests that there were at least two exemplary monks in the territory ruled by King Rājasiṃha I. Alagiyavanna's praise for great monks and his use of the occasional Buddhist technical term such as the "Four Divine Abidings" (*sivu bamba viharaṇin*) and the "Fourfold Morality Consisting of Purification" (*sivu pirisudu sil*) demonstrates his awareness and respect for the Buddha's teaching.[103]

However, *Sävul Sandēśaya* does not end here in the monastery. It instead proceeds along to make one final stop at the shrine of the god Saman. Called a "palace of the gods," this *kovil* or *devale* is the site of a major shrine dedicated to Saman, a local guardian deity who is also associated with the shrine to the Buddha's footprint relic on top of Śrī Pāda or "Adam's Peak." At this point in the work the poet praises in the *sähäli* meter the chief ritual officiant at this *devale*, a man named Nānambi Kuruppu.[104] This reference in Alagiyavanna's work possibly reveals that Hindu institutions received considerable support from the king and that Kuruppu eventually assumed leadership of the Saman Devale.[105] From lines such as these, it stands to reason that the Hindu tradition likewise enjoyed a high standing in the king's realm.

Alagiyavanna's work praises the officiating priest in a grandiose fashion. He is called "noble and very pure," he is said to be endowed with "great power like Viṣṇu," and he is said to have mastered all the arts and weapons to become a paradigmatic actor within the culture-power formation of Sri Lankan society.[106] Kuruppu is also said to have come under "the shadow of the resplendent foot" (i.e., authority) of King Rājasiṃha I, which suggests that the temple priest was a loyal favorite of the king.[107] The fact that Kuruppu is praised and identified by name in the work suggests he was a man who enjoyed a high social status. It also indicates something of the importance given to temple rites in the religious system and literary culture of the period. *Sävul Sandēśaya* places a premium on religious and cultural performances, ignoring the subtleties of doctrinal formulations. The cock is instead told to gaze on the young women who dance, chant, and make offerings according to the customs at the shrine. This description allows the poet to indulge further in aesthetic devices and literary expressions connected with female beauty. For religion, like poetry itself, it is the formal expressions that count most in the world of *Sävul Sandēśaya*.

Finally, the work ends with a lengthy poetic account of the image of the god Saman at the shrine. Saman, who again is the intended recipient of the message, is the deity associated with Śrī Pāda, the mountaintop shrine with the Buddha's footprint relic in the southern hills of the island. Often included in the pantheon of the Four Warrant Gods (*sataravaraṁ rajadaruvō*) who were entrusted to help protect the Buddha's dispensation in Sri Lanka, Saman is deemed worthy of veneration and shrines to him are found today in numerous Buddhist temples across the island.[108] In *Sävul Sandēśaya*, Saman is conventionally described in ornate terms from head to feet.

> The beautiful forehead, shining with golden cloth that diffuses color,
> Of the renowned majestic god, who is the peerless eye to the Three Worlds,
> And whose head is decorated with the resplendent lotus feet of the Well-Gone One,
> Took the appearance of a rain cloud containing streaks of lightning.
> The luminous pair of eyebrows of the majestic god,
> Shining like a pair of blue banners that flutter on top of a sapphire pole,
> Took on the splendor of two lines of bees that shine and play without separation,
> Decorating well the blue water lilies of his eyes.[109]

These verses and the many that follow them paint a vivid picture of an icon that inspires devotion and an aesthetic appreciation of beauty. In certain ways, however, the deity is not that different from other specimens of beauty described in the work. Other kings and gods are said to have traces of the Buddha's feet on their foreheads, and other women have been said to have eyes comparable with flowers. Saman inhabits the same world that is artfully fashioned through Sinhala verse, one shaped by the beauty and conventions of poetry, seemingly unaffected by the Portuguese presence in the island.

Linked to the Buddha herein, Saman appears as an exceptional deity, given the large number of verses and substantial praise dedicated to him. A few verses conflate certain attributes of the god—such as his boundless compassion (v. 191), his delightful speech (v. 193), and his renown throughout the ten directions (v. 199)—with those of the Buddha. When Alagiyavanna refers to Saman as the "peerless eye to the Three Worlds," he is unquestionably elevating an aspect of the god to a level usually reserved for the Buddha. The Buddha is traditionally held to possess five kinds of eyes, culminating in *samantacakkhu*, or the "all-seeing eye" that is equivalent to omniscience.[110] Alagiyavanna's exuberant praise for Saman, resulting in part from the desire to supplicate the god as well as the demands of the rhyming scheme he employs, leads him to borrow a few, select attributes of the Buddha to use for this important deity. Nevertheless, this conflation does not result in confusion, as it is Saman who is represented as bowing down to the Buddha and not the other way around. Near the beginning of the work, the Buddha is said to be "unique among *brahmās*, gods, and persons," which is to say that he is ultimately incomparable in terms of his virtues and accomplishments.[111]

Nevertheless, Saman is still deserving of veneration, according to Alagiyavanna. Saman is said to bestow all forms of wealth that delight the gods and persons, in a manner akin to the divine, wish-fulfilling tree of lore.[112] Devotees may thus venerate the deity and reasonably expect to achieve some form of worldly gain. Saman is also described as almost indescribably beautiful, which is also a reason to honor him. Using a familiar figure of speech in which the subject's indescribable qualities are nevertheless related by an excellent poet, the narrator rhetorically asks if anyone, short of another god, can describe the great splendor of Saman's shining body.[113] Of course, Alagiyavanna can and does, establishing both the grandeur of the god's appearance and the poet's impressive command of language.

Finally, in the last use of *sähäli* in the work, the poet interweaves praise for Saman with praise for the Buddha, establishing once and for all a seemingly incontestable claim to venerate both figures jointly. Although the worship of Saman cannot simply be labeled Hindu as such, it does point to an expanded repertoire of devotion and an expanded setting for religious practice in the early 1580s. Devotion shown to the Buddha is thus portrayed as regularly accompanied by devotion to other deities. So the narrator addresses the cock thus:

> Pay homage, noble friend, to the resplendent feet of the majestic god Sumana [Saman], whose mind is good,
> And whose ears are adorned with the collections of the Tripiṭaka Dharma,

And whose head is always decorated with the lotus of the feet of the Sage,
That shines with the pistils of the crowns of gods, *asuras*, persons, and *nāgas* who pay homage,
Gleaming with the petals of his distinctive, faultless red toes,
And being continually attended to by the bunch of swans of ascetics bereft of desire,
And [then] supplicate him always to protect,
The Dispensation of our Noble Sage and the beings of the world,
The strong-hearted King Rājasiṃha and his assembly of ministers,
And the renowned, extensive army of elephants, horses, chariots, and soldiers.[114]

In these lines, where devotion to the gods is seamlessly combined with devotion to the Buddha, the ultimate objective of the poem emerges. Divine protection for Buddhist, royal, and military institutions is sought—and presumably obtained—through aesthetically pleasing words of praise and ritual expressions of devotion. Following closely on the heels of a literary and religious culture centered on the Koṭṭe kingdom, where ornate verse and the veneration of deities were both prominent and celebrated, the *Sävul Sandēśaya* presents us with similar views and values. The world of Sinhala *kavi*, as faithfully refashioned by Alagiyavanna, treats Buddhist and Hindu worship as analogous, overlapping forms of religious expression.

In the early 1580s, therefore, there is no inconsistency seen when the cock venerates the chief Buddhist monk at the Saparagamuwa temple and then proceeds to the temple dedicated to the god Saman and venerates the chief priest and ritual specialist there. The fact that these actions appear so ordinary as to not require any sort of explanation suggests that such pluralistic forms of devotion were the norm in the early part of Alagiyavanna's career. As long as Rājasiṃha I could keep the Portuguese and their missionaries at bay, religious identity in the Sītāvaka kingdom could remain inclusive and loosely defined. Such is the devotion modeled by the cock in *Sävul Sandēśaya*. In addition, the glorification of worship at Buddhist and Hindu shrines also suggests that Alagiyavanna composed this poem before Rājasiṃha I allegedly turned against the local Buddhist institutions and embraced Śaivite Hinduism in their place.[115] Though the circumstances surrounding the king's "conversion" will be discussed in more length in the next chapter, *Sävul Sandēśaya* presents an image of religiosity that is uncomplicated by the lack of dogmatic assertions and formal expressions of religious allegiance. At this time, model devotees would, like the cock, venerate the Buddha, Umā, and Saman, among others in the religious world the work depicts.

Alagiyavanna's *Sävul Sandēśaya* illustrates a form of religious praxis in which the boundaries between different religious systems are blurred. Just as the cock is encouraged to worship at both Buddhist and Hindu sites without dwelling on what makes them different, the poem's audience is similarly encouraged to see the devotional practices at all such temples as coherent and consistent. Although neither unprecedented nor unchallenged in previous eras, such an inclusive attitude toward religious practice represents the thinking of a scholar for whom religious identity had not yet become problematic. Alagiyavanna's concerns lie instead in utilizing the full capacities of poetic language to evoke fame and power. His attention is given to local personages and landscapes, a world that exists concretely outside his poem but is made more beautiful and impressive by it. Far from being simply a flaw to be lamented by modern critics, the so-called derivative nature of *Sävul Sandēśaya* points to the author's resolute efforts to imitate and sustain the poetic ideals and political imagination of medieval Sinhala society.

3

Longing for the Dharma in Poem of King Dhammasoṇḍa

IN THE LATTER part of the 1580s, a number of marked changes began to take place in the Sītāvaka kingdom and in Alagiyavanna's poetry. As a poet in the court of King Rājasiṃha I, Alagiyavanna had a clear interest in sustaining the culture-power formation that reserved for the literati an integral role in spreading the fame and enhancing the power of kings. *Sävul Sandēśaya* was largely devoted to establishing the king's reputation as a mighty sovereign, as well as Alagiyavanna's own as a poet. As the decade wore on, however, military campaigns and internal conspiracies made it more difficult to sustain the classical poetic tradition of Sri Lanka. His next work, called *Dahamsoňḍa Kava* (*Poem of King Dhammasoṇḍa*), was written sometime in the latter half of the 1580s using an established poetic subject—the life story of the Bodhisattva or Future Buddha. But this work departed from *Sävul Sandēśaya* in several ways. The most likely explanation for this fact is that the warfare and intrigue that enveloped the kingdom generated new motivations and constraints for Alagiyavanna, some of which are reflected in *Dahamsoňḍa Kava*. This work reflects the early stages of a transition in Sinhala poetry away from the rich, ornate style of court poetry focused on aesthetic description to works with stronger narrative elements and religious concerns.

The powerful rule of Rājasiṃha succeeded in isolating the Portuguese and the convert king Dom João Dharmapāla of Koṭṭe, while it also weakened the threat posed by the Kandyan kingdom. But the military campaigns of Rājasiṃha exacted a stiff toll on his subjects. The nearly continuous warfare created heavy demands for labor and revenue that fell on Rājasiṃha's subjects in the form of service and taxes.[1] A number of nobles and members of the Sangha began to hatch a plan to assassinate the king and relieve the people of Sītāvaka from the burdens imposed on them. The Portuguese were also possibly involved in fomenting opposition against Rājasiṃha in an effort to weaken or get rid of their implacable and powerful foe.[2] Whoever shared responsibility for plotting against the king, we know at least that a plot to take his life was carried out. Sometime around 1585, there was an attempt to poison Rājasiṃha, but he recovered and took revenge against those he suspected of the crime.[3] Some conspirators fled to join the Portuguese side, but others were executed. The fact that this plot involved nobles and monks caused turmoil in the Sītāvaka court and among the Sangha. One tradition holds that the chief monk was stoned and cut to pieces, while his followers were buried up to their necks and had their heads ploughed off.[4] Another story claims that dozens of monks were thrown in a nearby river and drowned.[5]

The extended *Mahāvaṃsa* contains an unflattering account of Rājasiṃha I in which the king is alleged to have killed his father, Māyādunnē, to accede to the Sītāvaka throne. This charge of patricide was made also by a number of Portuguese chroniclers, who likewise had a very dim view of the king who caused much suffering and destruction to their army. Diogo do Couto, writing in Goa in 1593, asserted that for "Raju" or Rājasiṃha, "it was a great hindrance to his tyranny to have his father living: wherefore he determined to murder him in order to usurp the kingdom."[6] For early modern Portuguese chroniclers, Sinhala kings who resisted Catholicism and Portuguese power were regularly described as "tyrants," brutal men who were instinctively hostile to the Portuguese and the church in order to shore up their own power. Couto's account of how Rājasiṃha had his elderly father of eighty years poisoned is embellished with an aside asserting the "divine justice" in the fact that a tyrant like Māyādunnē, who conspired to kill his father—King Vijayabāhu VI—in 1521, would eventually die at the hands of his son.[7] Historical examination, however, casts doubt on the accounts of Māyādunnē's murder at the hands of his son. As C. R. de Silva points out, Māyādunnē's advanced age and the fact that Rājasiṃha has already been the virtual leader of Sītāvaka for many years makes the charge seem dubious.[8] There would have been little reason for Rājasiṃha to kill his father. Moreover, the work of Fernão de Queyroz, another Portuguese chronicler who wrote a comprehensive history of Portuguese Ceilão in the late seventeenth century, mentions that Rājasiṃha received news of his father's natural death in 1581.[9]

Subsequently, the *Mahāvaṃsa* claims further that Rājasiṃha converted to Śaivite Hinduism to allay his conscience and fears of future suffering due to his patricide. It notes that when Rājasiṃha asked the monks whether he could be freed from the results of his wicked deed, they replied that he could not undo his crime. Then when the king learned from some Hindu devotees of Śiva that it was possible to avoid the fate of his deeds, he is portrayed as having turned against Buddhist institutions.

> Having taken up devotion to Śiva, and destroying the dispensation of the Conqueror,
> Tormenting the order of the monks, and burning the books of the Dhamma,
> Having broken apart the monasteries, he concealed the way to heaven.
> And as one who had become a support for *saṃsāra*, he embraced false views.
> Moreover, in order to seize all the profits that arose at Adam's Peak,
> He committed that place to the ascetics possessing wrong action and false views. . . .
> At that time, out of fear of the king, the monks gave up their robes and left the order,
> And those among them who were fearful of *saṃsāra* went away to various other places.[10]

This dramatic account of how and why King Rājasiṃha I came to embrace Śaivism and to turn against Buddhist institutions likely exaggerates and distorts the events it purports to describe. The king's increased patronage of Hinduism may actually have been the result of the monastic opposition he faced rather than the original cause of it.[11] Although the picture of a king trying to assuage his guilt for killing his father is likely a literary device with little basis in truth, it is entirely possible that Rājasiṃha punished members of the Sangha for their alleged involvement in a plot to kill him. The account of the slaying of monks and destruction of books may be overstated, but it appears that Buddhist institutions faced harsh reprisals in the region under Rājasiṃha's control in the latter years of his reign.[12]

Royal support of Hindu persons and places may have increased in the Sītāvaka kingdom during the late 1580s, but it did not emerge out of nowhere. The Sinhala *sandeśa* poems, including *Sävul Sandēśaya*, speak of a vibrant presence of Hindu shrines and ritual officiants in Sri Lanka much earlier.[13] Of course this presence had typically been seen to complement rather than compete with longstanding Buddhist practices. But the king appears to have shown more favor to Hindu shrines in the years following the assassination attempt up to his accidental death in 1593. In the context of such important political events and cultural upheaval, along with the king's monumental efforts to lay siege again to the Portuguese fort in Colombo from May 1587 to February 1588 by personally commanding a force of more than thirty thousand men, one can assume that court life and poetic learning languished in the latter part of Rājasiṃha's reign.[14]

What remains to be seen, however, is how Alagiyavanna responded to the turmoil. It appears that he composed *Dahamsoňḍa Kava* either before or shortly after the king began to support Hindu interests more intently. One modern scholar claims that Alagiyavanna wrote this poetic work after the king and other leaders of Sītāvaka adopted Hinduism as an effort to open their eyes to the truth of the Buddha's Dharma.[15] Given the poem's more conspicuous emphasis on Buddhist figures and ideas, such an interpretation is not far fetched. However, it may be just as possible that the poet composed this work before the king's so-called conversion and in response to the growing influence of Brahmins in the court. Another scholar has suggested that Rājasiṃha's persecution of Buddhist monks and his burning of texts would have forced some scholars to vacate their posts at the court.[16] Oral tradition current among the living descendents of Alagiyavanna holds that the poet was forced to flee to the southern city of Matara after Rājasiṃha converted to Hinduism and ordered the poet to be killed.[17] The exact details in regard to how Alagiyavanna survived this difficult time remain unclear, but it seems reasonable to conclude that the shifts in tone and content of *Dahamsoňḍa Kava* reflect an environment in which the traditional preeminence of Buddhist institutions was being challenged.

Furthermore, in the early twentieth century an opinion arose that Alagiyavanna did not compose *Dahamsoňḍa Kava* at all. Writing in 1925, the esteemed scholar W. F. Gunawardhana put forth an argument for attributing *Dahamsoňḍa Kava* to Alagiyavanna's father, Pandit Dharmadhvaja. Despite the fact that Alagiyavanna's name appears in the closing verse of *Dahamsoňḍa Kava*, Gunawardhana claimed that the appearance of identical lines of verse in both *Dahamsoňḍa Kava* and *Kusa Jātaka Kāvya* (another one of Alagiyavanna's works) ought to disqualify the former from the list of Alagiyavanna's writings. In essence, he argued that authors would not reproduce parts of their own works verbatim elsewhere, but since Sinhala poets have long imitated the work of others to honor them, he claimed that Alagiyavanna appropriated the same stanzas from *Dahamsoňḍa Kava* to honor his father.[18] The lines in question, describing beautiful city women, appear as verse 34 in *Dahamsoňḍa Kava* and verse 29 in *Kusa Jātaka Kāvya*:

The women who walk about in that city,
With red lips like the tender leaves of the Na tree,
With a gait like female elephants,
Who is able to describe these ladies?[19]

However, Gunawardhana's dismissal of the possibility that the same author may have plagiarized himself is wholly arbitrary and without substantiation. Although this interpretation was influential for a while, most scholars have accepted the more likely view that Alagiyavanna was indeed the author of *Dahamsoňḍa Kava*. The attribution of authorship to Alagiyavanna in the work, its praise of his contemporary Samaradivākara, and the complete absence of any hint that it was written by Dharmadvaja should suffice to confirm that Alagiyavanna was the author of the work.

A significant feature of the *Dahamsoňḍa Kava* is the fact that Alagiyavanna offers relatively little praise for King Rājasiṃha in the work. Unlike *Sävul Sandēśaya* in which Rājasiṃha is extolled in several dozen verses, the king is mentioned in only one verse in *Dahamsoňḍa Kava*. King Rājasiṃha is described as "the flag atop the palace of the Solar Dynasty" and "like a powerful lion that destroys and casts aside the arrogance of the elephants of enemy kings."[20] Such praise is weighty, if formulaic, but the paucity of panegyric verses here clearly represents a departure from the *praśasti* style of poetic writing seen in *Sävul Sandēśaya*. The environment of the Sītāvaka court appeared to have changed enough to make a traditional *praśasti* poem dedicated to one's king seem out of place. Alagiyavanna instead chose to compose a handful of laudatory verses to his colleague and friend Samaradivākara, the grandson of a minister under King Bhuvanekabāhu VI and a *mukaveṭi* like Alagiyavanna under Rājasiṃha I.[21]

This magistrate and noble minister named Samaradivākara,
Who is a mine of compassion,
Who is a mine of the precious materials of excellent virtues,
[Is] endowed with fame like the moon.[22]

The piety of Samaradivākara is highlighted in another verse, one that relates what counted at that time as the characteristics of a devout Buddhist. Here Alagiyavanna cites his friend's inclination for religious pursuits and his sponsorship of practices depicting the Buddha in art and of copying Buddhist texts.

> Aspiring for the attainment of liberation,
> Inclining his mind towards wholesomeness,
> Causing figures and painted images of the Buddha to be made
> He had the delightful Tripiṭaka Dharma written down.[23]

Such poetic praise is noteworthy for its emphasis on religious virtues, which are aspects not typically eulogized in the classical *praśasti* genre that favors physical prowess and aesthetic refinement. Thus, from this early juncture in the poem, hints of Buddhist values and interests are at work.

Alagiyavanna describes his fellow magistrate chiefly in terms of his moral righteousness and intellect. Whereas, in his earlier work, Alagiyavanna praises the fame of King Rājasiṃha for spreading out in all directions, he singles out a different virtue in Samaradivākara.[24] He compares his colleague's "thoughts of loving-kindness" to the light of the full moon as something "that overspreads every place in the world."[25] These remarks demonstrate that moral character is given more consideration in *Dahamsoňḍa Kava* than fame and glory, the traditional basis for eulogistic praise in *praśasti* and *sandeśa* poetry. Samaradivākara's intellect is lauded, too, when it is suggested that he gives wise and correct judgments in legal cases "like the swan who separates milk from water" when they are mixed together.[26] His good judgment is also seen when Alagiyavanna praises his friend's practice of Buddhist precepts and detachment from worldly comforts.

> He does not smear his mouth with false speech and liquor,
> Which are like dreadful poisons,
> And all the time he thinks that the heaps of wealth belonging to others,
> Are like bits of broken potsherds.[27]

Here Alagiyavanna inverts the value of an attribute traditionally held up for praise in Sinhala *kavi*. Court poets often treated the possession of wealth, as evidenced by the opulent surroundings of royal living, as a sign of virtue. This was true also for Tamil *caṅkam* poetry where the king's ability to give royal endowments to Brahmins, to temples, and to poets was an occasion for eulogistic praise and the basis for his authority.[28] Alagiyavanna confirms the importance of wealth in his *Sävul Sandēśaya*, wherein Rājasiṃha is praised for possessing all forms of wealth and, in turn, lavishing riches on the world with great generosity.[29] Yet in *Dahamsoňḍa Kava* our poet decidedly lessens the importance of material wealth by remarking that such riches are ultimately without value, a position consistent with Buddhist ideals of renunciation.

For these reasons, *Dahamsoňḍa Kava* appears as a distinctly different work from *Sävul Sandēśaya*. The simpler verse style of the work together with the secondary status given to eulogistic praise of historical actors reveal the work to be the product of new authorial concerns and a changed social environment. The lack of attention given to Rājasiṃha I in *Dahamsoňḍa Kava* is partly explained by the genre of employing verse to recall one of the stories of the Buddha's previous lives as a bodhisattva. The poetic treatise *Siyabaslakara* asserts that Sinhala *kavi* should be concerned with the life of the Buddha generally. The use of this literary subject may have excused our poet from spending much time on lavishing praise on his king. But the work also mentions that Samaradivākara specifically asked Alagiyavanna to compose a poem about the Buddha's former lives.[30] This invitation from a new patron, along with the likelihood that Samaradivākara was an acquaintance if not a friend of the poet, is sufficient for explaining the eulogistic dedication of *Dahamsoňḍa Kava* to another magistrate.[31] Aside from the genre and invitation associated with this work, the fact that King Rājasiṃha recedes into the background of the poem suggests that the Sītāvaka court had become a less vibrant setting for presenting and reciting poetry in the latter 1580s. The idea of culture as defined by the norms and conventions of classical Sanskrit and Tamil poetry seems to have begun to lose its hold over the expressions of Sinhala royal power at that time.

In the context of these signs of a shift in Sinhala literary culture during the latter stages of Rājasiṃha's reign, the choice to use the story of King Dahamsoňḍa (Pali: Dhammasoṇḍa/Dhammasoṇḍaka) appears curious yet somehow fitting. This story does not appear in the canonical collection of 547 *Jātaka* stories preserved by the Sri Lankan Theravāda tradition, which makes it a "non-classical jātaka," to use Peter Skilling's terminology.[32] In contrast, many of the earlier Sinhala *kavi* are based on tales of the Bodhisattva found in the canonical collection. For example, the

Muvadevdāvata is based on the Makhadeva-Jātaka (no. 9 in the Pali *Jātaka* text), the *Sasadāvata* is based on the Sasa-Jātaka (no. 316), *Kavsiḷumiṇa* is based on Kusa-Jātaka (no. 531), *Kāvyaśēkhara* is based on Sattubhatta-Jātaka (no. 402), and the *Guttila Kāvya* is based on the Guttila-Jātaka (no. 243). The story of Dahamsoňḍa, a king who renounces his throne in order to hear the Buddha's Dharma appears instead in a few collections of Buddhist stories, none of which enjoys the canonical authority of the Pāli Tipiṭaka. Perhaps the earliest appearance of the Dahamsoňḍa story in Sri Lanka is found in the *Sahassavatthuppakaraṇa* (*Exposition of Delightful Stories*), a work likely composed sometime after 900 CE but before 1250 CE.[33] A longer version of this story appears in the *Rasavāhinī* (*Stream of Sentiments*) of Vedeha Thera, which was written in the thirteenth century. The *Rasavāhinī* was then adapted into Sinhala in the late fourteenth century by Dēvarakṣita Jayabāhu Dharmakīrti under the title *Saddharmālaṅkāraya* (*Ornament of the Excellent Teaching*). It is likely this Sinhala work that provided the most inspiration to Alagiyavanna for his poetic rendition of the story.[34] Another version of this story has circulated in Southeast Asia in certain collections of the "apocryphal" *Paññāsa Jātaka*, and an analogous story can be found in several Chinese texts.[35]

The narrative of the Dahamsoňḍa story is relatively short and can be briefly summarized. A virtuous king longs to hear someone preach the Dharma of the Buddha but is unable to locate a Dharma preacher in his realm. He decides to renounce his throne and wander in search of someone who knows the Dharma. While doing so, the god Śakra comes to know of the future Buddha's search and decides to test his resolve. The god takes the form of a ferocious, man-eating *rakṣa*, which is an evil being (often translated as a "demon") in Indic mythology. He appears before the Bodhisattva and offers to preach a line of the Dharma if he can eat him. By their agreement, the *rakṣa* begins to preach the Dharma while the Bodhisattva flings himself down a tall mountain into his mouth. At the last moment, however, Śakra changes back into his divine form, catches Dahamsoňḍa, and then takes him up to his heavenly realm to see its divine comforts. The Dharma is preached, and then Dahamsoňḍa returns to his position as a righteous king on earth.

Although the story of King Dahamsoňḍa lacked canonical authority, it seems to have been popular enough to be suitable for a poem on the life of the Bodhisattva.[36] The story's narrative theme—a righteous king who seeks out the Dharma, which had become scarce in his kingdom—may well have resonated with listeners at a time when the Buddha's dispensation was under pressure from Portuguese Catholic and Hindu influences. The work can be read as a commentary on the precarious condition of the Dharma at this point in the island's history. Therein, Alagiyavanna highlights the inestimable value of the Buddha's teachings as well as the importance of righteous kingship as a conduit for religious pursuits and social order.

Poetic Conventions and Innovations

Alagiyavanna's *Dahamsoňḍa Kava* is a work that rehearses certain formulaic qualities of Indic poetry while it moves to explore new visions for what Sinhala *kavi* can accomplish. Whereas the poet's *Sävul Sandēśaya* can be located within an older genre of court poetry characterized by ornate description, the reliance on conventional figures of speech, and the celebration of the culture-power formation found in much premodern Indic verse, the *Dahamsoňḍa Kava* gives less attention to these poetic requirements and seeks instead to promote specifically Buddhist values and ideas. The varied aesthetic choices and conventions employed by Alagiyavanna result in a poem that is difficult to categorize. Having been influenced by a tradition of Sinhala poetry with norms and conventions derived largely from Sanskrit and Tamil literature, part of his work acknowledges the aesthetic requirements that had been developed for Sinhala verse in treatises on poetics, meter, and the like. At the same time, he embraces a keener sense of narrative structure and moments of moral reasoning that distinguish *Dahamsoňḍa Kava* from many earlier Sinhala court poems.

It is clear from the work that Alagiyavanna had not yet abandoned his commitment to conventional poetic norms and aesthetic interests. He displays considerable efforts to compose a well-crafted poem that employs many familiar poetic figures of speech that were assumed to delight audiences and confirm the author's skill. If the status of the Sītāvaka court during the time of the work's composition and presentation is in question, there is still an indication in the poem that it was directed to a more elite audience.

> Learned persons, who are endowed with knowledge,
> If you perceive a fault in this work, disregard it,
> Being serenely joyful with respect to the Buddha's virtues,
> Turn both ears and listen with devotion today.[37]

The people to whom Alagiyavanna is speaking are "learned persons" (*viyatuni*) who display an awareness and appreciation of poetic merits.

Only those who are well versed in the art of poetry could be expected to be able to perceive the poetic faults (*doṣa*) that mar a work. Such defects might violate the rule of comprehensibility or grammatical intention, but in general they detract from the desired poetic effect of a text.[38] Many classical Sinhala poems modeled after the carefully prescribed norms of Sanskrit or Tamil works likewise sought to engender particular experiences, whether through the suggestion of ideas or the evocation of sentiments. Various literary theorists from classical India wrote pronouncements on distinguishing poetic virtues (*guṇas*) from faults (*doṣas*), and these distinctions were used by the educated to analyze poetry from an objective point of view and to judge its worth formally.[39] In the preceding verse, Alagiyavanna clearly shows an awareness of such formal criteria with which to judge the value of his work. By pleading for the tolerance and generosity of his learned audience, he nevertheless indicates his familiarity with classical poetic norms. By emphasizing the primary importance of the Buddha's virtues, he reinforces his religious aims.

Moreover, the style in which he composed *Dahamsoňḍa Kava* imitates certain features of the ornate court poetry that served to establish his identity as a great poet. Approximately the first third of the work is devoted to embellished description and praise. The ornate verses in this section describe not the Sītāvaka court but rather King Bambadat (Pāli: Brahmadatta) and the city of Baraṇas (Benares), where the Bodhisattva will be born. What is interesting here is that Alagiyavanna borrows from the conventions of *kāvya* and *praśasti* to praise an ancient king instead of his own.

In that excellent city, possessed of splendor,
There was a king named Bambadat,
Who was endowed with loving-kindness towards all beings,
And who knew no defect.
When the continuous fame of that king,
Spreads to the end of all directions alike,
Even Viṣṇu does not know to distinguish,
The blue ocean from the milky ocean.
That hero's fame, which was white and diffused outwards,
Took the form of a white parasol over the head of Brahmā,
Shading the entire world,
And shining with the staff of the heavenly river.
When the forest fire of that king's glory,
Burned the ten directions in a single manner,

Iśvara, while dancing from thinking it was an evening cloud,
Was completely deceived and sighed, "Alas!"[40]

These verses from *Dahamsoňḍa Kava* praise an ancient king in a manner similar to that used by the poet when praising Rājasiṃha I in *Sävul Sandēśaya*. The use of Hindu imagery, so prominent in *Sävul Sandēśaya*, reappears briefly here to extol a king in a conventionally poetic way. In the earlier work, Rājasiṃha's fame is also said to confuse a dancing Iśvara into thinking it was a row of evening clouds, while elsewhere it appears like the Milky Ocean and blue Kaliňdu River, as well as the white parasol over the head of Brahmā that has the heavenly river as its staff.[41]

Alagiyavanna's descriptions of Benares are similar, formally speaking, to the kinds of ornate verses he used to describe the places visited by the cock in *Sävul Sandēśaya*. This use of poetic tropes to establish a more aesthetically rich setting for a narrative was not new to Alagiyavanna, nor was it new to the poets who preceded him.[42] Alagiyavanna employs several poetic tropes in order to reposition his *jātaka* narrative within the aesthetic framework of Sinhala *kavi*. Such a move also distinguishes this work from the more straightforward narrative accounts of the Dhammasoṇḍa story in *Sahassavatthuppakaraṇa* and *Rāsavahinī*. Although King Rājasiṃha I and the Sītāvaka court largely disappear from view in *Dahamsoňḍa Kava*, analogous figures and assemblies take their place in the form of King Bambadat and the heavenly Suddharma Hall where the gods assemble under the reign of Śakra. The immediate, local references in Alagiyavanna's world have been supplanted by those that exist only in texts. This decision to embellish an "ideal" world instead of the "real" one possibly signifies the poet's disenchantment with what Sītāvaka had become—a city no longer deserving to be immortalized in verse.

However, the emphasis given in the text to the Bodhisattva did not eclipse the considerable continuity in Alagiyavanna's style of composition. He praises a king in ornate fashion, he incorporates many verses that vividly describe the settings of the story, and he employs several figures of speech, which are all features found in his earlier work. One of the examples of his continued reliance on conventional poetic tropes is seen in the reappearance of hyperbolic statements (*atiśayokti*) that raise doubt about the ability of any ordinary person to describe or conceive of the grandeur to which the poet alludes.[43] After describing the women, houses, gardens, and fourfold army in the city of Benares, the narrator asks:

Who except for Ananta or Śakra,
Is able to describe or behold,

All the riches in that city,
That shines with virtuous persons?[44]

The implication here, again, is that only a poet like Alagiyavanna could compete with the gods in describing the manifold riches of the city where the Bodhisattva was born. Alagiyavanna made similar claims for his poetic excellence in *Sävul Sandēśaya*. The words of all but great poets and the gods fail to capture the grandeur of cities both real and imagined.

Moreover, like he did in his previous work, in *Dahamsoňḍa Kava,* Alagiyavanna occasionally adopts material from poems that preceded his. Among the previous works that influenced his composition of this work are *Kavsiḷumiṇa,* especially, but also *Kāvyaśēkhara, Mayūra Sandēśaya, Muvadevdāvata,* and *Guttila Kāvya.*[45] While perhaps not quite as derivative as *Sävul Sandēśaya,* the *Dahamsoňḍa Kava* reflects in several places a fairly conservative outlook toward poetic composition. Alagiyavanna's ornate description of Benares seems based in large part on how *Kavsiḷumiṇa* describes the city of Kusāvātī in its narrative.

The crystal ramparts of that city,
Like coils cast by Ananta, the cobra,
Namely the tall gate,
Shine at all times up to the city of the gods.
The girdle tied fully around
The hips of the ramparts of the woman of the city,
Was a well-adorned moat filled with water lilies,
And encircled with noisy bees.
The full moon that appears in the sky of the city,
Rubbing its rays on the tips of the mansion turrets,
Captivated the eyes and minds of people,
Like a shining white parasol with a staff of gold and gems.[46]

Alagiyavanna's description of the kingdom of Benares is clearly derivative of the following *gī* verses or couplets from *Kavsiḷumiṇa* that describe Kusāvātī:

The crystal ramparts, warding off others, like a jeweled bracelet supporting the bowl of the sky,
Caused those journeying over the city, which put the earth to shame, to tarry.

The moat having lotuses and rows of noisy bees took the form of a girdle,
Around the waist of the ramparts erected continuously around the woman of the city.
The radiant, full autumn moon in the sky above that city, which shines with mansions,
Was shining like a white parasol atop the staff of the rays from the gems on the spires.[47]

Alagiyavanna's imitation of Parākramabāhu II's description of ramparts, a moat, and the moon above a fabulous city underline his efforts to compose poetry in the style of his celebrated predecessors. Thus the verses in which he describes or praises the poem's settings and esteemed subjects reflect more generally the style of *kavi* that had long been held up as the ideal form of aesthetically rich literary expression.

Nevertheless, there are some stylistic aspects of Alagiyavanna's *Dahamsoňḍa Kava* that represent departures from his earlier poetry. His stylistic choices, which were mainly new for him, help us to recognize some different interests and motivations in his second work. The poetic meters he utilized in the work signify some of these differences. His *Sävul Sandēśaya* relies mostly on the elaborate *samudraghoṣa* verse with quatrains in which each of the four lines (*padas*) has eighteen syllables. The result is longer, more embellished verses that are suitable for conveying aesthetically rich descriptions. In contrast, the *Dahamsoňḍa Kava* employs a greater variety of poetic meters but relies more on the *mahapiyum* meter that makes use of short quatrains with a syllablic pattern of nine, eleven, nine, and fourteen. The concise quality of the *mahapiyum* meter makes it particularly fit for conveying narrative accounts in a manner that keeps the story moving without getting bogged down in highly detailed descriptions.[48] Of the total 163 quatrains in the work, the first eighty-four and the last nineteen are composed in the *mahapiyum* meter, allowing the work to move steadily through its descriptive sections and facilitate the flow of the narrative. The *mahapiyum* verses, as a rule, also retain only the final *eḷisama* rhyming scheme and thus generally do without internal rhyming patterns that contribute to a more complicated, artful form of composition.

Alagiyavanna, however, employs fuller and more complex meters in a few sections of *Dahamsoňḍa Kava*. After the king resolves to find someone who can preach the Dharma to him, the poem shifts in the eighty-fifth verse to using a *padaka* meter consisting of quatrains with internal rhymes and sixteen syllables per *pada*. This shift gives greater emphasis to the section in the narrative where Dahamsoňḍa articulates his willingness to sacrifice his kingship, his wealth, and his life to hear the Dharma, resulting in the move to renounce his royal position and enter the forest in search of a Dharma preacher. This particular meter is sustained when the god Śakra takes the form of a ferocious and terrifying *rakṣa* to test the Bodhisattva's resolve. Alagiyavanna then changes the rhythm of his work again starting with verse 111. In the next fifteen verses, he employs a *padaka* meter consisting of four *pada*s of twelve syllables each, while retaining both the internal and external rhyming schemes from before. This shift marks out the significance of the event when the deity who is masquerading as a *rakṣa* suggests that the Bodhisattva throw himself off a mountain and listen to the Dharma being preached while he falls into the *rakṣa*'s mouth.

When it comes time for Dahamsoňḍa to accept the terms of this arrangement that will lead him to sacrifice his life in exchange for listening to the Buddha's Dharma, Alagiyavanna changes meters again. Beginning with verse 127, the poet employs the *samudraghoṣa* meter to mark the story's climax—including the *rakṣa*'s succinct recitation of the Dharma, as well as the Bodhisattva's aspiration to attain Buddhahood and his leap off the mountain down into the *rakṣa*'s horrifying mouth. As the narrative arc begins to move toward the resolution of the plot, wherein Śakra changes back into his actual form, catches Dahamsoňḍa in his arms, and whisks him up to his heavenly realm, Alagiyavanna retains the more elaborate metrical and rhyming schemes of the preceding verses. The vivid and beautiful descriptions of the Catumahārājika Heaven appear in the *samudraghoṣa* meter in order to help evoke the beauty of the world of the gods in a more aesthetically rich poetic fashion. Then, the poem makes the final switch back to the *mahapiyum* meter starting with verse 144, which marks where the resolution of the story begins. The gods praise and venerate the virtuous Bodhisattva and, in a dramatic change in roles, listen to Dahamsoňḍa preach the Dharma. Śakra advises the Bodhisattva on the nature of virtuous kingship and sends him back to the world of humans where he resumes his duties as king. The work is brought to an end, and the author identifies and praises himself.

Alagiyavanna's use of a variety of different meters, many of which are shorter and simpler in form than what is found previously in

Sävul Sandēśaya, suggest a heightened interest in the story's plot. Aesthetic description is retained, but it does not come at the expense of the development and progression of the narrative. The paracanonical *jātaka* story serves to praise the Bodhisattva—and by extension the Buddha—in the terms of its plot. At the same time, however, the diminished aesthetic grandeur of *Dahamsoňḍa Kava* in comparison to *Sävul Sandēśaya* may also suggest that the traditional Sinhala culture-power formation was at this point somewhat estranged from the royal court. Alagiyavanna's increased interests in narrative and simplified verse structure in *Dahamsoňḍa Kavu* suggests that the heretofore dominant paradigm of the culture-power formulation, measured in large part by one's command over poetic language and expression, was beginning to unravel in the latter part of Rājasiṃha's rule. Since literature in South Asia had for centuries served to distinguish cultural skill and political power, the stylistic differences in *Dahamsoňḍa Kava* indicate changes were taking place in the court and the literary cultures of early modern Sri Lanka.

Devotion to the Dharma

By giving less prominence to panegyric verse and complex composition in *Dahamsoňḍa Kava,* Alagiyavanna paved the way for the reintroduction and highlighting of religious objectives in Sinhala verse. Of course, from the preceding century, Śrī Rāhula's *Kāvyaśēkhara* contains material concerning Buddhist thought and ethics, and Vīdāgama Maitreya's *Lō Väḍa Saňgarāva* (*Treatise on the Welfare of the World*) reads as a lengthy, poetic admonition on the benefits of Buddhist morality, while his *Buduguṇālaṅkāraya* (*Ornament of the Buddha's Virtues*) extols the praiseworthy qualities of the Buddha. Leaving aside these works, however, most Sinhala *kavi* texts from the Koṭṭe period dwell more on aesthetic values than religious ones. *Sävul Sandēśaya* mentions Buddhist and Hindu sites in conjunction with each other, describing ritualized acts of devotion but offering little in the way of religious reflection or instruction. Sinhala poetry in this era emphasized aesthetic features that aimed to establish fame and power through modeling itself on the rich expressive resources of Sanskrit *kāvya.*[49]

Something happened in the 1580s, however, to cause Alagiyavanna to begin to turn away from the conventions that treated poetry mainly as an expressive form of cultural power. This transformation in

Alagiyavanna's poetry was neither dramatic nor complete, as he continued to value many of the poetic norms established by the classical poets who preceded him. However, the change in style and subject from *Sävul Sandēśaya* to *Dahamsoňḍa Kava* marks the beginning of a significant evolution in Alagiyavanna's work and in Sinhala *kavi* more generally. Martin Wickremasinghe described this point as the beginning of a new epoch, one in which Alagiyavanna straddled both the "slavish imitation" of Sanskrit *kāvya* so common among classical Sinhala poets and the more simple—for him, more genuine—versification of postclassical Sinhala poets.[50] If we can put aside Wickremasinghe's contempt for Indian influences on Sinhala Buddhist literature, we can acknowledge a qualitative shift in the style and objectives of Sinhala poetry taking place in the midst of Alagiyavanna's literary career. The emphasis given to religious subjects in *Dahamsoňḍa Kava* is evidence of Alagiyavanna's new interest in poetry as a tool of religious formation.

The first sign of Alagiyavanna's increased interest in religious matters appears at the beginning of the poem where he composed verses of praise for the Triple Gem of the Buddha, the Dharma, and the Sangha in the Buddhist religion. It is commonplace for Sri Lankan Buddhist texts to invoke the Triple Gem at the start of any work related to the Buddha's Dharma. The fact that Alagiyavanna did so in *Dahamsoňḍa Kava*, in contrast to his *Sävul Sandēśaya* where no such invocation is found, is one hint that he intended this work to address religious matters more directly. In the first verse, the Buddha is compared to a great rain cloud that dissolves the "dust of the mental defilements," destroys the "pollen of the heretics," and shines with the "rainbow of disciples" who follow in his footsteps.[51] Then, in verse 2, the Dharma is compared to a great river that is sought after by the "birds of the great disciples," that contains the "ambrosial liquid of the Paths and Fruits" leading to awakening, and that shines with the further "bank of liberation."[52] The natural metaphors continue when the Sangha is compared to a row of stars that shine with the "brilliance of moral discipline," that dwell in the "sky of the Good Dharma," and that attend to the "faultless moon of sages," or the Buddha.[53] Honoring the three most worthy objects of reverence in the Buddhist religion this way indicates the poet's aim to address religious matters. It also is consistent with views of writing that characterize the composing of Buddhist texts as a form of meritorious ritual activity.[54]

This concern with Buddhist values does not prevent Alagiyavanna from seeking the blessings of a variety of Indic deities after he venerates the Triple Gem. The worship of deities along with the veneration of the Buddha, the Dharma, and the Sangha was the prevailing custom in the Sinhala culture from the Koṭṭe Period if not earlier. Although the poet would later deviate from this inclusive stance, here he continues to promote a fairly heterogeneous view of religious identity. Thus, in the next verse, Alagiyavanna cleverly unites all those from whom he seeks blessings by focusing on their different sets of eyes.

> May the divine-eyes of the Five-Eyed Buddha, the thousand-eyed Śakra,
> The eight-eyed Mahābrahmā, the three-eyed Śiva, the twelve-eyed Skanda,
> The worldly eyed Sūrya, and the lotus-eyed Viṣṇu,
> Direct their focus on those with two eyes and offer them protection.[55]

The supplication of the Buddha—whose "five eyes" include the bodily eye, the divine eye, the eye of wisdom, the Buddha eye, and the universal eye—along with the deities affirms the belief that powerful beings can look out for those who need their assistance. This view of the Buddha as an intercessor does not easily square with the normative Theravāda position that holds the Buddha as having attained a state of final nirvana beyond any communication with the mundane world. Yet it is also possible that the Buddha's inclusion reflects a desire to honor him and to extend the metaphor.

Śrī Rāhula's *Kāvyaśēkhara* starts similarly with three verses that honor the Triple Gem, followed by a fourth verse that petitions help from some of the more powerful deities found in the Hindu pantheon. Coming several generations before Alagiyavanna was writing, it demonstrates that the poet was following a well-established convention when he propitiated the gods for protection.

> Brahmā, Śakra, and the conch-holding Viṣṇu,
> Bṛhaspati, Ganeṣa, and twelve-eyed Skanda,
> Sūrya, Sukra, Candra, and three-eyed Śiva—,
> May this collection of gods always effect prosperity and peace.[56]

Alagiyavanna was therefore emulating Śrī Rāhula and others who routinely dedicated a verse to the gods in exchange for their blessings of well-being. Alagiyavanna uttered similar expectations of the deities in *Sävul Sandēśaya* earlier. Given the rise in the status of Hindu religiosity near the end of Rājasiṃha's rule, it would not be surprising to witness the invocation of some deities. Nevertheless, aside from using Hindu imagery metaphorically in a handful of other verses, the *Dahamsoňḍa Kava* neither celebrates nor even mentions Hindu religious practices.

The focus, instead, is on the Bodhisattva and the Dharma, which the poet believes has been discovered and preached alike by all the Buddhas in the past. In extolling the Dharma and a bodhisattva king from the past rather than celebrating his contemporary ruler, Alagiyavanna distances his second work from the *praśasti* genre that had long affected the poetic intermingling of culture and power. He thus begins to balance aesthetic sentiments with religious ones in Sinhala *kavi*. Whereas Buddhism is unnamed and appears indirectly through ritual practices described in *Sävul Sandēśaya*, it assumes a more conspicuous identity in *Dahamsoňḍa Kava* in the form of the Dharma, the ambrosial speech that causes beings to reach liberation from the cycle of birth and death.[57] The term *Dharma* also appears in the Bodhisattva-king's name—Dahamsoňḍa, which means "desirous of, or devoted to, the Dharma." The poem supplies some folk etymology to explain why he was given this name:

> Because when that future Buddha was born,
> All the people in the world,
> Bore the mark of the Good Teaching in their hearts,
> Therefore that prince was called Dahamsoňḍa.[58]

Borrowing a well-established trope in Buddhist literature whereby the birth of a future Buddha is portrayed as a miraculous event, Alagiyavanna asserts that the Bodhisattva's birth affected all persons in a deeply personal way and readied them to embrace the teaching he would later expound to the world.[59]

Once the figure of the Bodhisattva is introduced one-third of the way into the poem, ample references to ideas and values liberally gleaned from the Buddhist religion follow. Like many other works that recall the Buddha's life story, Alagiyavanna's *Dahamsoňḍa Kava* combines narrative with religious edification. For instance, one verse outlines concisely which qualities make him a bodhisattva. He is said to have been "distinguished in giving, morality, and so forth," comparable to an "Eye to the Three Worlds" in terms of his omniscience, and he is said to have been "born with an accumulation of merit" (*piṅ*) after having fulfilled the perfections of a Buddha in previous lifetimes.[60] At the same time, the poet employs conventional images and phrases to praise the Bodhisattva's virtues and appearance. Much like King Rājasiṃha I in *Sävul Sandēśaya*, the Bodhisattva-prince is said to have learned the sixty-four arts, the delightful eighteen *Purāṇas*, and the use of many weapons.[61] Further, like all praiseworthy subjects in Sinhala *kavi*, the Bodhisattva is also attributed with the kind of fame to which only poetic figures of speech can point.

> Being an ocean of gems of good qualities,
> Being the moon for the white water-lilies of people's minds,
> Being Viṣṇu, the Lord of Devices, to the goddess Śrī,
> He existed with fame spreading throughout all of Dambadiva.[62]

Yet Dahamsoňḍa is distinctive not only for his royal virtues but also for his moral commitment and religious devotion. The poem's narrative affirms that Dahamsoňḍa rules righteously when he accedes to the throne after his father's death. The story it tells, however short and sparse in events, revolves around the great sacrifices that Dahamsoňḍa makes in order to hear someone preach the Dharma.

What makes the story compelling—and timely given the decline in Buddhist institutions near the end of Rājasiṃha I's reign—is how Alagiyavanna makes the king's thirst for the Dharma the central motivation behind the plot. While considering his royal majesty, the Bodhisattva concludes that nothing can be beautiful and delightful in the absence of the Dharma. To make this point, Alagiyavanna includes a few verses portraying the king as lamenting the absence of the Buddha's teaching in his realm.

> Like an ocean that has no shore,
> Like a sky that has no sun or moon,
> Like a house in which the lamps went out,
> Like a rutting majestic elephant without tusks,
> Like a lake that has no lotus flowers,
> Like a pearl necklace that has no gem pendant,
> Like a face on which the nose has been cut off,
> The world without Dharma is not beautiful.[63]

This poetic lamentation of Dahamsoňḍa's desire for the Dharma that is scarce or even missing from his kingdom succinctly expresses a similar notion found in *Saddharmālaṅkāraya*. Therein, the same King Dahamsoňḍa bemoans the lack of beauty when ruling over an earth without Dharma, comparing it to the sky without the sun or moon, a majestic elephant without its tusks, and a king without his ornaments.[64] Of particular interest here is Alagiyavanna's use of the simile concerning a face without a nose. Not found in *Saddharmālaṅkāraya* or *Rasavāhinī*, this image instead is suggestive of one of the punishments meted out to enemy soldiers at this time. While discussing the Portuguese cruelties that inspired Sinhala opposition, Queyroz also notes that the "Chingalaz sometimes gave occasion for some harshness and severity, by cutting off the noses, lips and ears, of some Portuguese and even of their own countrymen when they seized them in war or captured them."[65]

Aside from the cases of mutilation during the wars of that period, there is another manner in which the *Dahamsoňḍa Kava* gives expression to the current political and religious environments. It employs a concept of "longing in separation from the Dharma" (*daṁ-viyo*) embedded in the narrative as the pathos around which the plot unfolds. When the god Śakra's heavenly seat becomes hot, characteristically alerting him of the need for assisting the Bodhisattva in his path toward Buddhahood, he gazes down on the earth and recognizes that Dahamsoňḍa has decided to renounce his kingship and the world out of a longing "because of separation from the Dharma."[66] The suffering felt by the Bodhisattva, whose thirst for Dharma remains as yet unquenched, moves the deity to action. He assumes the form of a ferocious *rakṣa*—with rough hair, red eyes, crooked fangs, and sparks of fire spraying from his mouth—to test Dahamsoňḍa's sincerity in his task to give up everything for the Dharma. This plotline whereby Śakra appears in disguise as a malevolent figure is fairly common, and it is often used in Buddhist literature to celebrate the Bodhisattva's extraordinary heroism, the extreme purity of his generosity and compassion, and his exaltation above all other beings.[67]

The idea of separation from the Dharma, rather than one's lover or deity, marks an interesting departure from classical Indic poetry. It appears also in the *Saddharmālaṅkāraya* version of the Dahamsoňḍa story, wherein the Bodhisattva reflects on how displeasing royal splendors are when he is "endowed with the longing in separation from the Dharma" (*dharmaviyogayen*).[68] This painful existence without the Buddha's teaching represents a different take on one of the oldest and most common tropes in Indian verse—love in separation (*viraha/vipralambha*). In Sanskrit and Tamil poetry, the themes of separation and union are ubiquitous.[69] As seen in the previous chapter, Kalidāsa's *Meghadūta*, the model for *sandeśa* poetry, highlights the grief a *yakṣa* feels in separation from his wife, a feeling so painful that he employs a cloud to take a message to her. Lee Siegel has noted that the agony of separation from one's beloved is an essential facet of Sanskrit love poetry, the necessary precursor to the joy of union in sexual or divine love.[70] Martha Ann Selby has similarly pointed out that poems dealing with love in separation are comparatively more prevalent in ancient Sanskrit, Tamil, and Prakrit works than those dealing with lovers in union.[71] Hindu Vaiṣṇava poetry is often said to dwell on love in separation as the proper expression of love, the painful realization that the woman married to another or God himself is ultimately unattainable no matter how badly one longs for her or Him.[72] Likewise, much ancient Tamil poetry stressed the love in separation theme. A preoccupation with absence and its counterpart of presence appears throughout the *caṅkam* literature and much of the *bhakti* poetic genre.[73]

Thus, the common poetic trope of the agony of love in separation is skillfully refashioned by Alagiyavanna into an unbearable longing for the Dharma. The *Dahamsoňḍa Kava,* in this sense, substitutes religious sentiments in place of romantic ones, retaining all the while many of the poetic conventions that had been established by the erotic poetry of *kāvya*. This mixing of Buddhist and romantic features is not wholly unprecedented in the history of Sinhala poetry. Parākramabāhu II's *Kavsiḷumiṇa* took the *jātaka* story of King Kusa and used it as the basis for a *mahākāvya* that dwells on aesthetic embellishment and several erotic scenes of love play and descriptions of beautiful women. There is, however, little in the way of Buddhist notions or values in this poem, aside from the fact that the narrative concerns a bodhisattva. Śrī Rāhula's *Kāvyaśēkhara* represents another Sinhala work that combines the aesthetic requirements of a *mahākāvya*, including erotic descriptions of women at play, with Buddhist admonitions. The *Kāvyaśēkhara* includes more Buddhist material than *Kavsiḷumiṇa*, but these ideas generally appear in separate cantos with little relation to the main *jātaka* narrative.[74]

Alagiyavanna's *Dahamsoňḍa Kava*, in contrast, devotes relatively few verses to the physical beauty and charms of women. The majority of these verses describe the dancing girls and city women of Benares, and these only appear in the context of the seemingly obligatory poetic description of the city near the beginning of the poem. One formulaic verse on the wives of enemy kings employs the standard metaphor of swans to describe these women's breasts, which display agitation as a result of the glory of King Bambadat.[75] Then, the Bodhisattva's mother, the chief queen of King Bambadat, is briefly described as a "very beautiful woman." But aside from mentioning her "luminous body," she does not become an object for erotic description.[76] No mention is made, however, of a wife or consort of King Dahamsoňḍa, as he is a figure who appears without romantic feelings or erotic interests. He is a king willing to renounce all forms of worldly delight for the sake of the Dharma. Alagiyavanna thus chose to forgo poetic reflections on love and desire for physical pleasures. His work also explicitly asserts that the only beauty in the world appears with reference to the Buddha and his teaching. Bereft of the Dharma, Dahamsoňḍa rejects every material and sensual form of delight associated with his reign. Such a move directly contests the ethos of *kāvya*.

This reorientation of values away from eroticism and aesthetics as major poetic aims allows Alagiyavanna instead to emphasize the precious nature of the Dharma in a world in which it unappreciated or even absent. In the late sixteenth-century Sītāvaka kingdom, after years of intense warfare and the failure of the plot to poison King Rājasiṃha I, Buddhist texts and institutions had a more precarious existence. As the poem relates King Dahamsoňḍa's almost futile search to find someone in his kingdom who could preach the doctrine of the Buddha to him, it at once glorifies the Dharma and bemoans the society from which it is absent. The king indicates the value of the Dharma when he exclaims:

> Relate to me in full the Good Dharma,
> Preached by the Lord of Sages, the Teacher to the Three Worlds,
> Delighting the *brahmās*, gods, and humans,
> And manifesting the fruit of liberation.[77]

This verse conveys through the speech of the king a concise statement about the supreme value of the Dharma. This is necessary for the story since it sets up the plot point in verse 83, whereupon Dahamsoňḍa promises to offer immeasurable wealth and his kingdom to whomever recites the Buddha's doctrine to him. Alagiyavanna draws out this idea of a willingness to give up nearly everything for the sake of the Dharma, the most valuable treasure since it alone facilitates comfort in the next world and liberation from *saṃsāra*. The king, increasingly desperate, thus continues:

> If anyone relates the doctrine to me now,
> Either with a verse or even with a half or quarter of a verse,

From the Dharma preached by the Lord of Sages and endowed with ambrosia,
I will give numerous riches to him and increase the joy in his mind.
Giving ownership over my royal wealth
Such as distinctive and priceless pearls and gems worth 1,000 to 100,000 crores,
Along with the kingdom's ports,
Increasing his happiness, I will become his servant.[78]

As King Dahamsoňḍa indicates how much he is willing to give up for the Dharma, even offering his servitude to the one who possesses such knowledge, the poet reinforces the classical Sinhala Buddhist view that kings have a duty to serve and respect the Sangha.[79] By expressing the king's desire to hear the Dharma in verse form, Alagiyavanna reminds his audience about the value of Buddhist poetry as well.

Still failing to find one who knows enough of the doctrine to preach it to him, Dahamsoňḍa renounces his kingdom and goes off into the forest. This retreat signifies the king's willingness to part with wealth and power for the sake of the Dharma, a motif that reappears in many *jātaka* stories and the life story of the Buddha who first renounces royal life before attaining his awakening. In *Dahamsoňḍa Kava*, this dramatic step attracts the attention of the god Śakra, thus setting into motion the story's narrative arc. However Dahamsoňḍa's renunciation also provides the poet with another opportunity to display his skills of poetic embellishment. Verses that vividly describe elephants at play, peacocks dancing, and young deer nibbling on plants are included. He details the various birds that sing while feasting on nectar and fruits, before proceeding to list the kinds of trees that decorate the forest. But all is not so pleasurable or beautiful, as Alagiyavanna also describes the various dangers lurking in the forest.

Because of the greatness of [the Bodhisattva's] merit, he did not arrive at any danger,
From poisonous cobras, pit vipers, and Russell's Vipers,
From fearful lions, elephants, tigers, and bears,
Or from very dreadful *yakṣas*, *bhūtas*, *piśācas*, and robbers.[80]

Listing such threats undermines the aesthetic delight to be found in ornately described forests, which are a characteristic feature of classical *kāvya* works. However, Alagiyavanna has already indicated that he seeks to exalt the Dharma first and foremost. Naming such fearsome predators may succeed in generating the sentiment of fear (*bhāyāṅkara*) in an audience that could be expected to worry about encountering many of these creatures too. But it is likely that Alagiyavanna employs this verse chiefly to allude to the protective powers of merit (*piṅ*) associated with great beings.

Next, Dahamsoṅḍa, whose desire for the Dharma outweighs any fear he might otherwise have for the ferocious looking *rakṣa* in whose terrifying form Śakra has disguised himself, goes straight up to the *rakṣa* and asks to hear some part of the Dharma from him. The *rakṣa* is another malevolent spiritual being recognized in ancient Buddhist cosmology and a figure that would ordinarily be avoided. However, from this act we learn how valuable the Dharma really is, as Dahamsoṅḍa indicates a willingness to sacrifice his life on its behalf. The king thus addresses the *rakṣa*:

> If today you recited a verse of the doctrine,
> Spoken by the Lord of Sages, clearing up the suffering of existence,
> Accomplishing the welfare of both worlds without fail,
> I would offer you my kingly riches and my life.[81]

Śakra is eager to test the Bodhisattva's resolve and offers to relate the Buddha's teaching if he can release him from the agony of hunger. He suggests letting him feed "on the flesh of your body and your blood" to extinguish his hunger before napping and then preaching the Dharma for which he longs.[82] However, the wise Dahamsoṅḍa points out that he cannot listen to the Dharma if the *rakṣa* eats him first. The *rakṣa* then praises the Bodhisattva and proposes a novel idea to alleviate both his hunger and the king's thirst for the Dharma.

> Noble Future Buddha, who is extraordinary,
> Fulfilling the Full Thirty Perfections completely,
> And attaining faultless Buddhahood in the future,
> Delighting the *brahmās*, gods, and humans,
> Ascending this mountain with joy,
> And while jumping into my mouth,
> I will preach the Dharma to you,
> May you quickly ascend it to listen.[83]

At this point, King Dahamsoṅḍa pauses to reflect on the deal the *rakṣa* is offering and the sacrifice that he is required to make. These brief moments of reflection allow Alagiyavanna to devote some more verses to extolling the Dharma and summarizing some of its moral admonitions for his audience. This section in the narrative demonstrates once again how Alagiyavanna uses *Dahamsoṅḍa Kava* to express religious ideas as well as aesthetic aims. There is little reference to the Dharma in *Sävul Sandēśaya*, only descriptions of ritual practice and scattered words of praise for the Buddha and the gods. In *Dahamsoṅḍa Kava*, however, we find a new interest in offering moralistic instruction in verse form. While the Bodhisattva reflects on the teaching of the Buddha, which he recognizes was "assuredly for the sake of attaining worldly comforts and liberation and for obstructing the very dreadful misery of repeated existence," the poet recounts some of the tradition's moral precepts.[84]

> Rejecting the words spoken by virtuous persons,
> But accepting fully the words of stupid persons,
> Some persons who commit adultery,
> Suffer dreadful punishment and are destroyed.
> Some people, while speaking cruel and boastful speech,
> Having entered into the middle of a war while lacking bravery,
> Receiving the fierce blows of weapons,
> Are completely destroyed.
> Some people, not taking the speech of virtuous persons to heart,
> Going from place to place and committing theft,
> Suffering cruel afflictions and being destroyed,
> Will come to hell.[85]

These verses about wicked deeds indicate that people who heed the advice of those lacking knowledge or who ignore the words of the wise and virtuous (*sudanan*) will suffer misfortune. These verses hint at a broader dispute among competing religious doctrines. Alagiyavanna seems to be condemning those who follow teachings that run counter to the Buddha's Dharma. The only reason to warn people about the dangers of not listening to the advice of virtuous persons—a category that presumably includes the poet—is that at this place and time there were people in the Sītāvaka kingdom who had begun to abandon the Dharma.

This section of the work also includes a meditation on death that is offered as further evidence of why one should devote oneself to the Dharma.

Using the fear and the inevitability of death as a spur to encourage people to embrace the Buddha's teaching is a common practice in Buddhist literature.[86] Alagiyavanna follows suit by portraying the Bodhisattva as reflecting on how people die by falling into water, being struck by lightning, and jumping off mountain peaks (as he is about to do). The brutal imagery used to communicate the various means of death continues in verse 120:

> Some are destroyed by various kinds of poisoned food,
> Some by putting a rope around their necks,
> Some by drawing out and eating their own tongues,
> And some by stabbing themselves with their own hand.[87]

Such violent deaths would have resonated with people living in a period when warfare, torture, and execution were common. But the narrator uses them to illustrate how innumerable ignorant beings destroy themselves without "knowing the tranquility that arises in this world and the next" or the good fortune enjoyed by those who follow the Dharma.[88] This message is consistent with the discourse on impermanence (*anicca*) in the version of the story found in *Sahassavatthuppakaraṇa*, but it is made more vivid and concrete by the imagery of Alagiyavanna's text.[89]

King Dahamsoňḍa is aware of the many dangers in the world and of the inevitability of death in *saṃsāra*. He displays rare insight by recalling the many times he was destroyed in previous lives by lions, tigers, bears, and other threats. Thus, realizing that a life without the Dharma is subject to great risks and death anyway, the king agrees to the terms set by the *rakṣa* that would allow him to hear the Dharma before falling into that being's large and terrifying mouth.

> At this time I will offer my life with devotion
> To the noble Good Teaching of the Lord of Sages,
> Which gives the splendor of liberation that is without old age or death,
> To beings who listen with thoughts of reverence.[90]

The king's realization of the fragility of life only makes his devotion (*bäti*) to the Dharma that much stronger. Unlike other forms of South Asian poetry in which devotion is commonly shown to a personal lord or a lover, Dahamsoňḍa's devotion is reserved for the Buddha's Dharma. Alagiyavanna argues that death, a frighteningly common yet still mysterious event, need not be feared by those who are committed to a doctrine that promises freedom from death. According to the *Dahamsoňḍa Kava*, the Buddha's Dharma is such a doctrine and should be embraced reverently by those who wish to survive in tumultuous times.

At the top of the peak, as the king readies to throw himself into the *rakṣa*'s mouth in exchange for hearing a Dharma verse, the poet switches to the more elaborate *samudraghoṣa* meter to highlight the story's climax. Still disguised as a *rakṣa*, Śakra begins reciting verses of the Dharma, including the briefly stated line: "All constituent elements are impermanent" (*anita vara sakara*) from the famous speech given by the Buddha on his deathbed in the Mahāparinibbāna Sutta of *Digha Nikāya*.[91] This Pāli verse is quoted in other versions of the Dahamsoňḍa story, signifying both the climax of the narrative and the message it is meant to convey.[92] Alagiyavanna then describes the greatness of the Bodhisattva who, fearlessly longing for the Dharma, makes an aspiration to become a Buddha in the future.

> "May I shine with beautiful, thick six-colored rays,
> That radiate outwards as far as one can see to the topmost part of existence,
> And spreading throughout the center of the entire universe without measure,
> And emitting the radiant mix of colors from my body, as small as a sesame seed,"
> And thinking, "I will bring all beings who wander about in the ocean of existence,
> To the City of Liberation that is without old age and death,"
> Our Great Bodhisattva, who is deep in virtues,
> Aspiring for noble and marvelous Buddhahood,
> Like the setting sun with its yoke of 1000 rays,
> And like the full moon swallowed by the mouth of Rāhu,
> Quickly leapt from the mountain top into the *rakṣa*'s mouth,
> As if offering his life while listening to the extraordinary Dharma.[93]

The praise for the Bodhisattva as he throws himself down toward the *rakṣa*'s mouth is a distinctive addition to the narrative. Alagiyavanna's work describes the Bodhisattva as again sacrificing himself for the sake of developing the Perfections (*pāramitā*), or moral virtues, needed for attaining Buddhahood. *Dahamsoňḍa Kava* depicts this act of self-sacrifice as having been motivated by the Bodhisattva's wish to assist all beings in the attainment of liberation, which is an objective that is not directly mentioned in the other versions of this story. It is a motive, however, that is frequently found in other Buddhist *jātakas*, particularly those in Sanskrit and in some *Paññāsa Jātaka* collections, which contain more episodes of the Bodhisattva's self-sacrifice than in the *jātakas* of the Pāli Canon.[94]

Seconds before Dahamsoňḍa falls into the *rakṣa*'s mouth, Śakra assumes his real form and catches the Bodhisattva in his arms. Then, the deity whisks the Bodhisattva up to his heavenly realm where he can delight in the good fortune enjoyed by other meritorious beings. This tour of the Caturmahārājika Heaven, over which Śakra is said to preside in Buddhist cosmology, allows Alagiyavanna once again to insert more ornate verses to describe the beauty of this realm. Verses 137 to 145 describe in considerable detail the divine mansions, nymphs, trees, and so on in this heaven, adding many aesthetically rich details to earlier versions of the story. Further, in a curious reversal of roles, Dahamsoňḍa assumes the seat of honor in the midst of the assembly of deities and preaches the Dharma to them "as if pouring down the rain of ambrosia."[95] Alagiyavanna's account, whereby "our Bodhisattva declared the Dharma, with words that were suitable and well-spoken," is a marked departure from the older Pāli and Sinhala versions of the story, which suggest that the god Śakra was the one doing the preaching.[96] For Alagiyavanna, it is seemingly more appropriate for the Bodhisattva to preach the Dharma, despite the fact that earlier he had been in search of someone else to preach it to him.

A Buddhist aspiration appears at the end of the poem, right before Alagiyavanna identifies himself as the author, confirming the religious goals that pervade this work. The audience is reminded that King Dahamsoňḍa, the protagonist whose longing for the Dharma finally pays off at the end, would later in this auspicious eon become the Buddha named Gotama. Such an assertion mirrors the so-called story of the present that relates past characters to contemporary figures and that appears in all *jātaka* tales and links the narrative to the figure of the Buddha.[97] Then, Alagiyavanna's aspiration connects the present poem to the future attainment of valued religious goals among those who listen to *Dahamsoňḍa Kava*.

May all beings, who listen with esteem,
To the life-story of the Great Bodhisattva,
Being released from birth, old age, and death,
Remain having obtained the benefit of Nirvana.[98]

With this verse, Alagiyavanna dedicates his poem to the eventual liberation of all who listen reverently to it. The aspiration for the highest Buddhist goal imaginable categorically marks the *Dahamsoňḍa Kava* as a Buddhist text directed toward meeting people's religious needs. This goal appears in contrast to what is found in *Sävul Sandēśaya*, in which the narrator simply asks for protection and long life.[99]

The Virtues of Kingship

It is significant that Alagiyavanna's decision to compose a poem infused with devotion to the Dharma coincided with a period when Rājasiṃha I apparently put increasing pressure on Buddhist institutions after an assassination plot his life. In this sense, parts of *Dahamsoňḍa Kava* read like a defense of the righteousness and importance of the Dharma in the kingdom of Sītāvaka. At the same time, other parts offer advice to kings on how best to rule. The work's expressions of longing for the Dharma consistently involve statements on the proper rule of kings. The multiple meanings of the Sinhala words *dahaṁ* or *daṁ*(i.e., Dharma) in this work refer not only to the teaching of the Buddha and the name of the king. They are also occasionally used in conjunction with royalty, as in the compound *rajadahaṁ*, which means the "moral conduct or righteous rule of kings."

For instance, when Dahamsoňḍa accedes to the throne, the narrator states that he "practiced the righteous rule of previous kings" (*pera raja dahama piḷipäda*).[100] Later, when Śakra admonishes the Bodhisattva in heaven, he enjoins him to "live long in accordance with the righteous rule of ancient kings" (*pavatu vilasin porana raja daṁ*).[101] It is clear from these and other references that Alagiyavanna wishes to emphasize the virtue of following the conduct of righteous kings in the past. This message could also represent a subtle admonition to Rājasiṃha I, whose constant warfare and hostility to sections of the Sangha invited dissension within his realm. Examples of Sinhala resistance to the rule of Rājasiṃha I are seen in the assassination attempt on his life, the desertion of a number of his army captains to the Portuguese side, and the revolt of the Kandyan kingdom, all taking place after 1585.[102] While there is no clear evidence that Alagiyavanna ever opposed Rājasiṃha I, his verses on kingship in *Dahamsoňḍa Kava* could hardly have been addressed to anyone else. Rather than honor his king with abundant praise, the poet gently admonishes him on the qualities of a righteous king.

For example, verse 69 of *Dahamsoňḍa Kava* defines some of the ideal characteristics of kingship. This particular verse strings together several lists of qualities deemed desirable for a monarch. Unlike the previous verse in which the features of a good ruler are specified in terms of fame, strength, and compassion, the following description of an ideal king appears more abstract and clearly expects that readers and listeners would understand the components in each list.

> Being endowed with the Four Devices for Ruling,
> With the Threefold Powers, Six Virtues, and Seven Branches,
> And with the Four Ways of Showing Favor,
> He continued to protect the world with distinction.[103]

Dahamsoňḍa is said to rule by employing four devices: conciliation (*sāma*), generosity (*dāna*), causing division (*bheda*), and the threat of force (*danda*), which are techniques mentioned in Kautilya's *Arthaśāstra*—an ancient Hindu treatise on governance, for dealing with treachery.[104] The Threefold Powers comprise glory (*prabhava*), perseverance (*utsaha*), and consultation (*mantrana*), which the king may use to reach his desired ends.[105] The Six Virtues or methods of foreign policy are forming alliances (*sandhi*), entering hostilities (*vigraha*), preparing for war (*yāna*), concealment or staying quiet (*asana*), befriending a neighboring king to strengthen one's hand in hostilities against a rival (*dvaidha*), and seeking the protection of a more powerful army (*saṃśraya*).[106] The Seven Branches refer to the constituent elements of the state: the king, his councilors, the territory and population of the state, its allies, the treasury, fortified towns and cities, and the forces of defense and justice.[107] Finally, the Four Ways of Showing Favor are strategies used to win support, namely generosity (*dāna*), kind speech (*priyavacana*), a life of usefulness (*arthacaryyā*), and impartiality (*samānātmatā*).[108] These royal qualities combine to portray Dahamsoňḍa in a manner akin to how the *Arthaśāstra* defines the ideal king in ancient India. He thus appears as a powerful and just ruler, one who any actual king should emulate.

What makes Dahamsoňḍa an ideal Buddhist king is his willingness to renounce his throne for the Dharma, a common trait among other Bodhisattva-kings mentioned in the *Jātaka* text.[109] By highlighting this virtue, Alagiyavanna effectively makes the argument that royal power must always be subordinate to religious observance and devotion to the Buddha's dispensation. Longing for the Dharma, King Dahamsoňḍa abandons his kingdom, offering to give away the wealth of his position for a verse of the Dharma. This represents more than just a gesture of voluntary poverty that is typically idealized in the Buddhist religion as the most effective path to moral development and liberation.[110] In *Dahamsoṅḍa Kava*, the Bodhisattva's act of renunciation and self-sacrifice also entitles him to rule as king once more. As Reiko Ohnuma has argued, many gift of the body stories involve kings who move to the forest, pass a test by offering their own bodies, and then return to assume a form of renewed and legitimated kingship.[111] After Śakra ushers the Bodhisattva to heaven, Dahamsoṅḍa is seated like the king of the gods in Śakra's *paṇḍukambala* stone seat in the middle of the Suddharma Assembly Hall.[112] It is from this royal seat that Dahamsoṅḍa expounds on the Dharma to the heavenly beings in attendance.

Śakra subsequently advises Dahamsoṅḍa on how to be a virtuous and effective ruler. By preaching the Dharma, Dahamsoṅḍa is able to reclaim his royal standing. But before he returns to earth and to his reign, he is admonished on how to incorporate the wisdom of the Dharma into his own rule. Śakra instructs him thus:

> May you live long in the manner of the previous kings,
> With the collection of the Four Moral Virtues,
> And with the precious Ten Forms of Royal Conduct,
> Pleasing the minds of all beings.
> Fulfilling the moral conduct of a future Buddha,
> Increasing your love without limit,
> Toward all beings like the love for one's own child,
> May you live long in accordance with the moral conduct of ancient kings.[113]

This call to imitate ancient kings moves away from some of the classical Indic notions of kingship preserved in the *Arthaśāstra* to other royal attributes expressed in Buddhist sources. For example, the Ten Forms of Royal Conduct (*dasaraja-dahaṁ*) refer here to a list of Buddhist virtues comprising generosity (*dāna*), morality (*sīla*), sacrifice (*pariccāga*), uprightness (*ajjava*), gentleness (*maddava*), self-control (*tapo*), nonanger (*akkodha*), nonviolence (*avihiṃsā*), forbearance (*khanti*), and nonopposition (*avirodhana*).[114] This image of the ideal king has moved beyond the picture of the wily and powerful ruler supplied by the *Arthaśāstra*. He now appears as a moral and compassionate monarch for whom kingship provides the means for fostering Buddhist piety throughout the realm.

The figure of King Dahamsoňḍa personifies in Alagiyavanna's work two crucial dimensions of Sinhala kingship. He appears as both a future Buddha and as divine, at least in the sense of journeying to heaven and being invited to preach to the gods there. To be a bodhisattva and divine was the highest status attainable by beings who remain in *saṃsāra*, or the cycle of birth and death. These attributes were also traditionally associated with kings in early modern Sinhala society, as H. L. Seneviratne has described in relation to the traditional Kandyan kingdom.[115] While in heaven, Śakra calls on the king to aspire to Buddhahood and to reflect continually on the Three Marks of impermanence, dissatisfaction and no-selfhood, finally wishing for him to attain liberation from *saṃsāra*.[116] Alagiyavanna then describes Dahamsoňḍa's return to the throne in both heroic and ethical terms.

> And descending to the world of men,
> Returning to the splendor of his kingship,
> He preached the Good Dharma, pleasing all beings,
> In order to become a Buddha in the future.[117]

Again, the narrative then comes to an end by affirming that King Dahamsoňḍa would later succeed in becoming a Buddha, followed by the poet's aspiration that all who would hear this story should one day attain nirvana. However, for all the praise reserved for the Bodhisattva in *Dahamsoňḍa Kava*, much of it is cast in terms of him as a righteous ruler. Kings like Dahamsoňḍa who are praised by a poet like Alagiyavanna earn this stature by displaying their commitment to the Dharma of the Buddha and the dharma of kings. For Alagiyavanna, these two objectives are interconnected, and he clearly asserts that righteous kings ought to be concerned with both of them. The ideal king of *Dahamsoňḍa Kava* differs markedly from how he appears in *Sävul Sandēśaya* and many other poetic works that extol kingly power in Sanskrit or in a literary vernacular modeled on Sanskrit *kāvya*. The powerful, attractive king who excels in martial and erotic pastimes has been replaced in *Dahamsoňḍa Kava* by a king who appears as a preeminently moral figure who reveres the Dharma and rules in accordance with it.

Dahamsoňḍa Kava is a work of poetry that employs a traditional narrative that is somewhat removed from sixteenth-century Sītāvaka in terms of both time and space. Local landscapes and figures are supplanted by the Bodhisattva and a god in a tale that takes place in Dambadiva (i.e., India) long ago. Nevertheless, the narrative as rendered into Sinhala verse by Alagiyavanna provides an implicit commentary on the historical setting in which he lived. The glories of the Sītāvaka court and kingdom, extolled in great detail in *Sävul Sandēśaya*, disappear from view in *Dahamsoňḍa Kava*. Instead of a world of great aesthetic beauty and delight—a world in which a Buddhist poet could celebrate a king and the many forms of religious rites that occurred under his patronage—the world of this later poem is characterized by the decline of the Dharma and of morality as a whole. King Rājasiṃha I's persecution of his political opponents, including members of the Sangha in Sītāvaka and Kandy, apparently led to severe reprisals whereupon many monks were executed, monasteries were destroyed, and books were burned.[118] This image of religious decline is taken up and highlighted by the work in a poetic manner.

> Like a lamp that, having shone on top of Mt. Meru,
> Has gone out to extinction,
> When that Sage attained Final Nirvana,
> The delightful dispensation of the Sage went into decline.[119]

Within the frame of the poem's narrative, the Sage referred to is Kaśyapa Buddha, and within the cosmological framework of Buddhist thought on the cyclical existence of the Dharma, it is perfectly normal for the Dharma and dispensation to be periodically rediscovered and reestablished in the world by another Buddha.[120] But given what we know about the historical context in which Alagiyavanna composed this work, it is clear that Dahamsoňḍa's longing for the Dharma and Śakra's admonition for moral kingship represent a commentary on the world of the poet. Dahamsoňḍa's predicament appears to resonate with Alagiyavanna's observations of a society in decline and of Buddhist teachings in retreat.

4

On Love and Kingship in Poem of the Birth-Story of King Kusa

ALAGIYAVANNA'S Kusa Jātaka *Kāvya* (*Poem of the Birth-Story of King Kusa*) is arguably his most popularly and critically acclaimed work. Also called by the *eḷu* title *Kusadā Kava,* the work is by far the longest poem in Alagiyavanna's oeuvre, numbering between 685 and 691 verses depending on the edition. Here again he based his text on a *jātaka* story—the "Kusa Jātaka" (no. 531), found in the *Jātaka-aṭṭhavaṇṇanā* and its Sinhala translation, commonly called the *Pansiya Paṇas Jātaka Pot Vahansē* (*The Revered Book of the 550 Birth-Stories*), which was compiled in the fourteenth century. Unlike the Dahamsoňḍa story, the Kusa story is a "classical *jātaka*" from the Pāli Canon, and the love story therein made it an appropriate topic for a Sinhala *kavi.*[1] Alagiyavanna explains that the wife of a nobleman from the Sītāvaka court invited him to write a poem about the Bodhisattva. However, the year of completion given near the end of the poem cites the Saka year of 1532, which is equivalent to 1610 CE, more than a decade after Rājasiṃha's death and the fall of his kingdom.

The apparent lapse of time between the original invitation and the work's completion is significant and may account for the length and the complex interests evident in the poem. *Kusa Jātaka Kāvya* continues and accentuates the stylistic trends seen in *Dahamsoňda Kava* by further emphasizing simpler verse forms and moral messages. Yet it is also marked by both continuities and discontinuities in terms of style and subject. Questions about why Alagiyavanna wrote this text, which poetic styles it expresses, and how it addresses issues of love and morality on the one hand and Buddhism and power on the other all contribute to making *Kusa Jātaka Kāvya* a provocative work. The text represents a clear case of how Alagiyavanna reinterpreted the traditional culture-power formulation that defined classical

Sinhala poetry in medieval Sri Lanka. Alagiyavanna's *Kusa Jātaka Kāvya* comes to illustrate the new capacity of Sinhala poetry to expand its literary horizons and address a broader audience than it had previously known.

Multiple Motives and Versions

The stated impetus behind the work lies in the request of the noble lady Mäṇiksāmi, the wife of Arthanāyaka, who was a minister in the court of Rājasiṃha I.[2] She is also said in the poem to be the granddaughter of the Chief Minister Sēpāla who served King Bhuvanekabāhu VII of Koṭṭe.[3] Mäṇiksāmi is singled out for extensive praise in the poem's early verses. In terms of Buddhist observance, she is compared to Viśākhā, the famous female lay *upāsikā* from commentarial Pāli and Sinhala preaching texts.

> Faultless with respect to the Triple Gem,
> Full of pious confidence,
> Who else in this world except for Visākā,
> Is equal to this long-eyed lady?
> Always guarding without blemish,
> The Five Precepts and the Eight Precepts on *poya* days,
> She guards herself at all times,
> Like a lapwing guards its egg or a yak its tail.[4]

Evidently, Mäṇiksāmi's great Buddhist piety led her to ask Alagiyavanna to compose a poem on one of the lives of the Bodhisattva. Alagiyavanna thus credits her rather than Rājasiṃha for encouraging and supporting him to undertake this particular work. However, her connection to the Sītāvaka court notwithstanding, the *Kusa Jātaka Kāvya*'s status as a court poem is ambiguous. Originating in a royal court, it appears that the work was finished outside a royal environment under distinctly different circumstances.

Other verses, however, suggest there were also religious motives behind its composition. Alongside Mäṇiksāmi's request to hear a "beautiful story about a former existence of the Buddha" (*budun pera siritak soňda*), Alagiyavanna also mentions a couple of his own reasons for authoring *Kusa Jātaka Kāvya*.[5] Early on in the poem, in a remark duly intended to signal the author's humility, Alagiyavanna asserts:

> My bold intention to recite,
> The unfathomable virtues of Lord Buddha,

Is like trying to pierce Mount Meru at once,
With the proboscis of a mosquito.[6]

Here the poet represents his task in terms of being partly, if not chiefly, the recitation of the Buddha's qualities and accomplishments throughout his many lifetimes. This motive is consistent with a long line of Sinhala authors preceding him.[7] Alagiyavanna's words clearly recall a similar objective expressed by Vīdāgama Maitreya in the fifteenth-century *Buduguṇālaṅkāraya*.

My bold intention is to recite,
The unfathomable virtues of Lord Buddha,
Which great poets in the past,
Declared without reaching their limit.[8]

This similarity suggests that Alagiyavanna saw himself as a poet comparable to great poets in the past, likewise seeking to praise the Buddha. He suggests that the greatness of the Buddha's virtues depicted in his work ought to overcome any faults in its meter or meaning.[9]

Then, in the concluding verses of *Kusa Jātaka Kāvya*, Alagiyavanna declares that he composed this work to help him and others reach the highest Buddhist goal. As conventional as it is to state that one seeks to proclaim the virtues of the Buddha for the good of the many, it is equally typical to connect one's literary activity with the goal of attaining nirvana. Alagiyavanna thus writes that he "composed this beautiful *Kusadā Kava* in order to perceive the endpoint of *saṃsāra*."[10] In case anyone does not understand his intentions, he restates them in the final verse of the work:

On the Vesak Poya Day of 1532 in the year of Saka,
At the request of the noble lady named Mäṇiksāmi, who is like a goddess,
The renowned magistrate Alagiyavanna, profoundly well versed in poetry and drama,
Composed this fitting poem of the birth story of Kusa in the Sinhala language for the sake of liberation that is without old-age or death.[11]

Phrased differently, Alagiyavanna claims that his work can help realize the same ultimate goal of many other Buddhist texts—the attainment of nirvana. The recitation of the Buddha's virtues and the realization of nirvana are complementary goals to which Alagiyavanna explicitly aspires in his work. As such, if Mäṇiksāmi was primarily seeking entertainment and edification when she made her request, Alagiyavanna claims to be attempting to realize even greater objectives.

There are, however, other likely motives at work behind the composition of *Kusa Jātaka Kāvya*. These include efforts to enhance the author's poetic reputation and possibly, if oral histories are to be believed, to effect the reconciliation between his sister and her estranged husband. When Alagiyavanna chose the story of King Kusa on which to base his poem, he selected a popular narrative that formed the basis of as many as four older Sinhala poems. Three of the central treatises on Sinhala literature all cite verses from different works dealing with the Kusa story. The *Sidatsaṅgarāva*, a thirteenth-century Sinhala grammar, cites passages from an *eḷu* work concerning King Kusa and his wife, Prabhāvatī.[12] The *Siyabaslakara*, the treatise on poetics from about the ninth or tenth century, also quotes a Sinhala verse describing Kusa and Prabhāvatī at play.[13] Additionally, the treatise on meter called *Eḷu Sandas Lakuṇa*, a work from the thirteenth or fourteenth century, quotes a verse about Kusa to demonstrate the *yāgī* meter. It reads, "On that day, King Kusa, having come to the sandbank in the spotless park, /And while dwelling comfortably in the ocean of his virtues, was giving great blessings to the world."[14] The fact that all three of these poetic treatises quote verses about King Kusa from texts that are no longer extant suggests that there were once multiple works of Sinhala poetry based on the Kusa story. Because many of these works were central to any curriculum for learning to compose Sinhala *kavi*, it is likely that Alagiyavanna was exposed to these excerpts if not their originals.

The more famous, extant Sinhala text that relates the Kusa story, however, is surely Parākramabāhu II's *Kavsiḷumiṇa* from the thirteenth century. The *Kavsiḷumiṇa* reworked the Kusa story into a Sinhala version of a Sanskrit *mahākāvya*. The highly embellished retelling of the story in 769 couplets (*gī*) of Sinhala poetry is consistent with the aesthetic literary concerns of the period. As noted by Hallisey, Sinhala poets between the tenth and fifteenth centuries were shaped by and consciously borrowed from Sanskrit literary culture, even while insisting on the use of the local Sinhala language to express its ideas.[15] It is in this context that the *Kavsiḷumiṇa* reworked the Kusa story into an ornate and difficult poem, one that could present most of the stylistic conventions of a *mahākāvya* while retaining its Buddhist narrative. Among those conventions are that the poem: be based on an epic story and should be directed toward the attainment of the four *puruṣārthas* (*dharma, artha, kāma,* and *mokṣa*); relate the deeds of a heroic figure who is strong minded, handsome, self-respecting, and humble; contain embellishing descriptions of cities, seasons, sports, festivals of drinking and love, and battles, among other things; and primarily evoke the sentiment (*rasa*) of eroticism, heroism, or quietism. In addition, in keeping with the injunctions of the *Siyabaslakara*, a Sinhala *kavi* should be based on the life story of the Buddha.[16]

Significantly, the narrative of the Bodhisattva's life as King Kusa is often overshadowed by the highly stylistic poetic descriptions in *Kavsiḷumiṇa*. Such a feature is consistent with Sanskrit *mahākāvya* in general. Edwin Gerow points out that despite their epic theme, *mahākāvya* are for the most part sequences of poetic digressions in which the story is relatively unimportant.[17] The consignment of the Kusa narrative to the background allowed the poet to focus on aesthetic conventions and figures of speech. The first canto, for example, contains several couplets that describe the city of Kusāvatī in terms of gems, mansions, and crowds of beautiful women. The sixth canto contains couplets that describe a drinking festival and the erotic escapades of women in the king's harem in Sāgala. This festive scene, which incidentally does not appear in the classical *jātaka* story, carries over into stanzas describing the love play between the father of King Kusa and one of the harem girls.

> When his eyes descended upon her genitalia, she covered herself with her very red lotus hands,
> And when he removed her hands and looked again, she adorned his chest with the weight of her breasts.
> The hanging flower garlands, swaying with the breeze that blew through the holes of the jeweled netting,
> Impeded the lamp's illumination of the maiden's desire and captivated the hearts of the king and his beloved.
> While seeing her own reflection on his chest, which was moistened with sweat,
> Trusting in the words that he spoke, the maiden quickly embraced the king.[18]

Verses such as those above serve primarily to delight and generate the erotic sentiment (*sṛṇgāra-rasa*) in the minds of a learned audience. The poem's descriptions of lovely women in various states of dress and play are clearly meant to delight and titillate, while displaying the author's skill in handling meter and figures of speech. The subject of love is also presented in stanzas expressing the grief and longing felt in being separated from one's beloved—again, a common trope in the court poetry of the Indic world.[19] The twelfth canto is devoted to describing in poetically moving ways the grief King Kusa experiences after Prabhāvatī leaves him. He states: "O' dear one, is it not because of your love of one familiar to you, that you took my mind, my eyes, and my ears when you, who are gentle, went away from here?"[20] Then, Kusa addresses his absent love, Prabhāvatī, again, "Causing you to remain in the middle of my heart, which burns from the fire of separation, oh...let me now just guard the virtues of men."[21] The numerous stanzas devoted to erotic love and the grief of love in separation clearly show how *Kavsiḷumiṇa* generally emphasizes poetic sentiments more than narrative development.

Although in some respects the setting and subject of the Kusa Jātaka make it a fitting subject for a Buddhist *mahākāvya*, there are some awkward discrepancies that emerge in Parākramabāhu II's *Kavsiḷumiṇa*. Rather than acknowledge Kusa's ugliness and unseemly behavior, as illustrated in Pāli and Sinhala prose versions of the story, the author alters the story to maintain the integrity of the masculine hero. Kusa's unsightly appearance is never fully acknowledged, but rather he is said to enjoy sporting with the harem women at the royal park (vv. 472–491) and to have driven Prabhāvatī off by his boorish behavior instead of his looks (v. 578). Rather than throwing elephant and horse dung at Prabhāvatī, Kusa in *Kavsiḷumiṇa* throws clumps of grass, which must be judged as much less unseemly.[22] The work also downplays the determinative role of karma in the story. As such, it further distinguishes the Sinhala *mahākāvya* from the prose *jātakas* that resort to this teaching in order to explain the Bodhisattva's ugliness and Prabhāvatī's danger of being cut into seven pieces. Instead, these misfortunes are either elided or blamed on the fickle nature of women.[23] Moreover, the author of *Kavsiḷumiṇa* invents wholly new episodes of drinking festivals, water sports, and a battle between armies in order to satisfy the requirements of a *mahākāvya*.

The story of the Kusa Jātaka is transformed in *Kavsiḷumiṇa* to display its royal author's poetic skills. Its romantic aspects are retained and accentuated, while its inherent moral ambiguities are generally ignored. In addition, *Kavsiḷumiṇa* embraced what Hallisey has called the "practice of difficulty," whereby literary composition was made deliberately complex through displays of poetic virtuosity, including some verses that use only one consonant, others that use only one vowel, verses that could be read backward and forward, and other verses that could be arranged into diagrams that reveal deeper layers to the structure of particular verses in the poem.[24] The celebration of complexity in Sinhala verse marked an expectation that one's audience was more narrow and refined than the general public at large. Thus, in both form and content, the *Kavsiḷumiṇa* represented a departure from the original *jātaka* story on which it was based. Moral lessons are generally obscured by efforts to evoke poetic sentiments and acclaim for the author's poetic skills.

At the end of the sixteenth century, Alagiyavanna's decision to compose a poetic work on the Kusa Jātaka would thus have resonated within the Sinhala literary culture with which he tried to associate. Alagiyavanna, like other Sinhala poets before him, found in the Kusa story a rich narrative about the Bodhisattva that could be utilized to perform all the expressive functions of figuration, style, suggestion, and aestheticized emotion that Indian theorists of *kāvya* demanded of their genre.[25] Alagiyavanna composed his *Kusa Jātaka Kāvya* in approximately 686 quatrains in the *sivupada* style, using a variety of poetic meters. The work qualifies as a *khaṇḍakāvya*, which means that it is "fragmentary" in the sense that it does not contain all of the criteria required for a *mahākāvya* such as *Kavsiḷumiṇa*.[26] Nevertheless, parts of *Kusa Jātaka Kāvya* clearly evoke the ornate descriptions and aesthetic interests of *mahākāvya* poems more generally. To this extent, Alagiyavanna appears to have consciously modeled himself after the great Sinhala court poets of previous eras, some of whom also wrote poems on Kusa Jātaka.

Another possible motive for composing the *Kusa Jātaka Kāvya* has been preserved in some of the oral traditions of Sinhala folklore (*janapravādaya*) connected with Alagiyavanna's life. His renown as a poet combined with the survival of his descendants has led to the transmission of various legends about him. One of these traditions holds that Alagiyavanna composed the *Kusa Jātaka Kāvya* due to a family crisis. His younger sister and her husband reportedly had a falling out early in their marriage. One version of this story claims that once, when the couple returned to her parent's house for a visit, the husband described her as an immodest woman, which led her to resolve to live with her parents instead of him.[27] Another version holds that the younger sister came to have doubts about her new husband's caste and wealth, which led her to secretly return home to her family.[28] In both cases, as legend has it, Alagiyavanna composed the *Kusa Jātaka Kāvya* to effect the reconciliation between his sister and brother-in-law, a reconciliation supposedly modeled after the reunion of Kusa and Prabhāvatī.

The above folk tradition was likely little more than hearsay designed to embellish the circumstances around which the *Kusa Jātaka Kāvya* was composed. There is no good evidence pointing to the existence of a younger sister to Alagiyavanna. Even if there were, it would not prove the historical veracity of this legend. The folk account succeeds, however, in casting Alagiyavanna as a poet grounded in the local culture, a person who experienced and dealt with family squabbles like many others. Such an effort to popularize Alagiyavanna was consistent with certain changes in his poetic style as his career wore on. The *Kusa Jātaka Kāvya* retains a more local flavor in terms of style and tone, departing somewhat from the classical poetic features in earlier centuries. Although Alagiyavanna embraced a familiar subject for composing a poem, he used the narrative to pursue a more eclectic set of interests, including the popularization of a heretofore rather exclusive literary genre.

Between the Court and Village

If Alagiyavanna's motives for composing *Kusa Jātaka Kāvya* were multiple and somewhat ambiguous, the same qualities can be attributed to the style in which he fashioned this work. Because it appears that he began this work in the Sītāvaka court but did not complete it until after Sītāvaka was annexed by Koṭṭe and the Portuguese, we could expect that the stylistic changes in the work reflected the dramatic political and social changes that occurred between about 1590 and 1610. Alagiyavanna composed *Kusa Jātaka Kāvya* during the period in which the traditional culture-power formation was dismantled arguably once and for all in Sri Lanka. Not coincidentally, modern scholars and critics credit Alagiyavanna's *Kusa Jātaka Kāvya* for having combined ornate, classical features of Sinhala *kavi* with those of a more popular, village style of poetry (*gämi kavi*). This innovative form of Sinhala *kavi* has served to distinguish Alagiyavanna from other poets, effectively sealing for him an important role in the historical development of Sinhala poetry.[29] What is less clear, however, is whether Alagiyavanna's combination of the "great" tradition (*mahāsampradāya*) with the "little" tradition (*cullasampradāya*) of Sinhala *kavi* in this particular work was more the result of a clear stylistic choice or, alternatively, the result of a larger cultural shift taking place at the time.

One of the areas in which Alagiyavanna blurs stylistic categories is in his choice of poetic genres. The work represents a *kaṇḍhakāvya* poem, although it still occasionally aspires to poetic virtuosity. C. E. Godakumbura remarked that Alagiyavanna's *Kusa Jātaka Kāvya* contains ornate descriptions of cities, kings, ponds, and parks in much the same manner as a *mahākāvya* work.[30] It is in these descriptive verses that Alagiyavanna claims for himself the mantle of an excellent poet who is well versed in figures of speech and other literary techniques. Significantly, many of these more embellished verses are found near the beginning of the work. For instance, in describing the women in the city of Kusāvatī, the poet writes:

> The bees of the eyes of desirous ones,
> Wander about the lakes of the bodies of the women in that city,
> Whose sand banks of their hips shine with light,
> Having the red and blue lotuses of their faces and eyes.
> The women who walk about that city,
> With red lips like the tender leaves of the *nā* tree,
> With a gait like female elephants,
> Who is able to describe these ladies?[31]

Alagiyavanna here employs several poetic conventions to portray a stereotypical image of a city and the beautiful women said to inhabit it. The picture it paints could be that of any other ancient city in Indic poetry. Verses such as these work to evoke the aesthetic sentiments of a learned audience but contribute little to the narrative itself. Much of this classical descriptive style modeled after Sanskrit *mahākāvya* appears in the first two cantos of the work.

At the same time, however, other parts of the *Kusa Jātaka Kāvya* depart from the classical *mahākāvya* form. This is because Alagiyavanna's work adheres closely to the original *jātaka* story, including narrative sections that are otherwise deemed inappropriate for the *mahākāvya* genre. Wickremasinghe compliments Alagiyavanna for his work from the third canto onward, asserting that this material does not "slavishly and quite unnecessarily...follow the stock pattern of the Sanskrit *kāvya*."[32] Alagiyavanna is thus thought to have abandoned many of the more aesthetically rich features of Sinhala *kavi* in order to relate a more accessible narrative. By simplifying his style and meter, Alagiyavanna displays a greater commitment to telling a story that is more comprehensible and engaging to the average person.[33]

In the judgment of Wickremasinghe, *Kusa Jātaka Kāvya* was composed specifically to meet the tastes of the common person. The early cantos dedicated to poetic embellishment notwithstanding, this work was, for Wickremasinghe, evidence that Sinhala *kavi* could also be composed for a popular audience outside the royal court. He asserts, "True to the tradition of a ballad-maker, Alagiyavanna seizes every opportunity of inflaming the imagination of his unsophisticated audience, by dwelling at length on dramatic situations and playing on their simple feelings."[34] There may be something to this interpretation of the numerous verses with shorter meters and clearer syntax. In these, descriptions are muted, and the story is permitted to flow unencumbered. In one example, Alagiyavanna describes Prabhāvatī's royal father when he is presented with a gold image and an offer of marriage between his daughter and Kusa:

> Hearing the words that they spoke,
> And becoming filled with a joyous mind,
> Like a young man newly consecrated [as king],
> And on that day, [going] by a great royal procession,
> Taking and gifting the gold image,
> To the princess herself,
> And showing respect by giving abundant wealth,
> To the ministers that had come,
> He sent back gifts of various riches,
> To the lord of men, King Okāvas,
> Who had reached the highest position in Dambadiva,
> While increasing the loving-kindness in his mind.[35]

Such lines are fairly clear and straightforward. The only figure of speech—a simile—is short and uncomplicated. These kinds of verses function to move the narrative along with a minimum of descriptive material. Attention is focused instead on the sequence of narrative events, generating interest in the content of the story while relying less on aesthetic flourishes. This direct style would have been more accessible to a broader audience, particularly those outside the court for whom poetic conventions were unfamiliar.

At the same time, Wickremasinghe highlights the simplicity of Alagiyavanna's *Kusa Jātaka Kāvya* in order to advance his preference for a form of Sinhala verse that can appeal to people from every walk of life, a form that to him seems more native to his country than poems imitating classical Sanskrit norms from ancient India. His bias is clearly toward forms of Sinhala poetry that abandon the verbose, flowery conventions and ornate imagery that dominated poetry from the Koṭṭe period. Nevertheless, despite Wickremasinghe's view, Alagiyavanna's work retains several classical literary elements of Sinhala poetry. Poetic figures of speech continue to be employed, and verses of praise are occasionally dedicated to great men and women. For example, the work utilizes poetic tropes in praise of the city of Kusāvatī in a series of embellished verses. Thus, the foregrounding of the narrative in *Kusa Jātaka Kāvya* does not prevent Alagiyavanna from including panegyric descriptions of the city where the Bodhisattva resides.

> The army of horses that are without measure,
> With five limbs that touch the earth,
> Having the color of the waves of the Milky Ocean,
> Wander about the main road in that city.[36]

Here again, an aesthetically pleasing account of a city serves to magnify the praise for the heroic figure residing there. The greatness of the horses, including their "fifth limb" that refers to a male animal's sexual organ—a conventional image used to highlight masculine virility and strength—serves as a metonymical symbol of the greatness of King Kusa. It is possible to find other examples of poetic embellishment in *Kusa Jātaka Kāvya* beyond the first two cantos, which Wickremasinghe identified as the derivative and trite parts of the work. It would thus seem that *Kusa Jātaka Kāvya* presents a more complicated mix of poetic *mahāsampradāya* and *cullasampradāya* than the famous literary critic recognized.

In many ways, Alagiyavanna seems equally beholden to the values of accessibility and embellishment in *Kusa Jātaka Kāvya*. At certain junctures, he addresses the connoisseurs of poetry, while elsewhere he adopts an informal tone suitable to those who lack the training to appreciate Sinhala *kavi*. This stylistic ambiguity cannot be simply dismissed as evidence of the poet's lack of skill. Instead, if literature continues to be interpreted as an index to culture, the instability of literary genres in *Kusa Jātaka Kāvya* points to an analogous instability in the cultural representation of power and identity around the turn of the seventeenth century in Sri Lanka. If the idea of this work was hatched in a courtly context and if it was modeled on older subjects and conventions associated with the *mahākāvya* genre, this original setting soon disappeared after the Sītāvaka kingdom fell. Since the courtly setting that once sustained Sinhala *kavi* had disappeared from lowland Sri Lanka, it would have made sense for Alagiyavanna to speak to different audiences, some of whom were to be found in villages rather than courts.

Significantly, Alagiyavanna refused to wholly renounce the classical tradition of Sinhala *kavi* and its aspirations to express cultural power along the lines of Sanskrit poetry. He retains aspects of the panegyric style of older *kavi*, albeit without the lengthy praise of a contemporary ruler. Similar to the approach in his *Dahamsoňḍa Kava*, he reserves the bulk of his praise in *Kusa Jātaka Kāvya* for Buddhas, bodhisattvas, and the noblewoman who requested the poem in the first place. Panegyric verses in these contexts reflect the poet's commitment to the conventions of his craft and entitle him to an audience's esteem. The presence of some panegyric verses is therefore indicative of his aim to compose a work that could evoke the aesthetic flourishes of celebrated poems from earlier times. It is in this sense that he writes of his patron Mäṇiksāmi in ornate terms.

> Observing without doubt that Lakṣmi and Rati
> Were created first by Brahmā,
> This woman possessing the beauty of physical form,
> Was, moreover, created likewise.
> Having a mind akin to a wish-fulfilling gem,
> And two eyes that are a pair of blue sapphires,
> Therefore it is appropriate,
> That this lady be named *Mäṇiksāmi*.[37]

Here Alagiyavanna finds it fitting to praise her physical beauty by using the stock images and figures of speech of *kavi*. The former verse plays on the tradition that the god Brahmā's greatest creation was women. The other verse draws a pun out of her name, claiming that her name Mäṇiksāmi indicates how she is "connected" or "related" to jewels in terms of her generous thoughts and striking blue eyes. Her interest in poetry also confirms her greatness. Aside from the fact that she requested the poem be composed, another verse asserts that when reciting books in *eḷu*, Pāli, and Sanskrit, she pauses only at the designated caesuras like one well versed in the poetry of these languages.[38]

The thirteen verses praising Mäṇiksāmi near the start of the work fit the mode of panegyrics by praising her beauty, virtue, and learning. Other familiar and conventional verses of praise are dedicated to the cities of

Kusāvatī and Sävät (Sāvatthi), where Kusa once lived and where the Buddha later recalled the events of that former life. Both cities are said to shine with splendid crystal walls surrounded by a lovely moat of water.[39] Both cities are said to have been the homes of beautiful women who entranced all who glanced at them as they strolled about the roads and to have possessed large, splendid armies comprising elephants, horses, chariots, and foot soldiers that wander about in marvelous displays of power. In these ways, the two cities appear as replicas of each other, each testifying to the glory of the Buddha, Bodhisattva, and kings who reside in them. The poetic description of cities is a key feature of the ornate court poetry on which Alagiyavanna modeled his works.

Other verses praise religious figures, namely Buddhas and bodhisattvas. These verses frequently overlay religious ideas on aesthetic sentiments, broadening classical poetic conventions to recall the virtues of the Buddha (*buddhānusmṛti*) for the sake of delighting the minds of devotees. Alagiyavanna's verses on the so-called story of the present, marking the occasion when the Buddha originally told the story of King Kusa, include lines of poetry that embellish the Buddha's moral and physical qualities.

> The Lord of Sages, who has bestowed good fortune to the world,
> Sits on a pure couch,
> Spread out in the great perfumed chamber,
> That shines like a *brahmā* mansion.[40]

And again, while describing the Buddha's physical appearance, Alagiyavanna writes:

> When the Buddha's body was covered with the Well-Farer's robe,
> That shines like the fruit of the banyan tree,
> It assumed the splendor of the moon,
> Dwelling in a very red evening rain cloud.[41]

Later the Buddha is compared to a splendid autumn moon surrounded by the stars of his monastic disciples. The poet devotes several verses that describe how the six-colored Buddha rays emanate from his body and illuminate the ten directions and various features in the traditional Buddhist cosmology such as Mount Meru.[42] These descriptions blend poetic figures of speech with religious claims about the greatness of the Buddha as manifested in his physical nature.

Consistent with Alagiyavanna's esteem for poetic conventions, he occasionally praises the Bodhisattva in highly conventional ways for his royal majesty and other characteristics that have little to do with the moral perfections highlighted in the *jātaka* genre.[43] For instance, near the end of the work, he compares Kusa to Śakra, the King of the Gods, to highlight to glory of the Bodhisattva.

> Like the King of the Gods who, having climbed upon the majestic elephant Airāvaṇa, surrounded by the army of gods,
> Defeating the *asuras* and bringing Sujātā, who has excellent physical beauty, entered the city of the gods,
> King Kusa, while ascending the royal elephant that was tall and large, taking along Queen Pabāvati with her retinue,
> Entered the noble city with limitless royal splendor.[44]

This quatrain celebrating the Bodhisattva's royal majesty employs poetic figures of speech and a more intricate rhyming structure to highlight the poet's aesthetic skills. The verse celebrates King Kusa in a literary way for his martial prowess, a quality appropriate for kings. Any kind of moral excellence on the part of the Bodhisattva is disregarded here in place of other features that are more conducive to poetic embellishment.

The *cullasampradāya* sneaks back into the work, however, at places where the poet focuses more on narrative events. In such instances, the work usually employs the simpler, shorter *mahāpiyuṁ* meter and eschews ornate description and praise. Scholars of Sinhala literature have long recognized the *Kusa Jātaka Kāvya* for its greater accessibility and appeal beyond a court setting. Wickremasinghe has remarked that Alagiyavanna's *Kusa Jātaka Kāvya* reveals the poet's intention to make a "straightforward verse narrative of the *Kusa Jātaka*, keeping in mind all the time an audience that was mainly interested in the story."[45] Puñcibandara Sannasgala has similarly commented that this work's straightforward style arises from the fact that it does not have much ornamentation or panegyric writing.[46] A. V. Suraweera, for his part, has argued that the poetic embellishments in the *Kusadā Kava* (i.e., *Kusa Jātaka Kāvya*) were composed not to please scholars but rather to present words of praise straightforward enough so that even common people could understand it.[47] The idea consistent throughout all of these assessments is that Alagiyavanna composed *Kusa Jātaka Kāvya* in a simpler fashion so that everyone could enjoy and benefit from it.

This interpretation of Alagiyavanna as the prototypical folk poet is not without some justification. In comparison with the more richly complex writing in his *Sävul Sandēśaya*, the *Kusa Jātaka Kāvya* is on the whole a less ornate poem with a more developed story replete with characters that interact with each other to form discrete scenes. Unlike the *Kavsiḷumiṇa*, which employed the same story for its plot but excluded, condensed, and added various accounts to suit its *mahākāvya* structure, Alagiyavanna's *Kusa Jātaka Kāvya* retained all parts of the *Jātaka* story to present a poetic work that reads much like a *baṇapot* or Buddhist "preaching text."[48] Still, there may be other factors behind the popular assessment of Alagiyavanna as a Sinhala folk poet. Dramatic social and political changes following Sri Lanka's independence in 1947 saw, among other things, the old regime governed by genealogy and its privileging of notions of descent and rank being replaced by a new regime of citizenship that revolved around notions of rights and equality.[49] As populist and nationalist ideals gained currency in postindependence Sri Lanka, scholars of Sinhala literature displayed a tendency to place a premium on works that spoke to the Sinhala people as a whole in their native tongue shorn of "foreign" conventions associated with Sanskrit and other Indic literary norms. Wickremasinghe's efforts from the late 1940s to the early 1970s to isolate and extol works of Sinhala literature that allegedly reflected the people's unique tastes and experiences are representative of this trend. Following him, much of modern Sinhala literary criticism has embraced originality, parsimony, and sincerity as the criteria by which one evaluates and appreciates Sinhala literature.

In contrast, another scholar writing in the 1920s, a generation before the island's independence, noted the general accessibility of a work like *Kusa Jātaka Kāvya* without concluding that Alagiyavanna had become a poet for the common folk. E. Vimalasuriya Gunapala's short biography on Alagiyavanna describes the *Kusa Jātaka Kāvya* as a large work endowed with various meters, pleasing poetic embellishments, and unaffected language (*śithila bhāṣā*) that is easily understood.[50] Gunapala's assessment of Alagiyavanna differs from many postindependence writers in that he does not view Alagiyavanna's writings as being symptomatic of what later authors termed folk poetry (*jana kavi*) or village poetry (*gämi kavi*).[51] The most that Gunapala allows is that the *Kusa Jātaka Kāvya* contains melodious passages to delight the minds of readers and humorous touches to allay the suffering of the people who lived in his native region.[52]

Gunapala's view of Alagiyavanna as occasionally speaking to ordinary people from his privileged social position appears closer to the truth than those who view him as being emblematic of a larger movement of literary populism. It is one thing for a poet to adopt different styles of composition, some of which were more accessible or popular than others, and quite another thing for a poet to embody the identity and values of a "folk poet."[53] The dissolution of the Sītāvaka court and its audience of poetic connoisseurs clearly necessitated some changes in the way Alagiyavanna composed poetry. Yet the *Kusa Jātaka Kāvya* does not fully abandon the ornate features of classical Sinhala verse. It would be illogical to conclude that a privileged, landowning courtier such as Alagiyavanna would suddenly become a populist who sympathized with the interests of ordinary Sinhala folk. There is instead every reason to assume that Alagiyavanna continued to bolster his position and reputation by composing a poetic work in the tradition of great Sinhala *kavi*, while also addressing the particular effects of the political and cultural upheavals of his time. He appears here as a poet who embraces aesthetic conventions and the mundane interests of a local audience comprising both poetic connoisseurs and people outside the court.

Love in a Moral Sphere

As the Kusa Jātaka relates the story of love lost and regained, its romantic overtones made it a fitting subject for the ornate *mahākāvya* style replicated in *Kavsiḷumiṇa*.[54] The subject of love also plays a critical role in Alagiyavanna's less ornate *Kusa Jātaka Kāvya*, although the poet displays more ambivalence toward love in his work than what is seen in *Kavsiḷumiṇa*. The ideal of love as portrayed in the agony of separation from one's beloved and in the blissful reunion with one's beloved has been a consistent undercurrent in much of classical Indic poetry down through the centuries. Sanskrit verse works used the dynamics of love in separation and union as motifs around which to describe the desire for one's lover or one's lord, especially in the form of Kṛṣṇa.[55] Likewise, the long history of South Indian love poetry, in the Tamil *caṅkam* works through later devotional expressions toward a personal lord, focused its primary attention on themes of separation and distance between the narrator and the object of his or her longing.[56]

These antecedents make Alagiyavanna's choice to write about the Kusa Jātaka seem entirely appropriate. However, his treatment of love is complicated by his concern for supplying moral admonitions, including a distinctly ambivalent attitude toward women. This reticence to celebrate the passion of love is consistent with the original prose narrative of the classical *jātaka,* which also adopts a more cynical attitude toward love than what one often finds in court poetry. At times, the moralistic and somewhat misogynistic voices that appear in parts of *Kusa Jātaka Kāvya* counter the romantic undertones of the story. Unlike the *Kavsiḷumiṇa,* for which exploring and celebrating the joys and pains of love remain a prime consideration, Alagiyavanna's *Kusa Jātaka Kāvya* treats the subject of love unevenly and as one of several different themes to be presented. The outline of the narrative adheres closely to the story from the *Jātaka* text. A king and queen who have difficulty conceiving a child receive divine assistance from Śakra, which leads to the birth of two sons—one who is clever but ugly, the other one handsome but dense. The elder son and heir to the throne is the unsightly Kusa, the Bodhisattva. Reluctant to marry, he eventually gives in to his parent's wishes but asks to be wed to a woman as beautiful as a golden statue he fashions. A search for such a woman is undertaken, and the king's ministers eventually locate Prabhāvatī (or Pabāvati), the beautiful, eldest princess in the kingdom of Sāgala.

A wedding is arranged between the two royal families, but Kusa's mother invents an alleged family tradition whereby the bride and groom shall sleep together at night but not see each other in the daytime until they conceive a child. This was done to ensure that the beautiful Prabhāvatī does not reject her ugly husband, Kusa. However, after their marriage, both parties seek out chances to catch a glimpse of their partner. Kusa masquerades as a mahout and a groomsman, both times flinging a piece of animal dung at proud Prabhāvatī's back. Prabhāvatī, for her part, is permitted to see Kusa and his brother in royal procession but is cleverly able to discern which one is the real king. After Kusa startles Prabhāvatī by leaping out of a lotus pond and grabbing her hand, the latter resolves to leave her ugly and boorish husband.

Her return to her parent's mansion exposes Kusa to the agony of love in separation. He travels secretly to Sāgala and anonymously undertakes various odd jobs well beneath his status as a king in the hope of catching a glimpse of his beloved queen. When as a cook his delicious food pleases the king of Sāgala, he is given the duty of providing meals to the royal family. One day, while carrying a pingo load of vessels, he stumbles and falls outside Prabhāvatī's chamber, causing her to rush out and check him. Her concern over Kusa's condition is dispelled once Kusa opens his eyes and spits a mouthful of saliva into her face. She scolds him, but he persists in seeking her affection. After several months, once Kusa grows weary of his efforts to win back his beloved wife, he resolves to return to Kusāvatī alone. At this juncture, Śakra again gets involved and tricks seven neighboring kings into thinking that King Madu will give his daughter Prabhāvatī in marriage to them. The kings arrive with their respective armies outside Sāgala, furious that King Madu has apparently made them out to be fools. When each king demands to be given Prabhāvatī, King Madu, who is already angry with his daughter for having left King Kusa, decides that the only way to pacify the seven kings is to carve Prabhāvatī into seven pieces and to give one piece to each king.

Understandably alarmed at this situation, Prabhāvatī reveals to her parents that King Kusa has been living as a servant in their kingdom. They make her go and seek his forgiveness, which she does in the hope of sparing her life. Kusa makes her grovel by lying down in the mud but ultimately forgives Prabhāvatī and promises to save her and her kingdom. He rides out on a war elephant with his wife and scares the seven armies into submission with his mighty lionlike roar. His great victory is followed by his remarkable physical transformation into a handsome man, and he brings Prabhāvatī back to his kingdom where they live happily ever after.

Employing this narrative outline, Alagiyavanna composes his quatrains to increase the dramatic tension of the story, refusing to subordinate the narrative content to aesthetic forms. The main characters are described in vivid fashion, both in terms of their physical appearance and their psychological states. Because the relationship between Kusa and Prabhāvatī makes up the central part of the story, Alagiyavanna employs numerous verses to describe their respective feelings of love and grief, revulsion and fear. It would not be difficult to conclude, as did Thomas Steele, the British civil servant who translated *Kusa Jātaka Kāvya* freely into flowery English verse in 1871, that this poem is a "love-story" exhibiting "great beauty and tenderness of sentiment" in many places.[57] This interpretation, however, does not do justice to the other aspects of Alagiyavanna's work. If *Kusa Jātaka Kāvya* is a love story, it is one that exhibits literary ideals more than romantic ones and a story in which love must compete with morality and power for acclaim.

Alagiyavanna's treatment emphasizes the trope of love in separation and the suffering it produces. Prabhāvatī's decision to leave King Kusa provides the author with an excuse to wax poetically on the agony of being separated from one's beloved. The original prose account in the Pāli *Jātaka* pays scant attention to this motif, only remarking: "When Pabhāvati had gone, he became full of sorrow. The women who were left, while serving his needs in various ways, were not even able to look at him. Without Pabhāvati, his entire residence appeared as if it was empty."[58] The remaining account, however, does not portray Kusa as being too upset by Prabhāvatī's absence. He appears confident that he will win her back and accomplish his aims. The *Kavsiḷumiṇa*, however, devotes the entire twelfth canto to the sorrow Kusa feels in being separated from Prabhāvatī. The following two couplets give a taste of how Parākramabāhu II treats this theme.

> Seizing my eyes with her lovely appearance, my ears with sweet speech,
> And my body with her sensuous touch, how did she seize my heart without giving hers?
> These tears that fill my eyes not only prevented me from seeing the direction of her departure,
> But they also have increased the fire in my chest like boiling water over a heated rock.[59]

The Kusa figure in *Kavsiḷumiṇa* is thus transformed into a character that exhibits the intensity of love and longing that is fitting of the *mahākāvya* style. The sentiments he feels may likewise be strongly felt by others.

Alagiyavanna similarly dwells on the sorrows of a love that appears lost. Although he may not develop this theme as extensively or dramatically as the author of *Kavsiḷumiṇa*, he still devotes several verses to depicting love in separation, the theme par excellence of the *kāvya* style. His *Kusa Jātaka Kāvya* is less a treatise on love than a work of poetry that uses emotions connected with love for dramatic effect. It is in verses 361 through 370 that Alagiyavanna devotes the most attention to the idea of love in separation. He presents, among other things, the images of an empty bed and the burning fire of separation to illustrate how King Kusa felt after his wife had left him.

> O' when will I be able to lie on the bed,
> With the noble, adorned Princess Pabāvati,
> Who moves and shines like a fully blossomed golden creeper,
> Spreading soft and gentle light from her faultless face?[60]

Alagiyavanna continues to describe Prabhāvatī's beauty in conventional ways while he conveys Kusa's sorrow from being alone. Such a move opens him to critiques by modern literary critics. However, Alagiyavanna was surely less concerned with portraying a genuine sense of Kusa's sorrow than, for example, a Romantic poet would be. Instead, his treatment of love in separation allows him to dwell briefly on this motif for the sake of composing a more aesthetically complete poem. Another verse similarly describes Kusa's sorrow by inverting the significance of some common poetic images.

> The moon that arrived in the sky appeared like the sun at the end of an eon,
> The flower petals on the bed became like thorns,
> The dancing and singing of sweet young women did not cause any pleasure,
> The mansion of this king, who lacked Pabāvati, was empty.[61]

The above verse alludes to the Pāli *Jātaka* account but expands on it by describing how things that once caused Kusa to be happy could no longer do so in the absence of his beloved.

The Kusa Jātaka narrative, with its account of the departure of Prabhāvatī and Kusa's efforts to win her back, easily incorporates the motif of love in separation. There is some tension, however, in the fact that the pining lover in this case is the Bodhisattva, a morally accomplished being who, by definition, is committed to the selfless goal of helping all beings as a Buddha. Alagiyavanna was clearly aware of the idea of a bodhisattva as a moral exemplar, as in his earlier *Dahamsoňḍa Kava* he wrote: "This Great Bodhisattva of ours, shining with a treasure of virtues, /Aspired in this way for the glory of Buddhahood with loving-kindness towards all beings."[62] King Dahamsoňḍa represents an ideal bodhisattva, a person willing to value the Dharma above all else, including his wealth and his own life. But King Kusa, on the other hand, is a more problematic bodhisattva. He tends to act out of love and selfish desire. Throughout most of the story, he seeks only the love and companionship of Prabhāvatī, even though this causes him to suffer.[63]

Unlike the *Kavsiḷumiṇa*, which treats the pursuit of romantic love as a noble aim, the *Kusa Jātaka Kāvya* recognizes and even accentuates the tension inherent between acting out of love and acting for the sake of moral perfection. Alagiyavanna's decision to acknowledge King Kusa's contrary motives could perhaps be interpreted as a poetic flaw, wherein the hero appears to be inconsistent in his aims. But it is also possible to view the author's presentation of Kusa as an attempt to utilize the story's complexities for dramatic effect. This romantic figure, ill-behaved but resolute, is after all the Bodhisattva. From a Buddhist perspective, then, the story of his pursuit of Prabhāvatī should have greater moral significance and devotional relevance.

> Although fulfilling the Perfections, he will obtain Buddhahood in the future,
> And will raise all beings up from the dreadful ocean of *saṃsāra*,
> Remaining all alone in bed because of the separation from Pabāvati,
> How can I describe the way in which the Great Being was burning.[64]

The king who lies in bed, burning with sorrow and desire, is the same figure who will one day renounce all physical pleasures and teach beings the way to attain nirvana. Alagiyavanna qualifies this portrait of the lovesick king by reminding his audience that Kusa is the Future Buddha. Kusa's lamentation and deep longing for Prabhāvatī are not easy to reconcile with the standard image of the dispassionate Buddha or the resolute, selfless Bodhisattva. Nevertheless, for Alagiyavanna, this incongruity adds depth to the emotional state of the poem's hero and gives assurance that eventually the Buddha will see things correctly and abandon such desires.

In the meantime, however, King Kusa is depicted as acting primarily out of love for his estranged wife. It is not always clear whether Alagiyavanna sees love as a praiseworthy motive or a suspect one. Clearly, however, the Bodhisattva willingly subjects himself to various hardships—collecting firewood and water day and night, cooking food, carrying pingoloads of food, washing pots, and so forth—in order to receive a glimpse of and a word from his beloved Prabhāvatī. He refuses to leave her, even when she scolds and insults him for having a grotesque face.[65] Undeterred by her hostility, Kusa asserts that he would gladly give up all of his claims to royal prosperity for the chance to see his lovely wife at all times. Later, in an admission that does not appear in the Pāli *Jātaka*, Kusa specifically tells King Madu that he abandoned his kingdom and came to Sāgala, becoming a lowly cook in order to express his love for Prabhāvatī.[66]

Here the Bodhisattva's motives can be called into question. The desire for individual rewards would normally constitute an unacceptable motive for the Bodhisattva's sacrifices.[67] This problematic situation could be avoided, as it is in *Kavsiḷumiṇa*, by downplaying the ethical considerations behind one's actions and focusing instead on *kāma* or desire as one of the proper ends of human life (*puruṣārtha*). Alagiyavanna, however, incorporates a number of moral admonitions that weigh against taking his poem as simply a celebration of romantic love and aesthetic expression. Alagiyavanna made sure that there would also be ethical benefits to those who read or listened to *Kusa Jātaka Kāvya*. The work's moral admonitions are found scattered throughout, reminding people about impermanence, the fruits of one's deeds, the necessity of virtue, and the problems to be found in love.

The notion that impermanence overcomes the pleasures of life—and indeed life itself—is found in *Kusa Jātaka Kāvya*'s treatment of Prabhāvatī's lamentation about her impending fate, which is to be cut into seven pieces and distributed to each of the seven kings who came to marry her. The *Kavsiḷumiṇa* notably omits any mention of the threat made to carve up Prabhāvatī's body. Poetic references to the dissolution of such a beautiful physique would run counter to the work's commitment to evoking the erotic sentiment. Alagiyavanna, however, shows no such reluctance to depicting horrific images and displays his fidelity to the *Jātaka* account by including a similar soliloquy wherein Prabhāvatī laments her impending death in verse.

> Soon my distinctive tresses of hair,
> Beautiful like a cluster of peacock feathers,
> Increasing the pleasure in the minds and eyes of the people who see them,
> Will be pulled and cut off by *yakṣas*, *bhūtas*, and *piśācas*.
> My pair of eyes that increase the happiness in those who see them,
> And my two ears near the ends of those eyes,
> Which shine like radiant blue water lilies,
> Will today be plucked out and eaten by crows and kites.[68]

In these and other verses, Alagiyavanna starts out with conventional figures of speech to represent Prabhāvatī's beautiful form and then subverts the charm of such images by describing how those parts of her body will be grotesquely destroyed. We learn, for example, that her beautiful, full breasts will be cut off by executioners using sharp weapons, her lotus-like fingers will be severed by greedy birds, her entrails and guts will be ripped out by vultures and kites, and her lovely thighs will be eaten by demonic *rakṣasas* and *yakṣas*. The enemy kings will likewise cut off her shining arms, feet, neck, body, and breasts in a heartless display of cruelty of which some kings are apparently capable.[69]

The section on Prabhāvatī's lamentation is evidence of another kind of grief that arises from separation. Prabhāvatī's grief stems from her impending death and the separation it brings from one's loved ones and from the pleasures of life. Prabhāvatī should presumably know better. The existential facts of impermanence and the conditioned nature of all life would be familiar to all those acquainted with Buddhist teachings. For those who are exceptionally learned, Prabhāvatī's description of her looming dissection resonates well with other accounts of the physical makeup of the body in Buddhist discourses on meditation and the psychophysical constituents of life.[70] This analysis of her physical makeup serves to place the poetic descriptions of Prabhāvatī's beautiful form in a recognizably Buddhist context. Consistent with how the tradition portrays the Buddha's dying words, "All conditioned elements are subject to decay," Alagiyavanna reminds his audience that even things as lovely as Prabhāvatī's hair, eyes, breasts, and so on will one day come to dissolution.[71]

Beyond confirming the impermanence of the body, Alagiyavanna's *Kusa Jātaka Kāvya* goes further in suggesting that Prabhāvatī's difficulties were the consequences of her own actions. Both here and elsewhere in the work, Alagiyavanna presents us with admonitions about the fruits of karma. Prabhāvatī's impending fate, we learn, is the fruit (*vipākaya*) of her disdain for King Kusa earlier.

> Having rejected the noble King Kusa,
> Saying his physical beauty is deficient,
> And having put her own beautiful form to the fore,
> She exhibited to the world the fruit that has come [to her].[72]

Prabhāvatī's decision to spurn the love of the Bodhisattva is treated by the text as an immoral act that led to her miserable condition. In framing this plot point within a moral context, Alagiyavanna's text depicts Prabhāvatī in a less favorable light than she appears in in *Kavsiḷumiṇa*. Alagiyavanna emphasizes Prabhāvatī's disrespectful and dismissive attitude toward Kusa, depicting her without compassion, and he makes her reproachful words seem even more heartless.[73]

> You, with the grotesque face,
> It is not at all proper to aspire after me,

Just like with fire and water,
There is enjoyment in dwelling far apart.[74]

Alagiyavanna, thus, makes it seem as if her vanity and her severe attitude toward Kusa are blameworthy and the causes of her precarious condition. Conversely, despite the Bodhisattva's appearance and boorish behavior, he is not made out to be culpable for the couple's separation and his wife's sorry fate.

In contrast, the *Kavsiḷumiṇa* tends to portray Prabhāvatī in a more favorable light. She lacks the hardness and selfishness of Prabhāvatī in *Kusa Jātaka Kāvya*. Parākramabāhu II elides certain negative episodes from his *mahākāvya* poem including the scene in which Prabhāvatī scolds Kusa, her rejection of his ugly appearance, and her attempt to threaten her hunchbacked maidservant, all of which serve to redeem her from the moralistic judgments of the *Jātaka* text and *Kusa Jātaka Kāvya*.[75] In Alagiyavanna's work, Prabhāvatī reproaches her maidservant, who has been bribed by Kusa to arrange for their reconciliation. The maidservant appeals to Prabhāvatī, remarking on the suffering that the great King Kusa has undergone for her sake. She then adds a moralistic stanza admonishing Prabhāvatī for her callous behavior.

When a husband with whom one has lain,
In the same bed for [even] one day feels suffering,
There are limitless women in this world,
Who would dispel his suffering.[76]

Such reasoning is clearly meant to indicate something about a wife's responsibility to console and care for her husband. By including this verse, Alagiyavanna is commenting on both Prabhāvatī's deficiency and, more generally, about the duties of a wife. This admonition is not restricted to Prabhāvatī alone, as the verse instead describes the "limitless women in this world." As such, these lines extend the moral message of the verse out into the real world, suggesting that all wives should behave in a similar manner.

Another way in which Alagiyavanna injects a moralistic message into his poem is by explaining the karmic causes behind the present circumstances of Kusa's ugliness and Prabhāvatī's dispassion. This account runs around thirty verses, and it serves to teach the audience about the value of merit and the inevitability of karmic fruits. In previous lifetimes, Kusa was the brother-in-law to Prabhāvatī and resided with her and his elder brother in a village near Benares. One day, the sister-in-law cooked tasty oilcakes for her husband and brother-in-law, but when a *paccekabuddha* came to their home for alms, she gave the oilcakes to him as an offering. The brother-in-law (i.e., Kusa) returned home shortly thereafter to find that his sister-in-law had given his oilcakes away to earn merit. Angered, he ran after the *paccekabuddha* and snatched the offering of oilcakes from him. Saddened by this event, the sister-in-law went away and returned with some ghee to offer the ascetic. She then made an aspiration (*prārthanāva*) by the power of her meritorious deed always to be beautiful, to be born in noble lineages, and to be acquainted with virtuous persons (*sudanan*).[77]

The brother-in-law, for his part, witnessed the act of devotion done by his brother's wife and had a change of heart. He offered the oilcakes back to the *paccekabuddha*, venerated him, and made an aspiration in conjunction with this act of merit. He aspired always to be born rich and the chief king of Jambudvīpa (i.e., India), to have a deep voice that roars like a lion, and to marry his brother's wife in the future.[78] We are told that these acts of merit and the aspirations that accompanied them had a determinative effect on the subsequent fortunes of Kusa and Prabhāvatī. Alagiyavanna adds, however, that the brother-in-law's initial rudeness was the cause of his ugly, oilcakelike face in a later life.

Because he had taken the oilcakes,
From the noble *paccekabuddha* angrily,
One should understand that by that wickedness (*pav*),
The face of King Kusa was grotesque.[79]

Although consistent with the *Jātaka* account, the Bodhisattva's ugly appearance in *Kusa Jātaka Kāvya* presents a couple of potential problems. First, South Asian Buddhist thought has long associated moral virtue with physical beauty, and bodhisattvas, in particular, could be expected to be attractive as a result of the inestimable merit they earn from their virtuous deeds and thoughts.[80] The ugly, oilcake face of King Kusa must appear as an anomaly to the devotees of the Buddha, who would find it hard to conceive of the Bodhisattva engaging in *pav* (*pāpa*) when he would otherwise be expected to make progress toward developing the Ten Perfections and attaining Buddhahood.

The other problem with King Kusa's ugly face is that the heroes of *mahākāvya*-inspired poetry are expected to be without physical and moral blemishes. As such, the *Kavsiḷumiṇa* never explicitly acknowledges that Kusa is unattractive or that Prabhāvatī is repulsed by his looks. Since the *mahākāvya* genre requires that the protagonist possess beauty and glory, the *Kavsiḷumiṇa* presents Kusa as an attractive figure who is able to captivate the eyes and minds of an audience.[81] The tenth canto of this poem describes how a bevy of delightful young women play with King Kusa in a park and tempt his erotic nature with their flirtatious behavior. There is no indication that he might appear unattractive to Prabhāvatī or other women. Later, when he receives a gem pendant from Śakra after defeating the enemies of Sāgala, the poet who authored *Kavsiḷumiṇa* refuses to suggest that this gift was anything else but an award of honor from the deity to the Bodhisattva. There is no ugliness in Kusa to be removed by a divine gem in this poetic version.

In *Kusa Jātaka Kāvya*, however, the moral greatness of Kusa eventually contributes to his transformation into a handsome king. Following and expanding on the *Jātaka* account, Alagiyavanna describes how Śakra, greatly pleased with Kusa's bloodless victory over the enemy kings, bestows the Bodhisattva with a priceless gem, which triggers the removal of his ugliness.

> By the power in that precious gem that Śakra brought and placed upon his chest,
> And because he accomplished what he had aspired for on that day and expended the wickedness done previously,
> Possessing splendor in the manner of a royal deity who has descended to earth from the city of the gods,
> The Great Bodhisattva, full of merit, flourished with the beautiful splendor of his excellent and appropriate body.[82]

The significance in this verse is found in Alagiyavanna's explanation as to why Kusa suddenly becomes handsome. The account in the Pāli *Jātaka* is unclear, as it simply states that after having taken the gem, Kusa and Prabhāvatī were "equal in complexion and form."[83] The fourteenth-century Sinhala rendition of the *Jātaka* adds to this by stating that Kusa becomes endowed with splendor and majesty like a golden figure by the power in the precious gem.[84] But Alagiyavanna further states that it was because of the gem *and* the exhaustion of the effects from his wicked deed that Kusa was able to become handsome and to live happily ever after with his wife. The *Kusa Jātaka Kāvya* version of this event stresses the factors of karma and merit to explain Kusa's newfound physical beauty, thus recasting what once appeared simply as a mysterious, divine act into a lesson about the effects of one's deeds.

The moral admonitions in *Kusa Jātaka Kāvya* turn what is ostensibly a romantic love story into a text for ethical reflection. Not content to compose a court poem designed to celebrate and evoke erotic sentiments, Alagiyavanna produced a work that considers love to be conditioned by morality. The poet does not permit love in its romantic and erotic aspects to operate outside a moral sphere. Kusa may be motivated by love to undergo hardships and win back Prabhāvatī, but that same love does not obscure the imperative to act morally and to be ethically reflective. Therefore he inserts verses, such as the following quatrain, to offer moral admonitions.

> If one takes a pebble and casts it into the center of the sky,
> It will not end up anywhere else but on the earth,
> Likewise, the accumulation of wickedness (*pav*) and merit (*piṅ*),
> Will certainly be fulfilled in the manner to which one aspires.[85]

The didactic tone of this verse would be out of place in many examples of classical Sinhala *kavi*, but it is consistent here with Alagiyavanna's moral concerns. The fruits of meritorious and wicked acts possess a certainty that few other things do. The lives of Kusa and Prabhāvatī, as well as the readers and listeners of the *Kusa Jātaka Kāvya*, are assumed to be influenced by previous deeds. This conclusion, present in countless Buddhist texts, provides the audience of the work with an incentive to act righteously and in accordance with Buddhist teachings.

The *Kusa Jātaka Kāvya* also encourages the audience to reflect on some of the problems with love. This story of Kusa and Prabhāvatī, one that includes a fair share of insensitive behavior and verbal abuse, hardly functions as a simple, straightforward endorsement for romantic love. In contrast to the *Kavsiḷumiṇa*, wherein Prabhāvatī always seems genuinely to care for Kusa, having left him only because she feels disappointed and unfulfilled, the image of Prabhāvatī in the *Kusa Jātaka Kāvya* is one of calculated self-interest—she rushes to the fallen Kusa out of worry that she will be blamed for his accident, and she begs forgiveness from him only out of fear of her impending death.[86] Despite its apparent happy ending, we learn from this work that love does not necessarily conquer all.

> The two kinds of iron that burns and does not burn,
> May not be welded together,

Likewise, two people who have aversion and desire for the other,
Will not remain together.[87]

The couple originally becomes separated as a consequence of their own actions. It is only after Prabhāvatī's life is in danger and Kusa becomes transformed into a handsome king that their relationship appears happy and strong. Their love is thus qualified and contingent on extenuating circumstances. Even Kusa's determination falters when he momentarily decides to give up his efforts and return home without his wife after seven unsuccessful months of laboring to win her back.[88] The poet's story reveals to us an ambivalent attitude toward romantic relationships, one for which *kāvya*'s typical celebration and idealization of love is traded by him for a cooler skepticism about love's motivations and the questionable reliability of women.

For all of the Bodhisattva's longing for a glimpse, a sweet word, and a brief touch from his wife, Alagiyavanna continually presents a fairly negative view of women in general and of Prabhāvatī in particular. The main female characters in this narrative—including Prabhāvatī, the Queen Mother Sīlavatī, and the hunchbacked servant—all exhibit moral flaws. Prabhāvatī's conceit, stubbornness, and harsh speech are shown throughout the work. Kusa's mother tricks Prabhāvatī and her parents into marrying Kusa by devising a ruse to prevent her from seeing his ugly appearance. The hunchbacked servant greedily accepts an ornament of gems to intervene on Kusa's behalf. Even King Okāvas's nameless harem women—figures normally praised by *kāvya* poets for their beauty—are said to be without "even a little merit" as evinced by their inability to conceive an heir to the throne.[89] Alagiyavanna picks up his misogynistic tone from the *Jātaka* account, which adheres to the stated intent behind the original tale to admonish a monk about the dangers of women. He follows the latter, for instance, by having Sīlavatī warn her son about the "deceit of women" (*laňdun māyaṁ*) when he prepares to go and fetch his queen from Sāgala.[90] But he also exaggerates Prabhāvatī's mean, inconsiderate nature, perhaps to make the reader or listener admire the Bodhisattva's struggles and virtues that much more.[91]

The largely negative portrayal of women in the *Kusa Jātaka Kāvya* encapsulates the author's preference not to let poetic descriptions of love trump morality in the Kusa story. The prominence of the poetic tropes of romantic love and the pain of separation notwithstanding, Alagiyavanna elects to remind his readers and listeners that love can be unreliable and happiness can be difficult to find in the world of human relationships. It is a message that is surely more suitable to a *jātaka* story than a Sinhala *kavi*, particularly one that shows signs of emulating the *mahākāvya* works of earlier generations. To the extent that the *Kusa Jātaka Kāvya* celebrates love and the erotic sentiment of the *kāvya* genre, it tempers such exuberance with numerous moralistic verses that remind the audience about the fickle nature of women and the importance of virtue. The work's treatment of the themes of love and morals illustrates how the poet was working in a different cultural environment in which older literary norms and ideals were beginning to lose sway in the midst of significant political and societal change.

Praise for a Bodhisattva-King

When looked at as a whole, Alagiyavanna's *Kusa Jātaka Kāvya* represents a poetic work that was modeled partly after older *kavi* yet signals the poet's efforts to employ a more straightforward style and speak to different interests. Taking up some of the themes he introduced in *Dahamsoňda Kava*, Alagiyavanna continued to praise and idealize Buddhist heroes and a generic notion of kingship in place of a particular, contemporary king. His praise for King Rājasiṃha I is limited and indirect, a fact that is not surprising given the king's reputed persecution of Buddhist institutions and destruction of Buddhist texts, as well as the fact that he died in 1593, well before Alagiyavanna completed the work.[92] Yet Alagiyavanna remained committed to much of the stylistic formulas of *kāvya* poetry, through which his literary reputation could be reinforced and secured. In *Kusa Jātaka Kāvya*, however, the *praśasti* style of ornate praise awarded to the one who excels in aesthetic and martial feats is redirected to those who achieve a kind of moral greatness that exceeds others. This means that the Buddha, the Bodhisattva, and the notion of a righteous king are all idealized in Alagiyavanna's verses. Those who are singled out for praise are distinctive first and foremost for their moral deeds and qualities.

The *Kusa Jātaka Kāvya*'s regard for moral accomplishments over aesthetic excellence and royal grandeur reflects a transition away from that which the writers of Sinhala *kavi* were long expected to value and uphold. In place of a court filled with aesthetic connoisseurs, Alagiyavanna writes of a Dharma assembly (*dam sabā*) where disciplined monks sit around a seat decked with nettings of pearls and lustrous gemstones.[93]

Having come while remaining tranquil,
Without weakening the order of seniority,

[The monks] sit while reciting words with sweet sentiment (*rasa*)
About the virtues of the Buddha.[94]

With a Dharma seat substituting for a royal throne, the assembly of monks delight in a speech celebrating what the Buddha accomplished by means of his moral perfections. What makes this speech so evocative is its subject—the Buddha's marvelous qualities—more than any particular figures of speech. The appearance of the Buddha at this point in the poem allows Alagiyavanna to describe his virtuous conduct and wisdom. The Buddha gives blessings to the world, meditates, exhibits the splendor of great merit, and covers himself appropriately with his robe.[95] Whereas many examples of Sinhala *kavi* linger over descriptions of the radiant fame and majesty of kings praised in verse, the *Kusa Jātaka Kāvya* includes a lengthy description of the six-colored Buddha rays that emanate from the Buddha's body throughout the ten directions.

Alagiyavanna's *Kusa Jātaka Kāvya* also endeavors to spread the fame of the Bodhisattva in the figure of Kusa. As an ugly, playful, yet resolute king, Kusa is not always so easy to praise. Nevertheless, since he is a bodhisattva who is on the way to Buddhahood, the poet cannot help but extol his greatness. Thus at certain points, Alagiyavanna praises Kusa's splendor and glory, despite the fact that he still possesses a "grotesque" face.[96] By attributing Kusa with splendor that is said to be "beautiful" (*sonduru*), Alagiyavanna casts the Bodhisattva in a manner in which he should appear but, in this narrative, does not. Not coincidentally, the poet employs the *samudraghoṣa* meter and more embellishing figures of speech for this verse. The literary conventions at work in this part of the poem almost demand that the hero appear in a splendid fashion. Accordingly, Alagiyavanna does not transgress the style of his craft, suggesting that the king with a grotesque face is still glorious in appearance.

Elsewhere, Alagiyavanna goes further and suggests that Kusa's splendid appearance overshadows even that of Prabhāvatī. Her physical beauty, it seems, is no match for the perceptible quality of the Bodhisattva's moral greatness. In the scene in which Kusa and Prabhāvatī are said to enjoy the nighttime pleasures of their marriage, the poet finds another opportunity to praise the physical appearance of the king.

The greatness of that king's glory,
Caused the heap of brilliance emitted from,
The beautiful face of Pabāvati,
To not be seen, like a firefly in the sun.[97]

Although neither Kusa nor Prabhāvatī can see each other during the darkness of night when they are permitted to come together, Alagiyavanna suggests that even then Kusa's glory outshines the radiant beauty of his queen. This glory does so arguably because it is an extension of his virtue and the majesty he commands as the chief king of all Jambudvīpa. Even before Śakra gives him the gem that helps to dispel his ugliness, the poem cites this king's tremendous glory and limitless fame as he defeats the enemy kings who threaten his wife's kingdom.[98]

The praise reserved for the Bodhisattva in the *Kusa Jātaka Kāvya* illustrates how the poem glorifies the one figure whose kingly splendor and martial exploits are derived from his moral perfection. Recall, for instance, that Kusa's prosperity and the so-called lion's roar that causes the enemy kings to surrender are explained as the direct results of an aspiration made by the Bodhisattva in a previous lifetime after returning the alms he snatched away from a *paccekabuddha*.[99] The *Kusa Jātaka Kāvya* does not simply praise Kusa's power as inherent to his kingly status, but rather the poem casts his power as one of the fruits of the Bodhisattva's good deeds in the past. Poetic praise thus acquires an explicit moral dimension. It recognizes royal prosperity and power as the results of good karma. Kings are great not because of their wealth and success in war but because of their moral development.

Although the *Kusa Jātaka Kāvya* functions to sustain certain poetic conventions of classical Sinhala *kavi*, it also complicates and at times subverts what poetic works traditionally had to say about love and power. Early on, the work praises in highly conventional ways the king of the Kosala kingdom in which the Buddha and his disciples were residing. This king is lauded for his virtue and his fame in much the same way other kings are lauded in other works of Sinhala *kavi*.

> The ocean of this Best of Men,
> Endowed with the ambrosial water of speech,
> The gems of virtues and the waves of gift giving,
> Flourished without transgressing the shore of the Laws of Manu.[100]

Poetic figures of speech serve to highlight the good qualities of a king, making him appear as a paradigmatic ruler worthy of being memorialized in literature. He dispels his enemies, protects his subjects, and always follows the traditional laws and customs of previous kings. Yet, after a handful of verses, this king disappears from the work as the poet turns his attention to the Buddha and his career as the Bodhisattva.

Again, in the context of the Kusa story, the Bodhisattva's father, King Okāvas, is praised in highly conventional terms. His fame, we are told, shines throughout the world, so much that the narrator asks rhetorically if any simile is appropriate to describe such a king.[101] The power of this king is established by poetically describing how his fame triumphs over his enemies and makes their wives' eyes turn red from weeping. Further, in an allusion to Indic mythology, the sword he holds in his hand is compared to the demon Rāhu that seizes the sun and moon, namely the glory and fame of his foes.[102] Thus far, the description of kingship in the *Kusa Jātaka Kāvya* accords with much of the classical poetic praise found in *praśasti* poetry and the *kāvya* genre more generally. Power is briefly associated here with the figures of kings who embody prosperity and military prowess. Their ethical consciousness, moreover, is shaped by classical Indian treatises on kingship rather than by Buddhist ethical teachings.

But once the narrative shifts to deal with Kusa, the bodhisattva-king, Alagiyavanna's work presents an idea of kingship and power that deviates from older poetic ideals. Kusa's power lies less in his great wealth and responsibilities than in his willingness to undergo tremendous suffering while laboring in various menial jobs to catch a glimpse of his estranged wife. We learn that he rejected the manifold prosperity of kingship in order to express his love to Prabhāvatī.[103] His determination and resolve lead him to undertake activities that even he deems as improper for a king. To labor as a basketmaker, a potter, and a cook, among other things, is clearly inconsistent with the deeds thought to enhance the fame of a king. By engaging in such activities and yet remaining worthy of praise, the Bodhisattva presents us with a new model for kingship, one shaped by moral excellence rather than wealth, prowess, and nobility, which are qualities normally celebrated in Sinhala *kavi*.

Among the virtues of King Kusa singled out by Alagiyavanna, it is his forgiveness that receives much praise and attention. Forgiveness or forbearing (*kṣanti*) is recognized in the Theravāda tradition as one of the Ten Perfections that the Bodhisattva must develop on the path to Buddhahood. Forgiveness is an ethical attribute, but it is not often one for which a king is specifically praised in court poetry. So when King Madu calls on Kusa to forgive him and his family for allowing him to labor tirelessly and in anonymity, he is depicted as invoking the qualities specific to a bodhisattva.

Noble Lord! It would be good if you would forgive,
The wrong we did without knowing,

Not keeping it in your heart, like water on a lotus leaf,
Expressing many thoughts of loving-kindness.[104]

Such praise for King Kusa is based squarely on his ethical capacities. Alagiyavanna portrays Kusa as reflecting compassionately on how to comfort King Madu and avoid using harsh words that would gravely hurt him.[105] It is his ability to show forgiveness that increases his fame as a king, first by accepting Prabhāvatī's entreaties and later by pardoning the seven enemy kings who threatened his in-laws' kingdom.[106] The work even suggests that forgiveness is a necessary attribute of virtuous kings more generally.

Previous kings, possessing virtue,
Not taking to heart the faults that arose,
From fools, poets, children, and women,
Disregarded them.[107]

According to Alagiyavanna, then, it is King Kusa's ability to tolerate the faults of others that entitles him to widespread fame. Rather than conquering the enemy kings by force, he subdues them with a shout. It is his willingness to forgive them and arrange for them to marry Prabhāvatī's seven younger sisters that makes Kusa exemplary. The power he possesses and that makes him great is rooted in his morality. While he shows valor and versatility, what makes Kusa special and particularly worthy of praise is his virtue. In this way, Alagiyavanna introduces us to a distinctly different vision of power in the *Kusa Jātaka Kāvya*, a vision that adds to the qualities held up for praise in the *praśasti* genre of Sanskrit *kāvya* and classical Sinhala *kavi*. Power is no longer simply martial prowess as evidenced by how skillfully a king wields a sword and a bow. Alagiyavanna is suggesting that power now has more to do with one's strength of character, a quality that even Kusa with all his physical flaws and mischievous deeds amply demonstrates.

As illustrated in the story of King Kusa, power was infrequently expressed in the setting of the Sinhala court at the turn of the seventeenth century. Instead, power had begun to be associated more with moral virtues than the skillful use of aesthetics. When Kusa leaves his throne and kingdom behind to win back his estranged wife, he does not lose his claim to power and greatness. No longer manifested solely in cultural displays before a royal assembly, power for King Kusa is demonstrated by his many noble deeds in the city of Sāgala. Although Alagiyavanna retained the *kavi* genre with its meters and figures of speech to relate the story of King Kusa, he incorporated some aspects that would make it more accessible and popular among an audience outside a royal court. While doing so, he came to focus more on the moral virtues personified by a bodhisattva who abandons his throne and develops his character through hard work.

Alagiyavanna's *Kusa Jātaka Kāvya* problematizes many of the assumptions that had been the basis of the culture-power formation during the previous millennium across South Asia. Its values and views of kingship differ considerably from what he extolled some three decades earlier in *Sävul Sandēśaya*. In seventeenth-century Sri Lanka, however, the connoisseurs and practitioners of the poetic arts had dispersed from the court and either died in battle, disappeared into the countryside, or aligned themselves with a wholly new power formation tied to the Portuguese crown and cross. As a result, the poet began to qualify beauty rather than to celebrate it unreservedly, and in so doing he modified the values and style of Sinhala *kavi* to edify an audience rather than simply delight it. In such a context, it is not surprising that Alagiyavanna's interest in the aesthetics and status of poetry would gradually shift to an interest in morality, which offered a new basis for expressing power and claiming status in a colonial setting. Like Kusa who discovers new sources for power and fame beyond the court of his kingdom, Alagiyavanna was forced to look for new ways to distinguish himself and his poetic work after the fall of the Sītāvaka kingdom to the Portuguese.

5

Admonishing the World with Well-Spoken Words

FOLLOWING THE DEMISE of King Rājasiṃha I and the Sītāvaka court, the subsequent unraveling of the traditional relationship between poets and kings in Sinhala society had profound implications for Alagiyavanna. Accustomed to privilege and prestige, he found himself adrift between the remaining centers of power in Sri Lanka, located respectively in Koṭṭe under the Portuguese colonialists and in Kandy under King Vimaladharmasūriya I, a former Catholic convert who returned to Buddhism after he no longer needed the support of the Portuguese against Rājasiṃha. From Alagiyavanna's perspective, both of these powers were hostile to his former king and patron. It has been suggested that Vimaladharmasūriya would have distrusted officials who served under his enemy King Rājasiṃha I, and thus people like Alagiyavanna either went to work for the Portuguese or returned to their villages in retreat from government service.[1] There is scant evidence of what Alagiyavanna did between the death of Rājasiṃha in 1593 and the completion of *Kusa Jātaka Kāvya* in 1610. His poetic works, however, reveal an unmistakable shift away from primarily aesthetic interests to primarily ethical ones. Whereas his earlier works embraced the richly suggestive style of Sinhala court poetry, his later works began to highlight moral counsel and ethical reflection. Alagiyavanna's increasing focus on truth claims and moral norms reaches a high point in his *Subhāṣitaya* (*Well-Spoken Words*), a work consisting of around one hundred stanzas that give advice on how to live a good life in a difficult environment.

The title *Subhāṣitaya* mirrors the name frequently used for a literary genre of aphorisms and didactic teachings in verse that was popular throughout the Indic world from ancient times. Gnomic verses that convey practical wisdom or moral thoughts are generally found in a variety of ancient Sanskrit texts, including the *Ṛg Veda*, the *Aitareya Brāhmaṇa*, the *Upaniṣads*, the epics, and the *dharmaśāstras*.[2] Collections of verses generically known as *subhāṣitas* proliferated around ancient South Asia, offering worldly wisdom in pithy stanzas that could be memorized and repeated with ease. Such verses came to embody oral traditions of well-known truths that could become so commonplace and detached from particular texts that they could reflect conventional sayings whose original authors had been forgotten. Alagiyavanna's entry into this genre signals a clear expansion of his literary career and a stronger concern with admonishing people on proper behavior. Thus, again, the local and the translocal become thoroughly intermixed in Alagiyavanna's poetic use of the Sinhala language to express pan-Indic ideas. His poetic interests in composing well-crafted poetic works that conform to aesthetic judgments of skill and beauty continued, as seen in his retention of a poetic repertoire including meter and appropriate figures of speech. Nevertheless, the *Subhāṣitaya* takes the form of a literary work that responded more directly to the cultural encounter with the Portuguese and the subsequent dislocation of traditional Sinhala Buddhist cultural forms.

Over time, the first sustained encounter with a European power spurred significant changes in Sinhala Buddhist poetry. Its aesthetic forms could serve new purposes and be utilized to augment the persuasiveness of moral admonitions. Bereft of Sinhala royal patrons and a viable court culture, Alagiyavanna began to move away from highly embellished verses that celebrate kingship and the Bodhisattva toward embracing a more moralistic, didactic style of poetic composition. With *Subhāṣitaya*, Alagiyavanna signaled his bold entry into contemporary moral contests over truth. Its verses no longer highlight a story in narrative form. Instead, they comprise short, moralistic admonitions that were evidently of interest or relevant to the audience of his day. In this way, *Subhāṣitaya* stakes out moral claims on the proper sphere of correct behavior. The tone of the poem appears more defensive and polemical compared to most other poetic works in Sinhala from the fifteenth and sixteenth centuries. Alagiyavanna's voice in the *Subhāṣitaya* appears more discontent with the status quo, and he eagerly points out what is wrong with the world. He no longer condones the previously pluralistic attitude toward religion as seen in *Sävul Sandēśaya*. One might instead picture him engaging in debates over right action and truth with supporters of Śaivite Hinduism and Catholic Christianity.[3] The poet appears in this work to be defending and defining an early notion of Buddhism as a religious system to be embraced in place of other, rival systems. The significance of *Subhāṣitaya* thus lies in the fact that it introduces a more didactic, less flowery style of poetic expression and articulates a self-conscious notion of Buddhist identity at a time when Portuguese colonialism was gaining influence in the island.

The Dating of Alagiyavanna's Subhāṣitaya

Insofar as the *Subhāṣitaya* represents an early modern Buddhist response to the cultural dislocation wrought by intensive warfare and European cultural encounters, the questions that linger over the dating of the work must be resolved. Since we lack any original manuscript version of this text, estimating the date of its composition must rely on indirect forms of evidence. The modern scholarly community in Sri Lanka is divided over the issue whether the *Subhāṣitaya* was Alagiyavanna's first work or one of his last. Near the beginning of the twentieth century, a claim was made for viewing the *Subhāṣitaya* as the product of a younger, unskilled poet. W. F. Gunawardhana suggested in 1925 that the *Subhāṣitaya* was likely Alagiyavanna's first work, since his other works appear more polished in comparison to the "amateurish" verse of this work.[4] The criteria by which Gunawardhana arrives at this judgment are not specified, and he also praises the author for his clear language, concise diction, and effective style in the same work. Soon after, S. G. Perera and M. E. Fernando cited Gunwardhana in presenting their doubts over the 1611 date of composition for the *Subhāṣitaya*, as mentioned in some manuscript editions of the text. According to them, not only does the matter, style, and purpose of the *Subhāṣitaya* indicate that it is one of Alagiyavanna's earliest works, but the alleged fact that he was already working on the Portuguese *tombo*, or land register, by 1611 as a Catholic convert makes Perera and Fernando reject this later date of composition.[5]

This line of reasoning, however, is problematic and appears to reflect the editors' interest in portraying Alagiyavanna as a sincere Catholic believer. As a Jesuit priest, Perera could perhaps be expected to make a strong argument for Alagiyavanna's Catholic identity. At the same time, however, the dates in which Alagiyavanna converted and began work on the *tombo* for the Portuguese are unclear. While it is possible that he was baptized as a Catholic convert under the authority of Dom Jerónimo de Azevedo, the Portuguese captain-general who governed Sri Lanka from 1594 to 1612 and whose name was given to Alagiyavanna after his baptism, the name could still have been bestowed on Alagiyavanna after he left the island. Further, although the Portuguese *vedor* Antão Vaz Freire is thought to have arrived in Sri Lanka by early 1609 to work on the *tombo*, it does not follow that Alagiyavanna began his work for the Portuguese soon after. Records show that Vaz Freire did not commence work on the *tombo* until March 1613.[6] It should be recalled that the *Kusa Jātaka Kāvya* contains a verse signifying it was completed in 1610, and this work contains ample evidence of the poet's continuing adherence to the Buddha and his Dharma.[7]

Even if Alagiyavanna converted in 1612 along with a number of other high-class individuals, this does not rule out the year of 1611 for the composition of the *Subhāṣitaya*.[8] Alagiyavanna's name does not appear in the *tombo* as an assistant to the *vedor* until entries dated 1614 and 1616.[9] Upon further consideration, the year 1611 or thereabouts seems perfectly reasonable for the work. A number of other scholars also support this conclusion.[10] Perera and Fernando's objections to this year seem based on their desire to emphasize the validity of Alagiyavanna's embrace of the Catholic faith. In other words, dating the *Subhāṣitaya* to around 1611 and Alagiyavanna's conversion to Christianity in the following year is problematic only to those who wish to see his conversion as a monumental event that he undertook with great forethought and sincerity. It is entirely possible, however, that his decision to convert was made fairly quickly. Like other landowning Sinhalas in territories that recently came under Portuguese rule, Alagiyavanna may have calculated that his quality of life—that is, his status, security, and wealth—would increase if he accepted Christianity.[11] Nevertheless, the existence of pragmatic reasons for conversion does not rule out a true change of heart in the poet.

The content and tone of *Subhāṣitaya* provide stronger reasons for assigning this text to the early seventeenth century rather than the early 1580s. The *Subhāṣitaya* adopts a pointed and polemical tone in arguing for the value of the Buddhist religion next to its competitors. It denounces the Hindu god Śiva in verse 74, and it admonishes against following wicked kings in other parts of the work. Were *Subhāṣitaya* the first work of an aspiring poet seeking to gain a place in King Rājasiṃha's court at Sītāvaka, it would have been foolhardy and reckless to address such subjects before a powerful king with devotional interests in Śaivism. Instead, the *Sävul Sandēśaya*, with its elaborate praise of Rājasiṃha and its elaborate descriptions of various sites in the kingdom, including a Hindu temple dedicated to the divine consort of Śiva, would have been a much more logical choice to present before the king. The *Subhāṣitaya*, in contrast, seems like an improbable work to be composed during the height of King Rājasiṃha's power and glory in the 1580s. Instead it reads as a work composed in reaction to new pressures and challenges placed on adherents of the Buddha's religion during the expansion of Portuguese missionary activity and colonial rule in the early seventeenth century.

Portuguese Missions in Early Seventeenth-Century Ceilão

The history of Portuguese-sponsored Christian missions in Ceilão began, strictly speaking, in 1543 with the arrival of a few Franciscan friars at the invitation of the Sinhala Buddhist King Bhuvanekabāhu VII. Before this event, Portuguese priests and friars ministered to the Portuguese soldiers and settlers in the island and performed conversions for some Sinhalas who sought to establish closer relations with the Portuguese, but there was no systematic effort to evangelize until the 1540s.[12] The missionary efforts in Sri Lanka were part of a larger project to Christianize Portuguese India and were spurred by a revival in Catholic piety linked in part with the Counter-Reformation in Europe. At the time, Ceilão was considered part of the Portuguese *Estado da Índia*, and thus political and religious affairs were often directed by authorities in Goa. The apparent success of Francis Xavier in converting "gentiles" in southern India and the island of Mannar off the northwestern coast of Sri Lanka raised the hopes of Catholic authorities that more conversions to the faith could be obtained. The papacy had granted the Portuguese crown the rights and duties to serve as the patron of the Roman Catholic missions and ecclesiastical establishments in Asia (along with Africa and Brazil) in a series of papal bulls and briefs between 1452 and 1514.[13] Concurrent with this religious duty, there was a desire to expand Portuguese trading interests following the "discoveries" made by naval explorers in the fifteenth and sixteenth centuries. Indeed, the propagation of the Gospel was regularly invoked as a motive and as justification for the expansion of Portuguese power overseas.[14]

Despite the dedicated efforts of the Franciscan missionaries to spread the Christian faith in Sri Lanka, they encountered several obstacles that prevented them from making much headway with the local population. Aside from the substantial numbers of conversions from the *Karāva* caste who lived along the coast as fishermen, most other groups of Sinhalas and Tamils in Sri Lanka were slow to embrace the Christian faith. Bhuvanekabāhu refused to convert despite the repeated overtures of the

Portuguese, and many of his subjects likewise refused. However, as the Sinhalas learned that conversion also entailed being placed under the protection of the Portuguese crown, clear benefits appeared to local inhabitants who began to claim exemption from the taxes levied by the Sinhala king. Bhuvanekabāhu, for his part, appealed to the king of Portugal for the confirmation of his authority in Koṭṭe, and he undertook other steps to consolidate his rule by reclaiming the lands of Christian converts, an effort that struck the missionaries as akin to persecution of the faith.[15] Meanwhile, the rift between Bhuvanekabāhu and his younger brother Māyādunnē in the kingdom of Sītāvaka effectively closed off missionary activity inland for decades. Prior to Bhuvanekabāhu's death, the king had arranged for his grandson Dharmapāla to be his successor, a move that angered Māyādunnē and contributed to armed hostilities between the two kingdoms. The battles that broke out between the Portuguese-led army of Koṭṭe and Māyādunnē's army from Sītāvaka caused much destruction and the depopulation of villages between the two warring kingdoms. The goal of obtaining Christian conversions, which was seen as complementary to the objectives of increasing revenue through trade and security for Portuguese ships, receded in the face of stiff resistance from Sītāvaka.

Under Portuguese protection, Dharmapāla converted to Catholicism and was crowned king in 1557. He took the name Dom João Dharmapāla, and large numbers of his courtiers in Koṭṭe also embraced the Christian faith. Then, the Council of Goa in 1567 proclaimed that heathen temples in Portuguese territories should be destroyed, all non-Christian priests should be expelled, and their religious literature destroyed.[16] To the degree that this policy was implemented in Sri Lanka, it resulted in the flight of monks to the central highlands and the seizure of temple lands to be used for the maintenance of Catholic religious orders. Later, with Rājasiṃha's death in 1593, Portuguese missionaries were enabled to proselytize more widely. When Dharmapāla died in 1597, the Portuguese assumed direct control of Koṭṭe and acted on ambitions to conquer the entire island, including the highland kingdom in Kandy. Dom Jerónimo de Azevedo, the captain-general appointed to govern Ceilão for the crown, brought in Jesuit missionaries beginning in 1602. The lands controlled by the Portuguese were divided between Franciscans and Jesuits, and later the Augustinian and Dominican orders were granted pieces of territory as well. Working with limited numbers of Portuguese troops at the head of armies made up of native soldiers (or *lascarins*), Azevedo experienced both gains and losses in battles with the Kandyan army. Success in gaining conversions was directly related to Portuguese success on the battlefield. Thus, as Portuguese political influence expanded in the island after 1604, Christian missionaries increased the numbers of converts, in large part due to the work of the Jesuits and the work of the Franciscan friar Francisco Negrão.[17]

The convergence of these events set the stage for the substantial growth of Christianity in Sri Lanka in the early seventeenth century. Portuguese documents give us some indication of the efforts made by missionaries to turn the local population away from Buddhist and Hindu practices. Throughout Asia, Catholic missionaries engaged in a common strategy of representing and then refuting the "pagan" religion that they sought to replace with Christianity.[18] Among the more notable examples, Luís Fróis in Japan, Matteo Ricci in China, and António de Andrade in Tibet were all concerned with portraying the falsehoods of Buddhism to assist in spreading what they considered the true faith.[19] While often exaggerating their successes in the field in letters written to Goa and Lisbon, the missionaries also depicted the religions that they sought to undermine, usually in unflattering terms. Most missionaries in service of the Portuguese *Padroado* only learned about the beliefs of the natives for the sake of defeating them in debates and converting them. They usually dismissed their sacred books and beliefs out of hand as "heathen" and the work of the devil.[20]

Nevertheless, missionary accounts from around the first decade of the seventeenth century testify to those efforts made to convert the "pagans" and "gentiles" to Catholicism. They represent the missionaries' struggle to demonstrate the superiority and truth of their faith compared to what the natives followed. The Jesuits, who are famous for their written accounts of the mission field, described in 1601 how their fathers assumed three tasks of ministry in the forms of preaching, hearing confessions, alleviating poor living conditions, and so on to the Portuguese and native converts; education for youths in the human and divine letters; and, principally, conversion of the gentiles to the faith.[21] In such accounts, one reads of both startling successes that allegedly give evidence of God's providence and disappointing setbacks that reveal the work of the devil. Convinced that God was on their side, the fathers still encountered Christian converts who might lapse back into the "blasphemies" of their previous faith, especially since they were held to be prone to ignorance and pressure from family members.[22] The Jesuits who arrived in Colombo in 1602 claimed that they received a warm welcome from the locals and quickly began their service by preaching, hearing confessions, teaching children Latin, and studying Sinhala to assist in the conversion of the "infidels" (*infiéis*).[23] Their work included building churches and ministering to the needs of the Portuguese and the natives alike. Elsewhere, Jesuit accounts describe how their faith rendered miraculous events. The fathers are said to have healed sick children through baptism and to have cast out the devil from those afflicted with illness.[24]

Franciscan missionaries also left accounts of their struggles with overcoming the heathen faith of the Sinhalas in order to introduced the "truth" of the Christian faith. An account from Francisco Negrão who traveled to Sri Lanka in 1610 describes not only the large numbers of alleged converts to the faith but also the methods he used to accomplish this. One version of this report describes how Negrão had a fellow friar preach in Sinhala to "all those gentiles the truth of our holy Faith and the falsity of their idols."[25] The account goes on to relate that "those who were disabused of the falsity of their pagodas and illumined by the truth of the law of Christ" asked to become Christian and receive baptism.[26] Then, having been briefly questioned on their newfound faith, the Sinhalas were instructed in the main articles of the Catholic faith, the Ten Commandments, and the Five Precepts of the Church, and they were told to guard them.[27] A different version of Negrão's account mentions that the Franciscans had shown how the idols that the Sinhalas had adored were actually demons, and thus the converts subsequently renounced their "idolatries and superstitions" before being baptized.[28] The account enumerates that Negrão arranged for more than 7,500 conversions and baptisms across much of the southwestern and southern part of the island during his seven-month visit to Sri Lanka.

Thus, under the protection of an expanded Portuguese rule in the lowland regions of the island, Catholic missionaries in the early seventeenth engaged in vigorous efforts to educate and convert people to the "truth" of their "holy Faith." The discourse employed in these polemical texts of conversion necessarily required people to "choose" sides and purposely created controversy between Christian and non-Christian views.[29] Converts were encouraged, if not required, to renounce their former Buddhist beliefs and practices as "false," "superstitious," and "idolatrous" before being permitted to embrace the "true" religion of Catholic Christianity. Seeking evidence of a genuine inner transformation that exclusively belongs to that of the church, Portuguese missionaries refused to tolerate the traditional multireligious synthesis of outward religious practice.[30] Whereas it had been customary to venerate the Buddha and Hindu deities in Sri Lanka without making much formal distinction between the different religions, the new religious order insisted on exclusive adherence to the Christian faith. Their moral contests held in the name of truth could have only one winner. The expansion of the mission field and the entrance of Jesuits, Augustinians, and Dominicans into the island created an environment wherein the success of each religious order was largely measured in the number of baptisms performed and the number of churches built. Christian missions, frequent warfare, and the removal of royal support for the Sangha meant that Buddhist institutions in the late sixteenth and early seventh centuries in Sri Lanka lost ground in terms of their vitality and their prospects for survival in the island.

The heightened sense of exclusive religious identities were also evidenced by the spurts of religious violence that occurred beginning from the late sixteenth century and into the seventeenth century. In accordance with the proclamations from the church councils in Goa and in the heat of battle, Portuguese forces frequently resorted to destroying the temples and scriptures of Buddhist and Hindu communities. The more militaristic stance sanctioned by Portuguese political and religious authorities beginning in the latter sixteenth century generally resulted in greater intolerance for non-Christians and their traditional practices.[31] Conversions were prized not only for the salvation of people's souls but also because they were seen as methods to subjugate the natives and prevent rebellions by effectively turning them into vassals of the Portuguese crown.[32] However, the close coordination between the political conquest of land and the religious conquest of souls often meant that Sinhala resistance to the Portuguese was directed at both realms. Sinhala revolts to Portuguese rule often involved anti-Christian iconoclasm, including the destruction of churches and the occasional killing of priests, which suggests that the missionary impulse succeeded in hardening religious boundaries in Sri Lanka.[33] This violence mirrored the "scorched-earth" policy of Portuguese-led armies, which often involved the plunder and destruction of Buddhist temples and places of worship.[34] Lands seized from temples that had been deserted or destroyed were routinely used to build churches and to earn revenues for the support of Catholic orders in the island. In seventeenth-century Ceilão, Portuguese efforts to conquer the island were thus accompanied by efforts to win the souls of "heathens." Religious competition sharpened religious boundaries and spurred changes in how Sinhala Buddhism was understood and expressed.

Aesthetics for Ethics' Sake

Within the context of the expansion of Portuguese control over much of the low country in Sri Lanka, Alagiyavanna's *Subhāṣitaya* appears as a poetic response to the dramatic social and cultural upheavals of colonialism. The work echoes the tone of desperation and dismay, frequently alluding to problematic situations wherein kings may rule unjustly and people have doubts about the Buddha's Dharma. While the work retains the classical Sinhala poetic style of *sivupada* (quatrain) composition with the formal use of the *samudraghoṣa* meter (comprising four lines of eighteen syllables in each line) and the *eḷīsama* scheme of duplicating the final letters in each line of verse, it tends to privilege moral admonitions over aesthetically rich poetic embellishments. The work's aesthetic features are used to reinforce the normative claims it makes about truth and morality. There are scarce traces of verses devoted to celebrating the glory of kings, the magnificence of nature, and the beauty of cities and women. Instead, the author chooses to dispense worldly wisdom in the form of didactic verses to help people to live well in the present world. One is left with the impression that Alagiyavanna sees fairly little to celebrate at all in such a world. Rather than describing its beauties and marvels, the work counsels its audience on how best to survive and even flourish in a setting in which things are not as they should be.

There are those who argue that *Subhāṣitaya* was Alagiyavanna's response to the alleged conversion of Rājasiṃha to Śaivism and the resulting persecution of Buddhism in his realm. A. V. Suraweera suggests as much when he claims that the *Subhāṣitaya* must have been written during Rājasiṃha's time. According to him, the poem's reproaches for "false views" and "wicked persons" refers to the Hinduism that the king embraced when he sought reassurance for his alleged killing of his father King Māyādunnē. In this light, Alagiyavanna appears as a heroic voice that risked the wrath of the king for the sake of rescuing the society in Sītāvaka.[35] While it is certainly possible that the poet was reacting to a variety of foes to Buddhism, there are problems with seeing the work as primarily anti-Hindu. First, although the poem disparages Śiva in one verse, it also praises a number of Hindu gods in an introductory verse, including the Śaivite deities of Iśvara, Skanda, and Ganeṣa. Second, no other works of Alagiyavanna composed during Rājasiṃha's reign display hostility to Śaivism. Thirdly and most importantly, the historical evidence behind Rājasiṃha's alleged "conversion" to Śaivism is unreliable, appearing mainly in the monastic records of monks who experienced persecution during the king's reign.

This persecution, however, was part of a broader purge of Rājasiṃha's enemies, including some members of the Saṅgha, who were implicated in a plot to poison the king.[36] A punitive response to monastic conspirators and the king's patronage of Hindu temples do not, in themselves, definitively show that Rājasiṃha turned against Buddhism. Much of the alleged evidence for this fact comes from the Portuguese chronicler Couto, who was eager to portray the great enemy of the Portuguese in Sri Lanka as a bloodthirsty tyrant. Thus, despite the advanced age of Māyādunnē, Couto claims that Rājasiṃha murdered him and later killed numerous priests who had conspired against him.[37] However, the seventeenth-century Portuguese chronicler Fernão de Queyroz, who also viewed Rājasiṃha as an enemy, mentions instead that the tyrant king learned of his father's natural death after returning from a siege against the Portuguese in Colombo.[38] Thus, while it seems reasonable to presume that Rājasiṃha did severely punish some monks suspected of disloyalty, and that he did give favor to Brahmin priests in his court, it does not necessarily mean that Hinduism effectively supplanted Buddhism in the kingdom. There is in general little evidence that people had disassociated these two systems, which were generally seen as complementary, or felt the need to do so during Rājasiṃha's reign. Alagiyavanna's praise of the Three Jewels of Buddhism—the Buddha, Dharma, and Sangha—in his earlier works indicate that the religion continued to have a presence in Rājasiṃha's court. Moreover, there is no evidence from which to deduce that Alagiyavanna was courageous or foolhardy enough to spite the king, his powerful and ruthless patron.

On the contrary, *Subhāṣitaya* should be seen as a product composed in the absence of a royal court. Unlike his earlier works, there is no mention of a noble patron who requested Alagiyavanna to compose it. The aesthetically rich descriptions of courts, either contemporary or legendary, are missing entirely from this work. Instead of containing lavish praise or an entertaining narrative from the Bodhisattva's life, *Subhāṣitaya* compiles the good advice from a range of Indic texts, many of which are associated with Hindu culture, to instruct an audience on how to live righteously. Such a topic appears highly idiosyncratic next to the corpus of other Sinhala poems from the medieval period in Sri Lankan history. Aside from the *Lō Väḍa Saṅgarāva*, which contains verses praising the performance of acts of merit, there are few traces of morally didactic poetry in Sinhala literature before Alagiyavanna's *Subhāṣitaya*.[39] Furthermore, the *Lō Väḍa Saṅgarāva* casts its message clearly in the Buddhist terms of merit (*piṅ*) and demerit (*pav*), which stems from basic Buddhist teachings rather than generalized moral sayings. One either acts to accrue merit and good fortune in the future, or one's actions inhibit and jeopardize efforts to progress toward good rebirths and nirvana. The ethical imagination of this earlier poetic work is restricted wholly to traditional Buddhist ideas in regard to the good fortune that follows acts of merit and the suffering that follows wicked deeds. The tone of this work reflects a monastic view of what constitutes correct action and how it should be evaluated in terms of the Dharma.

Alagiyavanna's *Subhāṣitaya*, on the other hand, delivers moral admonitions drawn from a range of pan-Indic aphorisms. Many of the verses in this work have no discernible connection to Buddhist thought but instead convey generic advice on what constitutes righteous behavior. Alagiyavanna marshaled these aphorisms, translated them into Sinhala, and introduced some specifically Buddhist ideas in an effort to reach an audience under pressure to reject the Dharma in favor of other religious teachings. In doing so, he drew on the collective weight of ancient Indian wisdom to contest newer, competing claims from the Portuguese missionaries about the bases of knowledge and truth. The wise sayings of Indic civilization, when expressed through the Sinhala language, not to mention through references to the Buddhist religion, appear as both a condemnation of contemporary society and a rebuttal to those who brandished rival religious views. Such a focus on Indic gnomic sayings may also reveal something about the weakness of Buddhist institutions at that time. Rather than base his moral instruction solely on teachings from monastic texts, Alagiyavanna instead chose a wider corpus of literature from which to offer the good counsel of ancient scholars.

Poetic embellishments (*alaṅkāra*) in *Subhāṣitaya* are consistently used in a supportive and subordinate role to illustrate its discursive points. The aesthetic features of this work serve to enhance its literary quality and, by extension, the persuasiveness of its arguments. For example, verse 46 presents some practical wisdom on which people make fitting recipients for one's good deeds:

> If one does a small act of virtue (*guṇayak*) to knowledgeable persons,
> It continually remains like a letter carved in stone.
> But if one does any great act of virtue to dumb persons,
> That dissipates like a line drawn upon water.[40]

The similes of a letter carved in stone and a line drawn in water are used to display the effects of what is done to particular kinds of recipients. These similes are not in themselves sources of aesthetic delight, as they appear as fairly concrete, unembellished images with which the poet illustrates his point. The audience learns that a virtuous deed, however insignificant, has lasting effects when done on behalf of those who are wise, whereas that which is done for those who are ignorant will bring little fruit. The two examples of inscriptions, on stone and water, convey with clarity a message about for whose sake one should act. Such a statement, moreover, clearly contrasts with the Buddhist message of *Lō Väḍa Saṅgarāva*, which asserts that all good deeds are beneficial and increase joy to oneself and others. This distinction here resembles what James Egge has characterized as "sacrificial" and "karmic" discourse in Buddhist theories of giving. Sacrificial discourse recognizes the worthiness of the recipient in calculating the merit to be earned by giving, while karmic discourse determines the gift solely by the purity of the giver's intention.[41] Notably, however, the issue of merit is not even mentioned in the preceding verse from *Subhāṣitaya*. Its argument is based more on the common sense of worldly wisdom than on any specifically Buddhist teaching.

A verse containing a related message on the importance of associating with good people also illustrates the conventional, moralistic tone of *Subhāṣitaya*. Note how in verse 41, the poet uses an image of the king of cobras in juxtaposition with its mortal enemy the *garuḍa*, a mythical bird comparable to an oversized bird of prey, to make a point about how one lives better in the company of good people

> To the degree one associates with clever people who are renowned and worthy,
> Even if one is small in strength, one does not give heed to one's enemies.
> It is like being the proud king of the cobras dwelling around the neck of Iśvara,
> And asking the king of *garuḍas*, "Friend, what's new with you?"[42]

Such advice reflects practical wisdom that is not exclusive to the Buddhist thought of monastics. The exhortation to associate with good people may and even should be adopted by all, irrespective of one's religious views. By keeping good company, one may exist without fear, even in the face of one's enemies. At root, this poetic verse conveys a moral message that teaches people what comprises right behavior in a terse manner, reflecting the genre of South Asian didactic verse more generally.[43] This style of poetic writing thus marks a clear departure from the ornate praise of kings, cities, and women as found in earlier Sinhala works.

Alagiyavanna's aptly named *Subhāṣitaya* draws much of its moral advice from admonitions gleaned from oral traditions and the vast store of Indian *subhāṣita* collections. Such works represent compilations of wise sayings that circulated orally and in written form throughout a variety of different genres in Sanskrit, Tamil, Pāli, and other languages. Alagiyavanna apparently drew liberally from a variety of didactic texts and oral sayings to compose his *Subhāṣitaya*. He actually says as much in verse 5 of the work, wherein he describes how he will translate the wise sayings of old teachers who wrote in Sanskrit, Tamil, and Pāli into Sinhala for the sake of ordinary, unlearned beings.[44] Gunawardhana, in his early edition and commentary of the text, traced numerous verses adapted from other works. Among the Sanskrit texts identified as sources for Alagiyavanna's *Subhāṣitaya*, Gunawardhana identified the *Śārṅgadhāra*, *Hitopadeśa*, *Raghuvaṃsa*, *Vyāsakāraya*, and the three *śataka* poems of Bhartṛhari called *Śṛṅgāra Śataka*, *Nīti Śataka*, and the *Vairāgya Śataka*, among others.[45] Further, Godakumbura has noted that several verses from Alagiyavanna's work are based on the Tamil *Nālaḍiyār*, which similarly comprises quatrains of didactic verse.[46] Like other works of this genre, Alagiyavanna's *Subhāṣitaya* selects, quotes, paraphrases, and alters material attributable to other texts or oral traditions. The fact that so many of these texts were compiled by non-Buddhist authors reinforces the idea that unlike the treatment of Buddhist morality in earlier Sinhala poetic works such as *Lō Väḍa Saṅgarāva* and *Kāvyaśēkhara*, which were composed by monks, *Subhāṣitaya* engages in broader discussions on what it means to be righteous across South Asia. Not limited to Buddhist teachings, its advice is supported by good sense and everyday experience, as well as the repute of popular and seemingly timeless maxims.

Yet numerous verses in the *Subhāṣitaya* advocate accepting those same Buddhist truths as the basis for reorienting one's moral conduct in the world. This fact points to one of many tensions evident in the work. Alagiyavanna juxtaposes Buddhist ethics and universal ethics, virtuous persons (*sudana*) and wicked persons (*dudana*), and suitable acts versus immoral ones. In the absence of a Sinhala court that would recognize and patronize a learned poet such as him, Alagiyavanna seems to have responded to the social dislocation and political turbulence of the early seventeenth century by taking recourse in poetic verses that stress moral instruction and ethical development. To the extent that the *Subhāṣitaya* addresses general rules of conduct, the work engages in a moral struggle to define and defend a notion of morality that is not sustained by a just Buddhist king. The moralistic dimensions of the *Subhāṣitaya* reveal a new effort to anchor moral conduct outside the traditional Sinhala culture-power formation and instead within the seemingly irrefutable scope of pan-Indic common sense. Here the poet must rely not only on aesthetic skills but also on reason and persuasion to make a compelling case for patterning one's behavior in the world after the practical wisdom of South Asian traditions rather than the moral system being proffered by the Portuguese.

The Sway of Ignorance and Wickedness

One of the conspicuous features of Alagiyavanna's *Subhāṣitaya* is its critical view of contemporary society as a whole. The typically suggestive verses celebrating kings, women, and cities in an effusive and aesthetically rich manner are scarcely evident in this work. Although his *Dahamsoňḍa Kava* leaves hints about righteousness being hard to find and his *Kusa Jātaka Kāvya* plays up moral concerns, it is the *Subhāṣitaya* that redirects the poetic form of Sinhala *kavi* toward the problems of the world rather than its pleasures. As such, it is a work that appears to be a product of an era bereft of a powerful Sinhala Buddhist king who could promote peace, prosperity, and poetry throughout his realm. As mentioned above, the early seventeenth century was marked by the rapid expansion of Portuguese influence throughout much of lowland Sri Lanka. Following the widespread destruction of many Sinhala villages in the last years of the sixteenth century, the first decade of the seventeenth century witnessed continued warfare and devastation throughout the land.[47] The Portuguese experienced a setback in 1603 in its efforts to capture the highland city of Kandy, but then shortly afterward resumed its policy of expanding colonial rule across the island. Most Buddhist temples in Portuguese controlled areas were destroyed, and the temple lands were seized and awarded to the various Catholic orders operating in Ceilão.[48] Meanwhile, the newly arrived Jesuit priests had begun to set up mission stations in the hinterlands between the coastal areas and the central highlands, expanding the Christian presence in lands formerly controlled by the Sītāvaka kingdom. In the eyes of a Buddhist poet who had earlier enjoyed patronage and some measure of security under a powerful Sinhala Buddhist king, the events of the first decade of the seventeenth century must have appeared disturbing and grim.

The use of Sinhala poetry for cultural criticism, while atypical, was not unprecedented before the early seventeenth century. A verse work of Vīdāgama Maitreya, the fifteenth-century monastic author, contains occasional, harsh comments in regard to the Brahmanical worship of ostensibly Hindu deities. This work called *Buduguṇālaṅkāraya* depicts the offerings and worship given to Hindu Brahmins and their deities as ineffective and fraudulent. Fire sacrifices, offerings to Brahmins, and the worship of deities such as Śiva and Viṣṇu all come under attack by the author. Evidently, Maitreya used this work to ridicule and denounce the various Hindu practices that had become part of the popular religion in the centuries following Tamil Coḷa rule over parts of the island.[49] Maitreya's works poke fun at contemporary Hindu practices to reduce their popularity in Sri Lankan society. Although *Buduguṇālaṅkāraya* criticizes Hindu practices, it stops short of condemning the major social institutions of Sinhala society at that time.

However, Alagiyavanna's *Subhāṣitaya* paints a bleak picture of a society that has fallen under the sway of ignorance and wickedness in general. The maxims that appear in this work suggest a mood of lamentation and deprivation. It is not only a matter of people mistakenly following Hindu customs—as described by Maitreya in the fifteenth century. For Alagiyavanna in the early seventeenth century, there is a lack of proper moral guidance and a widespread failure of most people to grasp and practice the Buddha's teachings. The "well-spoken words" that he reproduces effectively serve to critique the status quo, while shining light on the collective failures of the society's political and religious institutions to promote virtue. All in all, there is an overwhelming sense of pessimism in *Subhāṣitaya* that stands in stark contrast to the poet's earlier works that celebrate kingship and the acts of the Bodhisattva.

Alagiyavanna seems to suggest that wicked kings are more prevalent in the contemporary world than righteous kings. His *Subhāṣitaya* finds fault with what these wicked kings do and with the harmful effects on the world around them.

> Having driven away those with knowledge in order to shelter the wicked,
> Not having grasped virtues within one's mind, like water on a lotus leaf,

Not being moderate and spending the days with jealousy,
There is no other danger for the king and that kingdom.
When many leaders who are endowed with cruelty come into the world,
There is no substantial benefit, only the destruction of this world.
At the time when the seven suns appear without pause at the end of an eon,
Lotuses everywhere will burn and will not bloom.[50]

These verses evoke a scenario in which kings, lacking virtue, threaten all of existence. Marked by jealousy, cruelty, and poor judgment, such kings affect the world in a manner comparable to the Buddhist vision of the end of the world, whereupon seven suns will one day rise and burn up the entire earth.[51] These malevolent rulers are said to reject those who are wise for those who are wicked. Such sentiments are nowhere found in Alagiyavanna's earlier works, in which the poet was writing about King Rājasiṃha I of Sītāvaka or the Bodhisattva when reborn as a just and heroic king.[52] From the point of view of *Subhāṣitaya*, however, wicked kings are all too real, and their harmful effects on society are predictable.

When the *Subhāṣitaya* speaks of good kings, it does so in theoretical terms without specifying anyone by name. Those "Lords of Men" (*niriňdō*) who reign righteously are said to use their virtues for the benefit of all. Such good kings are notable for their efforts to protect and provide for all beings under their rule, without causing undue hardships for them.

The Lords of Men, who protect the beings of the world and associate with virtuous persons,
Are renowned everywhere by their compassion, virtues, and knowledge.
Like bees that go and gently take pollen from flowers,
They collect revenue in accordance with the law without disturbing people's minds.
Just as one eats only enough to extinguish the fire of hunger in the belly,
Even though the food has the taste of ambrosia that increases one's vitality,

> The Lords of Men whose glory and fame are widespread,
> Do not accumulate extensive wealth except in order to protect the beings of the world.[53]

Rather than single out a king's excellent qualities in the fashion of a bard that sings the praises of a powerful lord and patron, these verses highlight the fairly ordinary virtues of kings who do not abuse their subjects by levying excessive taxes in order to acquire great wealth for themselves. By noting how righteous kings are careful about acquiring wealth, the poet implicitly criticizes those rulers who cause economic hardship in their domains. Whereas in panegyric verse, kings are often praised for their lavish surroundings, with the wealth that surrounds them symbolizing their majesty, these verses from the *Subhāṣitaya* make it clear that good kings have modest tastes. The ideal king in didactic poetry appears rather different from the king who is praised in panegyric poetry. He is a hypothetical king, not one that can be named and praised for particular attributes. He pursues policies that benefit all beings and does not seek to enhance his own stature.

Given the historical context in which Alagiyavanna likely composed *Subhāṣitaya*, the inclusion of verses that criticize wickedness on the part of kings and their advisers resonates with the plight of the poet who had lost his own royal patron in 1593 and was living betwixt and between the rival powers of the Portuguese captain-generals and the Kandyan kings. In a time of political upheaval and constant warfare, when the lands around Sītāvaka were frequent battlegrounds and the old court was discontinued, Alagiyavanna evidently found no rulers on whom he could lavish ornate praise. Instead, he warns of the damage caused by wicked kings and describes what good kings *would* do if they were around to do so. His poetic commentary on kingship invokes traditional discourse and ideals, enabling the poet to associate moral failure with the ruling powers of the times. With righteousness and wisdom judged to be lacking among the rulers of early seventeenth-century Ceilão, one could expect society to be overwhelmed by their faults and misconduct.

Many verses in *Subhāṣitaya* focus on the ignorance and immorality that appears to be rampant in the world. The poet suggests, moreover, that these problems are the effects of poor rulers. It is clear that Alagiyavanna generally sees the world as being deficient in wisdom and virtue. He writes in his work: "Like the endless sky, there is no limit to immoral people," and again: "Wicked persons who are lacking in the power of wisdom carry on according to the customs of the world."[54] This sentiment of resignation over widespread immorality is echoed in other verses found in *Subhāṣitaya*. Alagiyavanna repeatedly acknowledges the shortcomings of people, attesting to the prevalence of wickedness in a way that is unprecedented for him. The faults to be found in the world are, in one sense, predictable and wholly unavoidable.

> The moon has a blemish, there is a heap of snow on the Himalaya mountain.
> There is saltwater in the ocean, and the Lord of Poets wanders impoverished.
> It is fitting that things like these bear great shortcomings.
> It is only nirvana, which is renowned in the Three Worlds, that is very pure.[55]

Alagiyavanna maintains that imperfections in nature and society are in keeping with the transitory nature of existence in *saṃsāra*. Even a great poet like him might not receive the patronage of a king. But compared to the problems of life in the world, nirvana is taken to be the ultimate blessing that exists as a moral counterpoint to one's everyday experience. Alagiyavanna makes use of the concept of nirvana in this way, as it highlights the imperfection of all other types and manners of existence. The reference to nirvana here indicates the recognition that the world of experience is characterized by impurity and immorality, pain and death. This world is to be forsaken, not celebrated.

Owing to the unfortunate conditions of existence, the poet includes verses that acknowledge the trials of life in the world, while other verses offer advice on how to deal with the presence of wickedness. In the writing of *Subhāṣitaya*, Alagiyavanna comments on how virtuous persons are still subject to suffering due to the ignorance and immorality that surrounds them. At one point, he compares the lot of virtuous persons to the burning of metal, with those good people being left to experience misery and to sigh about their fates.[56] As opposed to other Buddhist writings that tend to emphasize the beneficial fruits that follow moral conduct, Alagiyavanna's *Subhāṣitaya* explicitly notes that even virtuous persons may suffer due to no real fault of their own. Their virtue, however, is said to persist even in the face of great difficulties.

> If noble ones, renowned, and endowed with limitless virtue and knowledge,

Obtain trouble without end, they do not become evil-minded.
Similarly when a bunch of beautiful sandalwood with a fragrance extending to the ends of all directions,
Is cut and crushed, it still emits its singular fragrance.[57]

By complimenting the resolve of virtuous persons, the text reasserts their virtue but also concedes that even good people suffer when the world is in disarray. Alagiyavanna's *Subhāṣitaya* admits that virtuous persons suffer trouble and affliction (*vehesa*) along with everyone else.

The danger that wickedness and ignorance pose to those who are virtuous is compounded by the existence of doubt and false views that lead people astray. Alagiyavanna points out that, in the context of the overwhelming ignorance of the age, there are many who fail to recognize the Buddha's Dharma and instead adhere to mistaken conceptions about the nature of the world.

Beings possessing false views do not take up the conventions (*samaya*) of the great King of Dharma,
Which effects the highest happiness of nirvana.
Just like a swarm of blue flies that do not travel through the lotus grove,
Which shines with splendor and emits limitless fragrance.[58]

In this verse, Alagiyavanna explains what constitutes ignorance—namely the misunderstanding or rejection of the Buddha's Dharma. Those persons who possess incorrect religious views are thus comparable to flies that fail to take notice of the sweet fragrance and nectar of lotus flowers. Alagiyavanna's criticism of the failure to grasp the Dharma could only be conceivable in a context in which substantial numbers of people did not embrace the Buddha's teachings.

Other verses in Alagiyavanna's *Subhāṣitaya* explain that those who reject the Dharma often do so in favor of worshiping other gods and following the conventions of other ritual systems. Such conduct is further evidence of the sway of ignorance under which Alagiyavanna and his audience existed in early modern Sri Lanka. Yet the poet is not content to allow these so-called false views go without being identified and refuted in his work.

Forsaking the refuge of the Great Sage, whose feet rest upon the heads of all gods and persons,

> And venerating other gods [instead], those beings,
> Who guard their false views for the sake of pure liberation,
> Are like those who struggle to draw water from the *dimbula* flower.[59]

This contrast drawn between the greatness of the Buddha, or "Great Sage," with the ineffectiveness of the "other gods" revolves around the issue of who can assist people in attaining liberation. Alagiyavanna clearly asserts that the worship of beings other than the Buddha is futile. In doing so, he also articulates a new, more exclusive way of relating to Buddhism. The Buddha here stands in place of other gods, not just aside or above them.

At the same time, *Subhāṣitaya* points to unmistakable signs of religious competition with the Buddha's Dharma. Not everyone appears to embrace the Dharma and live in accordance with its moral and ritual conventions. The work suggests that people's ignorance prevents them from recognizing the virtue and truth represented by practitioners of the Dharma. Even great beings who follow the Buddha may in time become taken for granted and disrespected by people who have grown accustomed to their presence in the world.[60] Elsewhere, the work similarly claims that "thick-headed persons" fail to recognize the goodness found in virtuous persons but instead behave like frogs in lakes that are ignorant of the fragrant lotus flowers.[61] In such an environment, it is possible for people to be misled into venerating such deities as Śiva (or Iśvara), whose grand appearance belies his more circumscribed power.

> If possessing so many things that cannot even be measured,
> One makes requests with a greedy mind in the manner of beggars,
> It is like Great Iśvara, endowed with an eye on his forehead and great glory,
> But who wanders about on the vehicle of a decrepit old bull.[62]

This parody of the god Śiva resembles some similar critiques found in other Buddhist works. It directly evokes an image from *Buduguṇālaṅkāraya*, which also mentions how Śiva travels around on the vehicle of a decrepit old bull (*mahalu gon vāhanen*), before going on to assert that offerings made to this god are fruitless.[63] Similarly, a Brahmin convert to Buddhism named Śaṅkarasvāmin also argued sometime in the first millennium in India for the inferiority of Śiva and other Hindu deities next to the Buddha, because they carry weapons such as a trident and cause destruction with their defiled minds.[64] Although it is unlikely that Alagiyavanna had knowledge of this earlier work, he still felt it was necessary to show that the god Śiva is an inappropriate recipient for worship.

The poet's disparagement of religious rivals to the Buddha and his Dharma illustrate something important about the religious environment in which he lived and wrote. By acknowledging the existence of other religious paths while seeking to discredit them, Alagiyavanna's *Subhāṣitaya* speaks to the perceived threats that other religious ideas posed to the Buddha's dispensation. If *Subhāṣitaya* is any indication of the diversity and competition of religious notions in early colonial Sri Lanka, Sinhala authors could no longer assume the predominance of Buddhist teachings in the society of that time. The criticism of rampant ignorance and the failure to venerate the Buddha suggest that these problems were serious enough to be denounced. From time to time, both before and after Alagiyavanna, Sinhala Buddhist authors have sought to express in clear terms the evident superiority of Buddhism over other religious systems. The poet's decision to reject other religious forms rather than tolerate or assimilate them is suggestive of the belief that Buddhism was under threat and required protection from harmful influences.

More broadly, the text expresses a sense of resignation over the fact that not everyone subscribes to the teaching of the Buddha. The recognition of doubts in regard to the Dharma invites a new kind of reading and engagement with the text. Specifically, *Subhāṣitaya* works to define and elicit a form of religious identity that stands in opposition to other forms.

> Great virtuous persons! Whether the next world exists or not,
> It is good if one forsakes wicked acts and expels them from one's mind.
> Therefore, if the next world does not exist, no harm will come about.
> But if it does, there will be misfortune for the one who does wicked deeds (*pav*) while thinking it does not exist.[65]

In this verse, Alagiyavanna strongly suggests that some people may have doubts over whether one's deeds in the present lead to some sort of afterlife. His verse recalls the Buddha's argument against the nihilist position in the Apaṇṇaka Sutta of *Majjhima Nikāya*.[66] Subsequently, the

Buddhist tradition, in Sri Lanka and elsewhere, has taken the theory of karma and rebirth as practically a given, requiring little evidence or support to be accepted. Like the Buddha some two millennia earlier, however, Alagiyavanna found himself confronted by skeptics who dispute the reality of karma and rebirth. He even supposes for the sake of argument that such notions may not have any effect on a person's life. Ultimately, however, Alagiyavanna wishes to convince his audience to dispel their doubts, false views, and worship of other gods. What is striking about this stance is the fact that few, if any, older Sinhala texts ever entertain positions that run so contrary to Buddhist thought. Whereas in such works as *Lō Väḍa Saṅgarāva* the concepts of merit and wicked deeds were taken for granted, in *Subhāṣitaya* they appear contestable and in need of legitimation. Such a stance only makes sense if there were Christians who questioned or disputed such a view.[67]

The "Religion" of the Buddha

The moral admonitions and cultural commentary found in *Subhāṣitaya* are typical of the content found within the broader genre of *subhāṣita* texts from premodern India. Such works endeavor to teach what was considered morally correct behavior, while vividly depicting the ways people lived in different historical periods.[68] Alagiyavanna's *Subhāṣitaya* is notable, however, for the efforts made by the author to articulate and promote a conception of Buddhism in Sri Lanka long before Orientalist scholars labored to "invent" a pan-Asian Buddhist tradition in the nineteenth century.[69] Included in his text are poetic verses that celebrate the teachings and practices of the Buddha, which are sometimes contrasted with those directed to other gods. The verses in which Alagiyavanna highlights Buddhist thought are rarely derived, even in part, from other identifiable literary sources. As such, his *Subhāṣitaya* represents one of the earliest known works that speak of a religious system linked to the Buddha—an allusion to "Buddhism"—rather than just relying on technical terms such as *Dharma* ("teaching") or *Sāsana* ("dispensation") from within the tradition itself.[70] Apparently moved by the perceived decline in righteousness and the concurrent rise in ignorance and immorality, Alagiyavanna went further to evoke a distinct and exclusive notion of the Buddhist religion as superior to all others.

The poet's calls to venerate the Buddha rather than other gods is consistent with a religious polemic that recognizes but also denigrates the religious practices dedicated to various non-Buddhist deities. Earlier, in the fifteenth century, Maitreya's *Buduguṇālaṅkāraya* similarly denounced Brahmanical worship given to various Hindu deities such as Śiva and Rāma, pointedly asking what is the benefit of doing so.[71] Alagiyavanna picks up aspects of this critique, yet he goes further in discussing not just the virtues of the Buddha but also a nascent conception of Buddhism. When compared to what other gods can offer, *Subhāṣitaya* extols the benefits of venerating the Buddha.

> Like ignorant merchants who do not know the price of a gem,
> Taking a lump of glass and greedily calling it a gem,
> Ignorant beings, wishing for liberation, make offerings,
> Venerating other gods besides the spotless Noble Sage.
> The effort made by ignorant beings that aspire to nirvana,
> Serving other gods and forsaking the delightful Lord of Sages,
> Is like pressing an oil machine on a sandy courtyard,
> While increasing in one's mind the desire to obtain oil.[72]

Next to the Buddha, the poet claims, there can be no divine source of aid that leads to liberation from the world. The "other gods" (*an suran*) are worshiped by those who are ignorant, and this effort is as useless as trying to work a press on a sandy spot of ground.

For Alagiyavanna, the Buddha is exceptional and alone worthy of veneration. The text explicitly notes that there are numerous beings who follow paths other than the Buddhist one. Although these unnamed "other gods" may include Hindu deities, in the context of the upsurge in Christian missions in the early seventeenth century, it stands to reason that Alagiyavanna may well have had the Trinity and various other Catholic saints in mind with this critique. This discourse could be a response to Portuguese missionaries who encouraged an exclusivist attitude toward religion and drew sharp distinctions between the "truth" of the holy Christian faith and the falsity of idolatrous, "heathen superstition." From this perspective, there could be no room for retaining aspects of Buddhist practice among converts to Christianity. In much the same way, the *Subhāṣitaya* seeks to articulate clear notions of religious difference and adherence to a particular religion. Its polemical critique of those who venerate other gods and repudiate the Buddha illustrates a step toward the rejection of rituals dedicated to other deities.

Alagiyavanna's move to mark boundaries and delimit truth illustrates a strikingly different attitude toward religious imagery and practices connected with the gods. In his *Sävul Sandēśaya*, the cock messenger is urged to visit Hindu *kovils* as well as Buddhist temples in order to venerate deities such as Umā at the Śaivite shrine in Sītāvaka, Saman at Saparagamuva, and other deities at a shrine in the Delgamuva Buddhist temple in Kuruviṭa.[73] The *Dahamsoňḍa Kava* employs the imagery of Hindu deities to praise the good qualities of the bodhisattva king.[74] Meanwhile, although *Kusa Jātaka Kāvya* includes scant references to Hindu rituals or imagery, it refrains from distinguishing a coherent, Buddhist tradition apart from other religious systems. These three poetic works from Alagiyavanna's earlier career do not depict a sense of rivalry or conflict between "Buddhist" and other religious systems. They do not attempt to distinguish adherence to the Buddha from other forms of religious practice.

In *Subhāṣitaya*, however, one encounters a substantive notion of Buddhism as a tradition of rites and beliefs associated with the Buddha as opposed to those linked with other deities. Long before the invention of Buddhism as a definable world religion alongside other so-called religious traditions such as Christianity, Hinduism, and others, the Sinhala poet Alagiyavanna articulated a kind of Buddhist identity that rivaled and could not be harmonized with other religious practices and beliefs.[75]

> Not accepting the conventions of the Lord of Sages, who is clear and very pure,
> The beings of the world, having deficient knowledge and accepting various false views,
> Will come to that City of Liberation,
> Whenever a blind man can see the feet of a fish in the sky.[76]

These so-called conventions of the Buddha (*muniňdu samaya*) express a notion of religious identity that is constructed in opposition to other religious forms. The ninth verse of the work, previously quoted in reference to the failure of those with false views to grasp the Dharma, similarly speaks of the "conventions of the King of the Dharma" (*dahaṁ raja samaya*). This coupling of terms for the Buddha and *samaya* is significant and noteworthy, given that a portion of the late sixteenth-century Sinhala text called *Alakeśvarayuddhaya* (*Battle of Alakeśvara*) that was written by a Christian author mentions adherence to *jesus kristu dēvasamaya*, or "the divine religion of Jesus Christ."[77]

Alagiyavanna's description of the *samaya* (i.e., "conventions" or "religion") of the Buddha thus represents what may be one of the first expressions of an exclusive notion of Buddhism found in Sinhala writing.[78] The linking of conventions with the Buddha represents an expansion of what is denoted by terms such as *Dharma* and *Sāsana*, that emerged from within a specifically Buddhist discourse and that were not, strictly speaking, attributable to other religious systems. The term emerges out of a comparative framework, reflecting a way of talking about Buddhism that presupposes the existence of other religious systems or movements.[79] Alagiyavanna's use of *samaya* in these two verses of *Subhāṣitaya*, particularly in contrast with the notion of "false views," indicates something sanctioned by the Buddha that may (or may not) be obtained or accepted. Alagiyavanna seems to imply that a person with correct views will embrace the Buddha's *samaya*, thereby taking up the thought and practice outlined by him. The *samaya* of the Buddha is thus comparable—albeit superior, in Alagiyavanna's view—to the beliefs and customs of other religious systems. When expressed in the context of a moral struggle over truth and who may claim to possess it, the depiction of a *samaya* connected with the Buddha comes to reflect a conception of religion that is not far removed from our modern understanding of the term. *Samaya* can even be translated as "religion" in modern Sinhala usage.

It is significant that the poet's construction of an idea that is roughly analogous to Buddhism invokes the notion of false views and the worship of other gods as its counterpoint. Verses 9 and 13, in which the concept of the Buddha's *samaya* is articulated, appear alongside other verses that decry the ignorance and futility that go along with venerating other gods in place of the Buddha. Alagiyavanna seems to be speaking of the idea of Buddhism rather than describing which features may be said to be representative of it. In other words, Alagiyavanna does not imitate the work of Śrī Rāhula in the fifteenth-century *Kāvyaśēkhara*, in which he presents and discusses such aspects of Buddhist thought and practice as the Five Precepts, the eleven types of wicked deeds (*pav*) that lead to miserable rebirths, the twelve types of merit (*piṅ*) and so on, in the ninth canto of this Sinhala *mahākāvya*. Śrī Rāhula speaks of some major features of Buddhist thought without explicitly positing an overarching label that comprises those features and to which one should adhere. Alagiyavanna, on the other hand, pays relatively little attention to specific features of the tradition and, instead, alludes to a conceptual superstructure founded on and incorporating those specific teachings and practices.

One does not learn much about what the conventions of the Buddha actually entail by reading *Subhāṣitaya*. Alagiyavanna's work is more ideological than practical, as it emphasizes moral rationales and ideals rather than specific instructions for practicing or understanding the Dharma. The *Subhāṣitaya* highlights and celebrates certain Buddhist virtues in a largely impressionistic manner, in which they appear more as symbols than as concepts for elucidation.

> The wish-fulfilling tree of merit, which yields the desirable fruits of heaven and liberation,
> Having the circle of branches, flowers, and buds of generosity, forbearance, and knowledge,
> Endowed with the trunk of virtues and the roots of pure precepts that have been fulfilled,
> Always grows from the water of loving-kindness in the minds of virtuous persons.[80]

Although this verse makes reference to Buddhist ideas, they are linked together poetically in the form of a serial simile around the subject of the mythological "wish-fulfilling tree" of Indic thought. Such a tree, which forms a common motif in Indic literature, illustrates several virtues without explaining them in detail. One simply learns that the development of certain virtues is conducive to merit and the attainment of heavenly rebirth or nirvana.

Elsewhere in *Subhāṣitaya*, Alagiyavanna urges his readers and listeners to listen to the Dharma being preached and to help others. Specifically, he argues that even a small thought made for the benefit of another leads one away from the cycle of rebirth to the eventual attainment of *mokṣa*—described as the "city of liberation."[81] The audience of Alagiyavanna's work is encouraged to do good works for the sake of others, not for their own sakes. The *Subhāṣitaya*, however, gives little direction beyond cultivating a regard for others that would assist the reader or listener in determining how certain practices lead to the attainment of nirvana. The work simply affirms that virtuous persons (*sudanō*) make efforts for others' happiness rather than for their own.[82] In Alagiyavanna's vision, the conventions of the Buddha revolve around correct practice and the adherence to moral principles.

The admonitions found in Alagiyavanna's *Subhāṣitaya*, while consistent with Buddhist teachings such as impermanence, are not always identified as such. This work presents verses containing generalized ethical advice about the benefits of compassion, generosity, and moral discipline, among other kinds of virtues that are not unique to Buddhism. For instance, one learns that persons endowed with compassion are not inclined to do evil deeds while under the influence of wicked persons.[83] Again, those who are generous and satiate the wants of beggars are praised for their knowledge and strength.[84] Those whose minds are steady and pure are not swayed by the false speech of those who are wicked and greedy.[85] Such admonitions contribute to the understanding of the Buddha's *samaya* by drawing on wise sayings that may likewise be embraced and adopted by his audience. In the context of other verses that praise the Triple Gem or "Three Jewels" of the Buddha, Dharma, and Sangha (vv. 1–3), as well as other verses that specifically mention Buddhist notions of merit or liberation, the insertion of universal ethical teachings in *Subhāṣitaya* enhances the utility and value of the Buddha's teachings.

Phrased differently, Alagiyavanna co-opts ethical teachings that he often draws from other Indic texts in order to present a moralistic vision of Buddhism that could appeal to persons seeking practical guidance for living well in a turbulent world. An example of this literary appropriation is seen in the following verse, the message of which is adapted from the *Śṛṅgāra-śataka* of Bhartṛhari,[86]

> If the ascetic who feeds continually on the wind, water, and grass,
> Sees a red water-lily of a woman, he would end his trance.
> If anyone, while feeding on food such as milk, oil, and curd, trains their sense-capacities,
> That one is like the *Maṅdara* Mountain that rises up from the ocean.[87]

On its face, this verse appears to extol the self-discipline of all those who succeed in controlling their senses. This message is consistent with Buddhist teachings on self-restraint, but it is not making a statement that is in any way distinctive to Buddhism and its monastic tradition. Although the identity of the ancient Sanskrit poet Bhartṛhari is far from clear, there is material in *Śṛṅgāra-śataka* that points to his association with Śaivism.[88] The actual religious identity of Bhartṛhari is, however, beside the point for Alagiyavanna, as the verse itself contains precisely the kind of useful, worldly wisdom that the poet wishes to associate with Buddhist ideals.

Alagiyavanna's use of gnomic verse from other sources accomplishes two important aims. First, his translation and adaptation of other Sanskrit,

Tamil, and Pāli sources functions to establish his credentials as a great poet who has a command over a wide body of literature and languages. In this respect, his motivation to convey the meanings of "great books on the study of moral laws" (*puvaḷa nīti sata gata*) in Sinhala for those not versed in other Indic languages signify, at the same time, his exceptional learning and altruism.[89] His erudition is demonstrated simply by being multilingual, an association established in previous centuries by such renowned poets as Śrī Rāhula, who was called the "lord of six languages."[90] Alagiyavanna similarly had a high estimation of his literary skills—in *Subhāṣitaya*, he refers to himself as the "best of poets" (*kiviyara*)—and thus sought to bolster his reputation by drawing on a multilingual corpus of didactic poetry. Likewise, by stating that he is composing *Subhāṣitaya* for the sake of "ordinary beings" who are unfamiliar with Sanskrit, Tamil, and Pāli, Alagiyavanna depicts himself as altruistically seeking to make important pieces of worldly wisdom available to Sinhala speakers. In short, his adaptation of material from *Śṛṅgāra-śataka* and other works is presented as proof of both his erudition and compassion. Such qualities befit a Buddhist author and are consistent with the religion's values.

The second aim for his use of Bhartṛhari and others is connected with his particular vision of Buddhism as a religion. Alagiyavanna's use of a wide range of didactic verse within the context of an identifiably Buddhist work has the effect of recasting the religion more broadly and along distinctively moralistic lines. *Subhāṣitaya* combines verses that praise Buddhist symbols and ideas with other verses that contain universal ethical admonitions. His representation of the Buddha's *samaya* revolves neither around canonical texts nor monastic practice. Instead, the didactic material adapted from various Indic texts is translated and repackaged by Alagiyavanna to supplement traditional Buddhist teachings with verses of worldly wisdom. The effect of these authorial moves is to render the *samaya* of the Buddha into a set of moralistic teachings with worldly applications and otherworldly aims. It is a form of Buddhism that may be practiced by laypersons without much guidance from monks and Buddhist texts, both of which had become relatively scarce in early seventeenth-century Ceilão. Unlike Alagiyavanna's earlier poems, as well as the classical Sinhala poetry from previous centuries, his *Subhāṣitaya* shifts its focus away from the praise of kings, deeds of the Bodhisattva, and explanations of basic Buddhist doctrines. The connoisseurs imagined and shaped by this text are expected to conduct themselves righteously and not just revel in the pleasures to be had by listening to well-composed poetic verse.

Moral concerns do not fully replace aesthetic interests, as Alagiyavanna still employs metaphor and meter to augment the persuasiveness and attractiveness of his verse. However, the text effectively subordinates the experience of poetry to that of cognitive ideas on what it takes to live a moral life. This shift of emphasis from aesthetics to ethics—as seen from Alagiyavanna's *Sävul Sandēśaya* to his *Subhāṣitaya*—evolved in conjunction with the growing marginalization of Sinhala literary culture in the court of Sītāvaka. The massive military campaigns in the latter stages of King Rājasiṃha's rule surely overshadowed the patronage and recognition given to poets. Hints of the displaced privileges once given to poetry and religion can already be glimpsed in Alagiyavanna's *Dahamsoňḍa Kava* and *Kusa Jātaka Kāvya*. The elaborate panegyric verses of *Sävul Sandēśaya* begin to slip away, and we might hypothesize that the poet's position vis-à-vis the royal court had much to do with this change. While comfortably ensconced in a place of power and privilege in Rājasiṃha's court, Alagiyavanna could compose poetry that lingered over aesthetically rich praise of the current king. However, as he found himself removed from this position following the wars and the eventual death of Rājasiṃha, Alagiyavanna was moved to employ poetry to new ends. Rather than simply celebrating power, Alagiyavanna began to criticize it and to change the terms in which one wields it.

Subhāṣitaya casts power less in terms of royal majesty or physical beauty and more in terms of righteousness and moral excellence. For it is within the sphere of morality that a Buddhist poet who found himself outside the centers of power—both Portuguese and Kandyan—in early seventeenth-century Sri Lanka could still make a claim for excellence. If he was no longer part of the traditional culture-power formation that combined literary achievements with the command of kings, Alagiyavanna could at least appeal to the moral teachings of the Buddha and wider Indic thought to create a place from which he could criticize his foes and redefine what is means to be Buddhist. In doing so, the poet actually took some of the first steps to articulate a reflexive Buddhist consciousness for people living in the early modern world. The verses of moral reflection in *Subhāṣitaya* work to interrogate the nature of identity, an effort that Sudipta Kaviraj has likened to engaging in "second order questions about morality."[91] The fact that Alagiyavanna explores notions of morality and religious identity in poetic verse during the same period when the Portuguese were actively expanding their control over the political and religious landscapes in lowland Sri Lanka demonstrates that *Subhāṣitaya* is a testament to a novel use of literature to contest power and to rethink Buddhist identity.

As far as the form of *Subhāṣitaya* is concerned, the adaptation of Indian didactic verse would have lent prestige and persuasion to Alagiyavanna's endeavors as a Buddhist poet to challenge the terms on which truth and morality were being determined during the expansion of Portuguese colonialism in the island. Alagiyavanna's work demonstrates an awareness of morality that is divorced from the power of kings and the supervision of monks. It is morality to which the poet resorts in an attempt to reassert the value of Buddhist teachings in a world in which their authority and privilege are no longer taken for granted. Moral criticism also becomes the basis for contesting powerful agents and institutions that deviated from the traditions of Sinhala Buddhist kingship, which nurtured monks and poets in previous centuries. By the early seventeenth century, however, Portuguese colonialists and missionaries exercised power in lowland Sri Lanka. Alagiyavanna, as a result, turned to composing poetry that critiqued power and defended local institutions over against foreign ones.

As a work that blended traditional literary forms with innovative uses of poetry, *Subhāṣitaya* demonstrates how poetry could be used to accomplish several different ends. Its adaptation of pan-Indic gnomic verses and Sinhala poetic conventions, in theory, reinforced Alagiyavanna's identity as a reputable poet during a time when few others could claim that standing. *Subhāṣitaya* served, in part, as a tool for enhancing the author's prestige and his ability to speak with authority. This could occur despite the fact that *Subhāṣitaya* tones down its aesthetic features and plays up its moral admonitions. In addition, the work stakes particular claims on truth and morality, arguing that its vision of both supersedes all rival systems. In this manner, Alagiyavanna's work constructs a vision of Buddhism as a religion that is grounded in ethical reasoning and moral conduct, something comparable but superior to other religious traditions. Related to this point, *Subhāṣitaya* also articulates ideological refutations of rival political and religious agents that were in ascendance at the time of its composition.

Alagiyavanna's work thus served much like what James C. Scott has termed a "hidden transcript," a form of discourse that resists and contests the claims of various power holders in early seventeenth-century Sri Lanka.[92] It vigorously resisted the official, normative accounts of what constitutes truth and righteousness as disseminated by Portuguese-sponsored missionaries. The degree to which Alagiyavanna was engaging Christian and Hindu rivals when composing *Subhāṣitaya* remains difficult to discern. Yet the conspicuous ethical interests and polemical tone of this work make it stand out among classical Sinhala poems as expressing a novel combination of moral concerns and religious identity through poetry. It would, however, become the last time Alagiyavanna argued for embracing a distinctively Buddhist identity and a moral foundation based on the teachings of the Buddha mixed with pan-Indic maxims. His social position and religious affiliation soon changed and led him to yet another novel use for Sinhala poetry.

6

Identity and Hybridity in The War of Constantino

THE SECOND DECADE of the seventeenth century witnessed an expansion of Portuguese power in Sri Lanka. Aside from the central highland kingdom of Kandy, which resisted periodic incursions by Portuguese-led armies, the bulk of the island's maritime territories, including Jaffna, came under colonial control. As the historian Tikiri Abeyasinghe has noted, there was a close correlation between the growth of the church and the expansion of Portuguese political power, as the latter provided both the impetus and the protection needed for churches to be built and baptisms to be performed.[1] Franciscan and Jesuit missionaries, as well as members from other religious orders, continued their efforts at preaching the Gospel and bringing the local inhabitants to the Holy Faith. The previous chapter illustrated how Alagiyavanna responded to the decline of Sinhala Buddhist kingship in the lowlands by emphasizing morality and a more circumscribed notion of Buddhist identity. This chapter, however, discusses the poetic work called *Kustantīnu Haṭana* (*The War of Constantino*), which represents a dramatically different response to the Portuguese encounter. Dated to around 1619, *Kustantīnu Haṭana* articulates a view that seeks to embrace and extol the resurgent Portuguese presence in the island.

Kustantīnu Haṭana embodies some of the contradictions inherent in early modern Buddhist responses to the disruptive influences of colonial power in Sri Lanka. It employs a familiar poetic style to celebrate the person and acts of a Portuguese captain-general named Constantino de Sá de Noronha (d. 1630), who suppressed a large Sinhala rebellion in 1618 and 1619. It borrows a variety of Indic cultural tropes, praising certain aspects of Catholicism while affirming some Buddhist ideas. The author—likely, Alagiyavanna—articulated hybrid forms of literary and religious expression in *Kustantīnu Haṭana*. This effort, in turn, is indicative of a more nuanced response to colonial power in early modern Sri Lanka. Portuguese kingship and Catholic religiosity are praised in this work, albeit in terms of Sinhala conventions and values rather than those of the colonizer.

The Poet and the Portuguese

As a renowned poet who composed literary works at the request of the Sītāvaka nobility under King Rājasiṃha I, Alagiyavanna was comfortable navigating the spheres of power in a Sinhala Buddhist kingdom. Yet after the king's death in 1593 and the fall of Sītāvaka soon after, Alagiyavanna suddenly found himself without the protection and patronage of a king. Signs of his response to becoming unmoored from the centers of power appear in the cultural criticism and the moralistic turn of his later works. Ultimately, however, the expansion of Portuguese authority and influence would come to interrupt these labors. The political landscape in the second decade of seventeenth-century Sri Lanka was highly unstable and subject to violent revolts and brutal campaigns to eliminate opposition to Portuguese rule. Added to this was the steady growth in converts to Catholicism beginning in the early seventeenth century due to Jesuit activities and the mission of Negrão, the Franciscan.[2] After 1610, for example, the Jesuits began setting up mission stations in the inner hinterlands of the island, which effectively brought more Sinhalas into the church.

Meanwhile, Portuguese interests in conquering the entire island were guided by various colonial strategies to consolidate their control. These strategies included the continuation of policies put in place to spread Christianity and to suppress the practice of Buddhism and Hinduism. This involved, among other things, training at least some missionaries to converse in the Sinhala and Tamil languages, building churches, and encouraging baptisms by rewarding those who became Christian with gifts, favors, and privileges to denote their vassalage to the Portuguese crown.[3] It also involved the destruction of temples and images—described as "idols," as well as preventing new temples to be constructed in areas under Portuguese control.[4] The more destructive acts committed for the sake of propagating the Christian faith did not, however, always have the desired effects. The Jesuit's annual letter of 1617 describes how two Portuguese priests were murdered by fifty Sinhala soldiers and speculates that this act, which is described as "martyrdom," was motivated by the arrest and execution of three Buddhist monks in the previous month and by the hatred for those who convert fellow Sinhalas.[5] Resistance to Christian missionizing was more frequently expressed in the vandalism of churches during the periodic revolts in territories away from the coast. Although Christian conversion was not without controversy or backlash, it remained a priority for the Portuguese during their colonial presence in the island.[6]

Neither the Portuguese-sponsored missions for the *propagação da fé* ("propagation of the Faith") nor the island's resources were the prime factors behind efforts to conquer Sri Lanka in the early seventeenth century. The more salient causes for the Portuguese attempt to gain control of the entire island relate to the role that Sri Lanka might play in the wider context of Portuguese possessions and trading networks in Asia. Jorge Flores has identified four main reasons for the Portuguese designs on conquering Ceilão in the seventeenth century: to defend and expand Asian territories under Portuguese rule, which could make up for the decline in the country's naval power; to respond to the Portuguese fascination with the land-based colonial expansion of Spain in the New World; to impede Dutch efforts to establish a maritime hegemony throughout the Indian Ocean; and to support the Portuguese positions in India that were coming under the threat of an expanding Mughal Empire.[7] Portuguese concerns for maintaining their influence in Asia as a whole led them to abandon their previous policy of guarding their maritime possessions to facilitate trade and adopt a newer policy of territorial acquisition and rule. Additionally, the union of the Portuguese and Spanish crowns under Philip II of Spain after 1580 also supported this new imperial model, one based on exercising direct sovereignty through a Portuguese captain-general, not an indirect suzerainty through a Sinhala vassal king.[8] In practice, this imperial model meant that the Portuguese began building fortifications and asserting their control throughout the lands governed previously by Sītāvaka kings. They also launched several expeditions to conquer the mountain kingdom of Kandy, including smaller raids directed by Azevedo to destroy villages and crops in Kandyan lands.[9]

These efforts to exert Portuguese control over territory by military campaigns and over people's souls by Catholic missions were complemented by other initiatives to strengthen the civil administration of the island and enhance its revenues. Azevedo reorganized the complex system of smaller districts (*kōralēs*) into larger provinces (*disāvas*), each to be ruled by a single official.[10] Meanwhile, particular land grants were made to Portuguese soldiers and colonists, Sinhala converts to Christianity, and Catholic orders operating in the island.[11] Such awards of land were in theory meant to reward and incentivize the efforts toward colonization and conquest by loyal subjects to the Portuguese crown. Some of these lands belonged earlier to Buddhist and Hindu temples but were converted to assist in the support of the Franciscans and Jesuits, as well as the smaller numbers of Dominicans and Augustinians in the island. Other lands were previously owned by the Sinhala king or by other private individuals. The allotment of lands by the Portuguese was important not only as a source of income but also to sustain their political control and to provide for the Portuguese who fought and resided on the island.

The central importance of land under Portuguese colonial control led to initiatives to compile a land register in order to ascertain the owners of specific lands and the revenues that they generated. Once the kingdom of Koṭṭe annexed the lands belonging to Sītāvaka in 1594, efforts to compile a land registration were begun. Following the preparation of a register of royal dues in 1599, a series of *tombos*, or "register of lands," was compiled between 1613 and 1622 for the Portuguese-controlled lands in the Koṭṭe kingdom.[12] This undertaking coincided with the development of direct Portuguese rule over lowland Sri Lanka. Based on native records and the testimonies of local officials, these registers comprised detailed surveys of the lands and resources under Portuguese control. The *tombos* recorded the number and names of villages, the extent of cultivable and cultivated land, the type of crops grown, the average yield per acre, the number of craftsmen in each village, and the customary duties owed to the king.[13] The primary objective of this undertaking was to arrive at a regularized system of taxes that would generate the revenues needed to support and sustain the Portuguese colonial presence in the island.

The *tombos* compiled in Sri Lanka became strategic tools for consolidating Portuguese power, as they largely succeeded in increasing the revenues obtained from the lands under their control. This land policy, furthermore, was intricately related to another colonial strategy, that of employing native elites to serve the Portuguese crown. With an extensive maritime hegemony over much of Asian waters and ports, not to mention sites in Africa and the Americas, the Portuguese were dependent on native manpower to supplement the relatively limited number of men who could govern and protect their interests abroad.[14] In Ceilão, this resulted in the need to recruit native soldiers, or *lascarins*, to fight under Portuguese captains to advance their colonial interests. The efforts to compile the *tombos* also depended heavily on the assistance of local Sinhala officials. Local records written in Sinhala on dried palm leaves would have been unintelligible to Portuguese revenue officials, who could not have pursued their work without Sinhala assistants to collect and evaluate the verbal testimonies of local chieftains.

Notably, one of the Sinhala assistants mentioned in parts of the Portuguese *tombos* was Alagiyavanna, who is named and cited in the *tombo* compiled in 1614 as "Dom Jheronimo Aliguiavan Mutiar *velho* (i.e. retired) who was serving the Tombo, aged 62, son of the late Yscali Pandita Ralla (correctly Hissalle Dharma dvaja Pandita rala)."[15] It is apparent that sometime around 1612 Alagiyavanna converted to Christianity and took employment under the Portuguese *vedor da fazenda*, or "revenue official," António Vaz Freire. His baptismal name was given after the captain-general Dom Jerónimo de Azevedo, before he left Ceilão in December of 1612 for Goa. He is also cited by name for assisting with a later *tombo* produced in 1622 under the *vedor* Miguel Pinheiro Ravasco.[16] This is, incidentally, the last mention of Alagiyavanna in the extent historical sources.

Alagiyavanna's conversion to Christianity and service to the Portuguese appears as a striking, but not necessarily surprising, historical fact. His strident defense of Buddhism in the *Subhāṣitaya* need not have prevented him from adopting a new religious identity once Portuguese authority and missions overtook the old socioreligious order. Elsewhere in the *Estado da Índia*, Portuguese colonialists promoted conversion as a strategy to consolidate their political control over the natives, awarding converts with certain gifts and privileges while punishing those who refused to become Christian.[17] The same method was applied in Sri Lanka, where offices, lands, and protection were offered to Christian converts.[18] Some early modern Sinhala sources specifically condemned this practice. *Rājāvaliya* (*Lineage of Kings*), a chronicle composed around the late seventeenth century, portrays the conversion of Sinhala Buddhists to Catholicism in opportunistic terms. It claims that many women of "low birth" consorted with Portuguese men and converted to Christianity out of greed for wealth.[19] Another Buddhist text from the period depicts Buddhist converts to Christianity in a similar fashion: "The infamous *Parangis*, the infidels, the impious ones . . . rich in cunning, endeavored by gifts of money and the like to get their creed adopted by others, led a life without reverence for the doctrine [of the Buddha]."[20] These Buddhist representations of Christian missions underscore the presumption that conversion was always motivated by bribery and accepted only by Sinhalas for material gain.

Not surprisingly, Christian missionaries did not agree with this cynical assessment. For those who believed in the transformative power of the Word of God and of sincere Christian faith, the conversion of the "gentiles" or "infidels" could only be expected when they were made to encounter what the Portuguese believed was the superior and true faith. Nevertheless, the missionaries recognized that some newly converted Christians were insincere in their faith, and they also noted obstacles in the form of "tyrant kings," non-Christian "priests," and even the devil, who were all thought to prevent more native inhabitants from accepting Christianity. As a rule, conversion was more alluring to those among the colonized who sought to ascend the new colonial hierarchies established by the Portuguese in their overseas territories.[21] When Christian conversion clearly resulted in enhanced social status and economic benefit, people from all levels of the local social order had strong incentives to become Christian. Alagiyavanna, the old court poet and landowner who exercised influence under the previous culture-power formation, became an excellent candidate for conversion. Ângela Barreto Xavier's remarks on how the local populations in sixteenth-century Goa often converted pragmatically apply equally to Sinhala Buddhists in sixteenth- and seventeenth-century Sri Lanka. Like in Goa, Sri Lanka witnessed the conversion of people from lower social groups who sought to break from the caste-based social order, the middle groups who sought new privileges to raise their standing, and the upper groups to retain their social supremacy.[22]

Deprived of his place and influence in the defunct Sītāvaka court, Alagiyavanna appears to have eventually resigned himself to regain his social standing and privilege under Portuguese rulers. The poet and former magistrate who had been removed from circles of power since the death of King Rājasiṃha I accepted a position working for Vaz Freire, the *vedor* who had arrived in late 1609 or early 1610 to administer the island's revenues. Another Portuguese source, which survives in a Dutch translation, names Alagiyavanna among a group of local officials who swore an oath on the Bible to make truthful statements for the purpose of collecting information on the various lands under Portuguese control for the *tombo*.[23] His conversion and subsequent oath of service under the colonial rulers is a striking example of how some Sinhala Buddhists eventually came to embrace the new religious and political orders in Ceilão. The adoption of a new religious identity, a new name, and a new appointment suggests that Alagiyavanna interiorized the dominant colonial narrative to pursue his aspirations for status and renewed influence within a new political order.[24]

His conversion and service under the Portuguese was evidently a celebrated event, since an account of it was circulated later in the seventeenth century by the French Protestant Jean-Baptiste Tavernier, who travelled in India and briefly visited Galle, Sri Lanka, in 1648. Tavernier's account of Alagiyavanna's conversion indicates something of the importance given to this event by the Portuguese Jesuits. His narrative below was likely based on reports that he heard from Jesuits in Goa some twenty years after the poet's death.[25]

> [A] very accomplished man and good native philosopher, named Alegamma Motiar, as one might say master of philosophers, after having conversed some time with the Jesuit Fathers and other priests of Colombo, was inspired to become a Christian. With this object he went to see the Jesuit Fathers, and told them that he desired to be instructed in the Christian faith, but he inquired what Jesus Christ had done and left in writing. He set himself then to read the New Testament with so much attention and ardor that in less than six months there was not a passage which he could not recite, for he had acquired Latin very thoroughly. After having been well instructed, he told the Fathers that he wished to receive holy baptism, that he saw that their religion was the only good and true one, and such as Jesus Christ had taught, but what astonished him was, that they did not follow Christ's example, because, according to the Gospel, he never took money from anyone, while they, on the contrary, took it from everyone and neither baptized nor buried anyone without it. This did not prevent him from being baptized and from working for the conversion of the idolaters afterwards.[26]

Tavernier's praise of Alagiyavanna as a prized native convert contains more than a trace of the French Protestant's disdain for the work of the Jesuits in Sri Lanka. To the extent that his account is accurate, Alagiyavanna appears as an intelligent, yet critical, convert to Christianity. As an educated writer whose reputation was apparently known even to the missionaries, Alagiyavanna's decision to embrace the Catholic faith marked a clear triumph for the Jesuits, who otherwise found Sri Lanka to be a difficult mission field.

Like other members of Sinhala Buddhist society who converted to Christianity after their lands came under direct Portuguese rule, Alagiyavanna surely recognized substantial benefits in embracing the new faith.[27] His conversion would have eased his way into a position within the colonial administration, and it would have helped to ensure that he would retain something of his lands and former status. As a new convert and employee of the Portuguese colonial apparatus in the early seventeenth century, Alagiyavanna personified what Vicente Rafael describes as the two registers in which native elites could move. Alagiyavanna submitted to the external demands of the colonizers while at the same time claimed a privileged position within his community.[28] Conversion allowed Alagiyavanna to regain influence within local spheres of power and to maintain his position as a respected landowner with access to those who ruled. Becoming a Christian and working for the Portuguese effectively reduced the distance between him and the colonizers, which gave rise to certain opportunities as well as tensions in his dealings with the Portuguese.[29] The reliance of the *vedor* on Alagiyavanna's knowledge and linguistic skills meant that the poet, as one of a number of local assistants, offered invaluable information concerning the ownership and revenues of land that came under the rule of the Portuguese, information necessary for collecting taxes.[30]

Alagiyavanna's success in regaining some measure of status and influence within the new ruling order also led him to take advantage of his position and register a complaint about a case of mistreatment at Portuguese hands. Even earlier the captain-general Azevedo had set up a tribunal of nobles to hear suits presented by the natives and whose decisions were ultimately subject to his approval.[31] Procedures to provide the inhabitants of the island with some recourse to justice were limited by the imperial nature of Portuguese rule. However, they were also made necessary by that same imperialist rule, as the power placed in the hands of Portuguese officials was liable to be misused for personal gain at the expense of the Sinhalas. Much of these complaints were connected to the abuses committed by Portuguese soldiers and settlers on local villagers, a fact regrettably expressed by the late seventeenth-century chronicler Fernão de Queyroz.[32] Azevedo was also criticized by his Portuguese contemporaries (and later generations of Sinhalas) for his harsh, repressive tactics for overcoming Sinhala opposition to direct colonial rule.[33] Although particular examples may have been exaggerated, the frequent criticism of Portuguese cruelties, even by some Portuguese writers, suggests that violent and repressive acts were not uncommon.

Alagiyavanna's cause for complaint was based on having been stripped of his lands and his title by the captain-general Nuno Alvares Pereira, who governed Ceilão between 1616 and 1618. During his short tenure in the island, Pereira witnessed a number of large-scale rebellions under the command of Sinhala leaders called Nikapiṭiya Banḍāra and Kuruviṭa Rāla. These rebels, respectively, challenged the power and authority of Portuguese rule, and Pereira grew distrustful of all Sinhalese leaders.[34] Subsequently, for reasons we can only guess, Pereira dismissed Alagiyavanna from service and seized some of the lands that he possessed. Sometime shortly after Pereira was recalled from Ceilão in 1618, Alagiyavanna wrote a formal appeal to King Philip III of Portugal asking for his title and lands to be restored to him. Evidence for this lies in a record of the king's written response to the viceroy in Goa on this matter:

> Count, viceroy, and friend—I, the king, send to you much greetings as one of whom I am fond. On behalf of Dom Jeronimo de Aliguiamana, *motiar* of the *tombo* of the lands and villages of the island of Ceilão, a petition has been made to me in which he asks for the title of *mutiar* of my treasury and that the factory [*o feitor*] of Columbo continues for him the allowance and maintenance expenses that the General and *vedor* of the Treasury had arranged for him, and that portions of the villages and lands that were taken from him by Dom Nuno Alvrez Pereira, while he was General of Ceilão, be reinstated to him, as confirmed by the chamber and council of villages [*mesa e junta das aldeas*]. And seeing this claim of his, I thought to dispatch it to you, charging you to examine it and advise me about what you recommend by the list of rulings. Written in Lisbon on March 24, 1620.[35]

Alagiyavanna's appeal to the Portuguese king is a striking indication of how much he had internalized his identity as a colonial subject. By 1618, Alagiyavanna had completed several years of service on the *tombo* as a Christian under the Portuguese *vedor*. In conjunction with his elite background and his reputation as a poet, Alagiyavanna's identity as a local official led him to seek assistance at the highest levels to have his position, salary, and lands restored. Like other colonial subjects who converted and served the Portuguese, he apparently believed that his new status could erase at least some of the distance between colonizer and colonized.[36] He had also apparently internalized his new identity and felt free to bring his grievances directly to the king. Colonial petitions lodged by local subjects exemplify a means of expressing dissent against the actions of the colonizer, and yet they also reinforced the latter's authority and control over local populations.[37] Thus, Alagiyavanna appears simultaneously emboldened but powerless; he could take his complaints to the king but was unable to remedy by himself the injustices done to him.

In the meantime, while Alagiyavanna waited for a response, the Portuguese viceroy appointed a new captain-general, Constantino de Sá de Noronha, to assume control of the island in the midst of native rebellions and an unyielding Sinhala kingdom in Kandy. As a young man 33 years old, Sá de Noronha arrived in Sri Lanka with the aim of achieving peace in the lowlands, which he would achieve by building forts, subduing uprisings, restructuring the Portuguese military apparatus, and gaining the confidence of the Sinhala chiefs of the thousands of native soldiers who fought alongside the Portuguese forces.[38] The early successes of his military endeavors were surely helped by his efforts to win the support of the Sinhalas under his rule. Sá de Noronha believed that kind and just treatment would help to reconcile the Sinhalas to Portuguese rule, as illustrated by his role in changing the land policy to allow land grants given to Sinhala subjects to extend beyond the lifetime of the grantee so as to allow his heirs to retain the property after his death.[39] Although we have no clear evidence showing Sá de Noronha restoring Alagiyavanna's lands, it is not unreasonable to hypothesize that he did.[40]

However, as much as Sá de Noronha tried to gain the favor of the Sinhalas under his rule, he also pursued a strategy to promote Catholic conversions in Ceilão, which entailed an increase in church building and missionary activity in the 1620s.[41] Sá de Noronha's apparent commitment to the faith and to its role in producing loyal subjects to the Portuguese crown also led him to continue the policies of suppressing native religious institutions. During his two terms as captain-general in Ceilão (1618–1621 and 1623--1630), Sá de Noronha endeavored to desecrate Buddhist and Hindu temples to suppress the "idolatry" of the natives.[42] Such acts, along with the demands he made on local inhabitants to construct fortifications and his inability to halt the abuses of Portuguese soldiers and settlers, eventually caused him to fail to win the loyalty of the local population.[43]

Nevertheless, Sá de Noronha's initial foray into pacifying the rebellion in the lowlands between 1618 and 1619 was largely successful. A revolt led by the former Sinhala Catholic António Barreto, who had previously fought on the side of the Portuguese, had threatened not only the Portuguese garrisons but also the kingdom of Kandy. Barreto, who was also called Kuruviṭa Rāla for his ascension to a leadership position in the Kuruviṭa region, led a revolt against the Portuguese and sought to establish as king of Sri Lanka a man named Māyādunnē who claimed to be a descendent of the Sītāvaka royal family. Sá de Noronha led a small force of Portuguese soldiers bolstered by native *lascarins* and drew out Barreto's forces in an ambush at the village of Lellopiṭiya. Barreto and his chiefs were captured, and many of the rebels were slain. Sá de Noronha's arrival in Sri Lanka and his successful battle against Barreto's rebel force make up the major events in what was likely Alagiyavanna's final poem—*Kustantīnu Haṭana*. Sá de Noronha was later recalled from Ceilão in 1621, after the new governor of the *Estado da Índia* installed his own son as *capitão-geral* in the island. The latter's ineptitude, however, led the viceroy to reinstate Sá de Noronha to his position in Ceilão in 1623.[44] The captain-general would then govern the island with the limited resources afforded by Goa and Lisbon until 1630, when he was killed by Sinhala forces at the Battle of Randenivela.

The Identity and Sincerity of the Author

The *Kustantīnu Haṭana* consists of approximately 189 quatrains that describe in Sinhala *eḷu* the great qualities and deeds of the Portuguese captain-general Constantino de Sá de Noronha. Because the work culminates in the victory of the Portuguese forces over Sinhala rebels led by António Barreto in late 1618 or early 1619 but makes no mention of Barreto's death in 1620, it seems clear that it was composed sometime around 1619.[45] As such, the *Kustantīnu Haṭana* represents the second known Sinhala war poem (*haṭana*) after the *Sītāvaka Haṭana* (*The War of Sītāvaka*), which was composed in 1585 by a Buddhist layman named Alahapperuma Mudali. Alahapperuma appears to have been an army officer who fought for King Māyādunnē and who claimed to be unfamiliar with high Sinhala or Pāli literature.[46] This work and subsequent *haṭan kavi* works such as *Kustantīnu Haṭana* share similar features. The genre appears in the turbulent colonial era of Sri Lankan history and functions chiefly to describe battles and to praise heroic figures.[47] Although written with varying levels of literary skill, the Sinhala war poems typically emulate aspects of panegyric *praśasti* verse on the one hand and the journeys through local landscapes that are characteristic of *sandēśa* poetry on the other. Kings and other great men are extolled for their martial prowess and their masculine virility, which is often indicated by associations with erotically charged women. War poems often replicate the flowery praise found in several examples of earlier Sinhala verse (notably the fifteenth-century

Pärakumbā Sirita), but they distinguish themselves by focusing on heroic and sometimes violent accounts of war.

The focus of Sinhala *haṭan kavi* on the personification and expression of power means that such works were composed close to the spheres of rulers. From a practical perspective, it is likely that *haṭan* poems were written and recited to describe to the king and his ministers what took place in battles and to glorify the deeds of the victors.[48] War poetry could also serve a more grandiose purpose, namely the renewal of kingship and to render the king more potent and like the gods to whom he was regularly compared in such texts.[49] The subject of emphasis marks a key difference between *haṭan kavi* and *praśasti kavi* in Sinhala literature. The latter form of poetry typically strings together highly embellished verses to praise the qualities and accomplishments of kings, extolling battles won without actually recounting them.[50] War poems, in contrast, incorporate eulogistic verses into detailed accounts of battles that are fought. They thus serve to generate the classical poetic sentiments (*rasas*) of disgust and fear in their accounts of the ferocity of fighting and the severed heads and mutilated bodies that are its results. A related characteristic is the frequent reference made to what Michael Roberts has described in terms of dichotomized, collective identities of Sinhalas versus a foreign and menacing other.[51] In numerous cases, Sinhala war poems such as *Sītāvaka Haṭana*, *Paraṅgi Haṭana* (*The War with the Portuguese*) and *Mahā Haṭana* (*The Great War*) portray Portuguese soldiers in unflattering terms as immoral, bloodthirsty, and even demonic beings opposed to the heroic Sinhala king and his army.

Kustantīnu Haṭana, however, is different in many ways from other Sinhala war poems. It stands out for celebrating not a Sinhala king but rather a Portuguese commander. Consistent with its partiality to the colonizers, the work also expresses distinctly Christian sentiments, starting with its opening invocatory verses that honor the Christian Trinity, Jesus Christ, and the Virgin Mary in place of the Three Jewels of Buddhism—Buddha, Dharma, and Sangha—that are typically saluted at the start of Sri Lankan Buddhist texts.

> I venerate with reverence the one God who is of three kinds,
> Namely the Father, Son, and Spirit,
> Who exists without expression and division
> Like the word, the letter, and the meaning.
> I venerate the noble lord Jesus Christ,

> Who is a treasure full with the virtue of loving-kindness,
> And who bestowed the lotuses of his resplendent feet,
> To the heads of the beings of the entire world.
> I venerate with devotion the noble lord who issued forth,
> From the womb of the Virgin Mary,
> In the manner of the fiery flames that issue forth
> From the sunlight stone.[52]

Along with the Christian figures for whom the work shows reverence and respect, *Kustantīnu Haṭana* also employs a more developed literary sensibility compared to other Sinhala war poems. For instance, the work displays the learned "great" tradition of Sinhala verse compared to the more simple, folk style (or "little" tradition) of the *Sītāvaka Haṭana*.[53] It also makes good use of classical poetic conventions, even while describing the events and scenes of the battlefield.[54]

It is the peculiarity of *Kustantīnu Haṭana* that raises questions about its authorship. The name of the author is not mentioned in the work, and his identity has been a point of speculation and contention in the modern study of Sinhala literature. Starting in 1885, on discovering a palm leaf manuscript of the little-known text, Luis de Zoysa concluded that the author of *Kustantīnu Haṭana* must have been a Portuguese Catholic because he venerates the Christian Trinity.[55] However, the improbability of a Portuguese author writing in a fairly accomplished style of Sinhala *eḷu* poetry rendered such a theory obsolete. Then, in 1894, F. W. de Silva asserted that it was the work of a Sinhala Christian who studied and was indebted to the work of Alagiyavanna for several of the ideas it contained.[56] This attribution was more acceptable and led later scholars to explore the connection between this work and other works by Alagiyavanna. S. G. Perera, a Sinhala Jesuit priest, began in 1923 to amass evidence to demonstrate that the author of *Kustantīnu Haṭana* was Alagiyavanna.[57] Perera presented his case in detail for Alagiyavanna's authorship in his 1932 critical edition and translation of the text. He highlighted numerous instances in which *Kustantīnu Haṭana* shares similar vocabulary, peculiar forms and expressions, and verse constructions with Alagiyavanna's *Sävul Sandēśaya, Dahamsoňḍa Kava, Kusa Jātaka Kāvya,* and *Subhāṣitaya*.[58] In presenting this case, Perera offered ample evidence showing a striking coherence between *Kustantīnu Haṭana* and Alagiyavanna's other works.

Scholarly opinions over the author's identity have varied, despite the extensive similarities noted by Perera. Martin Wickremasinghe affirmed

Alagiyavanna as the author based largely on the poem's allegedly genuine expression of Christian sentiments and what is known about his conversion to Catholicism.[59] Also agreeing with Perera was P. B. Sannasgala, who asserted that because of the closeness of *Kustantīnu Haṭana* to Alagiyavanna's other works, one may deduce that it is a text composed by the same poet.[60] Yet there are other Sinhala scholars who remain unconvinced about this identification. For instance, C. E. Godakumbura argues that the attribution of Alagiyavanna as the author of *Kustantīnu Haṭana* is based "only on the slender evidence of the similarity of some of the lines with those of this well-known poet" and points out that many later poets imitated Alagiyavanna as well.[61] K. H. de Silva also raised doubts because Alagiyavanna's other works mention his name and boast of his reputation, but the fact that the author does not reveal himself in *Kustantīnu Haṭana* prevents de Silva from concluding that it was the poet's work based on the use of some similar words.[62] Likewise, A. V. Suraweera argues that the questions surrounding the unidentified author of the work together with the penchant for Sītāvaka-period authors to imitate the works of others give us reason to be skeptical that *Kustantīnu Haṭana* was composed by Alagiyavanna.[63]

One of the main reasons for this debate over the author's identity is the fact that this work expresses Christian ideas. The question of identity is closely linked to the question of the sincerity of the Christian sentiments expressed by the author. For literary critics, it is not just a matter of whether Alagiyavanna wrote *Kustantīnu Haṭana* or not. For those who think that he did, there is also a range of views on whether he meant what he wrote about Christianity and the Portuguese. This debate about the author's sincerity is a subject that resonates in the modern, postcolonial world. As Webb Keane has discussed in his study of Calvinist missions in the Indonesian island of Sumba, Dutch missionaries privileged the question of sincerity when assessing the religious practices and beliefs of animistic natives. The faith and beliefs of individuals are seen to stand apart from the material goods they possess and the actions they perform.[64] Protestant discourse effects a separation between immaterial beliefs and material, cultural forms of a religion, making it possible to interrogate the "sincerity" behind all outward religious expressions. This move, reflecting what Keane calls the "moral narrative of modernity," constitutes what has become a worldwide project that values individual agency and inwardness over the rote performance of tradition and the self over its material and social entanglements.[65] It is consonant with what Talal Asad describes as a "modern, privatized Christian" conception of religion that identifies belief as a "verbalizable inner condition of true religion."[66]

This distinction between inner feelings and outer expressions is what allows the question of whether Alagiyavanna was sincere in his Christian faith to be asked in the first place. It presumes the modernist idea that the views and values of an author are illustrated in one's writing and that such views and values hold the key in unlocking and understanding a given text. Thus, for Martin Wickramasinghe, the *Kustantīnu Haṭana* can "bear the stamp of genuineness" due to the Christian sentiments expressed therein.[67] While W.L.A. Don Peter can similarly contend that "Christian sentiments have been incorporated in it and it unmistakably reflects the Christian faith of the author."[68] In a further defense of Alagiyavanna's authorship and sincerity in *Kustantīnu Haṭana*, M. E. Fernando explains away the appearance of Indic religious imagery in the work as simply belonging to poetic tradition and reaffirms that the Catholic author did not really believe in them.[69] All of these views assert a clear distinction between the author's views and his words.

However, the gulf posited to exist between inner sentiments and outer expressions allows other critics to argue that Alagiyavanna was not sincere in his Christian faith. Godakumbura, for example, suggests that the author sings the praises of the Portuguese to "find his bread by means of his verses."[70] This view that the author, whether Alagiyavanna or not, composed *Kustantīnu Haṭana* for personal gain from the Portuguese rulers, that he and many other Sinhala converts were only Christian in name, having engaged in Christian acts under Portuguese eyes but returning to worship in their temples outside Portuguese-controlled cities, is one that is shared by several contemporary Sinhala academics.[71] Moreover, the assumption that Alagiyavanna converted out of convenience and for self-preservation is consistent with what several of his living, Buddhist descendants also claim.[72]

In regard to the authorship question, Alagiyavanna ought to be posited as the author of *Kustantīnu Haṭana*. The similarities between the text and the poet's other works are strong enough to affirm a direct relationship. Meanwhile, the suggestion that the author was a different individual who made a close study of Alagiyavanna's works seems unnecessarily convoluted and improbable given that copies of these texts were likely few and hard to come by in the early seventeenth century under Portuguese rule. There are also no other candidates for notable Sinhala poets who shared close connections with Portuguese authorities at this time. The author of this work clearly shared certain characteristics and interests—namely, poetic skills, the knowledge of other Sinhala poems, and a dependence on Portuguese rulers—that Alagiyavanna would have also possessed. It is reasonable to treat the work as composed by Alagiyavanna, because it speaks directly to the views and experience of someone like him, namely a Sinhala Buddhist poet turned Catholic subject of Portuguese rule.

The absence of any self-reference to the author is somewhat puzzling and may be explained by the fact that Alagiyavanna was no longer writing for noble connoisseurs of Sinhala poetry and thus no longer expected to win fame through the quality of his poetry.[73] In the eyes of colonial officials like Sá de Noronha, merely the composing of *Kustantīnu Haṭana* would have been more useful and noteworthy than any aesthetic judgments that could be made about the work. The formal praise of the Portuguese served a performative function to signal loyalty and win favor, objectives that were not dependent on the recognition of poetic excellence by the ruling authorities of the time. As such, this work may have been written more as a symbolic gesture then as a text to be publicly recited in a courtly setting.

The questions surrounding the authenticity of Alagiyavanna's conversion may also be set aside since they are usually framed in terms of modern notions of exclusive beliefs and adherence to distinct religious traditions. In the modern, postcolonial age of conversion controversies and clearly delineated world religions, we usually expect individuals to adhere either to Buddhism or Christianity.[74] Scholars of Sinhala literature, both Buddhist and Christian, have likewise submitted their claims either to debunk or legitimize the authenticity of Alagiyavanna's conversion in order to render the poet either Christian or Buddhist, which would augment the standing of each community in modern Sri Lanka. Exclusive demands were also placed on religious identity by Portuguese missionaries in early modern Sri Lanka. These missionaries expected conversion to bring about a total transformation of the individual, a creation of a new identity that split from any association with one's past, indigenous practice.[75] Yet there is evidence in Portuguese sources that many Sinhalas did not interpret conversion to mean the complete rejection of their previous religious commitments. Writers such as Queyroz frequently complained about the "inconstant" and "untrustworthy" Sinhalas who "make religion a matter of convenience," and receive the Christian faith sincerely or in pretense, only to discard it when the occasion arose to try to throw off Portuguese domination.[76] Queyroz also disparaged the Sinhalas for being "notoriously obstinate" about holding on to the religion of their ancestors, believing that "one can go to Heaven by many ways" and preferring to embrace more than one faith.[77] More generally, Portuguese churchmen were concerned to ascertain whether conversions were genuine, as they recognized that one's inner faith was not necessarily demonstrated by external acts of participation in public rituals but could still be cancelled by the persistence of ancient customs among new converts.[78]

Scholars, however, are not obligated to discern an individual's genuine religious sentiments and identity like the missionaries of previous eras. Instead, the contents of *Kustantīnu Haṭana* invite consideration of a hybrid religiosity expressed by the author. Hybridity has become a popular concept among scholars influenced by postcolonial theory. Colonized peoples, it has been shown, have often retained some ability to respond to the evangelizing and so-called civilizing efforts of European powers by adapting the religions, cultures, and languages of the colonizers to their local, indigenous practices and traditions. Those who are subaltern, marginalized or disempowered by colonial agents, may still retain some agency in the face of their systematic subordination.[79] Scholars who seek to recover some evidence of resistance to colonial powers can find it in examples of hybrid cultural forms that challenge the purity and superiority of hegemonic cultures introduced from without and "hidden transcripts" that secretly express defiance to domination underneath the public mask of apparent, if grudging, consent.[80] In the case of early modern Sri Lanka, *Kustantīnu Haṭana* may be viewed as an example of religious and cultural hybridity—a literary work that adapts elements of Portuguese hegemony into a local cultural frame and that effectively celebrates the culture of the colonizer while validating the Buddhist tradition.

The concept of hybridity proves useful in analyzing *Kustantīnu Haṭana*, because it helps to account for elements of the work associated with, alternatively, Portuguese or Sinhala concerns. Previous scholars have dismissed the author's retention of Indic religious features as simply the formal adherence to poetic conventions or as examples of the "harmonization" of authentic Christian sentiments with quaint "mythological" native traditions.[81] Such theories may reinforce the author's Christian identity but do little to explicate the contents of the text. For those such as the seventeenth-century French missionary Tavernier, it is necessary to portray Alagiyavanna as a sincere convert to demonstrate the success of the missions to the island. Giving credence to the Buddhist elements of the text could therefore undermine the image of Alagiyavanna as promoted by the missionaries, that of a sincere convert who "worked for the conversion of the idolators" following his own baptism.[82] Yet, as noted elsewhere among historians of conversion, the actual conversions to Christianity were frequently incomplete processes, through which intended messages often failed to be transmitted and fundamental transformations of individuals often failed to be accomplished.[83] The dramatic conversion of an individual from one discrete religious identity to another was much less common than what many ecclesiastical writers have claimed.

Following Bhabha, those hybrid Buddhist elements can be read as implicitly challenging the vision of colonial authority and its concomitant rejection of local religion and culture.[84] To the extent that they understood the local Buddhist tradition, Portuguese missionaries and colonial agents tended to dismiss the religion as comprising "fables and nonsense" (*fabulas e disparates*) linked to the influences of the devil.[85] Buddhist monks could likewise be described as "teachers of cruelty" (*mestres da maldade*) whose ignorance did not prevent them from arrogantly holding fast to their mistaken opinions.[86] Meanwhile, Buddhists were often called "infidels" (*infiéis*) and "gentiles" (*gentios*) who were blamed and pitied for their adherence to a false doctrine out of blindness and ignorance. Queyroz also extended to the Sinhalas a strikingly backhanded compliment, "Let Europeans realize that these oriental peoples are not barbarians, except in their religion."[87] Such examples of disparaging comments from sixteenth- and seventeenth-century Portuguese observers show that any attempt to preserve aspects of Buddhist thought or Indic religious imagery could hardly have been met with approval by the Portuguese. The hybrid religious vision of *Kustantīnu Haṭana* thus runs counter to the differences and dichotomies developed by the Portuguese to juxtapose the alleged falsehoods and superstitions of the native Buddhist religion against what they considered to be the supreme truths and efficacious rites of the Christian faith. Compared to the clear-cut distinctions drawn by the Portuguese, the adaptation of Christian ideals to the cultural matrix of Sinhala Buddhist literature subtly yet effectively displaced the norms and presumptions of the colonizer.

Sinhala Visions of Portuguese Power

Kustantīnu Haṭana recognizes and responds to notions of power in Portuguese colonialism and Sinhala literary culture, although not in identical ways. Power in the Portuguese sphere is depicted as primarily institutional in the form of authorities that exercised influence over Alagiyavanna's life and control over the lands that he owned and inhabited. Meanwhile, power in the Sinhala sphere appears more abstract and ideological, found in the skills displayed by authors who exercised control over a textual corpus and the poetic conventions needed to compose works of literature. *Kustantīnu Haṭana* makes interventions in both spheres, extending older traditions of Sinhala poetry to celebrate Portuguese leaders at home and abroad. The work transforms Constantino de Sá de Noronha into a kingly, quasidivine figure akin to previous Buddhist rulers who were likewise celebrated in verse. "Righteous Lord" (*himi dähäm-in*), "Lord of Men" (*naraniňdu*), and "king" (*raju*) are among the titles with which *Kustantīnu Haṭana* describes and praises the captain-general.[88] He is repeatedly compared to South Asian figures of divine kingship such as Śakra and Viṣṇu. Elsewhere in the work, he is said to possess glory, splendor, and an extensive retinue, which are just a few of the traditional attributes of kingship found in Sinhala poetry.

The eulogistic verse used in praise of Sá de Noronha is related to the literary form of the *praśasti* poem, which extols certain great men in expressive verse. The use of poetry to describe and enhance the fame of kings has a long history in South Asian literary cultures, as seen in the numerous examples of acclaim and hyperbole used to extol kings in panegyric verses composed in Sanskrit, Tamil, and other Indic languages.[89] Among Sinhala works, *Pärakumbā Sirita* incorporates grandiose language and richly metaphorical images to celebrate the power and virtue of the fifteenth-century Buddhist king Parākramabāhu VI. Praise for the king serves to enhance his fame, which in theory augments his power and strengthens his rule.

> Like an elephant in rut, stomping the banana grove of other kings who have arrogantly entered into battle,
> Filled with fame like the kings Raghu and Rāma, and like the moonlight that has descended from the full moon,
> Like the God of Love, who is collyrium to the eyes of young women, with a physical form as if made from a mass of gold,
> May you, King Päräkum, the highest in merit, exist with a happy mind, enjoying diverse kinds of wealth![90]

This verse from *Pärakumbā Sirita* skillfully illustrates how a *praśasti* poem combines the virtues of might, fame, beauty, merit, and wealth in a single, celebrated figure. This example is instructive for an analysis of *Kustantīnu Haṭana*, because it, too, praises similar virtues in Sá de Noronha, who is transformed from a commander of the Portuguese to a ruler modeled after Sinhala Buddhist kingship.

If *Kustantīnu Haṭana* embodies some of the aims of *praśasti* poetry in describing and enhancing royal power, then it may be read as constructing a similar vision of power in Sinhala verse. The eulogies of Sá de Noronha and some other Portuguese figures imitate those composed about Sinhala kings in Alagiyavanna's *Sävul Sandēśaya* and in earlier works composed by others. One finds many of the same virtues of might, fame, beauty, merit, and wealth, which are conceptually linked in Buddhist thought, attributed here to Portuguese leaders.[91] Thus, after setting the backdrop of the rebellion led by António Barreto, the narrator depicts the Portuguese viceroy in Goa, inviting and praising Sá de Noronha before sending him off to Ceilão to subdue the rebels.

> If one considered your strength,
> The tall Meru Mountain is like an anthill.
> The great ocean is like a pond.
> And this Dambadiva [i.e., India] is like a courtyard for your door.
> If one were to compare you with something else,
> You are like the Meru Mountain to the ocean of battle.
> And a very strong diamond rampart,
> Protecting our many great armies.[92]

Here, Alagiyavanna attempts to refashion Sá de Noronha into a powerful native king. He is described and attributed with praiseworthy characteristics that are best recalled, from the author's perspective, in rich, expressive verse. Obviously, the actual Portuguese viceroy—Dom João Coutinho (r. 1617–1619)—would never use Sinhala *eḷu* and the symbol of Mount Meru, the axis of the traditional Indic cosmology, to praise the newly appointed captain-general. Yet, for an author such as Alagiyavanna, the use of such language is appropriate, even necessary, to honor the Portuguese ruler of the island.

One finds in *Kustantīnu Haṭana* numerous verses in which de Sá and other Portuguese leaders are praised in terms of the language and values of classical Sinhala poetry. Similar to the eulogies of masculine authority in *Sävul Sandēśaya*, this later work inserts praise for the captain-general's power and beauty throughout.

> Our distinctive noble Lord,
> Named Kustantinu da Sā,

Who is endowed with strength and fury,
Is like the sun in terms of his glory and command.[93]

The comparison of Sá de Noronha with the brilliance of the sun allows the poet to use a familiar, natural image to highlight the former's virtues and, by extension, his fitness to rule Sri Lanka. By employing this poetic image, the narrator establishes an aesthetically suggestive association between Sá de Noronha and the sun, which is used to confer the superlative characteristics of the latter on the Portuguese commander. Several other verses serve to illustrate and enhance his power by describing how he takes up weapons of war. Reminiscent of how King Rājasiṃha is portrayed grasping and striking with his sword in *Sävul Sandēśaya*, Sá de Noronha is depicted in *Kustantīnu Haṭana* as taking up a golden sword, a bright dagger, and a staff that usher enemy kings to their deaths.[94] By skillfully brandishing numerous weapons, Sá de Noronha appears to have mastered the arts of war like many praiseworthy kings in Indic literature.

The expertise in handling weapons is but one indicator of the power Sá de Noronha commands. Alagiyavanna also employs poetic conventions to compare him to various Hindu and Buddhist gods, in an effort to bestow suitable praise that elevates the captain-general to the divinelike status shared by great Indic kings. The comparisons drawn between kings and gods was not new to the seventeenth century, as numerous Sinhala and Pāli texts dating back at least a millennium often asserted or implied that a given Sri Lankan king possessed godlike powers and attributes.[95] In *Kustantīnu Haṭana*, Alagiyavanna extends the same courtesy and respect to Sá de Noronha, eulogizing him in terms of deities worshiped locally.

Entering the center of the battle without fear,
Displaying strength and courage,
Like Skandakumara and Viṣṇu,
I will display my might before you.[96]

Despite the unlikelihood of the Portuguese captain-general comparing himself to Skandakumara, the warrior son of Śiva, and Viṣṇu, the heroic king of Hindu dharma, this verse illustrates how the new ruler was associated with gods who represented his martial and royal attributes. Such use of mythological metaphors should not be simply explained away in terms of the author's adherence to poetic conventions.[97] The literary trope of the king embodying a quasidivine identity speaks to a broader conviction that the king truly is a powerful figure more capable of asserting his will in the world than any other human being. Glimpses of the divine natures often attributed to kings in premodern Sri Lanka precede the *praśasti* poems and may be seen in *vaṃsas*, which are historical writings or chronicles composed mainly between the fifth and fourteenth centuries CE.[98]

Comparing Constantino de Sá de Noronha to deities worshiped in the island was critical for bestowing the requisite praise on him as an imperial king. Broadly speaking, panegyric poetry everywhere relies on the power of its words to help bring about that which it describes, guaranteeing the authority and appropriateness of the leader by the force of its praise.[99] Invested with erudition and eloquence, poetic praise was assumed to make a difference in the world, leaving an impression that has actual effects in the world rather than simply giving a description that documents something that already exists.[100] In this sense, describing the Portuguese captain-general as a god suggests that this use of poetic language could actually endow him with godlike power.

> While exhibiting the appearance of the god Śakra made manifest,
> Who, having obtained victory in the war with the *asuras*,
> Entered the shining city of the gods,
> Being accompanied by his divine army, . . .
> Taking along his limitless great army,
> Engaging in victory games as he saw fit,
> The people's great king happily
> Entered the excellent city of Malvāna.[101]

Appearing like the divine King of the Gods named Śakra who returns to his divine city after vanquishing the enemy *asuras*, Sá de Noronha takes on the same divine glory when returning to his headquarters in Malvāna, having defeated the rebels led by Barreto. These verses serve to confirm how the captain-general should be seen, a majestic and valiant leader who has rid the world of a serious danger threatening its existence. In this context, it is significant that Sá de Noronha was divinized after his death and described as a "*deviyō*" in the Kandy area, an honor normally reserved for local kings.[102]

The poet's praise of the Portuguese captain-general employs the local language and literature to turn him into a figure resembling that of a local Sinhala Buddhist king. Many of the literary tropes used to honor and glorify Sá de Noronha imitate those used in praise of kings who ruled the island in previous centuries. These words of praise depict the king as the god Śakra and other divine figures. Alagiyavanna's *Sävul Sandēśaya* also employs divine imagery in praise of King Rājasiṃha, at one point depicting his glory and power as equal to that of Viṣṇu and Skandakumāra, to a degree that baffles even Śiva who looks on admiringly at the king.[103] *Kustantīnu Haṭana* similarly uses the images of gods to enhance the stature and power of Sá de Noronha, but it does not stop there. The work also speaks of him in ways that are otherwise reserved for Buddhist kings of the island. It imaginatively quotes Sá de Noronha as seeking the goal of "uniting this island of Laṅka under one parasol,"[104] which is the formula that traditionally signifies the political unification of all lands in the island under a single rule. Elsewhere, Sá de Noronha is described as having raised the royal insignia of a parasol and circle shield above his head, riding on a palanquin decorated with precious jewels and ivory while enjoying the breeze of chowries waved over him.[105]

The portrayal of the Portuguese captain-general as a Sinhala king is confirmed by the verses in *Kustantīnu Haṭana* that emphasize his erotic interests and appeal. Indic literature has long celebrated the masculine virility of kings and other great men whose power and beauty are said to attract the desire of beautiful women and who take pleasure in gazing at the female form. In this sense, erotic power complements martial power in the construction of great kings who are able to assert their will over their subjects. Ron Davidson's discussion of the apotheosis of ancient Indian kings, for whom panegyric Sanskrit verse was used to compare their military exploits to the erotic play of the gods, nicely illustrates a wide-ranging literary trope in South Asia that links sex with power in kingship.[106] Numerous Sinhala poems also pick up this theme, employing the popularity of love poetry that evokes the erotic sentiment (*śṛṅgāra rasa*) to extol the power and virility of kings through their associations with erotically charged females. The author of *Kustantīnu Haṭana* clearly draws on this poetic convention, depicting Sá de Noronha as possessing masculine beauty and as a voyeur who delights in the female form. Thus, during his march to war, Sá de Noronha is said to admire the beautiful, young women at play along the way.[107] The poet fittingly also describes women gazing at him, as if to confirm his beauty by comparing him to the God of Love, Anaṅga, whose own attractive form was burned by Śiva in Hindu mythology.

Because they remained looking without closing their eyes,
At our illustrious Lord of Men, who appeared with physical beauty,

That dazzled like the God of Love before he was incinerated,
The noble women of the outlying areas appeared like divine maidens.[108]

By recognizing and celebrating the physical beauty of de Sá in the depiction of women gazing longingly at him, *Kustantīnu Haṭana* imitates earlier poetic works that also equate masculine beauty with both power and moral excellence. A similar portrayal appears in *Kusa Jātaka Kāvya,* wherein city women gaze on King Kusa without blinking while appearing like divine maidens.[109] Elsewhere, *Pärakumbā Sirita* calls for "beautiful, unblinking eyes" to gaze on King Parākramabāhu VI's body at all times.[110] In this way, *Kustantīnu Haṭana* employs well-established conventions to mark Sá de Noronha as a figure comparable in physical beauty to great Sinhala kings and the Bodhisattva.

The author of this work enhances the figure of the Portuguese captain-general by including several erotic verses that depict beautiful women at play in his presence. Voyeuristic sexual imagery appears in numerous examples of Sinhala Buddhist poetry, often in order to depict the masculine power of a king or the Bodhisattva to whom the display of women's bodies is given. Desirable women are included in texts to illustrate the command of virile kings who take pleasure in looking at female forms. Mindful of the poetic conventions that extol the virility of kings through the use of erotic imagery, Alagiyavanna includes several verses wherein Sá de Noronha sits on a riverbank "like Śakra" surrounded by his army while he admires a group of women sporting in the water.

Being endowed with brilliant eyebrows, eyes, faces, and full breasts,
Because the young women play [in the water] while facing upward,
Although there are no [actual] rows of bees, blue lotuses, lotuses or swans,
It was as if there were rivers [containing these] everywhere.
Exhibiting the manner of lusty youth desiring love-play,
The women were splashing each other with very cold water,
Making their lips white and their blue eyes red,
And water lilies fall from their ears while they rubbed their large breasts.[111]

The first verse plays on the metaphorical relations between eyebrows and bees, eyes and blue lotuses, female faces and generic lotus flowers, and breasts and swans that are conventionally used in South Asian poetry. It is virtually identical to a verse in *Sävul Sandēśaya* that also describes semi-nude women splashing on their backs in the water.[112] Meanwhile, the second verse closely resembles the thirty-first stanza in the seventh *sarga* (or canto) of *Kāvyaśēkhara*, a *mahākāvya* from the fifteenth century.[113] The clear borrowing from other Sinhala works shows how the author employed the classical medium of poetry to celebrate and enhance the power of the Portuguese "king."

However fantastic the depiction of Sá de Noronha and his army taking a break from their march to war in order to gaze on female bathers appears, the image of the king as a sensualist is consistent with the imagery and ideology of kingship in premodern South Asia. Akin to the portrayal of Parākramabāhu VI in *Pärakumbā Sirita*, in which the king appears as conqueror of foes and of women, *Kustantīnu Haṭana* portrays Sá de Noronha as a ruler who subdues the rebels and gazes on beautiful women. In nearby Tamil Nadu, the Nāyaka rulers who reigned between the sixteenth and early eighteenth centuries shared similar features in early modern Tamil poetry. Absorbing the model of the divine Hindu king Rāma, the Nāyakas were cast in courtly literature as the paragons of an ideology of enjoyment (*bhoga*) stressing the king's physical charm and sexual prowess.[114] As a patron to poets, who dutifully praise him in highly conventional, figurative verse, the king is celebrated in verse for his aesthetic refinement and his command over that which pleases the senses. Therefore, when Alagiyavanna describes the lovely women who display their attractive bodies to Sá de Noronha, he is not only replicating poetic conventions designed to stir the erotic sentiments of an audience, but he is also enhancing the status of the captain-general by associating him with literary tropes that empower a ruler and make him worthy of reverence.

Alagiyavanna's portrayal of Sá de Noronha as a local king is the result of his reliance on conventional poetic methods of heaping praise on one's ruler and possible patron. The old poet sought to strengthen his ties to local powers, particularly following the misfortune he experienced when he lost his position, salary, and lands under the previous captain-general. The eulogistic tone of *Kustantīnu Haṭana* reinforces the image of a Sinhala poet who cast his lot with Portuguese authorities and who attempted to solidify this relationship through the traditional medium of poetry. Praise poems are, in general, literary works that carry an expectation of reward.[115] Whether Alagiyavanna actually presented this work to Sá de Noronha or received any reward for it remains unknown. However, the decision to employ traditional Sinhala poetic verse and imagery to celebrate the Portuguese captain-general is an unmistakable sign of the adaptation of local literature to translate colonial power into familiar, more manageable terms. *Kustantīnu Haṭana* works to enhance the power and status of Sá de Noronha, while at the same time encoding Sinhala ideas of kingship into the representation of colonial Portuguese power.[116] Portuguese efforts of Christianization in the *Estado da Índia* generally sought to substitute Christian signs for "gentile" ones and to transform the native's hearts and minds through repeated religious exercises.[117] In such a program there is practically no space for preserving local religious and cultural forms, as these would be seen to inhibit the religious and cultural conversions that the colonialists sought. Nevertheless, Alagiyavanna's *Kustantīnu Haṭana* effectively redeems local cultural expressions in the context of celebrating Portuguese power in Sinhala terms.[118]

Kustantīnu Haṭana also reserves praise for local Buddhist kings. King Rājasiṃha I, who fought vigorously against the Portuguese and who was described as cruel, bloodthirsty "tyrant" by Portuguese chroniclers, receives acclaim in the work. He is praised as a great king who united the island under one parasol of state and who enjoyed the splendor of his rule until his death and rebirth in the divine city of the gods.[119] This recognition of Rājasiṃha, the unyielding enemy of the Portuguese, is consistent with Alagiyavanna's praise for the Sītāvaka king in earlier works. In addition, King Senarat, the Buddhist king of Kandy at the time, is also praised. He is called blameless in the rebellion of Barreto, and he is said to possess the virtues of a bodhisattva.[120] The fact that local Buddhist kings are similarly praised in *Kustantīnu Haṭana* suggests that Alagiyavanna had an expansive vision of the rulers who deserve to be exalted in verse. It also reinforces the idea that in early modern Sri Lanka, royal power of all kinds was best expressed and understood poetically.

New Poetic Horizons

Portuguese colonialism shifted the ground on which native elites like Alagiyavanna sought status and recognition. Within the context of colonial rule, Alagiyavanna used his poetic expertise to negotiate a new sociopolitical order that accompanied the expansion of Portuguese authority in lowland Sri Lanka. It would be a mistake to interpret the poet's praise for Sá de Noronha as simply a means to ingratiate himself to the current ruler. To view *Kustantīnu Haṭana* as a cynical device for winning favor, through which he could "find his bread by means of his verses," ignores the range of options open to Alagiyavanna and overlooks the complexity of panegyric literature.[121] Poetic praise for the Portuguese entailed representing colonial power in accordance with Sinhala literary and cultural norms. It illustrates a reversion of the power relation between the "Oriental" and the "European," whereby the colonized could contain and represent the colonizer.[122] *Kustantīnu Haṭana* contains praise that simultaneously enhances and subverts Portuguese colonial power. It shores up the authority of the colonizer but does so by localizing it in the language and the customs of Sinhala Buddhists. Alagiyavanna's praise for Sá de Noronha makes the captain-general appear on par with great Buddhist kings, not above them. His composition of *Kustantīnu Haṭana* can thus be seen as an attempt to persuade Sá de Noronha to fulfill the traditional duties of a local ruler. Alagiyavanna's poetic praise would, in theory if not in practice, create obligations for Sá de Noronha and make him answerable to some degree to the Sinhala poet that extols him in verse. This use of poetry to express and extol Portuguese power is therefore not some sort of capitulation. Instead, it reflects the creative use of poetry to negotiate with that power and "build a life" within the crevices it creates by appropriating and translating its expressions into local literary terms.[123]

The poet's use of traditional panegyric forms to envision and celebrate Portuguese expressions of power does not mean that *Kustantīnu Haṭana* contains nothing new as far as Sinhala poetry is concerned. This work lies at another key juncture in the history of Portuguese colonialism in Sri Lanka, a point at which the new imperial order had successfully consolidated its hold over the maritime regions of the island. As such, *Kustantīnu Haṭana,* more than any of Alagiyavanna's other works, expresses a keen awareness of the presence of aliens in early modern Sinhala society, an expanded geographical vision of the world, and the destructive violence of warfare.[124] As much as Alagiyavanna found comfort in the traditional forms of Sinhala *kavi* and his role as a poet, the profound changes witnessed in the first two decades of the seventeenth century led to some novel features in his work. Thus, despite the many similarities of expression found between *Kustantīnu Haṭana* and the earlier works by Alagiyavanna, this latest work responds more clearly to the intensification of contacts between Sinhalas and Portuguese that marked the onset of early modernity in Sri Lanka.[125]

Leaving aside for the moment the veneration of the Christian God and other religious expressions, there are numerous other instances whereby

Kustantīnu Haṭana discloses a sense of dramatic change in the world beyond the text. It follows the *Sītāvaka Haṭana* in describing Portuguese soldiers and administrators engaged in a mission to conquer the island. The vast amount of material devoted to Constantino de Sá de Noronha and his army attests to the intensive and definitive encounters between Sinhalas and Portuguese at that time. Alagiyavanna's work stands apart from the earlier *Sītāvaka Haṭana* in that it recognizes the legitimacy of the Portuguese presence in the island

> This renowned Laṅkā came into the possession of,
> The steadfast king of Portugal,
> Whose essence of power crushed the pride of kings,
> Throughout the extensive land of Dambadiva.[126]

This verse explicitly affirms the validity of Portuguese colonial rule in the context of its maritime empire along the Indian Ocean. While it exaggerates the extent of Portuguese control over India, it rhetorically asserts the righteousness and supremacy of its rule throughout the region.

Furthermore, numerous verses that narrate the journey of Sá de Noronha and his army through the island's hinterland portray the significant encounters between the Portuguese and the island's inhabitants in various locations. Sá de Noronha and his soldiers are said to admire the local landscapes and the local women. Meanwhile, the Sinhalas also recognize and act on the presence of the Portuguese in their midst. In a verse that expresses a welcoming attitude toward the Portuguese troops, crowds of villagers are said to have prepared the roads and fords for the army and brought various gifts of food for them to enjoy.[127] *Kustantīnu Haṭana* does not dwell on these contacts, but they are still acknowledged throughout the narrative. Descriptions of the Portuguese encounter are complemented by the use of several Portuguese words in the poem. The novel use of these words in Sinhala poetry represents the presence of the Portuguese linguistically. One finds, for example, the word *pādiri* for "padre" or a Christian priest, *visurē* for "vice-rei" or the viceroy, *kappittan* for "capitão" or captain(s), *peragasa* for "pregação" or preaching, and *adāgaya* for "adaga" or dagger.[128] The inclusion of such words in the work makes clear the fact that Portuguese elements had impressed themselves on local Sinhala culture.

This Portuguese presence in *Kustantīnu Haṭana* also introduced an expanded geographical vision that is expressed in Alagiyavanna's text.

The horizons of the Sinhala literary world are stretched in new directions, encompassing distant sites that one can safely assume were never visited by the author or by most of his audience. Older Sinhala texts frequently mention "Dambadiva" (Jambudvīpa), or India, and several of its kingdoms and neighboring regions known to ancient Sri Lankan authors.[129] *Kustantīnu Haṭana,* however, articulates a recently acquired knowledge of new lands apart from the ancient Buddhist world. First and foremost, the new geographical imagination reflected in the text includes the land of Portugal, which is mentioned twice. First, the term *pratikal* appears in verse 9, in which the power of the country's king over Sri Lanka (*laka*) and India (*dambadiva*) is asserted and praised. In the second instance, the country of Portugal is said to be the place where Sá de Noronha was raised and where he "enjoyed all kinds of wealth in abundance."[130] These two brief references yield a sense of how Portugal appeared to the minds of Sinhalas in the early seventeenth century. Portugal is explicitly linked with notions of power and wealth, befitting of the sovereigns of the island. Similarly, Lisboa (*ḷuvisbōva*) is mentioned as an "excellent city" that is "decorated with great and small roads," where the great king of Portugal resides.[131] Clearly, Alagiyavanna had heard enough about Portugal to portray this distant center of imperial power in appropriately grand terms.

Meanwhile, the colonial capital of the *Estado da Índia*—Goa (*gōva*)—is also mentioned in a few verses, albeit shorn of the brief descriptive praise that Alagiyavanna inserts for Portugal and Lisbon. Instead, Goa is the location at which the Portuguese and local chiefs appeal for help from the viceroy in subduing Barreto's rebellion, as well as the place from which de Sá is dispatched to regain control in Sri Lanka.[132] The inclusion of some symbolic markers for the Portuguese imperial world in *Kustantīnu Haṭana* illustrates the adoption of new geographical knowledge into the imaginative horizons of the text. By 1619, and likely substantially earlier, people with extensive contacts with the Portuguese had seemingly obtained knowledge of a different map of the world. Older Sinhala texts typically replicated the traditional Indic cosmology that held that the great Mount Meru was the center of the world, surrounded by seven circular rings of mountains with seas in between them, followed by one great ocean with four large continents located in the cardinal directions, and encompassed by a circular wall of iron marking the perimeter of the world.[133] This vision of the world, however, is largely supplanted in *Kustantīnu Haṭana* with another vision that is informed by Portuguese imperial knowledge obtained through the extensive maritime explorations Portuguese sailors undertook beginning in the fifteenth century.

Encounters with the Portuguese military presence in Sri Lanka also spurred some novel features in *Kustantīnu Haṭana*. Large-scale battles had been fought under the command of King Rājasiṃha I in the late sixteenth century in what was ultimately an unsuccessful series of sieges to dislodge the Portuguese from their fort in Colombo. Portuguese-led raids of villages in the Sītāvaka kingdom also took place during Alagiyavanna's lifetime. However, after Rājasiṃha's death and the decision to conquer the entire island for the Portuguese crown, warfare in Sri Lanka became increasingly intense and destructive after 1590 and in the decades that followed.[134] The rise in violence and its spread across more territory in the island are evidenced by the correspondingly violent imagery found in *Kustantīnu Haṭana*.

The introduction of the new genre of war poetry in 1585 set the stage for more graphic accounts of violence, exceeding much of what preceded it in Sinhala literature.[135] The descriptions of battle and the use of guns, in particular, testify to the Portuguese presence in the island. Whereas the panegyric verses of *praśasti* poetry tended to stress the sentiments of heroism and eroticism, the *haṭan kavi* could also draw on other aesthetic sentiments known in classical treatises on poetics. The descriptions of pitched battles and the disposal of corpses in *Kustantīnu Haṭana* seem designed to arouse the sentiments of fear and disgust, which were also recognized as aesthetic responses to fine literature.[136] The text poetically describes the construction of forts by Sá de Noronha and the fiery destruction of the rebel headquarters, including Barreto's mansion, stables, storerooms, workshops, and temples. Although the devastation at the hands of the Portuguese army is complete, it is artfully portrayed by a metaphor comparing the flames that consumed the city with a spectacular, red evening cloud that confuses the god Śiva.[137]

However, not all accounts of the destructiveness of war are so charming. Other verses that describe the slaying of the rebels are unabashedly gruesome. The imagery of war permits Alagiyavanna to mention how the Portuguese forces "cut off and brought the heads of many enemies."[138] Several verses in *Kustantīnu Haṭana* describe in detail the actual carnage that took place when Sá de Noronha's forces ambushed Barreto's army.

> Some sliced the bodies of the enemies like yams and resin,
> Some severed and piled up the heads of enemies like coconuts,

Some, seizing the enemies forcefully, cut off their ears, noses, hands, and feet,
And some did not fall back without stabbing at least five or ten persons.
Some, taking their lances and stabbing the enemies, cast them aside,
Some fell two or three persons in one spot with one gun apiece,
Some, for the sake of merit (*piṅ*), did not lay waste to those prostrating at their feet,
And some, seizing without killing the enemies who turned tail, bound and brought them back....
When the large army of our Lord of Men who is endowed with spotless glory like the sun,
Won the battle, having severed and cast down one thousand lakhs of enemy heads,
The hawks, vultures, crows, dogs, and jackals, together with *rākṣasas*, *yakṣas*, *bhūtas*, and *pisācas*,
Engaged in a festival of frolicking here and there, eating their fill of human flesh and entrails.[139]

The violent imagery of these verses is characteristic of a work whose descriptions of warfare are pertinent to the aim of praising the heroic nature of a great man. Yet such verses portray the savagery of war in a fearful and disturbing manner to convey a sense of its brutality and to elicit both fear and disgust in its audience. Heads are severed, bodies are mutilated and devoured by animals, and numerous combatants die, although surely much less than the one thousand lakhs (or 100,000,000) of casualties estimated by the author. Although some of de Sá's soldiers show restraint, including some who are said to be mindful of the Buddhist concept of merit earned by sparing a life, the overall tone of the section is one of overwhelming destruction. Portuguese power, in this sense, required poetry to express the full force of its might. The changed character of political authority in the island generated correspondingly new features to panegyric verse.

Hybrid Religious Views

Other poetic innovations in *Kustantīnu Haṭana* mirror the religious changes that Alagiyavanna and many other Sinhala Buddhists came to express in the early seventeenth century. Questions on the religious sentiments expressed in this work are contentious and fraught with issues related to religion and the politics of identity in contemporary Sri Lanka. Scholars have debated whether the author of the text was a sincere Christian or a crypto-Buddhist, since the work contains references to both Christian and Buddhist concepts. In addition, there is a healthy dose of Hindu imagery employed in the work, particularly in the use of various poetic devices to signify power and majesty. Yet this debate rests on an assumption that modern, clearly defined, notions of religious faith and identity were consistently shared by Alagiyavanna and others in seventeenth-century Sri Lanka. Instead of presuming that he was either a Christian who used Buddhist concepts conventionally and superficially in his poetry or a Buddhist who was pretending to be Christian in order to gain approval and favors from the Portuguese, it is more helpful to consider that *Kustantīnu Haṭana* expresses a hybrid form of religiosity that drew selectively and purposefully from both traditions. Given Alagiyavanna's proclivity to refashion elements of Portuguese culture in terms of Sinhala Buddhist ideas and forms, it makes sense to hypothesize that the references to aspects of Christianity and Buddhism in the poem reflect his abiding interest in both.

The three opening verses of *Kustantīnu Haṭana* dedicated to the Trinity, Jesus Christ, and the Virgin Mary have been cited as evidence of the distinctiveness of the work. As a Sinhala poem written in accordance with classical literary forms, *Kustantīnu Haṭana* makes several references to the Christian God and to expressions of Christian piety in stock poetic ways. The figure of Christ, extolled in verse 2 for his virtue of loving kindness and his lotuslike feet, is depicted much like the Buddha. Sinhala Buddhist texts, including some of Alagiyavanna's earlier works, routinely describe the Buddha as embodying loving-kindness and possessing lotuslike feet to be venerated by gods and humans.[140] Another verse credits Lord Jesus (*yēsu devi*) with helping Constantino de Sá de Noronha travel safely to Ceilão, although it also mentions the positive effects of de Sá's own merit (*piṅ*) in this instance.[141] Given that Sinhala Buddhist literature typically subscribes to the Theravāda view of a Buddha who has passed away from the world of *saṃsāra* and is no longer able to help devotees in the world, the acknowledgment of Jesus's intervention in Sá de Noronha's journey seems in line with Christian views of divinity. However, Sri Lankan Buddhism also incorporated various bodhisattvas and Hindu deities beginning from around the fourteenth century, and these divine figures were quickly adapted to satisfy human needs in the current world.[142] In this way, Buddhists could appeal to powerful, divine beings for blessings and protection in the present while still venerating and following the Buddha to achieve otherworldly, transcendental goals of positive rebirths and liberation from *saṃsāra*.

This separation of duties, whereby Buddhas help people to obtain good rebirths and liberation while bodhisattvas and other heavenly beings offer assistance with this-worldly goals, is important to note. The portrayal of Jesus in *Kustantīnu Haṭana* appears in some verses much like a bodhisattva who looks after people's needs in the world of *saṃsāra*. In addition to the text's assertion of his help given to Sá de Noronha in his voyage to Ceilão, Jesus is portrayed as a compassionate figure who looks after beings in the world.

> Who is great in terms of virtue,
> Who is engaged in the protection of the world,
> And who possesses wondrous, supernatural powers,
> May the Lord Jesus Christ protect us![143]

The image of Jesus in this work fits well within the framework of a bodhisattva in the Buddhist tradition. Alagiyavanna makes no mention of Jesus's sacrifice and consequent removal of sin, nor is he praised for being the way to heaven and eternal life. Instead, Jesus is said to offer protection and prosperity to his devotees. He is called the "eye of the three worlds" (*tun lova äsa*), which is an epithet more commonly used with reference to the Buddha. The Buddha, as the Fully Awakened One or the Bodhisattva, is said to possess unobstructed knowledge of the world of desire (*kāma-loka*), the world of form (*rūpa-loka*), and the formless world (*arūpa-loka*), which together comprise the Buddhist universe. Alagiyavanna uses the same epithet in *Dahamsoňda Kava* to praise the Bodhisattva as being "like an eye to the three worlds."[144] Collectively these remarks show how the poet goes beyond simply using local figures of speech to express Christian sentiments. The view favoring Alagiyavanna's "harmonization" of Christian faith with the local Sinhala culture fails to recognize his transformation of that faith into a form that differs markedly from what Portuguese missionaries promoted.[145] Alagiyavanna re-envisions Jesus Christ as a kind of bodhisattva who likewise can assist his devotees while they are in *saṃsāra*. He answers the needs of people in this world, but there are scant signs of how he can help them in the next world.

Aside from the recognition of the Trinity and the mentions of Jesus and the Virgin Mary by name, Alagiyavanna was also familiar with a Christian conception of God and the creation of the world. It is well known that Buddhist texts definitively reject the notion of a creator god who brought the world of *saṃsāra* into existence. So when *Kustantīnu Haṭana* praises the "Great God who created the sky and earth" (*ahas poḷō mävū suriňdu*) and describes Sá de Noronha worshiping the triune god "who created the beings in the entire three worlds with loving kindness and compassion" (*muḷu tun lova mävu sata met kuḷuṇen-a*), the text is affirming Christian beliefs about divine creation.[146] However, the latter example shows that even this statement about the Christian God is conditioned by Buddhist views of the three worlds and the bodhisattva-like qualities of loving kindness and compassion. Elsewhere, the idea of God as creator appears in a verse describing Sá de Noronha's expression of Christian piety.

> And clasping his hands together on top of his head,
> Paying homage reverently to the resplendent feet of the illustrious Jesus Christ,
> Who created the diverse beings of the world in the sky and on earth,
> And protects them with compassion at all times.[147]

This verse reinforces the idea of God as the creator of the entire world, while portraying the captain-general as a pious devotee who worships God in the local custom of prostrating with one's hands on one's head. The assertion that Jesus created all beings runs counter to Buddhist conceptions of what a bodhisattva does, and thus it would be inaccurate to fold Alagiyavanna's Jesus fully into this Buddhist figure. One finds Christian ideas interwoven with Buddhist ones in this work. Although Jesus appears as a divine creator, he also protects beings with compassion like a bodhisattva.

The blending of Christian with Buddhist notions within a single frame of divine power signifies the hybrid religious vision of *Kustantīnu Haṭana*. The sincerity of Alagiyavanna's conversion need not be questioned in order to posit that he was either unable or unwilling to part with select Buddhist ideas and values while composing this work. The religiosity he promotes is transgressive in that it undermines more orthodox formulations of both Catholicism and Buddhism. To paraphrase Bhabha, the hybrid representation of religion in *Kustantīnu Haṭana* disturbs the hegemonic, discriminatory forms of knowledge belonging to the colonial authorities, making it dependent on local or "native" forms of knowledge for their expression.[148] The authority and status attributed to Christianity by the Portuguese can no longer be justified on its own terms. Alagiyavanna's text embraces certain features of Christian thought and symbolism but adds other Buddhist notions to it, a move that actually subverts the unrivaled authority and integrity of the Portuguese faith. The authority and integrity of Christianity are implicitly challenged by the work's recognition that the despised rebel António Barreto had once been a Christian "who had come to the religion of the Lord Jesus Christ."[149] Whether intentional or not, this brief comment raises questions about the effectiveness of Christianity if it cannot prevent a devotee of the faith from rebelling against Portuguese rule.

The Buddhist traces in *Kustantīnu Haṭana* that modify Christian doctrine entail more than just literary symbols thought to be external to genuine inner feelings. Sinhala Christian scholars have taken great pains to argue that the use of Buddhist-Hindu mythological elements in the text was merely due to poetic conventions, comparable to the use of Greek and Latin mythology by modern Christian authors.[150] However, this argument not only fails to recognize that poetic conventions are not universally meaningless and superficial, but it also overlooks important references made to karma and merit in the work. The Buddhist idea of merit appears in several places and is presented as an undisputable fact. Early on in *Kustantīnu Haṭana*, Alagiyavanna explains that the Kandyan king Senarat escaped without harm from Barreto's treachery "by the power of the Triple Gem, by the influence of the great gods, and by the power of the merit of that king."[151] The implication of this assertion is that merit, along with the Triple Gem and the local gods, can produce discernible, positive effects in the world. Such a position runs counter to stereotypical Portuguese claims from the sixteenth and seventeenth centuries that Buddhist beliefs are simply fables and diabolically inspired superstitions.[152] Alagiyavanna, in contrast, recognizes the validity and efficacy of such teachings.

The work attributes Sá de Noronha's safe journey to Sri Lanka to his own merit along with the divine assistance of Jesus. The assertion of his merit is noteworthy since it not only reinforces the validity of the concept, but it also reinforces the idea that the captain-general is worthy of reverence and respect like other beings who have earned merit by performing good deeds.[153] Verse 173, which declares that some Portuguese soldiers spared the lives of the rebels "for the sake of merit," further confirms the relevance of this idea. Elsewhere, in an important verse spoken by the followers of Māyādunnē while criticizing the claimant to the throne, merit is equated with knowledge as the basis for making correct decisions about moral conduct.

> Having adhered to the words spoken by António Barreto,
> And seeing now, Noble Lord, that you are defeated,
> If knowledgeable, renowned kings have done merit,
> Would they listen to the words spoken by wicked persons from here on?[154]

The operative assumption of this verse is that those who have performed acts of merit would not end up being misled by wicked persons who speak and act out of ignorance and malice. Doing merit is thus presumed to have an apotropaic effect, protecting the doer from harm and misfortune. The rebel Māyādunnē is not criticized for following a false religion but rather for not having done enough merit like good Buddhists do.

The verse also reflects the author's affirmation of the related Buddhist idea of karma. In a series of verses toward the end of the work, the soldiers who had been fighting on the side of Barreto and Māyādunnē turn in exasperation against the latter in the face of their defeat by the Portuguese-led forces. The implication here is that by following the treacherous and immoral Barreto, Māyādunnē and his forces have sown the seeds of their defeat. In a verse that recalls the experience of King Senarat of Kandy, whose kingdom suffered great destruction at the hands of Barreto's army, the vanquished soldiers proceed to draw a direct link between Māyādunnē's decision to join Barreto in seeking the island's throne and his eventual failure.

> Knowing well what happened to King Senarat, who gave him great wealth,
> But not remembering that [fact], Noble Lord,
> Having come [to Laṅkā] at the word of the wicked person named Barreto, who lacks virtue,
> This suffering has befallen you.
> In the past it has been said that many people were destroyed,
> Having taken to mind the speech declared by evil, wicked persons.
> Now we have observed beyond any doubt the disaster that has befallen you,
> Having listened to the speech declared by the nobleman Barreto.[155]

The scolding of Māyādunnē in *Kustantīnu Haṭana* suggests that the rebels' defeat is at least partly attributable to the immorality and illegitimacy of their cause. The suffering of the pretender and his forces is said to be due to his decision to follow the word of the wicked Barreto. The author presumes here that karma was a factor in their defeat. Their association with Barreto meant that they would inevitably experience the fruits of that wickedness. Further, these verses recall similar notions in *Subhāṣitaya*, in which it is said that those having virtue and knowledge ignore the words of wicked persons and thus avoid suffering, whereas evil kings cause destruction in their kingdoms.[156] These verses imply that karma, not some kind of divine intervention, is responsible for the defeat of the rebels. Barreto, too, obtains a just result, being apprehended and having all of his teeth knocked out as a punishment for opposing both God and the king of Portugal.[157]

The various direct and indirect references to Buddhist ideas and images suggest that they should not simply be written off as meaningless ornaments added to embellish the supposedly Christian religious sentiments of the work. Instead, there is evidence of a deeper adherence to certain Buddhist ideas alongside the pronouncements and descriptions of Christian piety. Scholars who have contended that the work demonstrates either Christian or Buddhist adherence have allowed themselves to be constrained by modern views of religious identity. But this seventeenth-century poem illustrates the possibilities by which a Buddhist subject of the Portuguese empire could appropriate elements from various religions to produce a hybrid religious identity. The retention of classical poetic forms and conventions, coupled with appeals to powerful ideas of local kingship and Buddhist morality, would in theory help Alagiyavanna make a case for reclaiming his exalted status as an excellent poet who is entitled to the patronage. The patron in this case is the Portuguese captain-general Constantino de Sá de Noronha. Notably, *Kustantīnu Haṭana* also draws on values associated with the Indic "*bhoga* ideology" of kingship by portraying Sá de Noronha as both an enjoyer of wealth and as generous to others.[158] After his victory over the rebels, he is said to have "rained a shower of gifts" on his army, awarding titles and hereditary rights over lands and villages.[159] Such a portrayal reinforced the grandiose image of the generous ruler who is praised in the conventions of Sinhala poetry, and it also set up expectations whereby Sá de Noronha might be similarly persuaded to reward his other subjects, including the poet who praises him.

Aside from the apparent motive of self-gain, which is a standard feature of classical panegyric poetry, the retention of selective elements of Sinhala Buddhist traditions could serve other purposes as well. The appearance of local religious values and ideas in the work suggests at the very least that Alagiyavanna's conversion to Catholicism did not entail the wholesale rejection of his previous religious identity. Yet early modern Portuguese religious values demanded a thorough, inner spiritual transformation that was exclusivist in nature, not permitting syncretistic forms of faith. Notwithstanding the more accommodationist missionary methods of Jesuits such as Valignano and Nobili, which encouraged the adopting of local cultural signs for promoting the Christian faith in Asia, the prevailing expectations of Portuguese missionaries well into the seventeenth century still assumed that successful conversions to Christianity required the complete adoption of the faith in its unadulterated Catholic form. This may explain why Tavernier's version of the Jesuit account of Alagiyavanna's conversion included the statement that this renowned local "philosopher" actively worked for the conversion of other "idolaters."[160] However, our reading of *Kustantīnu Haṭana* suggests that such a depiction of Alagiyavanna as a tireless promoter of the Christian faith was most likely an exaggeration. Instead, the text depicts an effort by the poet to combine, and thereby validate, certain aspects of both religions, resulting in a religious vision that was just as inclusive as the earlier cultural norms that permitted the worship of Hindu deities and performance of Brahmanical rites among Sinhala Buddhists in late medieval Sri Lanka.[161]

Nevertheless, Alagiyavanna's adoption of various Christian and Portuguese images and ideas in *Kustantīnu Haṭana* shows that he felt inclined to embrace the new political order and the religious identity it promoted. Seen in the light of historical evidence of the poet's conversion, his adoption of the Portuguese name Dom Jerónimo, and his service in compiling the *tombos*, the references in *Kustantīnu Haṭana* to the Christian faith can be seen as expressions of a more complex, multifaceted religiosity adopted by the poet in response to the imposition of colonial authority. Although a stance claiming that Alagiyavanna remained Buddhist in essence while being outwardly Catholic may be attractive to modern Sinhala Buddhists who remain resentful of Portuguese colonial history in Sri Lanka, there is no clear evidence to suggest that he did not develop some attachment to the Christian faith. Given that the work consistently exhibits visions of political power that are hybrid in nature, extolling Portuguese authorities in the manner of local Sinhala Buddhist kings, the author might similarly have been expected to have adopted hybrid religious views as well.

However, a hybrid form of religion does not necessarily involve a harmonization of traditions. Within the context of early modern Catholicism and Buddhism, there were numerous aspects of each that would have been objectionable to the other. Rather, in considering *Kustantīnu Haṭana* as a poetic response to Portuguese colonialism, its hybridity represented a challenge to the notion of fixed religious and cultural identities, as well as the idea of the disparateness of the other.[162] Such a vision that appropriated aspects of both religions and cultures could not succeed in reconciling the two traditions, which had already staked out claims to their respective truth and particularity. When seen in the light of his entire body of work, Alagiyavanna's *Kustantīnu Haṭana* appears as a creative synthesis of rival religious ideals to represent anew the traditional political-aesthetic order and restore the privileges of poets. It reversed the author's exclusive definition of religious identity in *Subhāṣitaya*, as the poet sought once again to praise colonial power rather than contest it. Although it is unknown whether Alagiyavanna ultimately succeeded in his aim of praising Sá de Noronha in verse, the composition of *Kustantīnu Haṭana* remains as a striking example of the manner in which poetic literature could be refashioned to enhance and negotiate colonial power, just as it did with royal power in previous eras.

Conclusion

Poetry and Buddhism

ALAGIYAVANNA MUKAVEṬI'S WORKS reveal much about how the composition of Buddhist poetry could express divergent notions of power and identity during a transformative period in Sri Lankan history. His poetry offers a unique lens through which one can begin to comprehend the effects of colonial encounters with Asian peoples in the sixteenth and seventeenth centuries. Alagiyavanna's career as a lay Buddhist poet coincided with an era of profound political and cultural upheaval, and thus his written works reflect some of the possible Buddhist responses to the expansion of European power in Asia. At one level, works such as *Sävul Sandēśaya, Dahamsoňḍa Kava, Kusa Jātaka Kāvyaya, Subhāṣitaya,* and *Kustantīnu Haṭana* can be read and enjoyed for their finely crafted verses that employ distinctive metrical forms and phonetic structures as well as aesthetically rich figurative speech. Even in translation, wherein much of the formal features of Sinhala *kavi* are obscured, such works can evoke an aesthetic appreciation for their evocative language and provocative ideas.

Aside from these aesthetic qualities, the historical settings in which Alagiyavanna lived and worked turns his poetic works into significant clues as to what it was like for Asian Buddhists to encounter European colonial power for the first time. Although traders and travelers from Western lands had visited Asian lands in earlier centuries, the expansion of Portuguese imperial power in the sixteenth century introduced novel and more intensive relationships between the colonizer and colonized in Sri Lanka and elsewhere. The examination of Alagiyavanna's works in historical sequence allows for the tracking of changing perceptions of self and society during this important era. One of the primary arguments throughout this book is that Alagiyavanna's poetry illustrates attempts to negotiate the transitions of early modernity and to develop new ways of being in a rapidly changing world. His writing career spanned an era that witnessed the steady decline in the authority of Buddhist kingship and the Sangha. At the same time, Portuguese ambitions to expand their trade and territories throughout the Indian Ocean were developed through the acquisition of lands by conquest or by forceful persuasion, bringing the Portuguese into close albeit fraught relations with various Asian communities.[1] The colonial encounters between the Sinhalas and Portuguese were characterized by both conflict and cooperation, giving rise to complex cultural and religious exchanges. Alagiyavanna's works thus exhibit efforts to utilize literary forms to gain some influence over new social and political conditions. His texts draw on and refashion traditional literary forms as a means to negotiate the decline of the Sinhala courts of Buddhist kings and the ascension of Portuguese imperial and missionary agents.

Alagiyavanna's works illumine some critical aspects of what scholars have termed *early modernity*. The idea of this historical epoch generally reflects the conviction that the years between roughly the late fourteenth and mid-eighteenth centuries were a time of pronounced changes on a global scale. Using keywords such as *networks, circulation,* and *flow,* scholars of early modernity typically seek to demonstrate how the cultural changes that accompanied the rise of national monarchies and colonial empires served as the catalysts for new understandings of self and society.[2] In the cases of Sri Lanka and Portugal, the social and political orders of both countries were transformed by their colonial encounters. As the sixteenth century wore on, increasing numbers of Sinhala Buddhists became intimately familiar with new conceptions of political power and religious identity. For their part, the Portuguese came to recognize the existence of significant religious and cultural differences in the "Orient" that informed their view of the world and their place in it.[3] Alagiyavanna was a figure who straddled two worlds that came into increasing contact and conflict near the end of the sixteenth century. As such, his poetic works also serve as resources with which to explore what Sanjay Subrahmanyam has described as "connected histories," which presumes that important historical events took place in the interactions between local and supralocal agents.[4] Alagiyavanna's poetry expresses and responds to this level of increased circulation and interaction between diverse cultural, religious, and political forms.

It is in this sense that Alagiyavanna appears as an early modern poet, not just because of the years of his life but also because of his location within both Sinhala and Portuguese spheres of power. He went from being a traditional bard in the court of a Sinhala king to a servant in the Portuguese colonial administration in Ceilão. His work illuminates some of the conjunctures wherein two distant countries were brought into contact and consequently changed by virtue of their encounter.[5] Like many products and effects of colonialism more generally, his poetry reflects the contestation and adaptation that takes place in forced cultural encounters.

False Dichotomies

The study of Alagiyavanna's works also invites the revision of some theoretical dichotomies that are common to scholarship in Buddhist studies and other humanistic fields. One such dichotomy contrasts historical agency with passive subjectivity in the study of historical figures in colonial contexts. To the extent that Alagiyavanna's works respond to the intensive interactions between previously distinct cultures, they may also serve to refine scholarly notions in regard to agency and cultural disruption under colonialism in Asia. The Sītāvaka Period of Sri Lankan history is conventionally described as a period of "darkness" when literary and cultural expressions were at their ebb.[6] This image has been used to frame most modern scholarly analyses of Alagiyavanna's work. Scholars of Sinhala literature regularly assert that Alagiyavanna was primarily, if not solely, responsible for preserving classical Sinhala literature at a time when monasteries and other educational institutes in lowland Sri Lanka had been abandoned if not destroyed.[7] This narrative casts Sinhala Buddhists and culture as the victims of Portuguese domination, although it is surely correct in noting that there are no extant works produced by Sinhala Buddhist monks from that time. The paucity of works of Sinhala literature from this period combined with scholarly interests in historical agency among subaltern groups make it easy to consider Alagiyavanna as an example of either colonial subjection or resistive agency on the part of the colonized.

However, instead of trying to fit Alagiyavanna into a preconceived box to make a larger argument about the nature of colonialism, we would be better served to use his example to break up those boxes on which scholars often depend. Alagiyavanna's varied career as a court poet and a colonial agent aptly illustrates Talal Asad's view that there are limits to the agency that scholars often wish to attribute to the people they study. The emphasis given to the agency of local Buddhists, which is to say their capacity to pursue courses of action by their own will, inhibits scholars from addressing relations of power that can limit their options. Asad urges scholars to recognize that there are "structures of possible actions" that are not controlled by a historical actor's conscious mind or voluntary will.[8] The implications of this for the present study require that we do not exaggerate the agency of a colonized subject such as Alagiyavanna. His works clearly attempted to engage and enhance various expressions of royal and colonial power on his own terms. Thus, from one perspective, his use of Sinhala literary conventions and Buddhist values in his texts supports the view expressed by Anne Blackburn that colonial discourses and identities did not always displace local ones in colonial Sri Lanka.[9]

On the other hand, the transformations in Alagiyanna's poetry and career remind us that he was still profoundly affected by colonial rule and often constrained in the choices and actions available to him. While we would be remiss simply to replicate the trope of active Portuguese domination over passive Sinhala victims, it would also be a mistake to overlook how Alagiyavanna was unable to resist the hegemony of imperialism altogether. Colonial power need not be overwhelming or internally consistent in its implementation to have an impact.[10] Likewise, it would be unwise to exaggerate the autonomy of colonized peoples during such significant cultural encounters. Alagiyavanna's poetry shows evidence of attempts to negotiate powerful social and political forces or, to paraphrase Frederick Cooper once again, of finding his way among the crevices of colonial power to deflect, appropriate, and sometimes reinterpret the teachings and preachings thrust on him.[11] Alagiyavanna's level of success in achieving his goals first as a poet and official under King Rājasiṃha I and later as a recorder under the Portuguese *vedor da fazenda* is ultimately beyond our knowledge. He secured some level of renown as a poet, and he likely enjoyed some privileges from his political patrons and superiors. Nevertheless, he expressed frustrations with religious and political institutions in *Subhāṣitaya*, and he ultimately converted to Catholicism to serve the colonial authorities. Later, he appears to have lost his title, salary, and lands, which caused him to appeal directly to the king of Portugal to have them restored. From any perspective, it is fair to say that Alagiyavanna enjoyed some measure of agency but remained a subject or a "patient" on whom others acted throughout his career.[12] He was at times a bard who praised kings and the Portuguese captain-general in aesthetically rich verse. At other times, when marginalized from centers of power, he was a voice for moral and cultural criticism. He was neither singly an agent nor a patient but rather a complex figure who sought to use his literary and linguistic skills to acquire what he could in terms of status, influence, and wealth. Therefore, we must qualify any notion of agency or passivity when it comes to Alagiyavanna, as he embodied both types of colonial subject—probably much like most other Sinhala Buddhists in this era.

Another dichotomy that may sometimes obscure more than it reveals comprises the distinction made between what is termed local and translocal. As historians and other scholars struggle to come up with terms to distinguish between communities of people that are brought together in cultural encounters, one increasingly finds oppositions made between local and translocal or global cultural forms. Subrahmanyam utilizes this distinction in theorizing about the "connected histories" between Indic, Persian, and European cultures during early modernity.[13] Pollock similarly contrasts "local languages" that use the vernacular with "cosmopolitan languages" such as Sanskrit and Latin to theorize about how during the second millennium of the Common Era authors of literary works transposed the universal ideals of cosmopolitan literary expressions onto local forms.[14] Although there can be some utility in such a distinction at the macro level, it is also true that the local-translocal dichotomy can be taken too far.

Several of Alagiyavanna's poetic works were composed in a vernacular written dialect of Sinhala, yet imitated certain conventions and themes that were found throughout the Indian subcontinent. His works are not simply "local" texts despite their use of what one might call a local language. Their concerns with aesthetic and moral excellence are explicitly adapted from wider, regional literary forms. Sinhala *kavi* developed through the imitation and vernacularization of Sanskrit *kāvya*. Verses of praise in *Sävul Sandēśaya* and verses of moral admonition in *Subhāṣitaya* may employ Sinhala words, but they reflect genres of literature that are anything but local. The local and translocal become so thoroughly intermixed in Alagiyavanna's poetry they are effectively indistinguishable. He also moved between local and translocal spheres of influence, showing the porous boundaries between them by juxtaposing Sinhala poetry and Portuguese authority. His career as a poet and a civil servant illustrates how neither the local nor translocal can be considered unique or absolute categories of experience and expression. Alagiyavanna thus reminds us that cultural forms rarely remain so singular and distinctive, and thus it is unwise to reify the local-translocal dichotomy or to expand it over increasing areas of social life.

In addition, another false dichotomy that is undermined by the study of Alagiyavanna's works concerns the one drawn between the world of texts and "everyday life." Scholars seeking to problematize the relation between text and context often choose to emphasize the purported difference between what is found in texts and what people actually do. One good example of the alleged gulf between the written word and bodily practice is seen in Gregory Schopen's skepticism about the actual significance of Sanskrit Buddhist texts on the behavior of ancient Buddhists in India. Responding to the longstanding scholarly focus on Buddhist scriptures, Schopen suggests that the "real religion," or that which Buddhists actually did irrespective of what their texts told them to do, must instead be found in the remains of archaeology and epigraphy.[15] Ethnographers and historians of other religions besides Buddhism often make comparable claims to be examining lived religion as actually practiced in everyday life. Robert Orsi, a scholar of American religious history, has popularized the idea of "lived religion" and defined it in terms of the intimate, everyday cultural practices wherein ordinary people make meaning out of their world.[16] Such a category privileges the empirical, quotidian, hybrid forms of religious practice, as opposed to what is normative and authorized by elite powers and texts.[17]

Such calls to examine the nontextual sources of religions are welcome, and the writings of Schopen and Orsi, among others, have made positive contributions to their respective fields. However, the materialist and empiricist approaches to religion are only valuable as long as they do not dismiss the cultural work that texts and ideas can perform. If the category lived religion is to remain useful, it must be theorized more clearly and stripped of its hidden presumption that the forms of a religion that are not immediately witnessed in the ordinary spheres of life are then "dead" and inauthentic. Even the category of the "everyday" is not nearly as natural and empirically evident as it seems to suggest. Rather it is actually an object of modern intellectual history, a term that appeals to those who reject language-based cultural models and macrostructural explanations of culture.[18] The everyday as a distinctive theoretical sphere emerged in the twentieth century with the work of thinkers such as Fernand Braudel, who used it to explore the historical infrastructure conditioning people's thought and action; Henri Lefebvre, who linked the everyday to the totality of social interactions that bring to bear the contradictions of modern, middle-class life; and Michel de Certeau, who saw in the everyday the means for individuals to tactically resist the mechanisms of control and protocol imposed on them by the state and other social institutions.[19] Now the everyday seemingly possesses the theoretical cache to demarcate the boundaries of cultural realities. It comprises the objects and practices that are presumed to be actual and authentic by virtue of their appearance in ordinary, nonofficial settings.

In such a framework, doctrinal and other elite texts enjoy no special privileges. The world of texts is instead commonly held in opposition to the world of practices, whereby what people actually do counts for more than the ideas, symbols, and values that often motivate and condition their actions. From the overlapping perspectives of lived religion and everyday life, the poetic works of an elite author such as Alagiyavanna might not be revealing of the so-called cultural world of early modern Sri Lanka. However, as shown throughout this book, Alagiyavanna's texts reveal a great deal about the cultural upheavals and transformations under colonial influences. Aside from his work on the Portuguese *tombo*, we may never know what Alagiyavanna actually *did* in his everyday life. Yet his poetry alerts us to his expression of discursive power (the kind of power that can influence and impose certain visions of reality) and his negotiations with institutional powers (the kind of power wielded by Sinhala kings and Portuguese officials who had a surplus of economic and military resources). The embellished, highly conventional nature of Sinhala Buddhist poetry retains usefulness in shedding light on people's lives in history. As Steven Collins has argued in respect to Pāli literature, "elite" texts can be sites of ideological power that articulate forms of religious and political order, shaping collective thought and individual impressions.[20] Therefore, contrary to the unstated implication behind the categories of lived and everyday religion, wherein textualized forms of religious expression are somehow invalid or inconsequential, our focus on the written works of Alagiyavanna illustrates that textual analysis remains an effective means for understanding the values, ideals, and aspirations that could be just as determinative for people's lives as so-called everyday practices and social encounters.

Furthermore, this study challenges the validity of drawing clear-cut dichotomies for religious identity in early colonial encounters. Alagiyavanna's poetic works illustrate varying, sometimes contradictory, examples of religious identity, making it difficult always to draw distinct boundaries between that which is Buddhist, Hindu, or Christian. His *Sävul Sandēśaya* depicts a pluralistic religious field wherein people participate in rituals held at Hindu and Buddhist temples to honor a variety of deities and the Buddha. The devotional offerings made to diverse extraordinary beings are not depicted as inconsistent with one another, although they are generally expressed in different social frames.[21] Subsequently, in

Subhāṣitaya, Alagiyavanna articulates a more circumscribed and exclusive notion of Buddhist identity, while denouncing those who follow different religious conventions apart from those connected with the Buddha. Here one finds efforts to distinguish that which is Buddhist from that which is not. However, this exclusive approach to religious identity is not sustained, as *Kustantīnu Haṭana* reintroduces a more complex picture. While working for the Portuguese, Alagiyavanna converted to Catholicism and apparently adopted a hybrid religious identity that drew in similar measures from Christian and Buddhist forms.

When examining his works, Alagiyavanna appears to have held shifting views on religious identity, moving from pluralism to exclusive demarcation to hybrid religious expressions. One could posit that a fluid notion of religious identity is one of the major effects of colonial encounters and results from the contact between different ideas about religious practice and adherence. The poet's portrayal of religion undergoes change, depending on his location in respect to the ruling power at the time. As such, religious identity was alternately blurred, sharpened, or blended in Alagiyavanna's works, but it clearly became a subject of conscious deliberation in the context of Christian missionary discourse about religious truths and falsehoods. In other words, religious identity became a matter for public representation and interrogation after various options were introduced and demands were made on adherents to model a specific religious identity as opposed to other ones. Alagiyavanna first sought to distinguish the truths and efficacy of Buddhism but later chose to identify to some degree with the Catholic faith of the Portuguese. Perhaps then the need to distinguish and choose between religious identities is a hallmark of early colonial encounters, but it is significant that with Alagiyavanna religious identity could still repeatedly shift and elude clear-cut distinctions.

The Power of Poetry

This study has also sought to focus attention on how Buddhist poetry was used to negotiate and refashion power in a historical period in which the traditional culture-power formation in Sri Lanka was tested and overturned. In previous centuries, Buddhist kings, monks, and poets could exercise power and influence over society in their respective positions. Kings enjoyed wealth, legal authority, and unparalleled ownership of land. Monks exercised religious and moral authority that rivaled the political authority of the king. In late medieval Sri Lanka, poets used their command of language to depict and confer power on themselves and others. Long understood as a vehicle for empowerment and self-assertion in South Asia, poetry had been fashioned as a discourse to express and authorize power long before Alagiyavanna used it in this way. For him, the composition and performance of poetry were a means of negotiating his position and influence under a Sinhala king, then in the absence of a Buddhist king, and finally under the Portuguese colonialists.

His poetic works display a keen awareness of which authorities—political and religious—could exercise power and, in Foucault's view, act to structure the possible field of action of others.[22] Kings and religious authorities, both living and deceased—as in the case of the Buddha—are consistently attributed with virtue and influence in the poet's works. By praising and describing them in poetic terms, Alagiyavanna was enhancing their abilities along with his own reputation and stature. Poetry thus possesses the capacity to refashion power in its own image, endowing the subjects and author of its verses with increased fame and influence. Whether speaking of Rājasiṃha I, the Bodhisattva, Constantino de Sá de Noronha, or a god, the poet focused his expressive talents on celebrating kings of various types. In doing so, Alagiyavanna was strengthening the ties that had long existed between sovereignty (*rājya*) and poetry (*kāvya*) in premodern Asia, wherein the practice of polity revolved in part around aesthetic practice.[23] For Alagiyavanna, Buddhist poetry (even when refashioned to celebrate Catholic figures) employed a discourse of power to gain access to and establish relations with people who exercised authority and influence over the society in which he lived.

The formal characteristics of Sinhala *kavi* are well suited for articulating certain expressions of power in political, religious, and social arenas. Verses may operate individually to deliver short ideological statements about what is excellent and true. Moreover, the semantic message of a verse is bolstered by the aesthetic and metrical features that serve to embellish and lend authority to its expressions. Poetry, whether Buddhist or not, is a genre wherein form is just as important as content. The skill and learning required to compose what might be called classical Sinhala poetry with all of its formal requirements thus would set certain authors apart from others. In Alagiyavanna's case, he commonly includes self-praise that distinguishes his literary skills. In *Sävul Sandēśaya*, he describes himself as a "very fine pandit" who "dove into the deep ocean of poetry and drama in Sanskrit and Pāli and who destroyed the elephants of poets who are his foes like a lion."[24] In *Dahamsoňḍa Kava*, he claims to be "renowned throughout the world" and "possessing the best of virtues."[25] Similarly, Alagiyavanna claims to have renown and the best of virtues while seeing the further shore of the Buddhist Tipiṭaka (i.e., the Three Baskets of Buddhist scriptures) according to the *Kusa Jātaka Kāvyaya.*[26] In *Subhāṣitaya*, among other qualities, he is the "best of poets" who speaks pleasingly like the goddess Sarasvatī and who splits open elephants, or other poets, like a lion.[27]

Such self-praise is far from unusual among authors of late medieval Sinhala poetry. Aside from its conventionality, however, such praise serves to reinforce the authority on which these works rest. The assumption widespread in premodern South Asia was that a skillful poet speaks words that are powerful enough to make reality conform to the speech that he (or less often, she) utters.[28] Alagiyavanna's panegyric verses about himself therefore function to confirm his reputation and to strengthen the claim that his verses have real effects on the world. Even *Kustantīnu Haṭana* draws on the skillful manipulation of rhyme, meter, and figures of speech to craft a literary work than can delight and persuade. In premodern Sri Lankan history, poetry often aspired to create a space within the domains of power in order to be recognized and rewarded. While much Sinhala poetry was composed to show reverence to the Buddha, beginning around the fifteenth century an increasing number of poetic works were produced to celebrate and secure blessings for kings. Thus, by the time Alagiyavanna began to compose poetry, he inherited a literary tradition that had been developed to praise figures of authority and represent symbols of power.

The influence of Alagiyavanna as a poet is glimpsed in the verses he wrote as well as the records that others wrote about him. He appears to us through the poetic works that he authored and a handful of references in Portuguese sources, along with remarks from the seventeenth-century French traveler named Jean Baptiste Tavernier. It is known that he was born the son of a reputable pandit in Hissälla, served under King Rājasiṃha I in Sītāvaka, and later converted to Catholicism and worked for the Portuguese on the *tombo*s or colonial land registers. Despite these details, Alagiyavanna remains an elusive yet compelling figure. The gaps in knowledge about him have permitted modern scholars to expand on his story and turn it into an allegory for contemporary concerns about religious and cultural identity in Sri Lanka. His power as a poet endures as modern scholars debate whether Alagiyavanna was either a hero or a traitor. To many, Alagiyavanna is noteworthy for his efforts to preserve the Sinhala poetic heritage when learning and literature went into steep decline.[29] He has been called the last author in the ancient line of Sinhala poets.[30] He has also been praised as "the shining star that illuminates the sky of the Sinhala language," one who is credited with having composed "immortal verses" that energize the Sinhala people.[31] Even though some critics consider Alagiyavanna's works to be derivative and undistinguished, he is still widely credited for having sustained Sinhala literature like a "solitary spark" in a time when many texts were lost and destroyed.[32]

Nevertheless, Alagiyavanna's later career makes him a problematic hero to some Sinhala Buddhists. The fact that he converted and worked for the Portuguese—a colonial order that is still widely reviled by Sinhalas to this day—generates feelings of ambivalence toward the poet. From the point of view of Buddhist nationalists—those Sri Lankans who posit an essential, age-old relationship between Buddhism and the nation that requires the energetic defense of both—Alagiyavanna forsook his devotion to Buddhism and the Sinhala nation to work for its greatest foes. In the light of contemporary conflicts over Christian missions and national sovereignty in Sri Lanka, the case of an early modern Sinhala poet who became a Catholic and praised the colonial overlords evokes strong resentments. One scholar's evaluation of Alagiyavanna as a traitor to his native country and religion, a person who was willing to convert opportunistically to the faith of whichever ruler in command, exemplifies some of the negative assessments of the poet.[33] Such a view resonates with contemporary Sri Lankan views of religious conversion, many of which associate the conversion to Christianity with self-interested acts done to raise one's economic standing in society.[34]

Contemporary evaluations of Alagiyavanna, however, do little to help us understand his writings. Most scholarly assessments of the author and his works are content to emphasize that he was a cultural hero for Sinhala literature. He is often read as a practitioner of the broader field of classical Sinhala *kavi*, a literary imitator whose works are chiefly interesting for what they replicate from other texts. This book has taken a different tack. The works of Alagiyavanna have been read and examined alongside one another to study the religious and cultural impact of Portuguese colonialism in Sri Lanka. The five poetic works discussed reveal much about the composition and pleasures of Sinhala poetry more generally. Any one of them could be fruitfully made into the subject of a monograph study. However, given that Alagiyavanna's entire career overlapped directly with one of the most tumultuous and consequential periods of colonial conquest in an Asian Buddhist land, what *Sävul Sandēśaya*, *Dahamsoňḍa*

Kava, Kusa Jātaka Kāvyaya, Subhāṣitaya, and *Kustantīnu Haṭana* tell us about important transformations in Buddhism and Sinhala literature in the early colonial era has been examined instead.

Alagiyavanna's texts illustrate for us poetic conceptions of what it meant to be Buddhist in the sixteenth and seventeenth centuries, while also displaying the range of poetic responses to Sinhala and Portuguese rules. The five works discussed in previous chapters represent some of the main types of poetic expression in Sinhala literature—a *sandēśa* or message poem, *jātaka* tales in verse, *upadeśa kāvya* or didactic verse, and the panegyric *praśasti* style of poetry. As such, Alagiyavanna's works represent many of the possible poetic themes and styles utilized by premodern Sinhala authors. The diverse poetic forms in which he wrote signify the diverse agendas that he had at different points in his career. Early on, Alagiyavanna wrote as a court poet to praise a king and his assembly, an approach that adhered to earlier poetic ideals that stressed the poet's crucial role in celebrating and strengthening the rule of kings. As time went on and as Buddhist institutions continued to deteriorate, Alagiyavanna's poetic works began to stress religious ideals and moral themes. Finally, near the end of his life, Alagiyavanna found himself dependent on Portuguese colonial authorities. The *Kustantīnu Haṭana,* which appears to have been his final work, expresses some of the ambiguities involved in siding with the colonizer at a time in which Portuguese imperialism was gaining influence in Sri Lanka. As a discourse that derived power from aesthetic conventions, the praise of great beings, and universal claims to moral and literary excellence, Sinhala poetry was an apt medium to establish relationships with political leaders and other elite authorities.

Moral Discourse and (Early) Modern Buddhism

Alagiyavanna's recognition that poetry could enhance fame and influence change was consistent with longstanding South Asian views of *kāvya.* But leaving aside the similarities between his literary work and earlier models, Alagiyavanna is notable for making Sinhala *kavi* accomplish new aims. What is particularly striking is his role in helping to construct what might be called modern Buddhism. Although many scholars tend to identify the phenomenon of modern Buddhism as a nineteenth-century product of the interaction between Buddhists and the British in Sri Lanka (and elsewhere), the examination of Alagiyavanna's works—particularly, *Subhāṣitaya*—suggest an earlier precedent for the development of a particularly modern view of Buddhism. The idea of modern Buddhism is likely more of an ideological construct than an empirical phenomenon. Nevertheless, a scholarly consensus is forming around the idea that the development of scientific discoveries and the spread of the discourses and values of modernity have given rise to distinctively new forms of Buddhism in the modern age.

Modern Buddhism has been defined as a system of rational and ethical philosophy divorced from daily practices that are traditional but now deemed superstitious.[35] Generally speaking, modern Buddhism seeks to recover the essential, allegedly rational core of the Buddha's Dharma and reject the tradition's more ritualistic and communal aspects for the sake of promoting worldly concerns of rational individuals living in an age of scientific truths.[36] The fact that increasing numbers of people are embracing modernist interpretations of Buddhism does not mean that more traditional, ritualistic forms of the religion are dying out. Like all religious persons facing pressure to conform to the values and technologies of the modern age, Buddhists may selectively adopt new features while retaining and revitalizing older forms of the tradition.

The varied expressions of modern Buddhism notwithstanding, scholars argue that its initial formulations were largely the result of encounters with Christian missionaries in the colonial period of Asian history. Donald S. Lopez, Jr. has singled out the series of debates that took place in 1873 between Buddhist monks and Christian missionaries in Sri Lanka as the starting point for the emergence of modern Buddhism.[37] Therein, Lopez locates the formulation of a new type of Buddhism that stresses its ancient philosophical roots and its universally applicable message. This modern version of Buddhism was thus forged in encounters with Christian interlocutors, many of whom accused Buddhists of following a superstitious, untrue faith. As a response, Asian Buddhists in the late nineteenth century and later began to espouse a Buddhism that claimed to be even more rational and scientifically oriented than Christianity. Lopez is, broadly speaking, correct in his description of the process by which modern Buddhism came to be articulated. However, we have seen here that the first expressions of what could be termed modern Buddhism occurred in fact much earlier. It is possible to argue that Alagiyavanna articulated a modern (or at least protomodern) Buddhist identity in the early seventeenth century when he fashioned a moralistic interpretation of the Buddha's religion over against other forms of theistic worship.

Alagiyavanna's *Subhāṣitaya* offers glimpses of an effort to construct a more exclusive and reflexive Buddhist identity in opposition to rival religious systems. Appearing shortly after the launch of an intensive missionary project in Sri Lanka, Alagiyavanna's defense of the Buddha's religion and denunciation of the "false" views of others appears as something of a turning point in the construction of Buddhist identity. His overt recognition of competing religious ideas signals both an awareness of other traditions and a willingness to combat them in order to reinforce the truth and vitality of the "tradition of the Buddha" (*muňindu samaya*).[38] The contrastive manner in which Alagiyavanna sets out to describe and defend this idea of Buddhism is noteworthy for its parallels with later, better known Buddhists such as the Anagārika Dharmapāla, who is almost universally credited with expressing a highly influential form of modern Buddhism around the turn of the twentieth century in Sri Lanka.[39] I do not wish to imply a direct link between Alagiyavanna and Dharmapāla as exponents of modern Buddhism in Sri Lanka. The latter is known to have employed a discourse of ethnic nationalism that is altogether absent in Alagiyavanna's thought. Yet, each was a lay Buddhist engaged in similar projects to delegitimize rival religious systems to Buddhism on the island. Dharmapāla's efforts to revitalize Buddhism were more intentional and comprehensive (not to mention more successful) than Alagiyavanna's comments in *Subhāṣitaya*. However, the latter work can be read as an early modern antecedent to later Sinhala Buddhist initiatives to reaffirm the validity of their tradition in comparison to others.

Alagiyavanna's *Subhāṣitaya* thus offers clear signs of the dawning of modern Buddhism in the early stages of colonial and missionary encounters in Asia. This work not only imagines and articulates a Buddhist tradition that competes with other religious traditions, it also recasts Buddhism in terms of one's adherence to moral teachings. By translating and presenting selective moral teachings on what followers of the Buddha should affirm, *Subhāṣitaya* depicts Buddhist adherence in terms of ethical practice and a self-reflexive commitment to this tradition's ideals. The focus on morality is significant, especially since such a theme was exceptional for Sinhala poetry at the time. Herein we see how moralistic appeals were used to shape and promote something akin to a modern Buddhist identity, much earlier than what most scholars have previously imagined.

In one sense, appeals to following Buddhist ethical codes of conduct are nothing new. After all, there are numerous ancient Pāli *suttas* in which the Buddha is said to encourage his followers to adopt various forms of moral practice such as selfless giving and the abstention from taking life. However, the emphasis that Alagiyavanna gives to moral teachings and ethical awareness in the light of his refutation of rival religious systems is suggestive of the use of moralism as the means to reassert the exclusive validity of Buddhism. Even forms of modern Buddhism in postcolonial Sri Lanka highlight the virtues of developing morality in order to trump the practices of non-Buddhists and reclaim a moral authority that exemplifies the superiority of Buddhism as a religion.[40] In *Subhāṣitaya*, we see moral instruction and criticism being used to reassert the value of the Buddha's teachings while undermining the views and practices of those people who follow different traditions. When such a stance is taken in the context of a decline in Sinhala Buddhist authority and sovereignty, it reflects an attempt to empower Buddhists who have been marginalized by the collapse of traditional centers of power and influence such as Buddhist monasteries and royal courts.

In the early seventeenth century, the expansion of Portuguese imperial control dismantled the traditional culture-power formation of Buddhist kingship and its mutually constitutive ties with monks and poets. When power could no longer be commanded by these traditional authorities, the attempt to regain it by means of asserting moral excellence must have become particularly appealing. Strictly speaking, the development of moral excellence is not dependent on royal patronage or monasticism. Moral development remained a viable path for Buddhist laypeople such Alagiyavanna, even in the midst of the cultural dislocation that accompanied the colonial transformation of political and religious authority. Like modern Buddhist reformers who composed texts urging moral behavior or critiqued Westerners for their immorality in drinking alcohol and eating beef in an effort to delegitimize colonial rule and to criticize Christianity, Alagiyavanna's *Subhāṣitaya* similarly emphasizes moral conduct and ethical reflection as a means of empowerment.[41] It is surely no coincidence that this "moral turn" coincided with the period when Sinhala Buddhists in the low country found themselves bereft of kings and monks who could sustain a social organization based on Buddhist norms and values.

However, Alagiyavanna's critical stance toward political and social formations in the seventeenth century disappeared after he converted and went to work for the Portuguese. His articulation of an early version of modern Buddhism was, as far as is known, short lived and effectively replaced by a more accommodating approach to colonial and Christian spheres of power as seen in *Kustantīnu Haṭana*. Assuming that Alagiyavanna authored this work, based in part on internal evidence as well as his unique position as a Sinhala poet who went to serve the Portuguese, there is a striking transition from the moralistic discourse of *Subhāṣitaya* to the panegyric style of *Kustantīnu Haṭana*. Once he found himself again within the sphere of a local, albeit colonial, ruling power, he turned away from giving moral admonitions and returned to the business of enhancing the fame and power of rulers.

One of the central themes uniting Alagiyavanna's works is his use of poetry to negotiate political power and cultural dislocation. Although the five works reflect various subjects and styles, they each express the poet's engagement with the world as it changed around him. His *Sävul Sandēśaya* conveys the interests and aspirations of a court poet seeking to solidify his position in the traditional culture-power formation that still existed under King Rājasiṃha I. The work celebrates the local king along with the religious pluralism and natural settings found throughout the kingdom of Sītāvaka. Not surprisingly, this early work contains a preponderance of images and phrases gleaned from previous authors, and this textual continuity likely reflects the perseverance of traditional social and religious formations that likewise spurred the composition of Sinhala *kavi* earlier. *Dahamsoňḍa Kava* and *Kusa Jātaka Kāvya* share several features as works that narrate *jātaka* stories and convey Buddhist concepts more directly. Each work cites the names of local elites who requested Alagiyavanna to compose a poetic work—the magistrate named Samaradivākara in the former case and the noblewoman Mäṇiksāmī in the latter.[42] Each work emerged from a court setting and addresses the interests of aesthetic connoisseurs with their evocative figures of speech and descriptive imagery. Yet in each of these works, signs of nostalgic longing and idealistic portrayals of Buddhist kings who bring the Dharma and peace to their respective realms are present. By dealing with such traditional narratives, Alagiyavanna could express his own longing for righteousness and harmony at a time marked by warfare and religious persecution.

The final two works attributed to Alagiyavanna contain conspicuous attempts to respond to the political and cultural upheaval that followed the fall of lowland Sinhala kings and the expansion of the Portuguese imperial project. *Subhāṣitaya* employs didactic verse to express particular ethical ideals in the face of political and social decline. Rather than simply celebrating powerful overlords, *Subhāṣitaya* is more concerned with criticizing immoral expressions of power and lamenting the breakdown of virtue in society. The work appears to mark a transitional period in Alagiyavanna's life, wherein he found himself dispossessed of the patronage and protection of a Sinhala king but not yet under the auspices of the Portuguese and the Catholic Church. Significantly, *Subhāṣitaya* contains comments that begin to define a distinctive religious system attributed to the Buddha and in opposition to others that revolve around deities.

Yet the strong support given to Buddhist values and adherence in *Subhāṣitaya* is largely overturned in *Kustantīnu Haṭana*, a work that deviates from the norms of Sinhala poetry by venerating Christian images of the divine and by praising Constantino de Sá de Noronha, the Portuguese captain-general in charge of Ceilão at that time. *Kustantīnu Haṭana* reverts back to some older poetic styles, drawing on both the panegyric comments of *praśasti* works and the motif of a journey through local landscapes that is reminiscent of *sandeśa* poetry. The key difference here is that the author utilizes his poetic skills to enhance the power of a colonial ruler and to solidify his position within a new power formation. The effect—if any—*Kustantīnu Haṭana* may have had on the Portuguese leaders in the island is unknown; nor do we know if Alagiyavanna benefited in any tangible way from it. However, the work offers clear evidence of the elderly poet's attempt to engage Portuguese political authority and negotiate with colonial spheres of power in early seventeenth-century Sri Lanka. Alagiyavanna adopts elements from local and colonial traditions to produce a complex hybrid vision of sovereignty and religiosity. The work enhances colonial power by refashioning it along the lines of Sinhala Buddhist ideals, a move that effectively undercuts many of the assumptions about religious and cultural superiority that accompanied Portuguese imperialism in the first place.

In each case, Alagiyavanna's poetic works enable us to see the varied responses available to local elites within a colonial context. Sinhala *kavi* at this point remained an aesthetic practice closely linked to the exercise of political power and expressions of cultural refinement. It was a genre that articulated expressions of power, usually in order to support and augment its specific manifestations. Like numerous authors of Sinhala poetry before him, Alagiyavanna constructed for himself an elevated social status based on his command of literary arts and his knowledge of texts. He appears in some poems as a confident author whose skill in composing poetry sets him apart from all others and makes him an invaluable agent in the wielding of power by local kings. He adopts the image of a lion that rips apart the elephants, which represent other, clearly inferior poets. Elsewhere, Alagiyavanna expresses religious motivations for composing his works. He encourages his audience to be serenely joyful in respect to the virtues of the Buddha as personified in the form of the Bodhisattva. He also aspires for some of his works to help facilitate the attainment of the comforts of heavenly rebirths and nirvana. Significantly, the poet draws on both aesthetic and moral excellence, in varying degrees from one text to another, in order to make an impact on the world. The celebration of power through the skillful use of language and imagery came in handy when Alagiyavanna wished to gain proximity and access to local rulers, who were in theory dependent on the praise of poets for respect and approval. Then when political power was being exercised to his detriment and to that of society, Alagiyavanna stressed morality as a symbol of and a sanction for authority.

In Alagiyavanna's hands, Buddhist poetry assumed the form of a literary tool that could fashion religious and social identities along with expressions of power in society. His poetry embodies a discourse of power that could either enhance or challenge the authority of various political and religious elites. The aesthetic values of poetry complemented its utility as a genre that would enhance the author's status while setting parameters for early modern conceptions for what it meant to be an adherent of the Buddha and his Dharma. Around the beginning of the seventeenth century, a Buddhist identity was being formulated in Ceilão in conjunction with and in contrast to other religious systems. Meanwhile, many of the resources that could help sustain a Buddhist identity were weakened and lost due to the imperial project and Catholic missions of the Portuguese. Aside from brief references to two leading monks in *Sävul Sandēśaya*, the Buddhist Sangha is largely absent from Alagiyavanna's works.[43] This is not wholly surprising given Portuguese efforts to repel and drive out all religious forms that appeared to be "heathen" and in competition with Christianity. The larger significance of this fact is that in the absence of monks from much of lowland Sri Lanka at this time, the practice of Buddhism was left to laypeople such as Alagiyavanna who tried to maintain their customs and beliefs despite the hostility of the colonizers. The focus of *Subhāṣitaya* on Indic gnomic verse rather than canonical Buddhist *suttas* gives a further hint of the weakness of monastic institutions. Although he was not the first layperson to write texts promoting Buddhist practice in Sri Lanka, the study of his career allows us to reflect on the important lay contributions to the history of Buddhism in Sri Lanka as well as to note that monks were not the only ones responsible for defining and preserving its traditions.[44]

The corpus of Alagiyavanna's works illustrates many things about the production and use of Buddhist poetry in early modernity. Although he lived at a time of political and cultural upheaval coinciding with the onset of direct colonial rule, he drew on the traditions and authority of Sinhala poetry to negotiate a place for himself and his religion. Even though he would ultimately convert to Catholicism and serve under the Portuguese in Sri Lanka, Alagiyavanna demonstrated the resourcefulness of literary traditions by composing poetic works in response to significant historical changes. His poetry, together with the scattered historical facts about him, fashion an image of a local elite who was constrained by the powers around him yet still able to articulate his interests in a compelling way. He resorted to the prestigious and influential art of poetry to express his personal goals and cultural values, even when it is unclear whether the political powers of the time responded to him in the way that he would have desired. Above all, the study of Alagiyavanna's works shows us how Buddhist literature could be used to negotiate with royal and colonial powers—some of which were hostile to Buddhism—and thus it survived the displacement of many other cultural forms in that place and time.

The picture of Alagiyavanna that emerges from this book tells a story of what it meant to be Buddhist during the onset of colonialism in Sri Lanka, experiencing and reacting to the pressures of the intensified contacts between peoples and religions in the early modern world. Often referred to as the last classical Sinhala poet, Alagiyavanna may also represent the first modern Buddhist, as seen in his works' early attempts to negotiate with a range of different authorities and cultural expressions that resemble the experiences of Buddhist practitioners in more recent centuries. The writing of poetic texts that both borrow from—and yet modify—past traditions allowed Alagiyavanna to fashion cultural and religious identities that enabled him to access and influence royal and colonial authorities. His use of literature to glorify kings and poets, to condemn the challenges to Buddhist cultural forms, and finally to assimilate new religious and political expressions is instructive when considering the various responses that modern Buddhists have employed to confront the disruptive effects of modernity on their religion in Sri Lanka.

Above all, Alagiyavanna's poetry and life story serve to illustrate contours of the dynamics of religious encounters in an early modern colonial setting. Volkhard Krech has defined the parameters for dynamics in the history of religion as the "intensified development and change of semantics and social structures" in religion.[45] The development and change witnessed in Alagiyavanna's poetry in response to the transformations in the social and political orders of Sri Lanka appear more in the semantic field and extend more broadly into other linguistic areas as well. His poetic works were sometimes highly conventional and derivative of older texts, while at other times he employed distinctly new poetic forms. Through the study of his works, one may note the dynamics in the transformation of literary expression and religious identity that resulted from the cultural pressures of Portuguese colonialism. Alagiyavanna and his works thus reflect how Sinhala Buddhist poetry could function not only as a medium for generating aesthetic sentiments but also for augmenting, contesting, and transforming expressions of power and religious adherence in an unstable colonial setting. It is through the writings of Alagiyavanna that some of the earliest traces of the consequences of colonialism on the Buddhist religion may be seen.

Notes

CHAPTER 1

1. One welcome exception to this situation is the attention given to the religious encounter between the Portuguese and the Sinhalas in the mid-sixteenth century by Alan Strathern's book *Kingship and Conversion in Sixteenth-Century Sri Lanka* (Cambridge, UK: Cambridge University Press, 2007).
2. Sanjay Subrahmanyam, "Connected Histories: Notes towards a Reconfiguration of Early Modern Eurasia," *Modern Asian Studies* 31/3 (1997), 736, 745.
3. One scholar helpfully compares Sanskrit praise poetry to ancient Vedic chants, inasmuch as they both are seen to be endowed with sacred speech, which in poetry is capable of increasing the glory of the object of praise. See Indira Viswanathan Peterson, *Design and Rhetoric in a Sanskrit Court Epic: The* Kirātārjunīya *of Bhāravi* (Albany: State University of New York Press, 2003), 11.
4. Michel Foucault, "The Subject and Power," *Critical Inquiry* 8/4 (1982), 790.
5. Donald S. Lopez, Jr., ed. *Curators of the Buddha: The Study of Buddhism under Colonialism* (Chicago: University of Chicago Press, 1995).
6. Richard Gombrich and Gananath Obeyesekere, *Buddhism Transformed: Religious Change in Sri Lanka* (Princeton, NJ: Princeton University Press, 1988), 215–218.
7. In addition to the work of Obeyesekere, other important studies on Protestant Buddhism may be found, for example, in Kitsiri Malagoda, *Buddhism in Sinhalese Society 1750–1900: A Study of Religious Revival and Change* (Berkeley: University of California Press, 1976) and George D. Bond, *The Buddhist Revival in Sri Lanka: Religious Tradition, Reinterpretation and Response* (Columbia: University of South Carolina Press, 1988).
8. John C. Holt, "Protestant Buddhism?" *Religious Studies Review* 17/4 (1991), 308–309.
9. Anne M. Blackburn, *Buddhist Learning and Textual Practice in Eighteenth-Century Lankan Monastic Culture* (Princeton, NJ: Princeton University Press, 2001), 199–201.
10. Anne M. Blackburn, *Locations of Buddhism: Colonialism & Modernity in Sri Lanka* (Chicago: University of Chicago Press, 2010), 202.

11. Elizabeth J. Harris, *Theravāda Buddhism and the British Encounter: Religious, Missionary and Colonial Experience in Nineteenth-Century Sri Lanka* (London: Routledge, 2006), 174–181.
12. Gregory Schopen, *Bones, Stones, and Buddhist Monks; Collected Papers on the Archaeology, Epigraphy, and Texts of Monastic Buddhism in India* (Honolulu: University of Hawai'i Press, 1997), 2–3.
13. Sheldon Pollock, *The Language of the Gods in the World of Men: Sanskrit, Culture, and Power in Premodern India* (Berkeley: University of California Press, 2006), 7–8.
14. I make a similar argument about Buddhist historiography in Stephen C. Berkwitz, *Buddhist History in the Vernacular: The Power of the Past in Late Medieval Sri Lanka* (Leiden, Netherlands: Brill, 2004). The idea of texts that can "make a difference," supplementing the empirical experience of reality by giving rise to such things as commitment, interpretation, and imagination is found in Dominick LaCapra, *Rethinking Intellectual History: Texts, Contexts, Language* (Ithaca, NY: Cornell University Press, 1983), 30. LaCapra's distinction here between the "worklike" and "documentary" aspects of texts has become influential in Buddhist studies.
15. Stephen Greenblatt, *Marvelous Possessions: The Wonder of the New World* (Chicago: University of Chicago Press, 1991), 12.
16. Jerome McGann, *The Textual Condition* (Princeton, NJ: Princeton University Press, 1991), 184.
17. Jerome McGann, "Rethinking Romanticism," *ELH* 59/3 (1992), 735–738.
18. A forthcoming work by Charles Hallisey, currently titled "Flowers on the Tree of Poetry: The Moral Economy of Literature in Buddhist Sri Lanka," promises to yield important reflections on the poetry of Śrī Rāhula.
19. A handful of other works has sometimes also been attributed to him—including *Mahā Haṭana* (*The Great War*), *Paraṅgi Haṭana* (*The War against the Portuguese*), and *Nīti Sāraya* (*Essence of Moral Instruction*), but these texts lack good evidence to be connected to our poet. For an older, more expansive list of Alagiyavanna's works, see D. W. Ferguson, "Alagiyavanna Mohoṭṭāla, the Author of 'Kusajātaka Kāvyaya,'" *Journal of the Royal Asiatic Society (Ceylon Branch)* 50 (1899), 116. Most scholars typically identify *Sävul Sandēśaya, Dahamsoňḍa Kava, Kusa Jātaka Kāvya, Subhāṣitaya,* and *Kustantīnu Haṭana* as the extant body of Alagiyavanna's works, although there is considerable debate over whether *Kustantīnu Haṭana* was actually composed by him.
20. Pollock, *Language of the Gods*, 24–26.
21. On the development and uses of Pāli poetry, see Steven Collins, "What Is Literature in Pali?" in *Literary Cultures in History: Reconstructions from South Asia*, ed. Sheldon Pollock (Berkeley: University of California Press, 2003).
22. Charles Hallisey, "Works and Persons in Sinhala Literary Culture," in *Literary Cultures in History: Reconstructions from South Asia*, ed. Sheldon Pollock (Berkeley: University of California Press, 2003), 694–695.

23. Pollock, *The Language of the Gods in the World of Men*, 2.
24. Nevertheless, as Hallisey shows, Buddhist religious values tended to exert their influences on Sinhala poetry as seen, for instance, by the insistence of *Siyabaslakara* that the proper subject of poetry should be the Buddha's previous lives as a *bodhisattva*. Cf. Hallisey, "Works and Persons," 703–704.
25. Pollock, *Language of the Gods*, 6, 18
26. Ibid., 25–27.
27. Hallisey, "Works and Persons," 698.
28. Berkwitz, *Buddhist History in the Vernacular*, 236–240. For examples of the "Sanskritized" language and conventions in Sinhala prose, see Stephen C. Berkwitz, *The History of the Buddha's Relic Shrine: A Translation of the* Sinhala Thūpavaṃsa (New York: Oxford University Press, 2007) and particularly the explanatory comments on this subject on pages 18–20.
29. Hallisey, "Works and Persons," 728.
30. Ibid.
31. Ibid., 733–740. One sometimes finds similar moves to compose difficult, complex verses in classical Sanskrit poetry. See, for instance, Peterson, *Design and Rhetoric*, 21–22.
32. Pollock, *Language of the Gods*, 184–185.
33. Ibid., 188.
34. Ibid., 419.
35. There are numerous, detailed studies of the Portuguese in Sri Lanka that may also be consulted. See, for example, Tikiri Abeysinghe, *Portuguese Rule in Ceylon 1594–1612* (Colombo: Lake House, 1966); Chandra Richard de Silva, *The Portuguese in Ceylon 1617–1638* (Colombo: H. W. Cave & Company, 1972); Paul E. Pieris, *Ceylon: The Portuguese Era*, vols. 1 & 2 (Dehiwala, Sri Lanka: Tisara Press, 1983); and Strathern, *Kingship and Conversion*; among other books on the subject.
36. Jorge Manuel Flores, *Hum Curto Historia de Ceylan: Five Hundred Years of Relations between Portugal and Sri Lanka*, (Lisbon: Fundação Oriente, 2000), 47.
37. C. R. de Silva, "The Rise and Fall of the Sitavaka Kingdom (1521–1593)," in *University of Peradeniya History of Sri Lanka: Volume II (c1500 to c1800)*, ed. K. M. de Silva (Peradeniya, Sri Lanka: University of Peradeniya, 1995), 63–73. As for Portuguese misdeeds, there were allegations made that Portuguese settlers often seized people's lands by force of arms, cut down jak and coconut trees in the local people's gardens for their own use, and engaged in unfair trading practices.
38. Zoltán Biedermann, "Tribute, Vassalage and Warfare in Early Luso-Lankan Relations (1506–1543)," in *Indo-Portuguese History: Global Trends*, ed. Fatima da Silva Gracias (Goa, India: Maureen & Camvet Publishers, 2005), 199–202.
39. De Silva, "Rise and Fall," 73–74.
40. See, for example, João de Barros and Diogo do Couto, *The History of Ceylon from the Earliest Times to 1600 AD*, trans. Donald Ferguson (Delhi, India: Navrang,

1993), 109–113; and Fernão de Queyroz, *The Temporal and Spiritual Conquest of Ceylon*, vol. 1, trans. S.G. Perera (New Delhi: Asian Educational Services, 1992), 114–120.

41. C. R. Boxer, "'Christians and Spices': Portuguese Missionary Methods in Ceylon, 1518–1658," *History Today* 8 (1958), 346.
42. Ibid., 347–349.
43. A. R. Russell-Wood, *The Portuguese Empire, 1415–1808: A World on the Move* (Baltimore: The Johns Hopkins University Press, 1992), 30–45.
44. De Silva, "Rise and Fall," 87.
45. Ibid., 96.
46. Barros and Couto, *History of Ceylon*, 308–387. Queyroz, *Temporal and Spiritual Conquest*, vol. II, 436–442.
47. Abeysinghe, *Portuguese Rule*, 32.
48. Abeysinghe, *Portuguese Rule*, 32–33.
49. De Silva, "Rise and Fall," 125–126.
50. V. Perniola, trans., *The Catholic Church in Sri Lanka: The Portuguese Period, vol. II, 1566 to 1619* (Dehiwala, Sri Lanka: Tisara Prakasakayo, 1991), 224.
51. E. Vimalasuriya Gunapala, *Kavīndra Alagiyavanna Mukaveṭi Caritaya* (Katugasthota, Sri Lanka: E. M. V. Gunapala, 1927), 25–26.
52. Flores, *Hum Curto Historia*, 73.
53. P. E. Pieris, *The Ceylon Littoral 1593* (Colombo: The Times of Ceylon, 1949), 9.
54. D. W. Ferguson, "Alagiyavanna Mohoṭṭāla," 116–118.
55. De Silva, *Portuguese in Ceylon*, 22–31
56. Ibid., 336–37.
57. See Gunapala, *Kavīndra Alagiyavanna Mukaveṭi Caritaya*, 29–30, and Ferguson, "Alagiyavanna Mohoṭṭāla," 118–119.
58. Flores, *Hum Curto Historia*, 75, and De Silva, *Portuguese in Ceylon*, 59.
59. An insightful critique of scholarly conceptions of power and agency appears in Ananda Abeysekara's essay "Buddhism, Power, Modernity," *Culture and Religion* 12/4 (2011): 489–497.
60. Jorge Flores, "'They Have Discovered Us': The Portuguese and the Trading World of the Indian Ocean," in *Encompassing the Globe: Portugal and the World in the 16th and 17th Centuries*, ed. Ana de Castro Henriques (Lisbon: Ministério da Cultura, Insitituto dos Museus e da Conservação, 2009), 234.
61. My attempt to define Buddhism in a more dynamic sense than usual owes much to work done on Buddhist identity by Ananda Abeysekara. He argues in his *Colors of the Robe: Religion, Identity, and Difference* (Columbia: University of South Carolina Press, 2002) for the need to view Buddhism as a relational discursive formation that becomes variously defined and disputed at specific, historically contingent moments (see pp. 3–4, 16–17).
62. Peter Skilling, "Theravāda in History," *Pacific World* 3rd Series/no. 11 (2009), 63.
63. Ibid., 62–64.

64. In Sri Lanka, these modern views have been in large part shaped by such reformers as the Anagārika Dharmapāla and Orientalist scholars as T. W. Rhys Davids, both of whom went far in presenting normative views of Buddhist practice and Buddhist texts to define Theravāda Buddhism. For more on this subject, see Stephen C. Berkwitz, "Buddhism in Modern Sri Lanka," in *Buddhism in the Modern World*, ed. David L. McMahan, 29–47. London: Routledge, 2011.
65. John Clifford Holt, *The Buddhist Viṣṇu: Religious Transformation, Politics, and Culture* (New York: Columbia University Press, 2004), 47–51, 57.
66. Thomas A. Tweed, "Theory and Method in the Study of Buddhism: Toward 'Translocative' Analysis," *Journal of Global Buddhism* 12 (2011), 27.
67. Pollock, *Language of the Gods*, 380.

CHAPTER 2

1. See Pollock, *Language of the Gods*.
2. David Shulman, *The Wisdom of Poets: Studies in Tamil, Telugu, and Sanskrit* (New Delhi: Oxford University Press, 2001), 63.
3. K. R. Norman, *Pāli Literature: Including the Canonical Literature in Prakrit and Sanskrit of All the Hinayana Schools of Buddhism* (Wiesbaden, Germany: Otto Harrassowitz, 1983), 58–59, 63, 75.
4. Pollock, *Language of the Gods*, 77.
5. Dehigaspe Pannasara, *Sanskrit Literature: Extant among the Sinhalese and the Influence of Sanskrit on Sinhalese* (Colombo: W. D. Hewavitarane Esqr., 1958), 109.
6. The tenth-century Sanskrit poet Rajaśekhara praised the author of *Jānakīharaṇa*, considering him second only to Kālidāsa as a poet. See Hallisey, "Works and Persons," 690. Noteworthy, too, is the fact that the manuscript used to reconstruct this ancient poetic work was written in the Malayalam script and may date from around the sixteenth century. See Pannasara, *Sanskrit Literature*, 106–107.
7. C. E. Godakumbura, *Sinhalese Literature* (Colombo: The Colombo Apothecaries Ltd., 1955), 144–147.
8. Cf. Stephen C. Berkwitz, "An Ugly King and the Mother Tongue: Notes on Kusa Jātaka in Sinhala Language and Culture," *parallax* 18/3 (2012), 59–61.
9. Hallisey, "Works and Persons," 700.
10. Godakumbura, *Sinhalese Literature*, 222–223.
11. Sheldon Pollock's list of characteristic features of *praśasti* poems can be found in Hallisey, "Works and Persons," 727.
12. Pollock, *Language of the Gods*, 134–143.
13. Shulman, *Wisdom of Poets*, 245–246.
14. Hallisey, "Works and Persons," 699.
15. W.L.A. Don Peter, "Portuguese Influence on a Sinhalese Poet," *Aquinas Journal* 6/1 (1989), 9. The renowned monastic poet Śrī Rāhula, for example, was

recognized as the chief incumbent of the Vijayabā Piriveṇa. He praises himself in his Kāvyaśēkhara:

> Listen happily to this doctrine,
> Spoken by the Chief Incumbent of the Vijayaba Pirivena,
> Who illuminates the ten directions with his fame,
> And who knows the Teaching of the Three Baskets well.

See Ratmalane Dharmakirti Sri Dharmarama, ed, *Śrī Rāhula Māhimiyan visin viracita Kāvyaśēkhara Mahākāvyaya*. Kelaniya, Sri Lanka: Vidyalankara University Press, 1966, v. 25.

16. Boxer, "'Christians and Spices,'" 348–349.
17. Ananda Kulasuriya, "Alagiyavanna Mukaveṭi Mohoṭṭāla: Kālina Tatu, Kaviyā hā Kavi Pabaňda," in *Sītāvaka Kaviya: Vivēcanāṭmaka Vigrahayak*, ed. Amara Hevamadduma et al. (Colombo: Department of Cultural Affairs, 1991), 6.
18. Gunapala, *Kavīndra Alagiyavanna Mukaveṭi Caritaya*, 3. Cf. Kulasuriya, "Alagiyavanna Mukaveṭi Mohoṭṭāla," 12.
19. Godakumbura, *Sinhalese Literature*, 349. Additionally, another description of *Svapnamalaya* describes this work as dealing with dreams as portents of things to come and mentions that it has been enlarged by a later author. See K. D. Somadasa, *Catalogue of the Hugh Nevill Collection of Sinhalese Manuscripts in the British Library*, vol. 5 (London: The British Library, 1993), 439–440. Elsewhere, W. F. Gunawardhana credits Dharmadvaja as being the real author of *Dahamsoṇḍa Kava*, although I will dispute this attribution in the following chapter. See W. F. Gunawardhana, *Subhashita Varnana: Being a Commentary on the Subhashita*, 2nd edit. (Colombo: Sri Bharati Press, 1925), ii–iii.
20. Gunawardhana, *Subhashita Varnana*, iii.
21. See, for example, Puñcibandara Sannasgala, *Sinhala Sāhitya Vaṁśaya*, 2nd ed. (Colombo: Department of Cultural Affairs, 1994), 342; and A. V. Suraweera, "Alagiyavanna Mukaveṭitumā," in *Gampaha District: Socio-Cultural Studies*, ed. A. V. Suraweera (Colombo: Department of Cultural Affairs, 1999), 190.
22. K.D.P. Wickramasinghe, *Haṁsa Sandēśaya* (Colombo: M.D. Gunasena, 1995), v. 56:

Vi mati	no vī dänagena adikaraṇa	arut
Pä vä tilesa ma kiyamin häma täna ma		surut
Nä vä ti	sitin akusal ava guṇat	borut
Si ṭi ti	paseka vāsala mukaveṭṭi	varut

23. Gunapala, *Kavīndra Alagiyavanna Mukaveṭi Caritaya*, 8. Gunapala settles on the term *registrar*. Rä. Tennekoon describes a *mukaveṭi* as a "secretary" but adds that he has some legal authority to decide minor cases. See Tennekoon, ed., *Sävul Sandēśaya* (Colombo: M.D. Gunasena, 1955), 139. I wish to thank my father Robert Berkwitz for his advice on the most appropriate legal term for *mukaveṭi*.
24. See, for example, Sannasgala, *Sinhala Sāhitya Vaṁśaya*, 2nd ed., 298; and H. V. Abahyagunawardhana, "Sävul Sandeśa Pilibaňda Vimarshanayak," in *Sītāvaka*

Kavi, ed. Amara Hevamadduma et al. (Colombo: Department of Cultural Affairs, 1991), 25.

25. Pollock, *Language of the Gods*, 14.
26. Abhayagunawardhana, "Sävul Sandeśa Pilibaňda Vimarshanayak," 29.
27. Tennekoon, *Sävul Sandēśaya*, v. 1:

Särade sävuliňdu saňda—ratamiṇi sadisi siḷuyut
Dimutu mutu kalambev—paḷaheḷa piya patara sädi

28. See, for example, Tennekoon, *Sävul Sandēśaya*, v. 5. I wish to thank P. B. Meegaskumbura for helping me to understand the importance of friendship in this work.
29. Ibid., v. 9:

Mituru hasalakaḷa kaḷa me rada rada visuḷa leḷa tarala miṇi sadisi vū
sabaňda miyuru rasa bas nusun vū ē asun kiyaṁ matu me dän topa
nikutvana sav isuru numutvana me purä sirisara vänuṁ miṇi koňṁol
ta savan sada.

30. Tennekoon, *Sävul Sandēśaya*, vv. 10–11:

Pähäsara	yasäti sē tā raka pati se du	ḷa
Muḷudiya	te ka mā tā vaka van näba	ḷa
Hämavara	siri di tā räka varaṇa ka	ḷa
Danuva	mitura sītāvaka pura laka	ḷa
Manahara	digata pätirena saňdakän ha	raṇa
Tarasara	tuňgu pavura räňdi piḷimiṇi ki	raṇa
Naravara	naraṇa raňdanā me nuvara ki	raṇa
Vaṭakara	ananta nārada lū väni da	raṇa

31. Velivitiya Sorata, *Śrī Sumaňgala Śabdakośaya*, part II (Mount Lavinia, Sri Lanka: Abhaya Publishers, 1970), 906.
32. The attacks on Sītāvaka occurred in early 1550 and again in late 1551. See some related comments on the imaginative vision of Alagiyavanna in Abhayagunawardhana, "Sävul Sandeśa Pilibaňda Vimarshanayak," 27.
33. Tennekoon, *Sävul Sandēśaya*, v. 15:

Me pura	vara visal salpil tuḷä udu	ḷa
Pa tara	anagi mutumiṇi räs ras visu	ḷa
E vara	'gatisi genä dilyen silil u	ḷa
Sa yura	vilas satahaṭa no hära paḷaka	ḷa

34. Velivitiya Sorata, ed., *Kalpalatā Vyākhyā Sahita Kavsiḷumiṇa* (Mount Lavinia, Sri Lanka: Abhaya Publishers, 1966), III. 14:

Ne visituru ruvanu—dula tarapatara keḷiyen,
Isihu silil uḷa siyal—ruvanāra dura lannā.

35. K.W.De A. Wijesinghe, ed. and tran., *Sälalihiṇi Sandeśa* (Colombo: Godage International Publishers, 2006), v. 54:

Diya kaňda	gämbara piri puvatara maha	sayu	ra
Muva raňda	lesin vata agatī'si kara	tamba	ra
Mana naňda	karana miṇi gaṇa men disi	eva	ra
Pähä nada	pahan ehi mahaveyä bala	mitu	ra

36. Bandusena Gunasekara, ed. *Tisara Sandēśaya* (Colombo: S. Godage and Brothers, 1986), v. 17:

Kaḷayen upan agatisi nam ekaku pe	ra
Ekäňdilini gat vara viyäḷiṇi sat sayu	ra

37. In contrast, Stephen Greenblatt affirms that the transition from feudalism to despotism in early modern western Europe fostered a new change in consciousness and a need for secretaries, ministers, and poets to find new ways to shape worlds and their characters. See Stephen Greenblatt, *Renaissance Self-Fashioning: From More to Shakespeare* (Chicago: University of Chicago Press, 1980), 162.
38. Tennekoon, *Sävul Sandēśaya*, v. 16:

Ni mal	miṇimäduruvala sīmäduru pa	ta
Ḷa kal	kalūn vatsiri narambā dimu	ta
Su pul	soňduru piyumäyi digukaramina	ta
Kuhul	sitin häsireti ehi mataňga ma	ta

39. Gunasekara, *Tisara Sandēśaya*, v. 12:

Nil mini mäňdurē sī mäňdurata säpa	ta
Kal baňda soňda vata dakimin mataňga ma	ta
Pul piyumeka kuhulin digu karata a	ta
Tul rahuväni sisi gänumaṭa gaman ga	ta

40. Hallisey, "Works and Persons," 718.
41. On the figurative device of the city's splendor dispelling the darkness of night, see Tennekoon, *Sävul Sandēśaya*, vv. 13 and 18.
42. Pollock, *Language of the Gods*, 184–186.
43. Tennekoon, *Sävul Sandēśaya*, v. 86:

Sa yu ra	ṭa	vadina gaṅ hō vilasa paḷa	ka ra
Ni si pa	ṭa	saḷu kapuru kasturu saňdun	ha ra
Ne ka ra	ṭa	valehi niriňdō puda paňduru	kä ra
Mona va	ṭa	siṭiti mudunat dī kara tam	ba ra.

44. Tennekoon, *Sävul Sandēśaya*, v. 83:

Ma ha	ta	sayura diya saha pas muḷu dera	ṇa
Ni si	ta	näṇin dänä kaḷa metekäyi pama	ṇa

Di ya	ta	vavana vahasala mukaveṭṭi ga	ṇa
Si ṭi	ta	supun sisi kän men saba kira	ṇa

45. Tennekoon, *Sävul Sandēśaya*, v. 84:

Gä mbu ru	saku magada heḷu demaḷehi puru	du
So ňdu ru	saňda lakara viyaraṇa dat kivi	ňdu
Mi yu ru	arut yodamin kav bäňda viri	du
A tu ru	nova kiyati sabaturehi narani	ňdu

46. Pollock, *Language of the Gods*, 186–187. Śrī Rāhula helped to authorize this image of the poet in Sri Lanka by referring to himself as having mastered all the sciences of learning, skilled in several languages, and fit to recite his work in the company of the learned. See Hallisey, "Works and Persons," 715–716.
47. Tennekoon, *Sävul Sandēśaya*, v. 34:

Hara turu rāja	vilasin yasäti no vita	ra
Nisi manu rāja	kulayen pävatena pava	ra
Rupu para rāja	mata gaja biňdi kesara yu	ra
Dina vara rāja	siha naraniňdu saňda me pu	ra

48. K. V. Zvelebil, *Tamil Literature* (Leiden, Netherlands: E. J. Bril, 1975), 7, 98.
49. Pollock, *Language of the Gods*, 145–46.
50. Ibid., 148.
51. Tennekoon, *Sävul Sandēśaya*, v. 36:

U vi ňdu	kiraṇa aḷalana saňdä nägi soba	na
Ta ri ňdu	amā situmiṇa suratura räge	na
Si ni ňdu	vata tepala sita ataṭa yodami	na
Pa si ňdu	me himi mävu väni maha bambu visi	na

52. Tennekoon, *Sävul Sandēśaya*, v. 53:

Di si aga raňga	miṇeka van rivi kula kiru	ḷa
Mu ḷu diya taňga	me niriňdu yasa räsa näba	ḷa
Duḷa suragaňga	yaṭa diya tek sevaṇa ka	ḷa
Bamba utumaňga	sē sat vilasa paḷa ka	ḷa

53. The image of Brahmā holding a parasol also evokes the image of the Buddha, who in many texts is portrayed as the one for which the parasol is being held. For example, the commentary to the *Buddhavaṃsa* states: "And the Brahmā Sahaṁpati stood holding a white parasol that was like another full moon, three leagues (*tiyojana*) in extent, above the Meritorious One." See Yagirala Pannananda, ed., *Madhuratthavilasini: Or the Commentary to the Buddhawansa* (Colombo: Simon Hewavitarne Bequest, 1922), 239. This same image is repeated several times in the thirteenth-century *Sinhala Thūpavaṃsa*. See Berkwitz, *History of the Buddha's Relic Shrine*, 58, 70, 111, 216.

54. Sorata, *Kavsiḷumiṇa*, I.52:

Ohu yese sesateka—siri rukuḷe bamba mudunē
Suragaňgayaṭāga raňdanā—diya tek sevaṇa baňdanā

55. Pollock, *Language of the Gods*, 185.
56. Tennekoon, *Sävul Sandēśaya*, v. 57:

Da sa	ṭa	avi sarama däna viridu biňda ha	ḷa
Da sa	ṭa	poraṇarut situsē puhuṇu ka	ḷa
Da sa	ṭa	pasidu me niriňdu rivi kula kiru	ḷa
Da sa	ṭa	desehi basa siya basa men hasa	ḷa

57. Similar praise of a king's intellectual and martial abilities is found in *Pärakumbā Sirita*, wherein King Pärakumbā is praised for "knowing through examination all of the arts, including poetics, drama, and the arts of various kinds of weapons." See D. G. Abhayagunaratna, ed., *Pärakumbā Sirita*, 1929, reprint (Colombo: Madhyama Saňskṛtika Aramudala, 1997), v. 121.
58. Tennekoon, *Sävul Sandēśaya*, v. 207:

Gä mbu ru	sakumagada kav naḷu siňdu kimi	dī
Mi tu ru	novana kivi gaja siha sirin bin	dī
Soňd uru	alagivan mukaveṭi namäti su	dī
Mi yu ru	pada rasäti me sävul asna ye	dī

59. In comparison, however, Śrī Rāhula was even less inhibited about engaging in self-praise in his *Kāvyaśēkhara*. See Hallisey, "Works and Persons," 715–716.
60. Tennekoon, *Sävul Sandēśaya*, v. 34.
61. Hallisey, "Works and Persons in Sinhala Literary Culture," 709–710.
62. Tennekoon, *Sävul Sandēśaya*, v. 37:

No hiṁ	saturu ganaňduru durä lamini ru	du
Dä guṁ	vata mesiri laka 'mbara me himi sa	ňdu

63. Ibid., v. 25.
64. Tennekoon, *Sävul Sandēśaya*, v. 39:

Sa ta ta	me himi kara maha meyini pähädu	ḷa
Ga sa ta	'sipata sena rupu niriňdu giri ku	ḷa
Di ga ta	pätirä yana yasa gigumata näba	ḷa
Pa ti ta	viya una 'mbu kara hara balā vä	ḷa

65. Abhayagunaratna, *Pärakumbā Sirita*, v. 94:

Laki su	ru surata lela kagapata vālaku	ḷē
Nira ti	ru näňgena evigasa palādigin ve	lē
Ami tu	ru niriňdu aňganan kōmala urata	lē
Piyo vu	ru tisara mutuhara neḷumbudali ha	lē

66. See, for example, the image of two leaves compared to the red eyes of grieving widows in Tennekoon, *Sävul Sandēśaya*, v. 48. Cf. Sorata, *Kavsiḷumiṇa* I. 43, where the red eyes of the enemies' widows are compared to leaves that grow from the fame of the king who defeated their husbands.
67. Shulman, *Wisdom of Poets*, 106.
68. Tennekoon, *Sävul Sandēśaya*, v. 31:

Sa ka ta	sa va ta	lesa buja bala vikuṁ yu	ta
Nu muta	sa ma ta	mahasen raňdanā sata	ta
Ma hata	sä pa ta	piri me purehi siri ana	ta
Va na ta	a na ta	narambata saka mut ke va	ta

69. Tennekoon, *Sävul Sandēśaya*, v. 201:

Sa ma ta	sura naran neta rasa aňdun yu	ta
Di mu ta	sumana suriňduge tunu siri vana	ta
Sa ta ta	savata suraguru gaṇi suru ana	ta
Sa ma ta	me sura misa an ke viyata sama	ta

70. See, for example, James Gair, *Studies in South Asian Linguistics: Sinhala and Other Languages*, ed. Barbara C. Lust (Oxford, UK: Oxford University Press, 1998).
71. Hallisey, "Works and Persons," 733.
72. Bourdieu contributes a similar, though broader argument about the social separation achieved by the arbiters of aesthetic taste in modern France. See Pierre Bourdieu, *Distinction: A Social Critique of the Judgement of Taste*, trans. Richard Nice (Cambridge, MA: Harvard University Press, 1984), 56–57.
73. Hallisey, "Works and Persons," 733–736.
74. For some dated but still helpful remarks about Sinhala *eḷu*, see James de Alwis, "On the Elu Language, Its Poetry and Its Poets," *The Journal of the Ceylon Branch of the Royal Asiatic Society of Great Britain & Ireland* 2–5 (1850): 241–315.
75. Hallisey, "Works and Persons," 736–737.
76. Tennekoon, *Sävul Sandēśaya*, v. 120:

Vä la ňda	aruṇu ras kasa vata peraga i	si
No maňda	lovaňganehi gana'ňdara kasaḷa rä	si
Ä ma ňda	eḷi karaṇa ganaran musun le	si
Sa ba ňda	kiraṇa kiňdu dula rivi balaga ri	si

77. Cf. Tennekoon, *Sävul Sandēśaya*, 170; Peliyagoda Aggavamsa Thera, ed., *Sävul Asna hēvat Sävul Sandēśaya* (Colombo: Sri Lankaloka Printers, 1925), 46; Udupila Dhammasiri and Sirisena Gamage, eds. *Alagiyavanna Mukaveṭitumāgē Sävul Sandēśa* (Colombo: Star Printers, 1968), 141.

78. When taken in their expressed word order, the words of this poem appear nonsensical:

> Wrapping-dawn's-rays-yellow-cloth-eastern-mountain-sage
> Large-world-courtyard-thick-darkness-rubbish-heap
> Sweeping-clean-solid-gold-broom-like
> Friend-rays-fibers-shining-sun-take a look-desire

79. Tennekoon, *Sävul Sandēśaya*, v. 151.
80. Tennekoon, *Sävul Sandēśaya*, v. 138:

> Miṇi mutu mal pabaḷu yutu sal pil dora ḷa
> Maha vidi tutu dada liya turu räv vata ḷa
> Siňdu vara varaṇa mihipā rada liya laka ḷa
> Vana pura vara siri sara naramba tamba si ḷa

81. The oral tradition among Alagiyavanna's living descendants specify seven villages originally granted him by King Rājasiṃha: Narangaspitiya, Boralangaspitiya, Ambagaspitiya, Malvatuhiripitiya, Lavulupitiya, Butpitiya, and Happitiya. A scholar writing earlier claims that he received these villages from King Rājasiṃha II (r. 1635–1687), but this seems unlikely. See Gunapala, *Kavīndra Alagiyavanna Mukaveṭi Caritaya*, 39. At least two scholars have asserted that Alagiyavanna also received his birth village of Hissälla as well. See Gunapala, *Kavīndra Alagiyavanna Mukaveṭi Caritaya*, 27, and K.D.G. Wimalaratne, *Personalities Sri Lanka: A Biographical Study* (Colombo: Ceylon Business Appliances, 1994), 8.
82. See Stephen C. Berkwitz, "Buddhism in Sri Lanka: Practice, Protest, and Preservation," in *Buddhism in World Cultures: Comparative Perspectives*, ed. Stephen C. Berkwitz (Santa Barbara, CA: ABC-CLIO, 2006), 45–47. For a sustained examination of the rhetoric of identity and difference in Sri Lankan Buddhism, see Abeysekara's *Colors of the Robe*.
83. Gombrich and Obeyesekere, *Buddhism Transformed*, 29–36. The work of Obeyesekere, in particular, has cast light on how the stresses of modern life have fueled the resurgence in cultic practices oriented toward gods in Sri Lanka. On Buddhist participation in spirit cults in Colombo and in Kataragama, see Gananath Obeyesekere, *Medusa's Hair: An Essay on Personal Symbols and Religious Experience* (Chicago: University of Chicago Press, 1981).
84. Stephen C. Berkwitz, "Resisting the Global in Buddhist Nationalism: Venerable Soma's Discourse of Decline and Reform," *Journal of Asian Studies* 67/1 (2008), 93–94. For a different interpretation of Soma's position against deity worship, see Holt, *Buddhist Viṣṇu*, 334–335, 348–350.
85. Martin Wickremasinghe, *Sinhalese Literature*, trans. E. R. Saratchandra (Colombo: M. D. Gunasena & Co., 1950), 142.
86. Ibid., 148–50.

87. C. R. de Silva, "Sri Lanka in the Early 16th Century: Political Conditions," in *University of Peradeniya History of Sri Lanka: Volume II (c1500 to c1800)*, ed. K. M. de Silva (Peradeniya, Sri Lanka: University of Peradeniya, 1995), 35–36.
88. Tennekoon, *Sävul Sandēśaya*, v. 45:

Sa ka ta	savata vikumäti me rajuge soba	na
Di ga ta	pätirä ya ta teda yugata nala me	na
Ti ne ta	saňda valā peḷayä yi salakami	na
Moho ta	raňgā vehesini avasara no dä	na

89. Tennekoon, *Sävul Sandēśaya*, v. 96:

Pavara tuňgutul hima—giri rajahaṭa nadana		vana
Basa'rut lesin ven novamin häma dava		sa
Sasandara baraṇa vetä raňdanā niti nido		sa
Tun yamehi gat tun—vesin tun lova parasidu		
Nama kaḷa	sura kiruḷu kemi ratäňgili dali	na
Sula kaḷa	siri saraṇa siya patini voraňda	na
Piyuṁ	yon uvindu hara sak ā̆ pava	ra
No hiṁ	suranhaṭa vara vara dena nito	ra
Utuṁ	guṇen yutu haraňganahaṭa pava	ra
Ḷa pem	vemin nama kärä rägena avasa	ra

90. Ibid., vv. 95–96. The remains of this temple, now known as the Bärendi Kovil, lie outside Avisawella, Sri Lanka.
91. Ibid., v. 118.
92. On various accounts of the circulation of the Tooth Relic, including one that holds it was kept at Delgamuwa for a period, see John S. Strong, "'The Devil Was in That Little Bone': The Portuguese Capture and Destruction of the Buddha's Tooth Relic, Goa, 1561," *Past and Present* 206, suppl. 5 (2010): 184–198.
93. Tennekoon, *Sävul Sandēśaya*, v. 123:

Bamba su ra	nara uraga kiruḷaga miṇi rasi	na
Häma va ra	pudana siri pā tambarin soba	na
Muni va ra	vadanambara sulakaḷa tariňdu me	na
Ma mitu ra	namadu daḷa dā himi haṭa bäti	na

94. Dharmaratna Herath. *The Tooth Relic and the Crown* (Colombo: Gunaratna Press, 1994), 162–163.
95. W. S. Karunatillake, "The Religiousness of Buddhists in Sri Lanka through Belief and Practice," *Religiousness in Sri Lanka*, ed. John Ross Carter (Colombo: Marga Institute, 1979), 27–28.
96. Tennekoon, *Sävul Sandēśaya*, v. 124:

Pa si du	utuṁ lakuṇen kaḷa muni ruva	da
Muni ňdu	dā nadan kärä kaḷa dā gäba	da

Vi hi du gana kuḷak baňdu rudu duma radu da
Na ma du mitura bätiyen tun sita pähä da

The "three moments of thought" (*tun sita*) refer to: the thought at the start of an action, the thought while the act is taking place, and the thought after the completion of the act. Thus the devotee will ideally experience serene joy throughout the entire performance of venerating the Buddha.

97. See Tennekoon, *Sävul Sandēśaya*, v. 125. Cf. Wijesinghe, *Säḷalihiṇi Sandeśa*, v. 97.
98. Tennekoon, *Sävul Sandēśaya*, v. 125.
99. The alleged dispute between the two most famous monks of the fifteenth century is alluded to in literary works from the period. Based on the satirical comments directed to Hindu gods and practices in *Buduguṇālaṅkara* (*Ornaments of the Buddha's Virtues*), Wickremasinghe casts Vīdāgama as a staunch opponent to Śrī Rāhula and his school that embraced Brahmanical religious and literary norms. See Wickremasinghe, *Sinhalese Literature*, 181. Hallisey, however, rightly points out that even Vīdāgama wrote a manual for composing poetry comprised of auspicious phonemes called *Kavlakuṇunmiṇimaldama* (*Garland of the Gems of the Characteristics of Poetry*) and thus could hardly have been as wholly opposed to Brahmanical culture as modern Sinhala critics often claim. See Hallisey, "Works and Persons," 740. Instead, the rivalry between these two monastic leaders may have arisen because of political affiliations more than cultural preferences. It appears that Rāhula was a vocal supporter of Jayabāhu II, who was a contender to succeed Parākramabāhu VI in 1467, whereas Vīdāgama supported the rival prince Sapumal (later Bhuvanekabāhu VI) in his efforts to become king. See H.B.M. Ilangasinha, *Buddhism in Medieval Sri Lanka* (Delhi, India: Sri Satguru Publications, 1992), 110–111.
100. Tennekoon, *Sävul Sandēśaya*, vv. 170–172.
101. Ibid., v. 173.
102. Ibid, v. 174.
103. Ibid.
104. Ibid, v. 176.
105. Abhayagunawardhana, "Sävul Sandēśa Pilibaňda Vimarśanayak," 36–37.
106. See Tennekoon, *Sävul Sandēśaya*, v. 176.
107. Abhayagunawardhana, "Sävul Sandēśa Pilibaňda Vimarśanayak," 36–37.
108. Gombrich and Obeyesekere, *Buddhism Transformed*, 30–31, 102–106.
109. Tennekoon, *Sävul Sandēśaya*, vv. 189–190:

Su ga tiňdu siri saraṇa sara päläňdi muduna ta
Pa ra si du sura raduge muḷu tediyaṭeka ne ta
Pä hä vidu ran paṭin hebi soňduru naḷala ta
Vidu kiňdu tora novana gana kuḷekä siri ga ta
Iňdu nil ya ṭa ga lela nil dada yuvala me na

Pähädul	bäma saňgaḷa sura raduge voraňda	na
Netupul	upul susadā tora novä keḷa	na
Mihilol	välan yuvaleka siri gati soba	na

110. Toshiichi Endo, *Buddha in Theravada Buddhism: A Study of the Concept of Buddha in the Pali Commentaries* (Dehiwela, Sri Lanka: Systematic Print, 1997), 24–29.
111. Tennekoon, *Sävul Sandēśaya*, v. 8.
112. Ibid., v. 195.
113. Ibid., v. 201.
114. Tennekoon, *Sävul Sandēśaya*, v. 202:

Namakaḷa sura asura—nara nā kiruḷu kemi dula

Vese s nido s	atäňgili petten te	vuna
A pi s tavu s	haskän nitten se	vuna

Muni saraṇa siyapata—mudunata pälaňdi hämasaňda

Sa van a ba ra ṇa	kaḷa tevaḷā dahaṁ kaňd	a
Su mana su ma na	suraraju siripada nämaň	da
Pa va ra	me apa munisasna da sat lova	da
Ḷa ta ra	rājasiha niriňdu da mäti gaṇa	da
Pa ta ra	ätas riya pābaḷa sen paba	ňda
Ni to ra	rakina lesa ayadin mituru sa	ňda

115. Suraweera, "Alagiyavanna Mukaveṭitumā," 191.

CHAPTER 3

1. K. M. De Silva, *A History of Sri Lanka* (Berkeley: University of California Press, 1981), 109.
2. P. E. Pieris, *Ceylon and the Portuguese, 1505–1658*, reprint [1920] (New Delhi: Asian Educational Services, 1999), 94.
3. C. R. de Silva, "Rise and Fall," 97.
4. Pieris, *Ceylon and the Portuguese*, 94.
5. This story was told to me by a caretaker at the Bärendi Kovil, at the site of the old Sītāvaka Kingdom in Avisawella, Sri Lanka, in 2006.
6. Barros and Couto, "The History of Ceylon," 271.
7. Ibid., 177, 272.
8. C. R. de Silva, "Rise and Fall," 95.
9. Queyroz, *Temporal and Spiritual Conquest*, vol. II, 438.
10. A. P. Buddhadatta, ed., *The Mahāvansa: Pali Text Together with Some Later Additions* (Colombo: M. D. Gunasena & Co., 1959), 584, vv. 10–12, 14:

Sivabhattiṃ gahetvāna nāsento jinasāsanaṃ/bhikkhusanghaṃ ca sātento jhāpento dhammapotthake

Bhindāpetvāna ārāme saggamaggampi chādayi/saṃsārakhāṇubhūto ca micchadiṭṭhim agaṇhi so.
Sumanakūṭamhi uppannaṃ sabbalābhaṃ hi gaṇhitum/niyojesi tahiṃ pāpamicchādiṭṭhikatāpase....
Tadā rājabhayeneva uppabbajiṃsu bhikkhavo/saṃsārabhīrukā tesu gatā āsuṃ tahiṃ tahiṃ.

11. C. R. de Silva, "Rise and Fall," 96.
12. Gunapala, *Kavīndra Alagiyavanna Mukaveṭi Caritaya*, 12.
13. On the "Hinduization" of Sri Lanka from the Koṭṭe Period, see Ilangasinha, *Buddhism in Medieval Sri Lanka*, 212–219. Cf. Strathern, *Kingship and Conversion*, 126–129.
14. C. R. de Silva, "Rise and Fall," 98.
15. Suraweera, "Alagiyavanna Mukaveṭitumā," 191.
16. Gunapala, *Kavīndra Alagiyavanna Mukaveṭi Caritaya*, 12.
17. This story was related to me by A.M.A. Herbert Kumar Alagiyavanna and his relatives in Kirindiwatte, Sri Lanka, in May 2006.
18. W. F. Gunawardhana, *Subhashita Varnana*, ii–iii.
19. Cf. Sorata, Velivitiye, ed., *Alagiyavanna Mukaveṭituman visin viracita Dahamsoňḍa Kava* (Colombo: Jinalankara Printers, 1934), v. 34; D. M. Samarasinghe, ed. *Alagiyavanna Mukaveṭituman visin racanā karana lada Kusa Jātaka Kāvyaya* (Colombo: Sri Lanka Publishing Company, 1964), v. 29:

Ratadarini nāliya
Gamanin sadisi nāliya
E pura sara ṇā liya
Kavuru naṁhäki vetiva ṇāliya.

20. Sorata, *Dahamsoňḍa Kava*, v. 9. Cf. Tennekoon, *Sävul Sandēśaya*, vv. 34 and 53, where King Rājasiṃha is described as one "who is like the lion who splits open the rutting elephants of enemy kings" and "who appears like the multicolored gem atop the crown of the Solar Dynasty."
21. Sorata, *Dahamsoňḍa Kava*, vv. 6–8. See also Gunapala, *Kavīndra Alagiyavanna Mukaveṭi Caritaya*, 9.
22. Sorata, *Dahamsoňḍa Kava*, v. 10:

Suguṇa ruvanā kara
Yasasiṅ sari sūdā kara
Me samaradivā kara
Mukaveṭṭi mätisaňda dayākara.

23. Sorata, *Dahamsoňḍa Kava*, v. 12:

Patā mok säpata ma
Situ natu kara kusalaṭa ma
Karavā peti piḷi ma
Liyavi tevaḷā dahaṁ manara ma

24. Tennekoon, *Sävul Sandēśaya*, v. 39.
25. Sorata, *Dahamsoňḍa Kava*, v. 14.
26. Ibid., v. 15. This same simile of the swan being able to separate milk from water when drinking also appears at the beginning of the thirteenth-century *Saddharmaratnavaliya*. See Dharmasena Thera, *Jewels of the Doctrine: Stories of the Saddharma Ratnavaliya*, trans. Ranjani Obeysekere (Albany: State University of New York Press, 1991), 3.
27. Sorata, *Dahamsoňḍa Kava*, v. 13:

    Boru tepala rahame ra
    Tuḍa no vakayi visa se go ra
    An satu dana pata ra
    Sitayi käṭakäbäliti se häma vara.

28. Shulman, *Wisdom of Poets*, 72. Shulman also notes here that the increasing importance for the king to find recipients of his wealth led to a new dynamic of kingship wherein the poet assumed more power in legitimating the authority of kings.
29. See, for example, Tennekoon, *Sävul Sandēśaya*, vv. 43, 67.
30. See Sorata, *Dahamsoňḍa Kava*, v. 17.
31. Gunapala, *Kavīndra Alagiyavanna Mukaveṭi Caritaya*, 9–10.
32. Peter Skilling, "*Jātaka* and *Paññāsa-jātaka* in South-East Asia," *Journal of the Pali Text Society* 28 (2006), 124, 130.
33. Oskar von Hinüber, *A Handbook of Pali Literature* (Berlin: Walter de Gruyter & Co., 1997), 189–191. Although the title of this work is sometimes called "Thousand Stories," its inclusion of ninety-five stories has led some scholars to suggest it *sahassa* ("thousand") should be read *sa-hassa* ("with delight"). See K. R.Norman, *Pāli Literature: Including the Canonical Literature in Prakrit and Sanskrit of All the Hīnayāna Schools of Buddhism* (Wiesbaden, Germany: Otto Harrassowitz, 1983), 154. Cf. Sharda Gandhi, ed., *Sahassavatthu-ppakaraṇaṁ* (Ghaziabad, India: Indo-Vision Private Limited, 1991), ii.
34. Godakumbura, *Sinhalese Literature*, 174.
35. See Toshiya Unebe, "Three Stories from the Thai Recension of the *Paññāsa Jātaka*: Transliteration and Preliminary Notes," *Journal of the School of Letters* 3 (2007), 2; and Arthid Sheravanichkul, "Self-Sacrifice of the Bodhisatta in the Paññāsa Jātaka," *Religion Compass* 2/5 (2008), 778. Skilling emphasizes the importance of seeing the *Paññāsa Jātaka* as comprising collections of stories that differ in contents, organization, and language; and then gives some examples of collections, not all of which even contain the Dhammasoṇḍaka Jātaka. See Skilling, "*Jātaka* and *Paññāsa-jātaka*," 138, 169–173. An analogous episode appears in Chinese sources, in which the Bodhisattva was a meditating ascetic seeking enlightenment in the Himālayas who offers his body to Indra in the disguise of a *yakṣa* in order to learn about the Dharma. The ascetic climbs a tree,

from which he leaps toward the *yakṣa*'s mouth, only to be caught by the god. This tale may be found in the Mahāyāna *Mahāparinirvāṇa Sūtra* from the fourth century, as well as the *Zangwai fojiao wenxian* 37.4 and the *Zhujing yaoji*, ch. 2. T. 2123.54, p. 13a. I wish to thank Henrik Sørenson for bringing the Chinese version of this story to my attention.

36. Sherry Harlacher has noted the relative popularity of this noncanonical *jātaka* story in visual forms during the late colonial period as well. Her survey of painted manuscript covers from Sri Lanka turned up at least two portrayals of the Dhammasoṇḍa story out of a limited number of manuscripts painted with *jātaka* story subjects. She also confirms that this story is frequently depicted in temple murals alongside paintings of canonical *jātakas* in the island. See Sherry Harlacher, *Picturing the Dhamma: Text and Image in Late-Colonial Sri Lanka*, PhD dissertation (Arizona State University, 2010), 86–88.
37. Sorata, *Dahamsoňḍa Kava*, v. 19:

Viyatuni näṇa paba	ňda
Hära mehi dosak duṭuva	da
Buduguṇayaṭa pähä	da
Asavu desavan namā bätin a	da

38. Edwin Gerow, *A Glossary of Indian Figures of Speech* (The Hague: Mouton, 1971), 33–34.
39. G. Vijayavardhana, *Outlines of Sanskrit Poetics* (Varanasi, India: Chowkhamba Sanskrit Series Office, 1970), 61.
40. Sorata, *Dahamsoňḍa Kava*, vv. 43–44, 46–47:

E puravara sirima	t
Sata veta pataḷa met yu	t
Kisi avaguṇa no da	t
Vīya niriňdek namiṅ bambada	t
E rajuge yasa paba	ňda
Dasata pätireta eka le	da
Kirisiňdu nil muhu	da
Eveṅ veṅ no ma dati ya pirisi	ňda
E viru yasa paḷa he	ḷa
Pätiri suragaňga yaṭa du	ḷa
Diya tek sevana ka	ḷa
Muduna bambu sēsateka les ka	ḷa
E rajuge teda läva	ga
Davata dasadiga ekara	ňga
Saňdavelasaňda ra	ňga
Ahō kara rävaṭune lu paňdera	ňga

41. Tennekoon, *Sävul Sandēśaya*, vv. 45, 52, 53.

42. Śrī Rāhula, in his *Kāvyaśēkhara*, employed many of the same conventions when describing the city of Sävät (Sāvatthi):

> The crowds of banners [in that city], while looking,
> At the mouth-lotuses of the city women,
> Were like crowds of *siddhas* who, having stumbled,
> Reclined when heated by the glory of the sun in the sky.

Cf. Dharmarama, *Kāvyaśēkhara*, 13, v. 33.

43. Vijayawardhana, *Outlines of Sanskrit Poetics*, 31–32.

44. Sorata, *Dahamsoňḍa Kava*, v. 42:

> Sudanaňgeṅ dimu t
> E purehi siyalu saṁpa t
> Vaṇata narambata ho t
> Anata saka mut kavuru pohosat.

45. A. D. Candrasekara, "Alagiyavannayi Dahaṁ Soňḍa Dā Kavayi," *Sītāvaka Kaviya: Vivecanatmaka Vigrahayak*, ed. Amara Hevamadduma et al. (Colombo: Department of Cultural Affairs, 1991), 18–20.

46. Sorata, *Dahamsoňḍa Kava*, vv. 26–28:

> Tuňgu gopura peṇa ka ra
> Nata lū daraṇaväla yu ra
> E pura piḷimiṇi vu ra
> Dileyi surapura hiṁ va hämavara
> Sahaguṁ biňgu vata ḷa
> Tambara piri piri sulaka ḷa
> Puramba mahavuru ku ḷa
> Räpäyi anubaňda baňdarasan vä ḷa
> Pahakotaga ras vä da
> Purambara disi supun sa ňda
> Ranmiṇiyaṭa vora da
> Sēsatev danamana nuvan ba ňda.

47. Sorata, *Kavsiḷumiṇa*, vv. 8–10:

> Deraṇa vulumbe purehi—nuba sarana 'sara dura lū
> Nubapā gat miṇivaḷa—mahavuru sēmiṇi vaḷā.
> Purakata nubaňda baňda—mahavuru ukuḷuvaṭahi
> Sahaguṁ biňguväla piyuṁ piri kiyalī rasandaṁ.
> Kärälimiṇiras yata—'gehi sēsat ev tevunē
> Vimanaudula e purä nubē—supunsarā sarāsaňda.

48. P. B. Meegaskumbura related this idea to me in a personal communication dating from July 2004 in Peradeniya, Sri Lanka.

49. Cf. Pollock, *Language of the Gods*, 89.

50. Wickremasinghe, *Sinhalese Literature*, 189–190.

51. Sorata, *Dahamsoňḍa Kava*, v. 1.

52. Ibid., v. 2.

53. Ibid., v. 3.

54. Stephen C. Berkwitz, "Merit and Materiality in Sri Lankan Buddhist Manuscripts," in *Buddhist Manuscript Cultures: Knowledge, Ritual, and Art*, eds. Stephen C. Berkwitz, Juliane Schober, and Claudia Brown (London: Routledge, 2009), 43–6.

55. Sorata, *Dahamsoňḍa Kava*, v. 4:

Pas neta	sahas	neta
Aṭa neta	tineta bara	neta
Diyaneta	kamala	neta
De neta	räka deta yomā diva	neta

56. Dharmarama, *Kāvyaśēkhara*, 3, v. 4:

Satata saka saka a	ta
Suraguru gaṇiňdu bara ne	ta
Rivi kivi saňda tine	ta
Medevigaṇa niti keret subaseta	

57. Sorata, *Dahamsoňḍa Kava*, v. 71.

58. Sorata, *Dahamsoňḍa Kava*, v. 59:

Bihi vata e budu ku	ru
Sav lō danō hada tu	ru
Sadaham lakuṇu dä	ru
Iň Dahamsoňda nam vi e kuma	ru

The poet is following a similar account in *Rasavāhinī* and *Saddharmālaṅkarāya*, in which it is stated that when the Bodhisattva was born, a perception of the Dharma arose in people's minds. See Sharada Gandhi, ed., *Rasavāhinī: A Stream of Sentiments* (Delhi, India: Parimal Publications, 1988), 2; and Migoda Paññaloka, ed., *Saddharmālaṅkarāya* (Dehiwala, Sri Lanka: Bauddha Samskritika Madhyasthanaya, 1997), 98.

59. For a comparable account in Sinhala prose of the miraculous nature of the Bodhisattva's birth and the significance behind his name *Siddhartha*, see Stephen C. Berkwitz, trans., *History of the Buddha's Relic Shrine*, 56–60. This account borrows some material from an older Pali account found in N. A. Jayawickrama, trans., *The Story of Gotama Buddha (Jātaka-nidāna)* (Oxford, UK: Pali Text Society, 1990), 70–71.

60. See Sorata, *Dahamsoňḍa Kava*, v. 57.

61. See Sorata, *Dahamsoňḍa Kava*, v. 61. Cf. Tennekoon, *Sävul Sandēśaya*, v. 57.

62. Sorata, *Dahamsoṅḍa Kava*, v. 62:

Suguṇamiṇi muhu du va
Satasatankoṅda tari ṅdu va
Sirisaṅdaṭa uvi ṅdu va
Visi muḷu dambadivhi pasi ṅdu va

63. Sorata, *Dahamsoṅḍa Kava*, vv. 74–75:

Ve la näti sayura mena
Rivisaṅda näti ahasa mena
Pahan nivi geya mena
Yuvala daḷa näti matagijiṅdu mena
Kamala näti vila me na
Taralamiṇa näti hara me na
Gahaṇasun vata me na
Dahaṁ näti lova no vē sasoba na

64. Paññaloka, *Saddharmalankaraya*, 100–101.
65. Queyroz, *Temporal and Spiritual Conquest*, vol. III, 1005.
66. Sorata, *Dahamsoṅḍa Kava*, v. 97.
67. Reiko Ohnuma, *Head, Eyes, Flesh, and Blood: Giving away the Body in Indian Buddhist Literature* (New York: Columbia University Press, 2007), 59–63.
68. Paññaloka, *Saddharmalankaraya*, 99. Cf. Gandhi, *Rasavāhinī*, 3 and Gandhi, *Sahassavatthu-ppakaraṇaṁ*, 2.
69. There are numerous examples of expressions of love in separation in Tamil, Sanskrit and Prakrit poetry, among other Indic languages. See Selby, *Grow Long, Blessed Night*, 71–4.
70. Lee Siegel, *Sacred and Profane Dimensions of Love in Indian Traditions: As Exemplified in the Gitagovinda of Jayadeva* (Oxford, UK: Oxford University Press, 1978), 70–71.
71. Selby, *Grow Long, Blessed Night*, 17.
72. Edward C. Dimock, Jr., "The Religious Lyric in Bengali," in *The Literatures of India: An Introduction*, Edward C. Dimock Jr. et al. (Chicago: University of Chicago, 1974), 159. The trope of longing for an absent lover also pervades the classical Sanskrit poem *Gītagovinda* by Jayadeva. See Barbara Stoler Miller, ed. and trans., *Love Song of the Dark Lord: Jayadeva's Gītagovinda* (New York: Columbia University Press, 1977), 78–85, 88–94.
73. Shulman, *Wisdom of Poets*, 15.
74. See, for example, the ninth *sargaya* or chapter containing Buddhist admonitions in the *Kāvyaśēkhara*. Dharmarama, *Kāvyaśēkhara*, 153–178.
75. See Sorata, *Dahamsoṅḍa Kava*, v. 48.
76. To objectify the Bodhisattva's mother in a sensual fashion would compromise the moral purity that a woman in her role must have according to the norms

of Buddhist literature. See *Dahamsoňḍa Kava*, vv. 53–55. For a description of the requisite virtue in Queen Mahāmāyā, the mother of Prince Siddhartha, see Berkwitz, *History of the Buddha's Relic Shrine*, 53–54.

77. Sorata, *Dahamsoňḍa Kava*, v. 82:

Muniňdu guru tilova	ṭa
Bambasuranaran tuṭu ko	ṭa
Mokpala pasak ko	ṭa
Desū sadahaṁ kiyālav ma	ṭa

78. Sorata, *Dahamsoňḍa Kava*, vv. 86–87:

Muniňdun	vadahaḷa dahamin amayu	t
Ga ya kin	vat in aḍinaḍakin va	t
Maṭa dän	kisiveku baṇa kiva tuṭu si	t
Vaḍamin	ōhaṭa demi neka sampa	t
Da ha s	paṭan keḷasuvahas hiṁ ko	ṭa
Ve se s	anagi mutumiṇi saha raṭa to	ṭa
Sa to s	vaḍana rajasiri dī himi ko	ṭa
Da ha s	bavaṭa pämiṇemi mama ōha	ṭa

79. H. L. Seneviratne has discussed the Sinhala concept of righteous rule in terms of the king's protection of the Buddha's dispensation, the practice of good government, and the performance of rites to the Tooth Relic. Numerous inscriptions and texts reference the view that kings have a sacred duty to ensure that the Dharma and Sangha continue to flourish in Sri Lanka. See Seneviratne, *Rituals of the Kandyan State* (Cambridge, UK: Cambridge University Press, 1978), 96–97.

80. Sorata, *Dahamsoňḍa Kava*, v. 94:

Vi sa da ra	nā telisap poḷaňgun ge	na
Bi ya ka ra	sī gaja vaga valasun ge	na
Go ra ta ra	yak bū pisas sorun ge	na
U va du ra	kaṭa no pämiṇa piṅ mahime	na

81. Sorata, *Dahamsoňḍa Kava*, v. 106:

De lo viṅ	väḍa sidu karaṇā novärā	da
Muniňduṅ	vadahaḷa bavaduk pirisi	ňda
Ta vi siṅ	baṇapadaya kiva hot a	da
Sa magiṅ	rajasiri ma divi kereṁ pu	da

82. See Sorata, *Dahamsoňḍa Kava*, v. 108.

83. Sorata, *Dahamsoňḍa Kava*, vv. 113–114:

Sapurā peruman sama ti	s
Keremin bambasuranara to	s

Matu budubava labana nido s
Budukuru himisaňdini vese s
Me gira ṭa näňgemin sahati ṭa
Ma kaṭa ṭa paninā atara ṭa
Topa ha ta daṁ desamä 'suma ṭa
Vi ga sa ṭa näňgevayi kī vi ṭa

84. Sorata, *Dahamsoňḍa Kava*, v. 115.

85. Sorata, *Dahamsoňḍa Kava*, vv. 116–118:

Sudanan kī bas pähä rā
Geṇa dada dana bas nā̆ rā
Kara samaharu paradā rā
Vänaset vada viňda gō rā
Migabas pavasamin kuri ru
Raṇa mäda väda no vamin su ru
Läba geṇa avipahara rudu ru
No maňda va vänaset samaha ru
Sudanan bas no geṇa sita ṭa
Täna täna gos sorakaṁ ko ṭa
Näsemin viňda ruduru gähä ṭa
Pämiṇet samaharu niraya ṭa

86. The referral to death in Buddhist poetry is seen in the Pāli *Telakaṭāhagāthā*, in which verse 25 reminds the reader to fear death:

Seeing this world, which is continually afflicted with fear and grief,
Overcome by anger, conceit, delusion, and old-age,
If not even a measure of fright is found in one,
Woe be to him, for that death is cruel.

See E. R. Gooneratne, ed., "Tela-kaṭāha-gāthā," *Journal of the Pali Text Society* (1884), 58. Likewise verse 26 from the fifteenth-century Sinhala poem, *Lō Väḍu Saňgarāva* also works to recall the inevitability of death:

Wherever one remains, one cannot avoid death,
As long as one has merit, one enjoys worldly comforts,
What a farce, game, joke, or laugh it is [to assume one can]
Traverse the sufferings of *samsara* without adhering to the doctrine of the Buddha.

See Devundara Vacissara, ed. *Bhāva sanna sahita Lō Väḍa Saňgarāva*. Colombo: M. D. Gunasena, 1991), 14.

87. Sorata, *Dahamsoňḍa Kava*, v. 120:

Samaharu vasavisa kā̆me na
Samaharu gele väl lā ge na

Samaharu tama diväda kami	na
Samaharu siyatin äna ge	na

88. See Sorata, *Dahamsoṅḍa Kava* v. 121.
89. Cf. Gandhi, *Sahassavatthu-ppakaraṇaṁ*, 4–5.
90. Sorata, *Dahamsoṅḍa Kava*, v. 123:

A da ra	sitin äsū sata	na
A ja ra	amara moksiri de	na
Pa va ra	sadahamaṭa muniṅdu	na
Me va ra	ma divi pudaṁ bäti	na

91. See T. W. Rhys Davids and J. Estlin Carpenter, eds., *The Dīgha Nikāya*, vol. II (Oxford, UK: Pali Text Society, 1995), 157.
92. The "all constituent elements are indeed impermanent" verse occupies a central place in the story told in *Sahassavatthu-ppakaraṇaṁ*, in which it appears as the only quoted verse and precedes a long exposition on the meaning of impermanence. See Gandhi, *Sahassavatthu-ppakaraṇaṁ*, 4–5. Cf. the appearance of this Pāli verse in Gandhi, *Rasavāhinī*, 9; and in Paññaloka, *Saddharmālaṅkarāya*, 113.
93. Sorata, *Dahamsoṅḍa Kava*, vv. 130–132:

Ta lä ṭak	pamaṇa siruren nikma pähäsa	ra
Pa maṇak	näti siyalu sakvaḷa gäba päti	ra
Ba va ak	dakina turu vihidī yana pata	ra
Sa va ṇak	gana räsin diliyeṁni manaha	ra
Sa sa ra	sayura saraṇā sav sa tā	yā
A ja ra	amara mok pura lami si tā	yā
Gämbara	guṇäti apa maha bō satā	yā
Pavara	asirimat budubava pa tā	yā
Sa ha s	räsbarin hunu dinakara lesa	da
Ta mas	muven gilihunu punsaṅda lesa	da
Ve se s	dahaṁ asamin divi pudana le	da
Ra kus	muvaṭa pinuvē girihisin se	da

94. Reiko Ohnuma has argued in her analysis of gift of the body stories that the only acceptable motive for the Bodhisattva to offer his life is to obtain Buddhahood and to thus liberate and give comfort to all beings. See Ohnuma, *Head, Eyes, Flesh, and Blood*, 102. On the popularity of this plotline in "nonclassical" *jātaka*s, see Sheravanichkul, "Self-Sacrifice of the Bodhisattva," 776–777. An exception is seen in the canonical Sasa Jātaka, which depicts the Bodhisattva as a rabbit who throws himself onto a burning fire to feed a beggar who is actually Śakra in disguise. See this episode from the Sasa Jātaka in V. Fausboll, ed. *The Jātaka: Together with Its Commentary*, vol. III (Oxford, UK: Pali Text Society, 1990), 54–55. The late twelfth-century Sinhala *mahākāvya* titled *Sasadāvata* takes this same tale

for its story. See Kusum Disanayaka, trans., *Sasa Dā Vata: Bodhisatva as a Hare* (Colombo: Godage International Publishers, 2004).

95. Sorata, *Dahamsoňḍa Kava*, v. 149.

96. Sorata, *Dahamsoňḍa Kava*, v. 149: "*tepalin nisi subäsi, me apa bōsat dahaṁ pävasi.*" Cf. Gandhi, *Sahassavatthu-ppakaraṇaṁ*, 4; Gandhi, *Rasavāhinī*, 8–9; Paññaloka, *Saddharmālaṅkarāya*, 113–14.

97. Naomi Appleton, *Jātaka Stories in Theravāda Buddhism: Narrating the Bodhisatta Path* (Surrey, UK: Ashgate, 2010), 147.

98. Sorata, *Dahamsoňḍa Kava*, v. 161:

Mahabōsat siri	ta
Adara va äsū sav sa	ta
Dā jarā mara mu	ta
Vesetvā läba nivan sampa	ta

99. Tennekoon, *Sävul Sandēśaya*, vv. 202, 206.

100. See Sorata, *Dahamsoňḍa Kava*, v. 66.

101. Ibid., v. 153.

102. C. R. de Silva, "Rise and Fall," 97.

103. Sorata, *Dahamsoňḍa Kava*, v. 69:

Satarak upāye	na
Tunsat saguṇa sataňgi	na
Sivusaňgarāvati	na
Yutu va lova räka vesē vesesi	na

104. Kautilya, *The Arthashastra*, ed. and trans. L. N. Rangarajan (New Delhi: Penguin Books, 1992), 166.

105. Sorata, *Dahamsoňḍa Kava*, 61.

106. Kautilya, *The Arthashastra*, 548–549.

107. Ibid., 119.

108. Sorata, *Dahamsoňḍa Kava*, 62.

109. An example of the motif whereby the Bodhisattva renounces his kingship for religious pursuits is found in the thirteenth-century *Sinhala Thupavamsa*'s account of the Cullasutasoma Jātaka. See Berkwitz, *History of the Buddha's Relic Shrine*, 75–76.

110. Donald K. Swearer has pointed out that a life of voluntary poverty represents the condition in which the virtues of moral perfections such as renunciation, generosity, and loving kindness are fully realized for the attainment of nirvana. Donald K. Swearer, "Buddhist Virtue, Voluntary Poverty, and Extensive Benevolence," *Journal of Religious Ethics* 26/1 (1998): 80–81.

111. Ohnuma, *Head, Eyes, Flesh, and Blood*, 242–243.

112. See Sorata, *Dahamsoňḍa Kava*, vv. 143–145.

113. Sorata, *Dahamsoňḍa Kava*, vv. 152–153:

Sivusaňgarā vati na
Maharu dasaraja dahami na
Sav satun sit ge na
Pavatu peranaraniňdun vilasina
Purā budukuru da ṁ
Sav satun veta no va hi ṁ
Vaḍavamini suta pe ṁ
Pavatu vilasin poraṇa raja da ṁ

114. See "*raja-dhamma*" in T. W. Rhys Davids and William Stede, *The Pali Text Society's Pali-English Dictionary* (Oxford, UK: Pali Text Society, 1995), 570.
115. Seneviratne, *Rituals of the Kandyan State*, 89. On medieval Sri Lankan kings as bodhisattvas, see also R.A.L.H. Gunarwardana, *Robe and Plough: Monasticism and Economic Interest Early Medieval Sri Lanka* (Tucson: University of Arizona Press, 1979), 171–172.
116. Sorata, *Dahamsoňḍa Kava*, vv. 154–155.
117. Sorata, *Dahamsoňḍa Kava*, v. 157:

Basamin nara lova ṭa
Pämiṇa tama raja säpata ṭa
Matu budu vana lesa ṭa
Desi sadahaṁ satan tuṭu ko ṭa

118. Ilangasinha, *Buddhism in Medieval Sri Lanka*, 121–122.
119. Sorata, *Dahamsoňḍa Kava*, v. 24:

Bäbalī sunera si ra
Nivī giya pahanak yu ra
E muni pirinivi va ra
Pirihini ya munisasuṅ manahara

120. For a discussion on the various Buddhist notions of the decline of the Dharma, see Jan Nattier, *Once upon a Future Time: Studies in a Buddhist Prophecy of Decline* (Berkeley, CA: Asian Humanities Press, 1991).

CHAPTER 4

1. Skilling, "*Jātaka* and *Paññāsa-jātaka*," 124.
2. Godakumbura, *Sinhalese Literature*, 158.
3. See D. M. Samarasinghe, ed., *Alagiyavanna Mukaveṭituman visin racanā karana lada Kusa Jātaka Kāvyaya* (Colombo: Sri Lanka Publishing Company, 1964), vv. 6–7. Cf. Sannasgala, *Sinhala Sāhitya Vaṁśaya* (1964), 301–302.

4. Samarasinghe, *Kusa Jātaka Kāvyaya*, vv. 11–12:

Teruvana veta nido	sa
Sapiri sädähäti me digä	sa
Visākāvan mi	sa
Venin sariveti kavurudiyaku	sa
Rakina tama biju va	l
Kirala semarev häma ka	l
Poho davasa aṭasi	l
Rakī niti pirisiduva pan si	l

On the literary figure of Visākhā, see Malalasekera, *Dictionary of Pāli Proper Names*, vol. II, (New Delhi: Munshiram Manoharlal, 1983), 900–904. Ranjani Obeyesekere also relates a lengthy Sinhala version of Viśākhā's story in *Portraits of Buddhist Women: Stories from the* Saddharmaratnāvaliya (Albany: State University of New York, 2001), 79–108. In Sri Lankan Buddhism, *poya* days are full-moon days that laypeople traditionally observe by following stricter codes of moral conduct.

5. See Samarasinghe, *Kusa Jātaka Kāvyaya*, v. 19.
6. Samarasinghe, *Kusa Jātaka Kāvyaya*, v. 20:

Sugatiňdu guṇa gämbu	ra
Ma kiyami sitana värasä	ra
Maduru naḷine 'kava	ra
Sunera viňdinaṭa tät karana yu	ra

7. For example, the twelfth-century *Amāvatura* by Guruḷugōmī was composed to promote one of the nine virtues conventionally ascribed to the Buddha—his identity as "a charioteer for the taming of men" (*purisadamma-sārathī*). This early Sinhala prose work relates multiple instances when the Buddha tamed hostile or undisciplined beings.
8. Kiri Elle Ñanavimala, ed., *Vyākhyā sahita Buduguṇa Alaṅkāraya* (Colombo: M. D. Gunasena, 1993), v. 6:

Maha kivivarun pe	ra
Pavasā no pat para te	ra
Sugatiňdu guṇa gämba	ra
Memā kiyami sitanu värasä	ra

9. Samarasinghe, *Kusa Jātaka Kāvyaya*, v. 21.
10. See Samarasinghe, *Kusa Jātaka Kāvyaya*, v. 686.
11. Samarasinghe, *Kusa Jātaka Kāvyaya*, v. 687:

Pava ra	sakavasine 'k dahas pansiya detis vamu vesaňga poho	dā
Ama ra	ňgana yuru mäṇiksāmi namäti laňda ayadamen noma	ňdā
Gämbura	kivi naḷu hasala alagiyavanna mukaveṭi tumā paba	ňdā
A ja ra	mara mok piṇisa sinhala basin kavi keḷe nisi me kusa	dā

12. Godakumbura, *Sinhalese Literature*, 138–139.
13. Ibid., 139.
14. Velivitiye Sorata, *Eḷu Sam̆däs Lakuṇa* (Colombo: Samayawardhana, 2005), 17:

> Kusaniriňdu e davasa—pivituru uyanataṭa väda,
> Väjamba vasata guṇamuhudu—no maňda diyataṭa seta dini.

15. Hallisey, "Works and Persons," 694.
16. The fourth stanza in *Kavsiḷumiṇa* states that poetry ought to be concerned with the deeds of the Bodhisattva.
17. Edwin Gerow, "The Sanskrit Lyric: A Genre Analysis," in *The Literatures of India*, ed. Edward C. Dimock, Jr. et al. (Chicago: University of Chicago Press, 1974), 153.
18. Velivitiye Sorata, *Kavsiḷumiṇa*, vv. 319–321:

> Heta duvanatä neta—sadata suratata tambarin
> Narambata ata kärä pahā—tanabarinura sädū yala.
> Miṇidäl siňdin van—nalanu lamba kusuṁdaṁ
> Kadahasa väṭup väruyen—piyadeviya da hidā gat
> Samaradelenada lehi—tamā piḷibimbu magamin
> Kiyū vadaneka adahā—välälū kal seda niriňdu.

19. See, for example, Daniel H. H. Ingalls, *Sanskrit Poetry: From Vidyākara's Treasury*. (Cambridge, MA: Harvard University Press, 1965), 147, 164–179.
20. Sorata, *Kavsiḷumiṇa*, v. 575:

> Piyagatni somi topa—gatin savaṇat net sit
> Metek me desin gatuyē—nonurā da e puruddan

21. Sorata, *Kavsiḷumiṇa*, v. 576:

> Viyodelenudulana—hida mädä ovun vasvā
> Vamō lu hā dän äpi—minis guṇa raknō naṁ

22. Sorata, *Kavsiḷumiṇa*, vv. 385, 390.
23. See, for example, Sorata, *Kavsiḷumiṇa*, vv. 693, 700, where Prabhāvatī is blamed for the threat facing Sāgala in the form of the seven hostile kings. However, this looming danger and Prabhāvatī's looming death are spoken of in terms of results (*laba*) but not specifically karma or the "fruits of karma."
24. Hallisey, "Works and Persons," 738–739.
25. Pollock, *Language of the Gods*, 76.
26. Ingalls, *Sanskrit Poetry*, 37.
27. Gunapala, *Kavīndra Alagiyavanna Mukaveṭi Caritaya*, 15–16.
28. S. B. Herath, "Kusa Jātaka Kāvyaya," in *Sītāvaka Kaviya: Vivēcanātmaka Vigrahayak*, ed. Amara Hevamadduma et al. (Colombo: Department of Cultural Affairs, 1991), 50.

29. Prof. Wimal Wijeratne expressed this scholarly assessment to me in a personal communication on May 30, 2006. Cf. Berkwitz, "Ugly King and Mother Tongue," 62–66.
30. Godakumbura, *Sinhalese Literature*, 158.
31. Samarasinghe, *Kusa Jātaka Kāvyaya*, vv. 28–29:

Vata neta kamalu pu	la
Duvan väli tala pähädu	la
E pura liya tunu vi	la
Sarati saleḷun nuvan mihilo	la
Ratadarini	nāliya
Gamanin sadisi	nāliya
E pura sara	nāliya
Kavuru naṁ häki vetiva	nāliya

32. Wickremasinghe, *Sinhalese Literature*, 189–190.
33. It has been said that *Kusa Jātaka Kāvya*'s straightforward style is based on its clear use of language and the reduction in its ornamentation and panegyrics. See Sannasgala, *Sinhala Sāhitya Vaṁśaya* (1964), 303.
34. Wickremasinghe, *Sinhalese Literature*, 195.
35. Samarasinghe, *Kusa Jātaka Kāvyaya*, v. 239–241:

Asā un kī ba	s
Lade 'v amutuva abise	s
Sita sapurā sato	s
Mahat raja peraharin e dava	s
Ran ruva paňḍuru ko	ṭa
Gena taman kumariya ha	ṭa
Ā e mätivaruna	ṭa
Nomada savsiri demin garuko	ṭa
Dambadivaṭa aga pa	t
Okāvas naraniňduṭa	t
Paňḍuru bäňda nanva	t
Piṭat kaḷe vaḍavamin met si	t

36. Samarasinghe, *Kusa Jātaka Kāvyaya*, v. 590:

Dara hasaḷa pasa ň	gaya
Pähäti kiri siňdu tara ň	gaya
E purehi vē ma ň	gaya
Saraṇa apamaṇa turaňga senaň	gaya

37. Samarasinghe, *Kusa Jātaka Kāvyaya*, vv. 14, 16:

Siri rati paḷamu ve	na
Säka hära mavā balami	na

Yaḷi loväduru visi	na
Mavā lū väni rusiru me kalu	na
Nisi situ ruvana ma	na
Nil miṇi yugaya denuva	na
Mäṇiksāmī ya	na
Naṁ yedeyi mē laňdaṭa e bävi	na

38. See Samarasinghe, *Kusa Jātaka Kāvyaya*, v. 17.
39. See Samarasinghe, *Kusa Jātaka Kāvyaya*, vv. 23, 81.
40. Samarasinghe, *Kusa Jātaka Kāvyaya*, v. 55:

Bamba vimane 'v udu	ḷa
Maha gaňdakili tuḷehi tu	ḷa
Yahanehi nikasa	ḷa
Muniňdu väḍahiňda lovaṭa set ka	ḷa

41. Samarasinghe, *Kusa Jātaka Kāvyaya*, v. 60:

Säňdä velakin sura	t
Vasane'v tariňdu pähäpa	t
Nuga pala van dimu	t
Sugat sivuren vasata buduga	t

42. See, for example, Samarasinghe, *Kusa Jātaka Kāvyaya*, vv. 61–68. The *Sinhala Thūpavaṃsa* contains a similar account, several centuries earlier, of Buddha rays emanating outward and bathing the entire world realm in a mixture of colors. See Berkwitz, *History of the Buddha's Relic Shrine*, 135–136.
43. Naomi Appleton makes a similar argument for reading earlier *jātaka* stories as being chiefly concerned with glorifying the Buddha, whereas their links to specific moral perfections arises only in later eras. See Appleton, *Jātaka Stories*, 53, 85.
44. Samarasinghe, *Kusa Jātaka Kāvyaya*, v. 640:

A ma ra	varaṇiňdu näňgī surasen pirivarā pera suran jayage	na
Pa va ra	rusiräti sujātāvan rägena surapura van suriňdu me	na
Pa ta ra	tuňgu maňguläṭuṭa naňgimin sapirivara pabavat biyova ge	na
Vi ta ra	noma vana rajasirin kusa rajatumā puravaraṭa vidimi	na

45. Wickremasinghe, *Sinhalese Literature*, 196.
46. Sannasgala, *Sinhala Sāhitya Vaṃśaya* (1964), 303.
47. Suraweera, "Alagiyavanna Mukaveṭitumā," 192.
48. Herath, "Kusa Jātaka Kāvyaya," 52. On the literary genre of *baṇapot*, see Mahinda Deegalle, *Popularizing Buddhism: Preaching as Performance in Sri Lanka* (Albany: State University of New York Press: 2006).
49. Nira Wickramsinghe, *Sri Lanka in the Modern Age: A History of Contested Identities* (Honolulu: University of Hawai'i, 2006), 156.
50. Gunapala, *Kavīndra Alagiyavanna Mukaveṭi Caritaya*, 17.

51. Sannsagala describes the rise of village poetry during the Sītāvaka Period in his *Sinhala Sāhitya Vaṁśaya* (1964), 296–297. Godakumbura, on the other hand, singles out the fifteenth-century *Guttila Kāvya* as having "set the style for a large number of poems composed by later writers for the edification of the masses." See Godakumbura, *Sinhalese Literature*, 156.
52. Gunapala, *Kavīndra Alagiyavanna Mukaveṭi Caritaya*, 17.
53. Martin Wickremasinghe describes Alagiyavanna as a "true ballad-singer" and a "folk poet" due largely to the latter's success in delighting ordinary listeners and readers with his poetic narration of *Kusa Jātaka Kāvya*. See Wickremasinghe, *Sinhalese Literature*, 190. The flaw in Wickremasinghe's view of Alagiyavanna is that he extrapolates Alagiyavanna's intention and values based on how the *Kusa Jātaka Kāvya* has been received by subsequent generations of his readers.
54. Godakumbura, *Sinhalese Literature*, 148–149.
55. Siegel, *Sacred and Profane Dimensions*, 142, 159.
56. Shulman, *Wisdom of Poets*, 332–333.
57. Thomas Steele, *Kusa Jātakaya, A Buddhistic Legend: Rendered for the First Time, into English Verse, from the Sinhalese Poem of Alagiyavanna Mohottala* (London: Trubner & Co., 1871), viii.
58. V. Fausboll, ed., *The Jātaka, Together with Its Commentary*, vol. V, reprint (Oxford, UK: Pāli Text Society, 1991), 289: *So Pabhāvatiyā gatāya sokappatto ahosi, nānākārehi paricaramānāpi naṁ sesitthiyo oloketum pi na sakkhiṁsu, Pabhāvatirahitam assa sakalam pi nivesanaṁ tucchaṁ viya khāyi.*
59. Sorata, *Kavsiḷumiṇa*, vv. 554–55:

    Tama yahadasanen—nuvan piya tepalen kan
    Pahasin gat genä kesē—mana no dī mā sit gat.
    Väḷakī me da piri—me kaňdaḷa e des dasnen
    Tat selehi silil men—leyi dala diyuṇu keḷe ha.

60. Samarasinghe, *Kusa Jātaka Kāvyaya*, v. 364:

Ni mal	vatin vihidena siniňdu somi kälu	ṁ
Su pul	raṇaliyaka men dilena vana däňgu	ṁ
Ḷa kal	pabāvati raja dū samaga utu	ṁ
Ki kal	läbē dō eka yahanatē lägu	ṁ

61. Samarasinghe, *Kusa Jātaka Kāvyaya*, v. 363:

Nu ba pa ta	saňda yugata rivi lesa	dis vīya
Ya ha na ta	atula mal peti kaṭu	les vīya
pi ya ka ta	dena räňguṁgī no ma	tos vīya
Pa ba va ta	näti me raja vimanata	his vīya

62. Sorata, *Dahamsoňḍa Kava*, v. 128:

So ba man	me apa mahabōsat guṇanada	na
Me le sin	patayi budusiri sataveta meti	na

63. Verses 75–78 of *Kusa Jātaka Kāvya* relate the backdrop for the story and reveal how the Bodhisattva once increased his desire (*loba*) in regard to women and experienced severe suffering (*duk*) as a result. The Pāli *Jātaka* includes a more pointed admonition, whereupon the Buddha tells a heartsick monk: "Do not, o' monk, subject yourself to passion. That woman is wicked. Resist having your mind enamored with her. Find pleasure in the Dispensation. Indeed, as a result of having minds enamored with women, even glorious pandits of old became powerless and arrived at misfortune and destruction." Cf. Fausboll, *Jātaka*, vol. V, 278.
64. Samarasinghe, *Kusa Jātaka Kāvyaya*, v. 367:

Häma sat	gora sasara sayuren goḍa naňga	na
Ä ti vatpun	peruṁ matu budu bava laba	na
Pa ba vat	venvuyen taniva ma iňda yaha	na
Mahasat	tävuṇu lesa mama kiyami kelesi	na

65. See Samarasinghe, *Kusa Jātaka Kāvyaya*, v. 441.
66. Ibid., v. 603.
67. Ohnuma, *Head, Eyes, Flesh, and Blood*, 100.
68. Samarasinghe, *Kusa Jātaka Kāvyaya*, vv. 548, 550:

Soňda nil gela pil kalambeka vila		s
Oda vaḍavana duṭu duṭu dana manä		s
Maňda kalekin māgē varalasa vese		s
Äda äda siňda lati yak bū pisa		s
Ni si le sa ṭa	dilena nilupul dimu	t
Neta veta ṭa	pämiṇa siṭi de savana	t
Duṭa satu ṭa	vaḍana mage yuga neta	t
A da upu ṭa	kapuṭu ukusō budi	t

69. See Samarasinghe, *Kusa Jātaka Kāvyaya*, v. 556.
70. Lists of psychic and physical elements are famously found in the texts of the Theravāda Abhidhamma. Other, more widely known discourses relating such material include the Mahāhatthipadopama Sutta of *Majjhima Nikaya* and the Mahāsatipaṭṭhāna Sutta in the *Dīgha Nikaya*. See, for instance, Bhikkhu Nanamoli and Bhikkhu Bodhi, trans., *The Middle Length Discourses of the Buddha: A New Translation of the* Majjhima Nikāya (Boston: Wisdom Publications, 1995), 278–285. See also Maurice Walshe, *The Long Discourses of the Buddha: A Translation of the* Dīgha Nikāya (Boston: Wisdom Publications, 1995), 335–50.
71. For the Pāli tradition's account of the Buddha's last words, see T. W. Rhys Davids and J. Estlin Carpenter, eds., *The Dīgha Nikāya*, vol. II, reprint (Oxford, UK: Pali Text Society, 1995), 156.
72. Samarasinghe, *Kusa Jātaka Kāvyaya*, v. 566:

Kusanara niňdu pava	ra
Rusiru maňda ya yi ata hä	ra

Tama ruva idiri ka   ra
Ā vipākaya lovaṭa paḷaka   ra

Cf. Samarasinghe, *Kusa Jātaka Kāvyaya*, v. 541.

73. Sucaritha Gamlath, *Kavsiḷumiṇi Vinisa*, [1966] reprint (Colombo: S. Godage and Brothers, 1995), 238–243.
74. Samarasinghe, *Kusa Jātaka Kāvyaya*, v. 465:

Visuḷu muva yut to   pa
Patanu noma yutu veyi a   pa
Vilasin hutäs a   pa
Durin duruvama vasanumäyi säpa

75. Gamlath, *Kavsiḷumiṇi Vinisa*, 248.
76. Samarasinghe, *Kusa Jātaka Kāvyaya*, v. 502:

Da va sak   lägi eka yahana   ta
Hi mi yak   haṭa duk pämiṇe   ta
O hu duk   dura lū me diya   ta
Pa maṇak   näti aṅganō ä   ta

77. See Samarasinghe, *Kusa Jātaka Kāvyaya*, vv. 343–348.
78. Ibid., vv. 350–353.
79. Samarasinghe, *Kusa Jātaka Kāvyaya*, v. 355:

Pasē munisaňdu ge   na
Kävuṁ gatten sarosi   na
Kusa niriňduge vuva   na
Visuḷu vū bava danuva e pavina

80. Susanne Mrozik, *Virtuous Bodies: The Physical Dimensions of Morality in Buddhist Ethics* (New York: Oxford University Press, 2007), 66–68.
81. Gamani Dela Bandara, *Saṁbhāvya Sinhala Sāhityaya* (Kelaniya, Sri Lanka: Sambhavya Prakasana, 1998), 98.
82. Samarasinghe, *Kusa Jātaka Kāvyaya*, v. 639:

Su ra   rada genävit ura lū miṇi ruvanehi anuhasinu   t
Pe ra   kaḷa pav gevī e dina pätuvā siduvana bävinu   t
Su ra   purayen deraṇaṭa baṭa suriňdaku vilasin sirima   t
Va ra   nisi tunu rusiren väjambiṇi pinsara maha bōsa   t

83. Fausboll, *Jātaka*, vol. 5, 311: *samānavaṇṇarūpena*. The commentary on page 312 glosses this compound: *samānavaṇṇarūpenā' ti vaṇṇena ca rūpena ca samānā hutvā*.
84. Nagoda Ariyadasa Seneviratne, ed., *Pansiyapaṇas Jātaka Pot Vahansē*, vol. 3 (Dehiwala, Sri Lanka: Buddhist Cultural Center, 1995), 1826.
85. Samarasinghe, *Kusa Jātaka Kāvyaya*, v. 357:

Käṭak gena nuba ku   sa
Dämuva no raňdayi bima mi   sa

E men pav pin rä	sa
Siduvīma niyataya pätū le	sa

86. Gamlath, *Kavsiḷumiṇi Vinisa*, 240, 245–248.
87. Samarasinghe, *Kusa Jātaka Kāvyaya*, v. 464:

Yā deka norata ra	ta
Samaga pāsīmek nä	ta
E lesin virata ra	ta
De dena samahaṁ vī iňdinu näta	

88. Samarasinghe, *Kusa Jātaka Kāvyaya*, vv. 525–527.
89. Ibid., v. 121.
90. Ibid., v. 377. Note that the Pāli *Jātaka* represents the Queen Mother as warning her son: "If that is so, son, may you remain diligent. Women have impure inclinations" (*tena hi tāta appamatto bhaveyyāsi, mātugāmo nāma asuddhāsayo*). See Fausboll, *Jātaka*, vol. V, 289.
91. Gamlath, *Kavsiḷumiṇi Vinisa*, 246. Although Sucaritha Gamlath argues that the author of the *Kavsiḷumiṇa* exhibits a much more positive attitude toward Prabhāvatī than Alagiyavanna, an attitude that he attributes to a clearer understanding of her situation as a young, married woman, he appears to overlook instances of misogyny in the older *mahākāvya* poem. For example, the work presents King Madu praising Kusa for magnanimously forgiving for his ill-mannered daughter: "Very childish, fickle, prone to anger, shortsighted, / O' king, this is the true nature of women, if you look, there is no truth in them." Sorata, *Kavsiḷumiṇa*, v. 719: *Nomaňda bolaňda sala—täräsuṁ no duru närämbuṁ// naraniňduni piyan säbäv—visinata nätōn säbäv.*
92. See, for example, verse 8 of *Kusa Jātaka Kāvya* in which Rājasiṃha is named as the famous king under whose splendid foot the minister Attanayaka, or Mäṇiksāmī's husband, subjects himself in loyal obedience.
93. See Samarasinghe, *Kusa Jātaka Kāvyaya*, v. 52.
94. Samarasinghe, *Kusa Jātaka Kāvyaya*, v. 53:

Saṁsun vemīn a	da
Mahalu piḷiveḷa no vihi	da
Buduguṇaya piḷiba	ňda
Miyuru rasa bas pavasamin i	ňda

95. Ibid., vv. 55–58.
96. Ibid., v. 304:97 Samarasinghe, *Kusa Jātaka Kāvyaya*, v. 268:

Mahimen e raja te	da
Pabavata vuvanatin so	ňda
Nikmena käluṁka	ňda
Adisi veyi rivi duṭu kadō le	da

98. Ibid., v. 636.
99. Ibid., vv. 351–352.
100. Samarasinghe, *Kusa Jātaka Kāvyaya*, v. 37:

Vadan ama rasi	nā
Guṇa miṇi tiḷiṇa raḷi	nā
Me naravara diya	nā
Väjambi manunaya veraḷa nopänā	

101. Ibid., vv. 95–96.
102. Ibid., v. 98.
103. Ibid., v. 603. Unlike some *Jātaka* stories that relate the renunciation of the throne to the worthless, inconsequential nature of kingship and worldly gain, the Kusa Jātaka does not question the value of royal prosperity. This fact makes the narrative especially suitable for a poetic genre that was developed in royal courts across South Asia.
104. Samarasinghe, *Kusa Jātaka Kāvyaya*, v. 600:

No däna 'pa kaḷa vara	da
No gena pokuramba men ha	da
Met sit kara noma	ňda
Kamā kaḷa hot yeheki himi sa	ňda

105. Ibid., v. 601.
106. Ibid., vv. 614, 646–647.
107. Samarasinghe, *Kusa Jātaka Kāvyaya*, v. 618:

Dadun kiviňdun ge	na
Biliňdūn saha laňdun ge	na
Vū varada noma ge	na
Haḷō pera rajatumō sat gu	ṇa

CHAPTER 5

1. Gunapala, *Kavindra Alagiyavanna Mukaveṭi Caritaya*, 13.
2. Ludwik Sternbach, "Indian Wisdom and Its Spread beyond India," *Journal of the American Oriental Society* 101(1981), 98–100.
3. A. V. Suraweera, *Gampaha District: Socio-Cultural Studies* (Battaramula, Sri Lanka: Department of Cultural Affairs, 1999), 192
4. W. F. Gunawardhana, *Subhashita Varnana: Being a Commentary on the Subhashita* (Colombo: Sri Bharati Press, 1925), 1–2, xi–xii.
5. S. G. Perera and M. E. Fernando, eds. and trans., *Alagiyawanna's Kustantinu Haṭana (The Campaign of Don Constantine)* (Colombo: Catholic Press, 1932), vi–vii
6. Abeyasinghe, *Portuguese Rule in Ceylon 1594–1612*, 131.

7. Perera and Fernando recognize this fact but choose to discount it in favor of seeing this verse as another extraneous addition to the original text. They assert that Alagiyavanna would have already come under the influence of the Portuguese by 1610 in Sītāvaka, but they do not consider that the very lengthy work may have been started earlier and finished in 1610 away from the ruins of Sītāvaka. See Perera and Fernando, *Alagiyawanna's Kustantinu Haṭana*, viii–ix. The lengths to which the editors go to dismiss certain verses with inconvenient dates are noteworthy.
8. Abeyasinghe, *Portuguese Rule*, 204.
9. Perera and Fernando, *Alagiyawanna's Kustantinu Haṭana*, x.
10. Puñcibandara Sannasgala has written that the relative lack of praise for King Rājasiṃha in *Subhāṣitaya* suggests that the work was at least composed after the king's death in 1593. He also notes that some copies of the work contain a final verse that mentions 1611 as the year of its composition. See Sannasgala, *Sinhala Sāhitya Vaṁśaya* (1964), 303. An early twentieth-century study of Alagiyavanna's career likewise maintains that the 1611 date is correct. See Gunapala, *Kavindra Alagiyavanna Mukaveṭi Caritaya*, 20. Another biographical note on Alagiyavanna, assigns *Subhāṣitaya* to 1611, and it also estimates that Alagiyavanna converted and went to work for the Portuguese sometime between 1611 and 1612. See Gonahene Jotipala, ed., *1981 Rājya Sāhitya Utsavaya Kāragala: Siyaṇā-Lēkhakayō* (Colombo: Cultural Affairs Department, 1981), 5.
11. Chandra R. de Silva, "Algumas reflexões sobre o impacto português na religião entre os singaleses durante os séculos XVI e XVII," *Oceanos* 34 (1998), 108.
12. Strathern, *Kingship and Conversion*, 86.
13. C. R. Boxer, *The Church Militant and Iberian Expansion 1440–1770* (Baltimore: The Johns Hopkins University Press, 1978), 77–78.
14. João Paulo Oliveira e Costa, "A Diáspora Missionária" in Carlos Morreira Azevedo, ed. *História Religiosa de Portugal, Volume 2: Humanismos e Reformas* (Lisbon: Círculo de Leitores, 2000), 261.
15. Strathern, *Kingship and Conversion*, 110–111.
16. Abeyasinghe, *Portuguese Rule*, 206.
17. Abeyasinghe, *Portuguese Rule*, 212–213. Negrão was said to have learned Sinhala and was familiar with local manuscript sources. Other authors cite his work, called *Crónica da Província de São Tomé*, which likely contained a wealth of information on his impressions of Sinhala Buddhist culture. Yet this valuable text seems to have been lost in the disastrous 1755 earthquake in Lisbon. Cf. Ines G. Županov, "Jesuit Orientalism: Correspondence between Tomás Pereira and Fernão de Querois," in *Tomás Pereira, S.J. (1646–1708): Life, Work and World*, ed. Luís Filipe Barreto (Lisbon: Centro Científico e Cultural de Macau, 2010), 52.
18. Ines G. Županov, *Disputed Mission: Jesuit Experiments and Brahmanical Knowledge in Seventeenth-Century India* (Oxford, UK: Oxford University Press, 1999), 111.

19. Cf. Luis Fróis, *EuropaJapão: um diálogo civilizacional no século XVI: tratado em que se contêm muito sucinta e abreviadamente algumas contradições e diferenças de costumes entre a gente de Europa e esta província de Japão (...)* (Lisbon: Comissão Nacional para as Comemorações dos Descobrimentos Portugueses, 1993); Matteo Ricci, *The True Meaning of the Lord of Heaven (T'ien-chu shih-i)*, eds. and trans. Douglas Lancashire, Guozhen Hu, and Edward Malatesta (St. Louis : Institute of Jesuit Sources, 1985); Hugues Didier, *Os Portugueses no Tibete: Os Primeiros Relatos dos Jesuítas (1624–1635)*, trans. Lourdes Júdice (Lisbon: Comissão Nacional para as Comemorações dos Descobrimentos Portugueses, 2000).
20. Boxer, *Church Militant*, 49–50.
21. Fernão Guerreiro, *Relação Anual das Coisas que Fizeram os Padres da Companhia de Jesus nas suas Missões*, vol. I: 1600 a 1603 (Coimbra Portugal: Imprensa da Universidade, 1930), 2–3.
22. Ibid., 18–19.
23. Ibid., 326.
24. Joseph Wicki, ed. *Documenta Indica* XVII (1595–1597) (Rome: Institutum Historicum Societatis Iesu, 1988), 407–408.
25. Paulo da Trindade, *Conquista Espiritual do Oriente*, ed. Fernando Félix Lopes, vol. III (Lisbon: Centro de Estudos Históriocs Ultramarinos, 1967), 170.
26. Ibid.
27. Ibid.
28. V. Perniola, *Catholic Church in Sri Lanka*, 291–292.
29. Županov, *Disputed Mission*, 45–46. Županov, for her part, chooses to emphasize the debates that took place between Christian missionaries on the nature of the societies in which they worked.
30. Strathern, *Kingship and Conversion*, 87.
31. Costa, "A Diáspora Missionária," 278–279.
32. Guerreiro, *Relação Anual das Coisas que Fizeram os Padres da Companhia de Jesus nas suas Missões*, vol.II: 1604 a 1606 (Coimbra, Portugal: Imprensa da Universidade, 1930), 344–345.
33. Strathern, *Kingship and Conversion*, 242–243.
34. Abeyasinghe, *Portuguese Rule*, 207.
35. Suraweera, *Gampaha District*, 191–192.
36. De Silva, "Rise and Fall," 95–96.
37. Barros and Couto, *History of Ceylon from*, 271–273, 284–285.
38. De Silva, "Rise and Fall," 95–96.
39. Although some people have dated the work of moralistic verse called *Lōkōpakāraya* (*Assistance to the World*) to the fifteenth century, I agree with Godakumbura and Sannasgala, both of whom date this poem to around 1799 ce, See C. E. Godakumbura, *Sinhalese Literature* (Colombo: The Colombo Apothecaries' Co., 1955), 214; and Sannasgala, *Sinhala Sāhitya Vaṁśaya* (reprint), 515.

40. Munidasa, ed., *Subhāṣitaya*, reprint (Colombo: M. D. Gunasena, 2001), v. 46:

Näṇä ti	danan haṭa mañda guṇayak kaḷa		da
Pava ti	galä keṭū akurak men	niba	ñda
Vima ti	danan haṭa kaḷa kisi guṇa	noma	ñda
E nä ti	vēyä diyä piṭä äñdi irak	le	da

41. James R. Egge, *Religious Giving and the Invention of Karma in Theravāda Buddhism* (London: Curzon, 2002), 19–20, 42–43. Reiko Ohnuma has developed a similar model of Buddhist motivations for giving that employs the phrases *giving up* to great beings and *giving down* to unworthy recipients as a testament of one's compassion. See Ohnuma, *Head, Eyes, Flesh, and Blood*, 153.

42. Munidasa, *Subhāṣitaya*, v. 41:

Pa ra si du	pabu danan sevi pamaṇin	maha	ru
Belenu du	mañda vuvat no kereti rupun sa		ru
Baraṇiñdu	gele vasana nā rada vemin	ga	ru
Guruḷiñdu	atin äsi kima yahaḷu tora	tu	ru

Cf. Gunawardhana, *Subhashita Varnana*, v. 40.

43. Ludwick Sternbach, *Subhāṣita, Gnomic and Didactic Literature* (Wiesbaden, Germany: Otto Harrassowitz, 1974), 7.

44. Munidasa, *Subhāṣitaya*, v. 5.

45. Kotmale K.B.E. Edmond, "*Subhāṣitaya*," in Amara Hevamadduma et al., eds. *Sītāvaka Kaviya: Vivēcanātmaka Vigrahayak* (Battaramula, Sri Lanka: Department of Cultural Affairs, 1991), 63–64.

46. C. E. Godakumbura, "The Dravidian Element in Sinhalese," *Bulletin of the School of Oriental and African Studies* 11/4 (1946), 838.

47. Abeyasinghe, *Portuguese Rule*, 32–33.

48. Ibid., 112–113.

49. D. E. Hettiaratchi, "Civilisation of the Period (Continued): Literature and Art," In *University of Ceylon History of Ceylon*, ed. H. C. Ray (Colombo: Ceylon University Press, 1960), 777. Cf. Holt, *Buddhist Viṣṇu*, 58–60.

50. Munidasa, *Subhāṣitaya*, vv. 31–32:

Nu va ṇät	tavun paha koṭa dudanan	sevu	na
Nomä gat	sitä tulehi guṇa pokuramba	lesi	na
Mäda hat	no vä masuru guṇayen davas	ari	na
Raju ṭa t	e raṭaṭat aturek näta	veni	na.
Pämi ṇeta	lovaṭa buhu nā guṇa yutu	napu	ru
Me diyata	nasinu misä yahapata novē	sa	ru
No näväta	yugatä pat vū sañdehi sat	hi	ru
Vi ka si ta	novī dā yeyi säma tänä	tambu	ru.

51. The doctrine on the seven suns and the eventual destruction of the world by fire appears in E. Hardy, ed., *The Aṅguttara-Nikāya* IV (Oxford, UK: Pali Text Society, 1999), 100–106, and is again referenced in Henry Clarke Warren and Dharmānanda Kosambi, eds., *Visuddhimagga of Buddhaghosācariya* (Delhi, India: Motilal Banarsidass, 1989), XIII.32–41. Buddhist thought holds that for those eons destroyed by fire, multiple suns rise up in the sky over a long period of time, clouds disappear, and then rivers, lakes, and oceans dry up before the entire world catches fire and is incinerated.
52. It should be noted that several *Jātaka* stories present a negative image of kingship in general, due largely to the recognition that kings must sometimes engage in negative, harmful acts in line with their royal duties. The Mūgapakkha Jātaka (no. 538) is a fine example of a story in which the Bodhisattva forsakes his right to the throne in order to renounce the life of a householder and avoid rebirth in hell following a lifetime as a king. See, for example, Berkwitz, *History of the Buddha's Relic Shrine*, 86–92.
53. Munidasa, *Subhāṣitaya*, vv. 26–27:

Kulu ṇi n	guṇen nuvaṇin pasiňdu häma	tä	na
Su da nan	sevuna niriňdō lōsata	raki	na
Dehi ru n	malin ron genä yana men	seme	na
Ni ya min	aya ganiti sata sita no	taḷami	na
A ma yu t	rasa ahara vat vaḍavana	oda	sa
Ku sa gat	gini nivana pamaṇaṭa budina	le	sa
Ted a ki t	pataḷa niriňdō nomaňda dana	rä	sa
No ke ret	lovä satan rakinā vitara	mi	sa.

54. Munidasa, *Subhāṣitaya*, v. 67: no paṇat aya anata ahasev näta niya ma; and v. 73: siri tin lovä päväti näṇa bala mada dudana.
55. Munidasa, *Subhāṣitaya*, v. 83:

Sa la pa ya	ta ri ňdu	himi räsa veyi hima	giri	ňdu
Karambaya	mu hudu	diliňdu vä ävidiyi	kivi	ňdu
Nisi de ya	mebaňdu	uvaduru däruyē	ru	du
Me tediya	pa si ňdu	apavaga mä yä	supirisi	du.

56. Cf. Munidasa, *Subhāṣitaya*, v. 38.
57. Munidasa, *Subhāṣitaya*, v. 47:

A mi ta	guṇa nuvaṇa yutu utumō	pabaň	da
A na ta	vehesa laduvat no mä veti	duha	da
Di ga ta	pataḷa suvaňdäti soňda saňdun kaň		da
Si ňdita	maňḍita eka lesa pätireyi	suvaňi	da.

58. Munidasa, *Subhāṣitaya*, v. 9:

U tuṁ	nivan säpa sapayā dena	maha	ta
Dahaṁ	raja samaya no ganiti kudiṭu	sa	ta

No hiṁ suvaňda vihidena siri räňdi dimu ta
Pi yuṁ venehi nila mäsi käla no häsire ta.

59. Munidasa, *Subhāṣitaya*, v. 12:

Sa ka la sura naran muňdunatä sädū pa da
Vi pu la muni saraṇa härä an suran väň da
Ni ma la mok piṇisa sata surakinu dula da
Dimbula mala nisā vehesenu väni diyä da.

60. Cf. Ibid., v. 75.
61. Cf. Ibid., v. 39.
62. Munidasa, *Subhāṣitaya*, v. 74:

Neka vat ätat me tekä yi yama pamaṇa nä ti
Loba sit vamīn ilvanu yadiyan siri ti
Daḷä net niyutu mehesuruhu da tada tedä ti
Jara pat mahalu gon vāhanayen sara ti.

63. Cf. Ñanavimala, *Buduguṇa Alaṅkāraya*, v. 160. This work proceeds in verses 172–173 to try and dissuade its audience members from making offerings to Śiva altogether:

Leaving aside the shape of a phallus,
That causes disgust in some people,
And increases lust in the minds of others,
What use is there in offerings made to it?
Offerings that are made to Iśvara,
Who is no field of merit to this world,
By one with a mind polluted by wicked conduct,
Are like seeds that are sown on a rock.

64. Michael Hahn, "Śaṅkarasvāmin's *Devatāvimarśastuti*," in *Vividharatnakaraṇḍaka: Festgabe für Adelheid Mette*, eds. Christine Chojnacki, Jens-Uwe Hartmann, and Volker M. Tschannerl (Swisttal-Odendorf, Germany: Indica et Verlag, 2000), 319–321. I give thanks to Ulrike Roesler for bringing this work to my attention.
65. Munidasa, *Subhāṣitaya*, v. 17:

Ät a t nätat para lova sudaneni mahata
Haḷot yeheki pav kaṁ no tabā mä sita
Nätot e para lova in vana aväḍa näta
Ät o t nätäyi pav kaḷa haṭa veyi vipata.

66. Specifically, the Buddha is said to argue whether there is another world or not, the person who acts as if there is will be praised by the wise, if not also reborn in a fortunate state. For one who acts as if there is no other world, he or she will be denounced by wise persons and, as it happens, reborn in a state of woe and

suffering. See V. Trenckner, *Majjhima-Nikāya*, vol. I (London: Pali Text Society, 1888), 403–404.

67. One example of the early modern Portuguese rejection of karma and rebirth, through which such ideas are denounced as "brutish" and fatalistic, effectively denying human free will and entertaining beliefs such as the passage of the souls of sinners into animals, appears in A. de Silva Rego, ed. *Documentação Ultramarina Portuguesa I* (Lisbon: Centro de Estudos Históricos Ultramarinos, 1960), 251–252.

68. Sternbach, *Subhāṣita*, 7.

69. Cf. Philip C. Almond, *The British Discovery of Buddhism* (Cambridge, UK: Cambridge University Press, 1988), 10–13. Almond and other scholars who conclude that Buddhism was invented as a world religion by Europeans in the nineteenth century have overlooked not only indigenous Buddhist conceptions but also earlier writings by Portuguese missionaries from the sixteenth and seventeenth centuries. The Jesuit Luís Fróis described Japanese Buddhism as a "*religião*" even in the 1580s, and other missionaries sponsored by the Portuguese crown recognized the widespread presence of Buddhist monks and devotees across Asia long before the nineteenth century. Luís Fróis, *Historia de Japam*, vol. I., ed. José Wicki (Lisboa: Biblioteca Nacional de Lisboa, 1976), 168. See also David N. Lorenzen, "Gentile Religion in South India, China, and Tibet: Studies by Three Jesuit Missionaries," *Comparative Studies of South Asia, Africa and the Middle East* 27/1 (2007): 203–213.

70. On indigenous terms used in place of *religion* in premodern Sri Lanka, see Sven Bretfeld, "Resonant Paradigms in the Study of Religions and the Emergence of the Theravāda Buddhism" *Religion* 42/2 (2012), 279–282.

71. Cf. Ñanavimala, *Buduguṇa Alaṅkāraya*, v. 157:

> Miserable Brahmin folk,
> Making offerings to the fire god,
> In order to receive wealth for themselves,
> What fruits are achieved for the world by this worship?

72. Munidasa, *Subhāṣitaya*, vv. 10–11:

Ru va n	miḷa nodat anuvaṇa dana	veḷa	ňda
Lo bi n	kadā käṭi miṇi yäyi rägat	le	da
Pa san	muni varan härä an suran	vä	ňda
Ni va n	patā anuvaṇa sata kereti	pu	da
Naňdana	muniňdu härä an suranaṭa	pävä	ta
Ni va na	patā anuvaṇa sata karana	tä	ta
La ba na	piṇisa tel loba vaḍavamini	si	ta
Maňḍina	vännä välimalu lamini	teliya	ta

73. Cf. Tennekoon, *Sävul Sandēśaya*, vv. 96, 118, 202.

74. Cf. Sorata, *Dahamsoňḍa Kava*, vv. 44–47, 62.
75. On the invention of Buddhism, see Tomoko Masuzawa, *The Invention of World Religions: Or, How European Universalism Was Preserved in the Language of Pluralism* (Chicago: University of Chicago Press, 2005), 121–126. Masuzawa's theoretical argument is compelling, but she is incorrect about Europeans and native "practitioners" not recognizing a single Buddhist religion out of the divergent rites across Asia before the nineteenth century.
76. Munidasa, *Subhāṣitaya*, v. 13:

Pa sa k	muniňdu samaya mä no genä sunima	la
A ne k	kudiṭu genä lō sata näṇa vika	la
Ē mok	puraṭa pämiṇeta yaṁ kalä e ka	la
Aňdek	däkkä heyi min pada da nuba ta	la.

77. Strathern, *Kingship and Conversion*, 135. It is also worth noting that the term "*yesus kiristū devisamaya*" appears in Alagiyavanna's *Kustantīnu Haṭana*, v. 11. This text will be examined at length in chapter 6.
78. The Sinhala term *samaya* comes from the word *sammata*, which is used to refer to "poetic conventions" (*kavi sammata*) or poetic norms on which there is general agreement over their use in literary compositions. I wish to acknowledge Professor P. B. Meegaskumbura for bringing this to my attention.
79. One finds analogous uses of the term *samaya* in Pāli and Prakrit sources, in which it connotes the idea of a convention in the sense of general consent and practice based on it. However, it later acquires the meaning of a system, doctrine, or religious movement. See Adelheid Mette, "Notes on *Samaya* 'Convention' in Pali and Prakrit," in *Middle Indo-Aryan and Jaina Studies*, ed. Colette Caillat (Leiden, Netherlands: E. J. Brill, 1991), 69, 74.
80. Munidasa, *Subhāṣitaya*, v. 14:

Pu n	pirisidu sil mul guṇa kaňdin	yu	ti
Da n	kama näṇa 'kuru mal sā maňḍulu	ä	ti
Pi n	kap tura sagamok pala dena	kämä	ti
Ma n	sudanan met sililin väḍeyi	ni	ti.

81. Cf. Ibid., v. 34.
82. Cf. Ibid., v. 85.
83. Cf. Ibid., v. 22.
84. Cf. Ibid., v. 80.
85. Cf. Ibid., v. 44.
86. W. F. Gunawardhana, *Subhashita Varnana*, 62.
87. Munidasa, *Subhāṣitaya*, v. 42:

Sata tin	paṭan amba koḷa budina	tavasa ra
Dähä nin	midē duṭa leḷa dena liya	tamba ra
Budi min	yamaku kiri tel dī ā̈̄	aha ra
Iňdu ran	damata siňdu ipile 'v maňdara gi ra.	

88. A. Berriedale Keith, *A History of Sanskrit Literature*, reprint [1928] (Delhi, India: Motilal Banarsidass, 1993), 176–177. Although Barbara Stoler Miller is less willing to speculate about Bhartṛhari's identity, her translation of the poet's *Śatakatrayam* includes verses that give homage to the god Śiva. See Miller, trans., *Bhartrihari: Poems* (New York: Columbia University Press, 1967), 4, 137.
89. Cf. Munidasa, *Subhāṣitaya*, v. 5.
90. Hallisey, "Works and Persons," 734.
91. Sudipta Kaviraj, *The Unhappy Consciousness: Bankimchandra Chattopadhyay and the Formation of Nationalist Discourse in India* (Delhi, India: Oxford University Press, 1998), 13, 171 n31.
92. James C. Scott, *Domination and the Arts of Resistance: Hidden Transcripts* (New Haven, CT: Yale University Press, 1990), 4–5.

CHAPTER 6

1. Abeyasinghe, *Portuguese Rule*, 212–213.
2. Ibid., 213.
3. Guerreiro, *Relação Anual*, vol. 2, 344–345
4. C. Gaston Perera, *The Portuguese Missionary in 16th and 17th Century Ceylon: The Spiritual Conquest* (Colombo: Vijitha Yapa, 2009), 141–146.
5. Perniola, *Catholic Church in Sri Lanka*, 431–434.
6. João Paulo Oliveira e Costa points out that there was a close association more generally between Christian missions and Portuguese colonial expansion from the mid-sixteenth century through the first quarter of the seventeenth century. See Costa, "A Diáspora Missionária," 260.
7. Jorge Flores, "Ceilão," in *Dicionário de História dos Descobrimentos Portugueses*, vol. I, ed. Luís de Albuquerque (Lisbon: Caminho, 1994), 231.
8. Zoltán Biedermann, "The Matrioshka Principle and How It Was Overcome: Portuguese and Hapsburg Imperial Attitudes in Sri Lanka and the Responses of the Rulers of Kotte (1506–1598)," *Journal of Early Modern History* 13 (2009), 294, 298–299, 308.
9. C. R. de Silva, *Portuguese in Ceylon*, 14–15.
10. Ibid., 12.
11. Abeyasinghe, *Portuguese Rule*, 106–107.
12. A *tombo* for the lands of Jaffna began to be compiled under the Portuguese in 1623, although a more complete and extant *tombo* for the Jaffna region was undertaken between 1633 and 1637. In contrast, there were no efforts made to register lands found in the Kandyan areas, the Uva region in the southeast hill country, or the eastern coastal areas. See Karunasena Dias Paranavitana, "The Portuguese *Tombos* as a Source of Sixteenth- and Seventeenth-Century Sri Lankan History," in *Re-Exploring the Links: History and Constructed Histories between Portugal and Sri Lanka*, ed. Jorge Flores (Wiesbaden, Germany: Harrassowitz Verlag, 2007), 64–67.

13. C. R. de Silva, *Portuguese in Ceylon*, 171.
14. The population of Portugal between the mid-sixteenth century and 1640 ranged between 1.5 and 2 million persons, and it has been estimated that the number of able-bodied Portuguese who served the crown overseas by the end of the sixteenth century did not exceed 10,000. See Russell-Wood, *Portuguese Empire*, 60.
15. Pieris, *Ceylon Littoral 1593*, 9.
16. C. R. de Silva, *Portuguese in Ceylon*, 174.
17. Ângela Barreto Xavier, "Disquiet on the Island: Conversion, Conflicts and Conformity in Sixteenth-Century Goa," *The Indian Economic and Social History Review* 44/3 (2007), 280.
18. The offering of tangible, material benefits to converts by the Portuguese is often condemned by Sri Lankans today as a cynical and coercive attempt to make a person choose a new religion without exercising free will. See, for example, C. G. Perera, *Portuguese Missionary*, 203, 322.
19. A. V. Suraweera, *Rājāvaliya* (Ratmalana, Sri Lanka: Sarvodaya Vishva Lekha, 2000), 76.
20. Quoted in K. D. Paranavitana, "Suppression of Buddhism and Aspects of Indigenous Culture under the Portuguese and the Dutch." *Journal of the Royal Asiatic Society of Sri Lanka*, N.S. 49 (2004), 4.
21. Costa, "A Diáspora Missionária," 303.
22. Xavier, "Disquiet on the Island," 284–285. Among the those Sinhalas who converted in large numbers to Catholicism, the *Karāva* caste of fishermen stands out as one of the communities who embraced the Portuguese religion most enthusiastically and who received clear benefits in terms of economics and status for doing so. For an in-depth study of this history, see Michael Roberts, *Caste Conflict and Elite Formation: The Rise of a Karāva Elite in Sri Lanka, 1500–1931* (Cambridge, UK: Cambridge University Press, 1982).
23. Ferguson, "Alagiyavanna Mohoṭṭāla," 117–118.
24. Cf. Ângela Barreto Xavier, *A Invenção de Goa: Poder Imperial e Conversões Culturais nos Séculos XVI e XVII* (Lisbon: Imprensa de Ciências Sociais, 2008), 24–25.
25. Peter, "Portuguese Influences," 14. Cf. V. Ball, trans., *Travels in India by Jean Baptiste Tavenier*, vol. II (London: Macmillan and Co., 1889), 188–189.
26. S. G. Perera and Fernando, *Alagiyawanna's Kustantinu Haṭana*, x–xi.
27. Abeyasinghe, *Portuguese Rule*, 204.
28. Vicente L. Rafael, *Contracting Colonialism: Translation and Christian Conversion in Tagalog Society under Early Spanish Rule* (Durham, NC: Duke University Press, 1993), 164.
29. Cf. Xavier, *Invenção de Goa*, 26.
30. Paul E. Pieris relates an account from an early *tombo*, wherein Alagiyavanna is depicted as testifying to the *vedor* about the details concerning the village Mandampe on the basis of some *ola* (palm leaf) manuscripts that he possessed. See Pieris, *Ceylon Littoral*, 9–10.

31. Paul E. Pieris, *Ceylon: The Portuguese Era*, vol. 2 (Dehiwala, Sri Lanka: Tisara Press, 1983), 85.
32. Queyroz, *Temporal and Spiritual Conquest*, vol. 2, 620.
33. Abeyasinghe, *Portuguese Rule*, 32–33.
34. De Silva, *Portuguese in Ceylon*, 36–37. While the Portuguese considered António Barreto a "rebel," he may have been viewed rather differently by some Sinhalas. In contemporary Sri Lanka, Kuruwita Rala is portrayed positively as a "warrior who fought the Portuguese to save the country." See, for instance, the newspaper editorial titled "Political Councils as Political *Ambalamas* [wayside rests]" in http://www.island.lk/2008/07/15/editorial.html.
35. António da Silva Rego, ed., *Documentos Remetidos da Índia: Ou Livros das Monções*, vol. VII (Lisboa: Imprensa Nacional-Casa da Moeda, 1975), 69–70.
36. Xavier, *Invenção de Goa*, 443.
37. Nira Wickramasinghe, "La petition coloniale: objet de contrôle, objet de dissidence," *Identity, Culture & Politics*, 7/1 (2006), 9, 16.
38. Flores, *Hum Curto Historia*, 75.
39. De Silva, *Portuguese in Ceylon*, 59, 80–81.
40. This hypothesis may be held in part due to the legacy of lands belonging to Alagiyavanna's descendants scattered around the Gampaha District in modern Sri Lanka. I was shown some of these lands by descendants sharing Alagiyavanna's name as their surname in 2006. Reference to some of Alagiyavanna's grant villages is made in K.D.G. Wimalaratne, *Personalities Sri Lanka: A Biographical Study (15th-20th Century) [1490–1990 A.D.] A–Z* (Colombo: Ceylon Business Appliances, 1994), 8. M. E. Fernando also asserts that de Sá restored Alagiyavanna's post and salary but does not specifically mention what was done with his lands. See Fernando, ed., *Alagiyavanna Mukaveṭitumā visin viracita Kustantīnu Haṭana* (Galle, Sri Lanka: St. Aloysius' College, 1933), iii.
41. De Silva, *Portuguese in Ceylon*, 82–83.
42. Jorge Flores and Maria Augusta Lima Cruz, "A 'Tale of Two Cities,' a 'Veteran Soldier,' or the Struggle for Endangered Nobilities: The Two *Jornadas de Huva* (1633, 1635) Revisited," in Jorge Flores, ed., *Re-Exploring the Links: History and Constructed Histories between Portugal and Sri Lanka* (Wiesbaden, Germany: Harrassowitz Verlag, 2007), 118–119.
43. De Silva, *Portuguese in Ceylon*, 82.
44. Jorge Manuel Flores, *Os Olhos do Rei: Desenhos e Descrições Portuguesas da Ilha de Ceilão (1624, 1638)* (Lisbon: Commissão Nacional para As Commemorações dos Descobrimentos Portugueses, 2001), 25.
45. E. Hector Perera, *Sinhala Haṭan Sāhitya* (Colombo: Ratna Pot Prakāśakayō, 1961), 63. Cf. S. G. Perera and Fernando, *Alagiyawanna's Kustantinu Haṭana*, xiii.
46. Ambagaspitiye Wimalahimi, *Siṅhala Haṭan (Kavi) Sāhitya Vimarśanaya* (Colombo: S. Godage and Brothers, 1998), 90. Cf. Rohini Paranavitana, ed., *Sītāvaka Haṭana* (Colombo: Madhyama Saṅskṛitka Aramudala, 1999), x–xi.

47. Wimalahimi, *Sinhala Haṭan (Kavi)*, 88. There is a much older tradition of war poetry in the *puṟam* genre of Tamil verse from the first centuries of the Common Era. See, for example, A. K. Ramanujan, trans., *Poems of Love and War: From the Eight Anthologies and the Ten Long Poems of Classical Tamil* (New York: Columbia University Press, 1985). There is, however, little evidence of Tamil war poems exhibiting a direct influence on Sinhala poetry, other than their frequent praise for kings and the shared theme of the glorification of war. On these ideas, see George L. Hart III, *The Poems of Ancient Tamil: Their Milieu and Their Sanskrit Counterparts* (Berkeley: University of California Press, 1975), 38–40, 212–213.
48. R. Paranavitana, *Sītāvaka Haṭana*, viii–ix.
49. Michael Roberts, *Sinhala Consciousness in the Kandyan Period 1590s to 1815* (Colombo: Vijitha Yapa, 2003), 111.
50. Cf. my translation of the praise of King Parākramabāhu VI's military exploits in *Pärakumbā Sirita*, which confirm his victories without supplying details of the battles fought:

> Being renowned throughout the entire world, like golden flags raised high,
> King Päräkum, who excels in the strength of merit,
> Crushed with his customary might the arrogance of the Kannaḍi kings,
> Who did not retreat even a foot because of the pride in their minds.

D. G. Abhayagunaratna, ed., *Pärakumbā Sirita*, reprint, [1929], (Colombo: Madhyama Saṅskṛtika Aramudala, 1997), v. 51. Editions, without gloss, of this work and several other comparable works are found in J. E. Sedaraman, *Praśasti Kāvya Rasaya* (Colombo: M. D. Gunasena, 1970).

51. Roberts, *Sinhala Consciousness*, 117–118.
52. Fernando, *Alagiyavanna Mukaveṭitumā visin viracita Kustantīnu Haṭana*, vv. 1–3:

Basakara aruta me	na
Venasa noma pā̆ pavati	na
Piti put vīdi ya	na
Tevak eksura vaňdiṁ adari	na
Sav lev sat mu	du n
Siya siripā kamala	du n
Met guṇa piri na	du n
Vaňdiṁ yēsus kristu suri	ňdun
Rivikän pahaṇaki	na
Nikut nalasiḷu vilasi	na
Kanni mari kusaye	na
Pahaḷa suriňdun vaňdiṁ bätiye	na

W.L.A. Don Peter explains the mythological symbolism of the "sun-stone" as an example of an Indic symbol used as a simile to portray Christ's virgin birth in his "Portuguese Influence," 21.

53. R. Paranavitana, *Sītāvaka Haṭana*, liv.
54. Wimalahimi, *Siṅhala Haṭan (Kavi)*, 103.
55. Perera, S. G. and Fernando, *Alagiyawanna's Kustantinu Haṭana*, ii.
56. F. W. de Silva, "Kostantinu Hatana," *Journal of the Royal Asiatic Society (Ceylon)* 13 (1894), 135.
57. S. G. Perera, "Alagiyawanna Mohottala," 46.
58. Perera, S. G. and Fernando, *Alagiyawanna's Kustantinu Haṭana*, xiv–xxiv.
59. Wickramasinghe, *Sinhalese Literature*, 197.
60. Sannasgala, *Sinhala Sāhitya Vaṁśaya* (1964), 307.
61. Godakumbura, *Sinhalese Literature*, 228.
62. K. H. de Silva, *Siṅhala Haṭan Kavi* (Colombo: Sri Lanka Publishing Society, 1964), 64.
63. Suraweera, "Alagiyavanna Mukaveṭitumā," 194.
64. Webb Keane, *Christian Moderns: Freedom and Fetish in the Mission Encounter* (Berkeley: University of California Press, 2007), 20, 62–63.
65. Ibid., 201.
66. Talal Asad, *Genealogies of Religion: Discipline and Reasons of Power in Christianity and Islam* (Baltimore: The Johns Hopkins University Press, 1993), 47–48.
67. Wickramasinghe, *Sinhalese Literature*, 197.
68. Peter, "Portuguese Influence," 17.
69. Fernando, *Kustantīnu Haṭana*, vi.
70. Godakumbura, *Sinhalese Literature*, 226.
71. Gunapala, *Kavīndra Alagiyavanna Mukaveṭi Caritaya*, 32–33. Another scholar holds that Alagiyavanna publicly "converted" numerous times, from Buddhism to Hinduism to Catholicism and to Calvinism out of convenience but remained Buddhist "in his heart." See Kosgoda Karunadasa Silva Dunusinghe, *Alagiyavanna Mukaveṭi Vicāraya saha Don Jerōnimōgē Konstantīnu Haṭana Kāvyaya* (Colombo: S. Godage and Brothers, 1997), 39–40.
72. The notion that Alagiyavanna died a Buddhist in his ancestral lands was shared with me by A.M.A. Herbert Kumar Alagiyawanna, A.M.A. Paulis Apphuamy, and A.M.A. Gunathilake Alagiyawanna, all of whom are Buddhists and share the honorific names Alagiyawanna Mohotti Appuhamilage and the family custom in noting descent from this famous Sinhala poet.
73. It has been suggested elsewhere that his anonymity may be due to the fact that he did not wish to ruin his reputation among his fellow Lankans as the author of a work that extols Portuguese Christians. See Gunapala, *Kavīndra Alagiyavanna Mukaveṭi Caritaya*, 33.
74. For studies on the modern controversies over Christian conversion, see the essays in Rosalind I. J. Hackett, ed., *Proselytization Revisited: Rights Talk, Free Markets and Culture Wars* (London: Equinox, 2008). For a different view on the possibility of being both Buddhist and Christian, see Rose Drew, *Buddhist and Christian? An Exploration of Dual Belonging* (London: Routledge, 2011).

75. Strathern, *Kingship and Conversion*, 121–122.
76. Queyroz, *Temporal and Spiritual Conquest*, vol. II, 699.
77. Ibid., 700.
78. Costa, "A Diáspora Missionária," 306.
79. Robert J. C. Young, *Postcolonialism: A Historical Introduction* (Oxford, UK: Blackwell, 2001), 354–355.
80. On hybridity as a form of resistance, see Homi Bhabha, *The Location of Culture* (London: Routledge, 1994), 159–165. On hidden expressions of resistance to official and elite power, see Scott, *Domination and the Arts of Resistance*, 4–16.
81. Fernando, *Kustantīnu Haṭana*, vi; Peter, "Portuguese Influence," 22–24.
82. S. G. Perera, "Alagiyawanna Mohottala," 46–47.
83. Kenneth Mills and Anthony Grafton, *Conversion: Old Worlds and New* (Rochester, NY: University of Rochester Press, 2003), xi–xii.
84. Bhabha, *Location of Culture*, 163.
85. António da Silva Rego, ed., *Documentação Ultramarina Portuguesa* (Lisbon: Centro de Estudos Históricos Ultramarinos, 1960), 251–254. On the issue of early Portuguese incuriosity of Buddhism, see Alan Strathern, "Re-Reading Queirós: Some Neglected Aspects of the *Conquista*," *Sri Lanka Journal of the Humanities* 26/1–2 (2000), 12.
86. Trindade, *Conquista Espiritual do Oriente*, vol. III, 31.
87. Queyroz, *Temporal and Spiritual Conquest*, vol. 2, 440.
88. Cf. Fernando, *Kustantīnu Haṭana*, vv. 102, 127, 141.
89. Ingalls, *Sanskrit Poetry*, 211; Ramanujan, *Poems of Love and War*, 287–289.
90. Abhayagunaratna, *Pärakumbā Sirita*, v. 81:

Van meden yuda an	radon	rambaran täḷuṃ madamat	gajāṇeni
Pansaňdin saňda kän	lesin	baṭapun yasin raguraṁ	rajāṇeni
Rankaňdin kaḷa men	ruvin	rasaňdun ḷaňdun netamin	dajāṇeni
Nan sirin viňdaman	tosin	iňdupin utuṁ päräkum	rajāṇeni.

91. On the associations drawn between religious and masculine virtues in South Asian Buddhist thought, see John Powers, *A Bull of a Man: Images of Masculinity, Sex, and the Body in Indian Buddhism* (Cambridge, MA: Harvard University Press, 2009). For a closer study of the association between physical beauty and moral excellence, see again Mrozik, *Virtuous Bodies*.
92. Fernando, *Kustantīnu Haṭana*, vv. 48–49:

Me topa situvot vä	ra
Tumbaseka tuňgu sunera gi	ra
Kiňdaleka mahasayu	ra
Me dambadiva miduleka taman do	ra
Me topa sari kaḷasa	ka
Raṇa samuduraṭa sunera	ka

Apa mahasen no ye	ka
Rakina tarasara viduru pavure	ka.

93. Fernando, *Kustantīnu Haṭana*, v. 71:

Vikum yutu	saros	sā
Tedaṇin yutu	siya rä	sā
Kustan ti nu	da	sā
Namäti apa himi tumā vese		sā.

94. Cf. Tennekoon, *Sävul Sandēśaya*, 59–63. The verses describing de Sá's weaponry appear in Fernando, *Kustantīnu Haṭana*, vv. 85–87.
95. Roberts, *Sinhala Consciousness*, 44–45. Note also the comparison made between King Parākramabāhu VI and the god Rāma in the verse excerpted from *Pärakumbā Sirita*, cited in n90.
96. Fernando, *Kustantīnu Haṭana*, v. 80:

Pā vikum di	ri	yē
Raṇamäda väda nobi	ri	yē
Kan̆da uvin̆du sa	ri	yē
Vikum pānem̆ topa idi	ri	yē.

97. For an example of how the images of Indic deities represent merely the local "literary and cultural heritage" overlaid on sincere Christian convictions, see Peter, "Portuguese Influence," 22–24.
98. Sedaraman, *Praśasti Kāvya Rasaya*, ix–x. For another example of a king being compared to a god, see the description that models King Duṭṭhagāmaṇī (Sinhala: Duṭugämuṇu) after Śakra, the King of the Gods, in *Sinhala Thūpavaṃsa*. Cf. Berkwitz, *History of the Buddha's Relic Shrine*, 233.
99. Morton E. Bloomfield and Charles W. Dunn, *The Role of the Poet in Early Societies* (Cambridge, UK: D. S. Brewer, 1989), 120–23.
100. On the productive distinction made between documentary and worklike texts, see LaCapra, *Rethinking Intellectual History*, 29–31.
101. Fernando, *Kustantīnu Haṭana*, vv. 184–185:

Asura yuda jay age	na
Sura senan̆ga pirivarami	na
Surapura van soba	na
Pasak sakdevi vilasa pāmi	na
Mahasen gena nomi	ni
Vijaya keḷi keḷa mana me	ni
Janamaharaja tosi	ni
Pavara malvāna nam̆ pura va	ni.

102. Flores, *Os Olhos do Rei*, 29. One cannot establish whether Alagiyavanna's work had a role in the divination of Sá de Noronha.

103. Cf. Tennekoon, *Sävul Sandēśaya*, v. 45.
104. Fernando, v. 77.
105. Ibid., vv. 88–89.
106. Ronald M. Davidson, *Indian Esoteric Buddhism: A Social History of the Tantric Movement* (New York: Columbia University Press, 2002), 68–70.
107. Fernando, *Kustantīnu Haṭana*, vv. 98–100.
108. Fernando, *Alagiyavanna Mukaveṭitumā visin viracita Kustantīnu Haṭana*, v. 130:

No da han	peramada rajumen babaḷa	na
Ru sir en	disi apa naraniňdu sasoba	na
Ba la min	äsipiya no heḷā siṭiye	na
Su ramban	sirisilu piṭisara kulaňga	na.

109. Cf. Kiri Elle Ñanavimala, ed. *Alagiyavanna Mukaveṭi Kiviňdun visin viracita Kusa Jātaka Kāvyaya* (Colombo: M. D. Gunasena), v. 673.
110. Abhayagunaratna, *Pärakumbā Sirita*, v. 100.
111. Fernando, *Kustantīnu Haṭana*, vv. 114–115:

Pä hä na da	bäma net vuvanat pirita	na
Yu tu ḷa ňda	uḍukuru vemin keḷinu ye	na
Bi ňgu ro da	nilupul siyapat tisaru	na
Nä ti va da	ätimen viya gaňga häma tä	na
Su du van	käradara ratu kära netu ni	l
He ḷa min	kanupul pirimäda tana tu	l
Un un un	aňganō isi diya sihilä	l
Sa le ḷun	siripaḷa kara rati keḷa lo	l.

112. Cf. Tennekoon, *Sävul Sandēśaya*, v. 159. My translation of this stanza, which is the likely source for the corresponding verse in *Kustantīnu Haṭana*, reads:

Endowed with moonlike faces, high eyebrows, blue eyes, and full breasts,
Because the women play [in the water] while facing upward,
Although there are not [actual] lotuses, clusters of bees, blue lotuses, or swans,
It was if there were rivers [containing these] everywhere.

113. Dharmarama, *Kāvyaśēkhara*, VII.31. My translation reads:

The women were splashing each other with streams of cool water,
Smearing the sandalwood paste on their bodies and making the water lilies fall from their ears,
As they caressed their cheeks and rubbed their excellent breasts while increasing desire,
Making their shiny red lips turn white, moaning continuously like husbands in love- play.

114. Velcheru Narayana Rao, David Shulman, and Sanjay Subrahmanyam, *Symbols of Substance: Court and State in Nāyaka Period Tamilnadu* (Oxford, UK: Oxford University Press, 1992), 66–67.
115. Bloomfield and Dunn. *Role of the Poet*, 126–127.
116. Cf. Rafael, *Contracting Colonialism*, 21–22. Rafael's theories and terminology found in his discussion of the deflection of Spanish power through the use of the vernacular Tagalog in the Philippines seems particularly apt here.
117. Xavier, *Invenção de Goa*, 205–206. There were, of course, exceptions to the intolerant stance toward local religions and culture as preached by many Portuguese missionaries. A few notable missionaries sponsored by the Portuguese, Alessandro Valignano and Roberto Nobili, for example, made a distinction between religious and cultural signs, permitting the retention of the latter as the means for facilitating conversions to Christianity. For more on this once controversial approach, see Županov, *Disputed Mission*.
118. The poet also praises the Portuguese king as well as the army commanders Phillip de Oliveira and Luis Teixeira. See Fernando, *Kustantīnu Haṭana*, vv. 9, 167.
119. Ibid., v. 8.
120. Ibid., v.164.
121. Cf. Godakumbura, *Sinhalese Literature*, 226.
122. This formulation reverses what Said has said about European efforts to define the Oriental. See Edward Said, *Orientalism* (New York: Vintage Books, 1979), 40. Of course, in his subaltern position Alagiyavanna did not enjoy the same degree of power that Said attributes to the European Orientalist.
123. I am borrowing the image of the colonized subject who builds a life within the crevices of colonial power from Frederick Cooper in his *Colonialism in Question: Theory, Knowledge, History* (Berkeley: University of California Press, 2005), 16.
124. Contemporary Tamil literature recognized similar social realities in this period and likewise strove to respond to them. See Rao, Shulman, and Subrahmanyam, *Symbols of Substance*, 12.
125. Biedermann, "Matrioshka Principle," 266.
126. Fernando, *Kustantīnu Haṭana*, v. 9:

    Dambadivatala pata ra
    Rajuneḍi mäḍi vikum sa ra
    Pratikal rajuṭa ti ra
    Me laka atpat vīya puvata ra.

127. Ibid., v. 129.
128. Cf. Ibid., vv. 31, 33, 53, 84, 86.
129. Cf. Berkwitz, *History of the Buddha's Relic Shrine*, 144, 158.
130. Fernando, *Kustantīnu Haṭana*, v. 42.

131. Ibid., v. 44. The extravagant descriptions of Portugal in this work were surely an exaggeration of the country's conditions at this point in history. The country was a maritime power but was historically much less prosperous than much of the rest of western Europe. See Sanjay Subrahmanyam, *The Portuguese Empire in Asia 1500–1700: A Political and Economic History* (London: Longman, 1993), 144.
132. Fernando, *Kustantīnu Haṭana*, vv. 32–33, 44.
133. See W. Randolph Kloetzli, *Buddhist Cosmology: Science and Theology in the Images of Motion and Light* (Delhi, India: Motilal Banarsidass, 1983), 24–25. References to Mount Meru, the *cakravaḷa* perimeter, and the continent of Jambudvīpa are particularly common in ancient and medieval Sinhala Buddhist literature.
134. Biedermann, "Matrioshka Principle," 302.
135. The thirteenth-century *Sinhala Thūpavaṃsa* contain prose accounts of battles fought by King Duṭugämuṇu and his warriors against an invading Tamil army, in which the slaying of enemy soldiers by swords, spears, and arrows is portrayed. See, for example, Berkwitz, *History of the Buddha's Relic Shrine*, 163, 166, 187–189.
136. Wimalahimi, *Siṅhala Haṭan (Kavi)*, 102–103.
137. Fernando, *Kustantīnu Haṭana*, v. 157.
138. Ibid., v. 140.
139. Fernando, *Kustantīnu Haṭana*, vv. 172–173, 176:

Samaharek	rudurupun baňda alamada vilasaṭa polu gasa	t
Samaharek	tal pol lesin rupun is taraṁ siňda goḍa gasa	t
Samaharek	rupu balen alvā kannāsa at pā kapa	t
Samaharek	dasa pasdenā haṭa äna misak aḍi pasu no la	t
Samaharek	saturanṭa äna lansayaṭa gena ahakaṭa dama	t
Samaharek	eka eka veḍillen detundena eka täna heḷa	t
Samaharek	tama de pā väňdiyan pin piṇisa no koṭāhari	t
Samaharek	piṭipā rupun no marāma alvā bäňda gene	t
Saha s ras les	nidos tedayutu me apa niriňduge sen vipu	l
Daha s suvahas	gaṇan rupun is siňda damā yuda dinū ka	l
Raku s yakbūpisas	samaňgin ukus gijukā balu siva	l
Mini s mas kus	purā budimin kaḷō täna täna keḷi magu	l.

140. For example, the opening verse of *Subhāṣitaya* instructs the audience to "venerate the lotus-feet of the Buddha," who "has loving-kindness that has arrived for all beings." See Munidasa, *Subhāṣitaya*, v. 1.
141. Ibid., v. 60.
142. For more on the historical appropriation of bodhisattvas and deities in late medieval Sri Lanka, see John Clifford Holt, *Buddha in the Crown: Avalokiteśvara in the Buddhist Traditions of Sri Lanka* (New York: Oxford University Press, 1991).

143. Fernando, *Kustantīnu Haṭana*, v. 186:

Guṇayen maha	t tu
Lova räkumehi niyu	t tu
Asiri iduma	t tu
Rakī sura yesus kiri s tu.	

144. Sorata, *Dahamsoňḍa Kava*, v. 57.
145. See, for instance, Peter, "Portuguese Influence," 20.
146. Fernando, *Kustantīnu Haṭana*, vv. 178, 126.
147. Fernando, *Kustantīnu Haṭana*, v. 83:

Lova nan	sata saha nubatala deraṇa	da
Mavamin	rakinā kuḷunen häma sa	ňda
Sobaman	yēsus kristus siri pa	da
A da rin	namakara mudunatädili bä	da.

148. Bhabha, *Location of Culture*, 164.
149. Fernando, *Kustantīnu Haṭana*, v. 11.
150. S. G. Perera and Fernando, *Alagiyawanna's Kustantinu Haṭana*, xxvi–xxvii. See also Peter, "Portuguese Influence," 22–24.
151. Fernando, *Kustantīnu Haṭana*, v. 22.

Teruvan mahimenu	t
Suravaran anuhasinu	t
E raju pin belenu	t
Uvadurak noma vemin maňdaku	t.

152. Barros and Couto, *History of Ceylon*, 110–113. For additional examples of Portuguese critiques of Buddhism in the seventeenth century, see Alan Strathern, "Representations of Eastern Religion: Queyroz and Gonzaga on the First Catholic-Buddhist Disputation in Sri Lanka," *Journal of the Royal Asiatic Society of Sri Lanka* XLIII (2000), 56–57. Interesting Portuguese condemnations of Buddhism may also be found in Flores, *Os Olhos do Rei*, 53–54, 181.
153. Cf. Alagiyavanna's words in verse 97 of *Subhāṣitaya*: "Knowledgeable beings make offerings to one having great merit." The assumption at work in this statement is that meritorious beings have developed great virtue and justifiably enjoy the fruits of their good conduct.
154. Fernando, *Kustantīnu Haṭana*, v. 163:

A n	toni baretto kī basa aba	ddā
Dän	bala balā himisaňda oba pärā	ddā
Pin	kaḷa näṇäti niriňdō naṁ pasi	ddā
Min	matu dudana pävasū bas asa	ddā.

155. Fernando, *Kustantīnu Haṭana*, vv. 161–162:

Ma ha t	isuru dun senerat naraniňdu	ṭa
Pä vä t	ta raňga däna däna ē sihi no ko	ṭa
Ba re t	tu naṁ guṇa maňda du danā basa	ṭa
Ä vi t	me duka viya himi saňdini me numba	ṭa
A sa t	dudana pävasū bas gena sita	ṭa
Ma hat	aya nasiti kī tepula pera si	ṭa
Ba ret	tu mäti pävasū bas asā oba	ṭa
Vi pat	vuven säkahära duṭimu atpi	ṭa.

156. Munidasa, *Subhāṣitaya*, vv. 22, 31–32, 44. Verse 78 in the *Dhammapada* reiterates this principle: "Do not associate with wicked friends, do not associate with ignoble persons, Associate with beautiful friends, associate with noble persons" (*na bhaje pāpake mitte na bhaje purisādhame, bhajetha mitte kalyāṇe bhajetha purisuttame*). See Hinüber, and Norman, *Dhammapada*, 22.
157. Cf. Fernando, *Kustantīnu Haṭana*, v. 178.
158. Rao, Shulman, and Subrahmanyam, *Symbols of Substance*, 67.
159. Cf. Fernando, *Kustantīnu Haṭana*, vv. 180–183.
160. S. G. Perera, "Alagiyawanna Mohottala," 47.
161. Ilangasinha, *Buddhism in Medieval Sri Lanka*, 189–190, 212–219.
162. Robert J. C. Young, *Colonial Desire: Hybridity in Theory, Culture and Race* (London: Routledge, 1995), 4.

CONCLUSION

1. A. R. Disney, *A History of Portugal and the Portuguese Empire. From Beginnings to 1807, Volume Two: The Portuguese Empire* (Cambridge, UK: Cambridge University Press, 2009), 146–147.
2. Cf. Björn Wittrock, "Early Modernities: Varieties and Transitions," *Daedalus* 127/3 (1998), 26–27.
3. C. R. de Silva, "Beyond the Cape," 296–297. See also Ana Paula Avelar, "The Orient in 16th-Century Portuguese Historiography," in *Europe and the World in European Historiography*, ed. Csaba Lévai (Pisa, Italy: Pisa University Press, 2006), 149–151.
4. Subrahmanyam. "Connected Histories," 745.
5. Sanjay Subrahmanyam, "Hearing Voices: Vignettes of Early Modernity in South Asia, 1400–1750," *Daedalus* 127/3 (1998), 99–100.
6. See, for example, Sannasgala, *Sinhala Sāhitya Vaṁśaya*, 2nd ed., 339; Kulasuriya, "Alagiyavanna Mukaveṭi Mohottala," 15; and Gunawardhana, *Subhashita Varnana*, xi.
7. See, for example, Kulasuriya, "Alagiyavanna Mukaveṭi Mohoṭṭāla," 12,15. Similar comments are found in Sannasgala, *Sinhala Sāhitya Vaṁśaya* (1964), 308 and Suraweera, "Alagiyavanna Mukaveṭitumā," 189.

8. Asad, *Genealogies of Religion*, 15–16.
9. Blackburn, *Locations of Buddhism*, xii.
10. Abeysekara, "Buddhism, Power, Modernity," 493.
11. Cooper, *Colonialism in Question*, 16.
12. Cf. Asad, *Genealogies of Religion*, 4.
13. Subrahmanyam, "Connected Histories," 745–746.
14. Pollock, *Language of the Gods*, 142–143.
15. Schopen, *Bones, Stones, and Buddhist Monks*, 9.
16. Robert Orsi, "Everyday Miracles: The Study of Lived Religion," in *Lived Religion in America: Toward a History of Practice*, ed. David D. Hall (Princeton, NJ: Princeton University Press, 1997), 7.
17. Cf. Orsi, "Everyday Miracles," 15. See also Robert Orsi, "Is the Study of Lived Religion Irrelevant to the World We Live In?" Special Presidential Plenary Address, Society for the Scientific Study of Religion, Salt Lake City, November 2, 2002," *Journal for the Scientific Study of Religion* 42/2 (2003), 171–172. Although Orsi does not explicitly label what constitutes the "authorized order" against which practices of lived religion resist and subvert, one may assume that he is referring to recognized religious authorities that define a tradition's orthodoxy.
18. Derek Schilling, "Everyday Life and the Challenge to History in Postwar France: Braudel, Lefebvre, Certeau," *diacritics* 33/1 (2003), 23–24.
19. Schilling, "Everyday Life," 26–27, 31–34, 35–36.
20. Steven Collins, *Nirvana and Other Buddhist Felicities: Utopias of the Pali Imaginaire* (Cambridge, UK: Cambridge University Press, 1998), 40, 57.
21. Charles Stewart, "Relocating Syncretism in Social Science Discourse," in *Syncretism in Religion: A Reader*, eds. Anita Maria Leopold and Jeppe Sinding Jensen (London: Equinox, 2004), 280.
22. Foucault, "Subject and Power," 790.
23. Pollock, *Language of the Gods*, 18.
24. Tennekoon, *Sävul Sandēśaya*, v. 207:

Gämbu ru	sakumagada kav naḷu siňdu	kimi dī
Mi tu ru	novana kivi gaja siha sirin	biň dī
Soňdu ru	alagivan mukaveṭi nämäti	su dī
Mi yu ru	pada rasäti me sävul asna	ye dī.

25. Sorata, *Dahamsoňḍa Kava*, vv. 162–163.
26. Ñanavimala, *Kusa Jātaka Kāvyaya*, vv. 685–686.
27. Munidasa, *Subhāṣitaya*, v. 100. Alagiyavanna may have borrowed this image from the late fifteenth-century *Kōkila Sandeśaya*, which appears to compare a "troupe of the lords of poets" (*kiviňdu käla*) to "a lion that continually splits open the frontal globes of the elephants of *asuras*" (*perasura dirada kumbu biňda sī lesa nitora*). See P.S. Perera, ed., *Kokila Sandeśaya*, 1906, reprint (Colombo: S. Godage and Brothers, 2009), v. 30.

28. This idea, widespread throughout the ancient Indic world, is given expression in South Indian thought. See Velcheru Narayana Rao and David Shulman, trans., *A Poem at the Right Moment: Remembered Verses from Premodern South India* (Berkeley: University of California Press, 1998), 11–13
29. H. M. Moratuvagama, ed., *Alagiyavanna Mukaveṭi Pabaňda* (Colombo: S. Godage and Brothers, 2000), xxii.
30. Wickramasinghe, *Sinhalese Literature*, 198.
31. Gunapala, *Kavīndra Alagiyavanna Mukaveṭi Caritaya*, 42–43.
32. Sucaritha Gamlath, *Saṁbhāvya Sinhala Kāvyayē Vikāsanaya*, 2nd ed. (Nugegoda, Sri Lanka: Sarasavi Prakāśakayō, 2004), 340.
33. Dunusinghe, *Konstantīnu Haṭana Kāvyaya*, 39–40.
34. On the contemporary debates about conversion in the island, see Berkwitz, "Religious Conflict," 207–211.
35. Donald S. Lopez, Jr., ed., *A Modern Buddhist Bible: Essential Readings from East and West* (Boston: Beacon Press, 2002), xvii.
36. Cf. David L. McMahan, *The Making of Buddhist Modernism* (Oxford, UK: Oxford University Press, 2008), 42–44.
37. Lopez, Jr., *Modern Buddhist Bible*, vii–x.
38. Munidasa, *Subhāṣitaya*, v. 13.
39. For more on the career and teachings of Dharmapāla, see H. L. Seneviratne, *The Work of Kings: The New Buddhism in Sri Lanka* (Chicago: University of Chicago Press, 1999).
40. Two of the more influential Buddhist reformers in modern Sri Lanka have also made explicit appeals to the central importance of moral instruction in Buddhist discourse. On Dharmapāla's concerns with morality, see Seneviratne, *Work of Kings*, 45–48. More recently, the late Venerable Gangodawila Soma could be seen making analogous moral critiques of Sri Lankan society and politics. See Stephen C. Berkwitz, "Resisting the Global in Buddhist Nationalism: Venerable Soma's Discourse of Decline and Reform." *Journal of Asian Studies* 67/1 (Feb. 2008), 90–96.
41. On the rise of ethical writing in response to the dislocations of French colonialism in Cambodia, see Anne Ruth Hansen, *How to Behave: Buddhism and Modernity in Colonial Cambodia, 1860–1930* (Honolulu: University of Hawai'i Press, 2007), 148. For a critique of the immorality associated with British colonialists, see Anagarika Dharmapala, *Return to Righteousness: A Collection of Speeches, Essays and Letters of the Anagarika Dharmapala*, ed. Ananda Guruge (Sri Lanka: Department of Cultural Affairs, 1991), 494–495.
42. Cf. Sorata, *Dahamsoňḍa Kava*, vv. 10–18; Ñanavimala, *Kusa Jātaka Kāvyaya*, v. 7–19.
43. Despite being conventionally praised along with the Buddha and Dharma in the openings of the first four texts, the Sangha as an actual historical phenomenon is hardly encountered in Alagiyavanna's works.

44. References are made to several lay authors of Buddhist texts in *Nikāya Saṅgrahaya* and *Rājaratnakāraya*, two Sinhala works from the fourteenth and fifteenth century respectively. See Berkwitz, *Buddhist History in the Vernacular*, 72.
45. Volkhard Krech, "Dynamics in the History of Religions—Preliminary Considerations on Aspects of a Research Programme," in *Dynamics in the History of Religions between Asia and Europe: Encounters, Notions, and Comparative Perspectives*, eds. Volkhard Krech and Marion Steinicke (Leiden, Netherlands: Brill, 2012), 32.

Bibliography

Abeyasinghe, Tikiri. *Portuguese Rule in Ceylon, 1594–1612*. Colombo: Lake House, 1966.

Abeysekara, Ananda. "Buddhism, Power, Modernity." *Culture and Religion*. 12/4 (2011): 489–497.

Abeysekara, Ananda. *Colors of the Robe: Religion, Identity, and Difference*. Columbia: University of South Carolina Press, 2002.

Abhayagunaratna, D.G., ed., *Pärakumbā Sirita*. 1929. Reprint. Colombo: Madhyama Saṅskṛtika Aramudala, 1997.

Abhayagunawardhana, H. V. "Sävul Sandēśa Pilibaňda Vimarśanayak." In *Sītāvaka Kavi*, edited by Amara Hevamadduma, et al., 23–37. Colombo: Department of Cultural Affairs, 1991.

Aggavamsa, Peliyagoda, ed. *Sävul Asna hēval Sävul Sandēśaya*. Colombo: Sri Lankaloka Printers, 1925.

Alden, Dauril. *The Making of an Enterprise: The Society of Jesus in Portugal, Its Empire, and Beyond, 1540–1750*. Palo Alto, CA: Stanford University Press, 1996.

Almond, Philip C. *The British Discovery of Buddhism*. Cambridge, UK: Cambridge University Press, 1988.

Alwis, Premachandra, trans. *Lokopakaraya*. Colombo: Sooriya Publishers, 2006.

Appleton, Naomi. *Jātaka Stories in Theravāda Buddhism: Narrating the Bodhisatta Path*. Surrey, UK: Ashgate, 2010.

Asad, Talal. *Genealogies of Religion: Discipline and Reasons of Power in Christianity and Islam*. Baltimore: The Johns Hopkins University Press, 1993.

Avelar, Ana Paula. "The Orient in 16th-Century Portuguese Historiography." In *Europe and the World in European Historiography*, edited by Csaba L évai, 149–160. Pisa, Italy: Pisa University Press, 2006.

Ball, V., trans., *Travels in India by Jean Baptiste Tavenier*. Vol. II. London: Macmillan and Co., 1889.

Barros, João de and Diogo do Couto. *The History of Ceylon from the Earliest Times to 1600 AD*. 1909. Reprint. Translated by Donald Ferguson. Delhi, India: Navrang, 1993.

Berkwitz, Stephen C. "Buddhism in Modern Sri Lanka." In *Buddhism in the Modern World*, edited by David L. McMahan, 29–47. London: Routledge, 2011.

Berkwitz, Stephen C. "Buddhism in Sri Lanka: Practice, Protest, and Preservation." In *Buddhism in World Cultures: Comparative Perspectives*, edited by Stephen C. Berkwitz, 45–72. Santa Barbara, CA: ABC-CLIO, 2006.

Berkwitz, Stephen C. *Buddhist History in the Vernacular: The Power of the Past in Late Medieval Sri Lanka*. Leiden, Netherlands: Brill, 2004.

Berkwitz, Stephen C. *The History of the Buddha's Relic Shrine: A Translation of the* Sinhala Thūpavaṃsa. New York: Oxford University Press, 2007.

Berkwitz, Stephen C. "Merit and Materiality in Sri Lankan Buddhist Manuscripts." In *Buddhist Manuscript Cultures: Knowledge, Ritual, and Art*, edited by Stephen C. Berkwitz, Juliane Schober, and Claudia Brown, 35–49. London: Routledge, 2009.

Berkwitz, Stephen C. "Religious Conflict and the Politics of Conversion in Sri Lanka." In *Proselytization Revisited: Rights Talk, Free Markets, and Culture Wars*, edited by Rosalind I. J. Hackett, 199–229. London: Equinox Press, 2008.

Berkwitz, Stephen C. "Resisting the Global in Buddhist Nationalism: Venerable Soma's Discourse of Decline and Reform." *Journal of Asian Studies*. 67/1 (Feb. 2008): 73–106.

Berkwitz, Stephen C. "Some Observations on the Study of Buddhist Literature in Sinhala." In *Arcana: Prof. M.H.F. Jayasuriya Felicitation Volume*, edited by Ven. Navagamuwe Revata et al., 61–84. Colombo: S. Godage and Brothers, 2002.

Berkwitz, Stephen C. "An Ugly King and the Mother Tongue: Notes on Kusa Jātaka in Sinhala Language and Culture." *Parallax*. 18/3 (2012): 56–70.

Bhabha, Homi. *The Location of Culture*. London: Routledge, 1994.

Biedermann, Zoltán. "The Matrioshka Principle and How It Was Overcome: Portuguese and Hapsburg Imperial Attitudes in Sri Lanka and the Responses of the Rulers of Kotte (1506–1598)." *Journal of Early Modern History*. 13 (2009): 265–310.

Biedermann, Zoltán. "Perceptions and Representations of the Sri Lankan Space in Sixteenth-Century Portuguese Texts and Maps." In *Re-Exploring the Links: History and Constructed Histories between Portugal and Sri Lanka*, edited by Jorge Flores, 235–260. Wiesbaden, Germany: Harrassowitz Verlag, 2007.

Biedermann, Zoltán. "Tribute, Vassalage and Warfare in Early Luso-Lankan Relations (1506–1543)." In *Indo-Portuguese History: Global Trends*, edited by Fatima da Silva Gracias, 185–206. Goa, India: Maureen & Camvet Publishers, 2005.

Blackburn, Anne M. *Buddhist Learning and Textual Practice in Eighteenth-Century Lankan Monastic Culture*. Princeton, NJ: Princeton University Press, 2001.

Blackburn, Anne M. *Locations of Buddhism: Colonialism & Modernity in Sri Lanka*. Chicago: University of Chicago Press, 2010.

Bloomfield, Morton E. and Charles W. Dunn. *The Role of the Poet in Early Societies*. Cambridge, UK: D. S. Brewer, 1989.

Bond, George D. *The Buddhist Revival in Sri Lanka: Religious Tradition, Reinterpretation and Response*. Columbia: University of South Carolina Press, 1988.

Bourdieu, Pierre. *Distinction: A Social Critique of the Judgment of Taste*, translated by Richard Nice. Cambridge, MA: Harvard University Press, 1984.

Boxer, C. R. "Captain João Ribeiro and his History of Ceylon, 1622–1693." *Journal of the Royal Asiatic Society*. 87/1 – 2 (1955): 1–12.

Boxer, C. R. "'Christians and Spices': Portuguese Missionary Methods in Ceylon, 1518–1658," *History Today*. 8 (1958): 346–354.

Boxer, C. R. *The Church Militant and Iberian Expansion 1440–1770*. Baltimore: The Johns Hopkins University Press, 1978.

Bretfeld, Sven. "Resonant Paradigms in the Study of Religions and the Emergence of Theravāda Buddhism." *Religion*. 42/2 (2012): 273–297.

Buddhadatta, A. P., ed. *The Mahāvansa: Pali Text Together with Some Later Additions*. Colombo: M. D. Gunasena & Co., 1959.

Candrasekara, A. D. "Alagiyavannayi Dahaṁ Soṅḍa Dā Kavayi." In *Sītāvaka Kaviya: Vivēcanātmaka Vigrahayak*, edited by Amara Hevamadduma et al., 16–22. Colombo: Department of Cultural Affairs, 1991.

Collins, Steven. *Nirvana and Other Buddhist Felicities: Utopias of the Pali Imaginaire*. Cambridge, UK: Cambridge University Press, 1998.

Collins, Steven. "What Is Literature in Pali?" In *Literary Cultures in History: Reconstructions from South Asia*, edited by Sheldon Pollock, 649–688. Berkeley: University of California Press, 2003.

Cooper, Frederick. *Colonialism in Question: Theory, Knowledge, History*. Berkeley: University of California Press, 2005.

Costa, João Paulo Oliveira e. "A Diáspora Missionária." In *História Religiosa de Portugal, Volume 2: Humanismos e Reformas*, edited by Carlos Morreira Azevedo, 255–313. Lisbon: Círculo de Leitores, 2000.

Davids, T. W. Rhys and J. Estlin Carpenter, eds. *The Dīgha Nikāya*. Vol. II. Reprint. Oxford, UK: Pali Text Society, 1995.

Davids, T. W. Rhys and William Stede. *The Pali Text Society's Pali-English Dictionary*. Oxford, UK: Pali Text Society, 1995.

Davidson, Ronald M. *Indian Esoteric Buddhism: A Social History of the Tantric Movement*. New York: Columbia University Press, 2002.

De Alwis, James. "On the Elu Language, Its Poetry and Its Poets." *The Journal of the Ceylon Branch of the Royal Asiatic Society of Great Britain & Ireland*. 2–5 (1850): 241–315.

Deegalle, Mahinda. *Popularizing Buddhism: Preaching as Performance in Sri Lanka*. Albany: State University of New York Press: 2006.

Dela Bandara, Gamani. *Saṁbhāvya Sinhala Sāhityaya*. Kelaniya, Sri Lanka: Saṁbhāvya Prakāśana, 1998.

De Silva, Chandra R. "Algumas Reflexões Sobre o Impacto Português na Religião entre os Singaleses Durante os Séculos XVI e XVII," *Oceanos* 34 (1998): 104–116.

De Silva, Chandra R. "Beyond the Cape: The Portuguese Encounter with the Peoples of South Asia." In *Implicit Understandings: Observing, Reporting, and Reflecting on the Encounters between Europeans and Other Peoples in the Early Modern Era*, edited by Stuart B. Schwartz, 295–322. Cambridge, UK: Cambridge University Press, 1994.

De Silva, Chandra R. *The Portuguese in Ceylon 1617–1638*. Colombo: H. W. Cave & Company, 1972.

De Silva, Chandra R. "The Rise and Fall of the Kingom of Sītāvaka (1521–1593)." In *University of Peradeniya History of Sri Lanka: Volume II (c1500 to c1800)*, edited by K. M. de Silva, 61–104. Peradeniya, Sri Lanka: University of Peradeniya, 1995.

De Silva, Chandra R. "Sri Lanka in the Early 16th Century: Political Conditions." In *University of Peradeniya History of Sri Lanka: Volume II (c1500 to c1800)*, edited by K. M. de Silva, 11–36. Peradeniya, Sri Lanka: University of Peradeniya, 1995.

De Silva, F. W. "Kostantinu Hatana." Journal of the Royal Asiatic Society *(Ceylon)*. 13 (1894): 135–41.

De Silva, K. H. *Siṅhala Haṭan Kavi*. Colombo: Sri Lanka Publishing Society, 1964.

De Silva, K. M. *A History of Sri Lanka*. Berkeley: University of California Press, 1981.

Dhammasiri, Udupila and Sirisena Gamage, eds. *Alagiyavanna Mukaveṭitumāgē Sävul Sandēśa*. Colombo: Star Printers, 1968.

Dharmapala, Anagarika. *Return to Righteousness: A Collection of Speeches, Essays and Letters of the Anagarika Dharmapala*, edited by Ananda Guruge. Sri Lanka: Department of Cultural Affairs, 1991.

Dharmarama, Ratmalane Dharmakirti Sri, ed. *Śrī Rāhula Māhimiyan visin viracita Kāvyaśēkhara Mahākāvyaya*. Kelaniya, Sri Lanka: Vidyalankara University Press, 1966.

Dharmasena Thera. *Jewels of the Doctrine: Stories of the Saddharma Ratnavaliya*, translated by Ranjani Obeysekere. Albany: State University of New York Press, 1991.

Didier, Hugues. *Os Portugueses no Tibete: Os Primeiros Relatos dos Jesuítas (1624–1635)*, translated by Lourdes Júdice. Lisbon: Comissão Nacional para as Comemorações dos Descobrimentos Portugueses, 2000.

Dimock, Jr., Edward C. "The Religious Lyric in Bengali." In *The Literatures of India: An Introduction*, edited by Edward C. Dimock Jr. et al., 157–165. Chicago: University of Chicago Press, 1974.

Disanayaka, Kusum, trans. *Sasa Dā Vata: Bodhisatva as a Hare*. Colombo: Godage International Publishers, 2004.

Disney, A. R. *A History of Portugal and the Portuguese Empire. From Beginnings to 1807, Volume Two: The Portuguese Empire*. Cambridge, UK: Cambridge University Press, 2009.

Drew, Rose. *Buddhist and Christian? An Exploration of Dual Belonging*. London: Routledge, 2011.

Dunusinghe, Kosgoda Karunadasa Silva. *Alagiyavanna Mukaveṭi Vicāraya saha Don Jerōnimōgē Konstantīnu Haṭana Kāvyaya*. Colombo: S. Godage and Brothers, 1997.

Edmond, Kotmale K.B.E. "*Subhāṣitaya*." In *Sītāvaka Kaviya: Vivēcanātmaka Vigrahayak*, edited by Amara Hevamadduma, et al., 61–69. Battaramula, Sri Lanka: Department of Cultural Affairs, 1991.

Egge, James R. *Religious Giving and the Invention of Karma in Theravāda Buddhism*. London: Curzon, 2002.

Endo, Toshiichi. *Buddha in Theravada Buddhism: A Study of the Concept of Buddha in the Pali Commentaries*. Dehiwala, Sri Lanka: Systematic Print, 1997.

Fausboll, V., ed. *The Jātaka: Together With Its Commentary*. Vols. I–VII. Oxford: Pali Text Society, 1990–91.

Ferguson, D. W. "Alagiyavanna Mohoṭṭāla, the Author of 'Kusajātaka Kāvyaya." *Journal of the Royal Asiatic Society (Ceylon Branch)*. 16 (1899): 115–120.

Fernando, M. E., ed. *Alagiyavanna Mukaveṭitumā visin viracita Kustantīnu Haṭana*. Galle: St. Aloysius College, 1933.

Flores, Jorge Manuel. "Ceilão." In *Dicionário de História dos Descobrimentos Portugueses*. Vol. I, edited by Luís de Albuquerque, 226–232. Lisbon: Caminho, 1994.

Flores, Jorge Manuel. *Hum Curto Historia de Ceylan: Five Hundred Years of Relations between Portugal and Sri Lanka*. Lisbon: Fundação Oriente, 2000.

Flores, Jorge Manuel. *Os Olhos do Rei: Desenhos e Descrições Portuguesas da Ilha de Ceilão (1624, 1638)*. Lisbon: Commissão Nacional para As Commemorações dos Descobrimentos Portugueses, 2001.

Flores, Jorge Manuel. "'They Have Discovered Us': The Portuguese and the Trading World of the Indian Ocean." In *Encompassing the Globe: Portugal and the World in the 16th and 17th Centuries*, edited by Ana de Castro Henriques, 233–244. Lisbon: Ministério da Cultura, Insitituto dos Museus e da Conservação, 2009.

Flores, Jorge and Maria Augusta Lima Cruz. "A 'Tale of Two Cities', a 'Veteran Soldier', or the Struggle for Endangered Nobilities: The Two *Jornadas de Huva* (1633, 1635) Revisited." In *Re-Exploring the Links: History and Constructed Histories between Portugal and Sri Lanka*, edited by Jorge Flores, 95–124. Wiesbaden, Germany: Harrassowitz Verlag, 2007.

Foucault, Michel. "The Subject and Power." *Critical Inquiry*. 8/4 (1982): 777–95.

Fróis, Luís. *EuropaJapão: Um Diálogo Civilizacional no Século XVI: Tratado em que Se Contêm Muito Sucinta e Abreviadamente Algumas Contradições e Diferenças de Costumes entre a Gente de Europa e Esta Provincía de Japão (...)*. Lisbon: Comissão Nacional para as Comemorações dos Descobrimentos Portugueses, 1993.

Fróis, Luís. *Historia de Japam*. Vol. I. Edited by José Wicki. Lisbon: Biblioteca Nacional de Lisboa, 1976.

Gair, James W. *Studies in South Asian Linguistics: Sinhala and Other Languages*, edited by Barbara C. Lust. Oxford, UK: Oxford University Press, 1998.

Gallagher, Catherine and Stephen Greenblatt. *Practicing New Historicism*. Chicago: University of Chicago Press, 2000.

Gamlath, Sucaritha. *Kavsiḷumiṇi Vinisa*. 1966. Reprint. Colombo: S. Godage and Brothers, 1995.

Gamlath, Sucaritha. *Saṁbhāvya Sinhala Kāvyayē Vikāsanaya*. 2nd ed. Nugegoda, Sri Lanka: Sarasavi Prakāśakayō, 2004.

Gandhi, Sharada, ed. *Rasavāhinī: A Stream of Sentiments*. Delhi: Parimal Publications, 1988.

Gandhi, Sharada, ed. *Sahassavatthu-ppakaraṇaṁ*. Ghaziabad, India: Indo-Vision Private Limited, 1991.

Gerow, Edwin. *A Glossary of Indian Figures of Speech*. The Hague: Mouton, 1971.

Gerow, Edwin. "The Sanskrit Lyric: A Genre Analysis." In *The Literatures of India*, edited by Edward C. Dimock, Jr. et al., 144–156. Chicago: University of Chicago Press, 1974.

Godakumbura, C. E. "The Dravidian Element in Sinhalese." *Bulletin of the School of Oriental and African Studies* 11/4 (1946): 837–841.

Godakumbura, C. E. *Sinhalese Literature*. Colombo: The Colombo Apothecaries' Co., 1955.

Gombrich, Richard and Gananath Obeyesekere. *Buddhism Transformed: Religious Change in Sri Lanka*. Princeton, NJ: Princeton University Press, 1988.

Gonçalves, Manuel Pereira. "Presença Franciscana na Índia no Século XVI." In *Portugal no Mundo*. Vol. 3, edited by Luís de Albuquerque, 104–134. Lisbon: Publicações Alfa, 1989.

Gooneratne, E. R. ed. "Tela-kaṭāha-gāthā." *Journal of the Pali Text Society* (1884): 49–68.

Greenblatt, Stephen. *Marvelous Possessions: The Wonder of the New World*. Chicago: University of Chicago Press, 1991.

Greenblatt, Stephen. *Renaissance Self-Fashioning: From More to Shakespeare*. Chicago: University of Chicago Press, 1980.

Guerreiro, Fernão. *Relação Anual das Coisas que Fizeram os Padres da Companhia de Jesus nas Suas Missões*, 2 Vols. Coimbra, Portugal: Imprensa da Universidade, 1930–1931.

Gunapala, E. Vimalasuriya. *Kavīndra Alagiyavanna Mukaveṭi Caritaya*. Katugasthota, Sri Lanka: E. M. V. Gunapala, 1927.

Gunasekara, Bandusena, ed. *Tisara Sandēśaya*. Colombo: S. Godage and Brothers, 1986.

Gunawardana, R.A.L.H. *Robe and Plough: Monasticism and Economic Interest Early Medieval Sri Lanka*. Tucson: University of Arizona Press, 1979.

Gunawardhana, W. F., ed. *Subhashita Varnana: Being a Commentary on the Subhashita*. 2nd ed. Colombo: Sri Bharati Press, 1925.

Hackett, Rosalind I. J., ed. *Proselytization Revisited: Rights Talk, Free Markets and Culture Wars*. London: Equinox, 2008.

Hahn, Michael. "Śaṅkarasvāmin's *Devatāvimarśastuti*." In *Vividharatnakaraṇḍaka: Festgabe für Adelheid Mette*, edited by Christine Chojnacki, Jens-Uwe Hartmann, and Volker M. Tschannerl, 313–329. Swisttal-Odendrof, Germany: Indica et Verlag, 2000.

Hallisey, Charles. "Roads Taken and Not Taken in the Study of Theravāda Buddhism." In *Curators of the Buddha: The Study of Buddhism under Colonialism*, edited by Donald S. Lopez, Jr., 31–61. Chicago: University of Chicago Press, 1995.

Hallisey, Charles. "Works and Persons in Sinhala Literary Culture." In *Literary Cultures in History: Reconstructions from South Asia*, edited by Sheldon Pollock, 689–746. Berkeley: University of California Press, 2003.

Hansen, Anne Ruth. *How to Behave: Buddhism and Modernity in Colonial Cambodia, 1860–1930*. Honolulu: University of Hawai'i Press, 2007.

Hardy, E., ed. *The Aṅguttara-Nikāya*. Part IV. 1899. Reprint. Oxford, UK: Pali Text Society, 1999.

Harlacher, Sherry. *Picturing the* Dhamma*: Text and Image in Late Colonial Sri Lanka*. PhD Dissertation. Arizona State University, 2010.

Harris, Elizabeth J. *Theravāda Buddhism and the British Encounter: Religious, Missionary and Colonial Experience in Nineteenth-Century Sri Lanka*. London: Routledge, 2006.

Hart III, George L. *The Poems of Ancient Tamil: Their Milieu and Their Sanskrit Counterparts*. Berkeley: University of California Press, 1975.

Herath, Dharmaratna. *The Tooth Relic and the Crown*. Colombo: Gunaratna Press, 1994.

Herath, S. B. "Kusa Jātaka Kāvyaya." In *Sītāvaka Kaviya: Vivēcanātmaka Vigrahayak*, edited by Amara Hevamadduma et al., 38–60. Colombo: Department of Cultural Affairs, 1991.

Hettiaratchi, D. E. "Civilisation of the Period (Continued): Literature and Art." In *University of Ceylon History of Ceylon*. Vol. I, Part II, edited by H. C. Ray, 770–778. Colombo: Ceylon University Press, 1960.

Hinüber, Oskar von. *A Handbook of Pali Literature*. Berlin: Walter de Gruyter & Co., 1997.

Hinüber, O von and K. R. Norman, eds. *Dhammapada*. Oxford, UK: Pali Text Society, 1995.

Holt, John Clifford. *Buddha in the Crown: Avalokiteśvara in the Buddhist Traditions of Sri Lanka*. New York: Oxford University Press, 1991.

Holt, John Clifford. "Buddhist Rebuttals: The Changing of the Gods and Royal (Re) legitimization in Sixteenth- and Seventeenth-Century Sri Lanka." In *Re-Exploring the Links: History and Constructed Histories between Portugal and Sri Lanka*, edited by Jorge Flores, 145–169. Wiesbaden, Germany: Harrassowitz Verlag, 2007.

Holt, John Clifford. *The Buddhist Viṣṇu: Religious Transformation, Politics, and Culture*. New York: Columbia University Press, 2004.

Holt, John Clifford. "Protestant Buddhism?" *Religious Studies Review*. 17/4 (1991): 307–312.

Ilangasinha, H.B.M. *Buddhism in Medieval Sri Lanka*. Delhi: Sri Satguru Publications, 1992.

Ingalls, Daniel H. H. *Sanskrit Poetry: From Vidyākara's Treasury*. Cambridge, MA: Harvard University Press, 1965.

Jayawickrama, N. A., trans. *The Story of Gotama Buddha (Jātaka-nidāna)*. Oxford: Pali Text Society, 1990.

Jotipala, Gonahene, ed. *1981 Rājya Sāhitya Utsavaya Kāragala: Siyaṇä-Lékhakayō*. Colombo: Cultural Affairs Department, 1981.

Karunatillake, W. S. "The Religiousness of Buddhists in Sri Lanka through Belief and Practice," *Religiousness in Sri Lanka*, edited by John Ross Carter, 1–34. Colombo: Marga Institute, 1979.

Kautilya. *The Arthashastra*. Edited and translated by L. N. Rangarajan. New Delhi: Penguin Books, 1992.

Kaviraj, Sudipta. *The Unhappy Consciousness: Bankimchandra Chattopadhyay and the Formation of Nationalist Discourse in India*. Delhi, India: Oxford University Press, 1998.

Keane, Webb. *Christian Moderns: Freedom and Fetish in the Mission Encounter*. Berkeley: University of California Press, 2007.

Keith, A. Berriedale. *A History of Sanskrit Literature*. 1928. Reprint. Delhi, India: Motilal Banarsidass, 1993.

Kloetzli, W. Randolph. *Buddhist Cosmology: Science and Theology in the Images of Motion and Light*. Delhi, India: Motilal Banarsidass, 1983.

Krech, Volkhard. "Dynamics in the History of Religions—Preliminary Considerations on Aspects of a Research Programme." In *Dynamics in the History of Religions between Asia and Europe: Encounters, Notions, and Comparative Perspectives*, edited by Volkhard Krech and Marion Steinicke, 15–70. Leiden, Netherlands: Brill, 2012.

Kulasuriya, Ananda. "Alagiyavanna Mukaveṭi Mohoṭṭāla: Kālina Tatu, Kaviyā hā Kavi Pabaňda." In *Sītāvaka Kaviya: Vivecanātmaka Vigrahayak*, edited by Amara Hevamadduma et al., 6–15. Colombo: Department of Cultural Affairs, 1991.

LaCapra, Dominck. "Is Everyone a *Mentalité* Case?: Transference and the 'Culture' Concept," *History & Theory*. 23/1 (1984): 296–311.

LaCapra, Dominck. *Rethinking Intellectual History: Texts, Contexts, Language*. Ithaca, NY: Cornell University Press, 1983.

Lienhard, Siegfried. *A History of Classical Poetry: Sanskrit—Pali—Prakrit*. Wiesbaden, Germany: Otto Harrassowitz, 1984.

Lopes, Fernando Félix. "A Evangelização de Ceilão desde 1552 a 1602." *STVDIA*. 20–22 (1967): 7–73.

Lopez, Jr. Donald S., ed. *Curators of the Buddha: The Study of Buddhism under Colonialism*. Chicago: University of Chicago Press, 1995.

Lopez, Jr. Donald S., ed. *A Modern Buddhist Bible: Essential Readings from East and West*. Boston: Beacon Press, 2002.

Lorenzen, David N. "Gentile Religion in South India, China, and Tibet: Studies by Three Jesuit Missionaries," *Comparative Studies of South Asia, Africa and the Middle East.* 27/1 (2007): 203–213.

Mahinda, S., ed. *Vistarārtha Vivaraṇa sahita Subhāṣitaya.* 1936. Reprint. Colombo: S. Godage and Brothers, 1999.

Malagoda, Kitsiri. *Buddhism in Sinhalese Society 1750–1900: A Study of Religious Revival and Change.* Berkeley: University of California Press, 1976.

Malalasekera, G. P. *Dictionary of Pāli Proper Names.* Vol. II. Reprint. New Delhi: Munshiram Manoharlal, 1983.

Masuzawa, Tomoko. *The Invention of World Religions: Or, How European Universalism Was Preserved in the Language of Pluralism.* Chicago: University of Chicago Press, 2005.

McGann, Jerome. "Rethinking Romanticism." *ELH.* 59/3 (1992): 735–754.

McGann, Jerome. *The Textual Condition.* Princeton, NJ: Princeton University Press, 1991.

McMahan, David L. *The Making of Buddhist Modernism.* Oxford, UK: Oxford University Press, 2008.

Mette, Adelheid. "Notes on *Samaya* 'Convention' in Pali and Prakrit." In *Middle Indo-Aryan and Jaina Studies,* edited by Colette Caillat, 69–80. Leiden, Netherlands: E. J. Brill, 1991.

Miller, Barbara Stoler, trans. *Bhartrihari: Poems.* New York: Columbia University Press, 1967.

Miller, Barbara Stoler, ed. and trans. *Love Song of the Dark Lord: Jayadeva's Gītagovinda.* New York: Columbia University Press, 1977.

Mills, Kenneth and Anthony Grafton, eds. *Conversion: Old Worlds and New.* Rochester, NY: University of Rochester Press, 2003.

Moratuvagama, H. M., ed. *Alagiyavanna Mukaveṭi Pabaňda.* Colombo: S. Godage and Brothers, 2000.

Mrozik, Susanne. *Virtuous Bodies: The Physical Dimensions of Morality in Buddhist Ethics.* New York: Oxford University Press, 2007.

Munidasa, Kumaratunga, ed., *Subhāṣitaya.* 1952. Reprint. Colombo: M. D. Gunasena, 2001.

Nanamoli, Bhikkhu and Bhikkhu Bodhi, trans. *The Middle Length Discourses of the Buddha: A New Translation of the* Majjhima Nikāya. Boston: Wisdom Publications, 1995.

Ñanavimala, Kiri Elle, ed. *Alagiyavanna Mukaveṭi Kiviňdun visin viracita Kusa Jātaka Kāvyaya.* Colombo: M. D. Gunasena, 1961.

Ñanavimala, Kiri Elle, ed. *Vyākhyā sahita Buduguṇa Alaṅkāraya.* Colombo: M. D. Gunasena, 1993.

Nattier, Jan. *Once upon a Future Time: Studies in a Buddhist Prophecy of Decline.* Berkeley, CA: Asian Humanities Press, 1991.

Nehamas, Alexander. "Writer, Text, Work, Author." In *Literature and the Question of Philosophy,* edited by Anthony J. Cascardi, 265–291. Baltimore: The Johns Hopkins University Press, 1987.

Newitt, Malyn. *A History of Portuguese Overseas Expansion, 1400–1668*. London: Routledge, 2005.

Norman, K.R. *Pāli Literature: Including the Canonical Literature in Prakrit and Sanskrit of All the Hīnayāna Schools of Buddhism*. Wiesbaden, Germany: Otto Harrassowitz, 1983.

Obeyesekere, Gananath. *Medusa's Hair: An Essay on Personal Symbols and Religious Experience*. Chicago: University of Chicago Press, 1981.

Obeyesekere, Ranjini, trans. *Jewels of the Doctrine: Stories of the Saddharma Ratnāvaliya*. Albany: State University of New York Press, 1991.

Obeyesekere, Ranjini, trans. *Portraits of Buddhist Women: Stories from the* Saddharmaratnāvaliya. Albany: State University of New York Press, 2001.

Ohnuma, Reiko. *Head, Eyes, Flesh, and Blood: Giving away the Body in Indian Buddhist Literature*. New York: Columbia University Press, 2007.

Orsi, Robert. "Everyday Miracles: The Study of Lived Religion." In *Lived Religion in America: Toward a History of Practice*, edited by David D. Hall, 3–21. Princeton, NJ: Princeton University Press, 1997.

Orsi, Robert. "Is the Study of Lived Religion Irrelevant to the World We Live In?" Special Presidential Plenary Address, Society for the Scientific Study of Religion, Salt Lake City, "November 2, 2002." *Journal for the Scientific Study of Religion*. 42/2 (2003): 169–174.

Paññaloka, Migoda, ed. *Saddharmālaṅkarāya*. Dehiwala, Sri Lanka: Bauddha Samskritika Madhyasthanaya, 1997.

Pannananda, Yagirala, ed., *Madhuratthavilasini: Or the Commentary to the Buddhawansa*. Colombo: Simon Hewavitarne Bequest, 1922.

Pannasara, Dehigaspe. *Sanskrit Literature: Extant among the Sinhalese and the Influence of Sanskrit on Sinhalese*. Colombo: W. D. Hewavitarane Esquire, 1958.

Paranavitana, Karunasena Dias. "The Portuguese *Tombos* as a Source of Sixteenth- and Seventeenth-Century Sri Lankan History." In *Re-Exploring the Links: History and Constructed Histories between Portugal and Sri Lanka*, edited by Jorge Flores, 63–78. Wiesbaden, Germany: Harrassowitz Verlag, 2007.

Paranavitana, Karunasena Dias. "Suppression of Buddhism and Aspects of Indigenous Culture under the Portuguese and the Dutch." *Journal of the Royal Asiatic Society of Sri Lanka*. N.S. 49 (2004): 1–14.

Paranavitana, Rohini. "Sinhalese War Poems and the Portuguese." In *Re-Exploring the Links: History and Constructed Histories between Portugal and Sri Lanka*, edited by Jorge Flores, 49–61. Wiesbaden, Germany: Harrassowitz Verlag, 2007.

Paranavitana, Rohini, ed. *Sītāvaka Haṭana*. Colombo: Madhyama Saṅskṛitika Aramudala, 1999.

Perera, C. Gaston. *The Portuguese Missionary in 16th and 17th Century Ceylon: The Spiritual Conquest*. Colombo: Vijitha Yapa, 2009.

Perera, E. Hector. *Sinhala Haṭan Sāhitya*. Colombo: Ratna Pot Prakāśakayō, 1961.

Perera, P.S., ed. *Kokila Sandeśaya*. 1906. Reprint. Colombo: S. Godage and Brothers, 2009.

Perera, S. G. "Alagiyawanna Mohottala," *Ceylon Antiquary and Literary Register*. 9/1 (1923): 45–48.

Perera, S. G. and M. E. Fernando, eds. and trans., *Alagiyawanna's Kustantinu Haṭana (The Campaign of Don Constantine)*. Colombo: Catholic Press, 1932.

Perniola, V., trans., *The Catholic Church in Sri Lanka: The Portuguese Period, vol. II, 1566 to 1619*. Dehiwala, Sri Lanka: Tisara Prakasakayo, 1991.

Peter, W.L.A. Don. "Portuguese Influence on a Sinhalese Poet." *Aquinas Journal*. 6/1 (1989): 9–26.

Peterson, Indira Viswanathan. *Design and Rhetoric in a Sanskrit Court Epic:* The Kirātārjunīya of Bhāravi. Albany: State University of New York Press, 2003.

Pieris, Paul E. *Ceylon: The Portuguese Era*. Vols. 1 & 2. 1914. Reprint. Dehiwala, Sri Lanka: Tisara Press, 1983.

Pieris, Paul E. *Ceylon and the Portuguese, 1505–1658*. 1920. Reprint. New Delhi, India: Asian Educational Services, 1999.

Pieris, Paul E. *The Ceylon Littoral 1593*. Colombo: The Times of Ceylon, 1949.

Pollock, Sheldon. "The Cosmopolitan Vernacular." *Journal of Asian Studies*. 57/1 (1998): 6–37.

Pollock, Sheldon. *The Language of the Gods in the World of Men: Sanskrit, Culture, and Power in Premodern India*. Berkeley: University of California Press, 2006.

Pollock, Sheldon, ed. *Literary Cultures in History: Reconstructions from South Asia*. Berkeley: University of California Press, 2003.

Powers, John. *A Bull of a Man: Images of Masculinity, Sex, and the Body in Indian Buddhism*. Cambridge, MA: Harvard University Press, 2009.

Queyroz, Fernão de. *The Temporal and Spiritual Conquest of Ceylon*. Vols. 1–3. Translated by S. G. Perera. 1930. Reprint. New Delhi: Asian Educational Services, 1992.

Rafael, Vicente L. *Contracting Colonialism: Translation and Christian Conversion in Tagalog Society under Early Spanish Rule*. Durham, NC: Duke University Press, 1993.

Ramanujan, A. K., trans. *Poems of Love and War: From the Eight Anthologies and the Ten Long Poems of Classical Tamil*. New York: Columbia University Press, 1985.

Rao, Velcheru Narayana and David Shulman, trans. *A Poem at the Right Moment: Remembered Verses from Premodern South India*. Berkeley: University of California Press, 1998.

Rao, Velcheru Narayana, David Shulman, and Sanjay Subrahmanyam. *Symbols of Substance: Court and State in Nāyaka Period Tamilnadu*. Oxford, UK: Oxford University Press, 1992.

Rego, António da Silva, ed. *Documentação Ultramarina Portuguesa*. Lisbon: Centro de Estudos Históricos Ultramarinos, 1960.

Rego, António da Silva , ed. *Documentos Remetidos da Índia: Ou Livros das Monções*. Vol. VII. Lisbon: Imprensa Nacional-Casa da Moeda, 1975

Ricci, Matteo. *The True Meaning of the Lord of Heaven (T'ien-chu shih-i)*. Edited and translated by Douglas Lancashire, Guozhen Hu, and Edward Malatesta. St. Louis, MO: Institute of Jesuit Sources, 1985.

Roberts, Michael. *Caste Conflict and Elite Formation: The Rise of a Kārava Elite in Sri Lanka, 1500–1931*. Cambridge, UK: Cambridge University Press, 1982.

Roberts, Michael. *Sinhala Consciousness in the Kandyan Period 1590s to 1815*. Colombo: Vijitha Yapa, 2003.

Russell-Wood, A. R. *The Portuguese Empire, 1415–1808: A World on the Move*. Baltimore: The Johns Hopkins University Press, 1992.

Sá, Isabel dos Guimarães. "Ecclesiastical Structures and Religious Action." In *Portuguese Oceanic Expansion, 1400–1800. A Collection of Essays*, edited by Francisco Bethencourt and Diogo Ramada Curto, 255–282. Cambridge, UK: Cambridge University Press, 2007.

Said, Edward. *Orientalism*. New York: Vintage Books, 1979.

Samarasinghe, D. M., ed. *Alagiyavanna Mukaveṭituman visin racanā karana lada Kusa Jātaka Kāvyaya*. Colombo: Sri Lanka Publishing Company, 1964.

Sannasgala, Puñcibandara. *Sinhala Sāhitya Vaṁśaya*. Colombo: Lake House, 1964.

Sannasgala, Puñcibandara. *Sinhala Sāhitya Vaṁśaya*. 1964. 2nd ed. Colombo: Department of Cultural Affairs, 1994.

Schilling, Derek. "Everyday Life and the Challenge to History in Postwar France: Braudel, Lefebvre, Certeau." *Diacritics*. 33/1 (2003): 23–40.

Schopen, Gregory. *Bones, Stones, and Buddhist Monks; Collected Papers on the Archaeology, Epigraphy, and Texts of Monastic Buddhism in India*. Honolulu: University of Hawai'i Press, 1997.

Scott, James C. *Domination and the Arts of Resistance: Hidden Transcripts*. New Haven, CT: Yale University Press, 1990.

Sedaraman, J. E. *Praśasti Kāvya Rasaya*. Colombo: M. D. Gunasena, 1970.

Selby, Martha Ann, trans. *Grow Long, Blessed Night: Love Poems from Classical India*. Oxford, UK: Oxford University Press, 2000.

Seneviratne, H. L. *Rituals of the Kandyan State*. Cambridge, UK: Cambridge University Press, 1978.

Seneviratne, H. L. *The Work of Kings: The New Buddhism in Sri Lanka*. Chicago: University of Chicago Press, 1999.

Seneviratne, Nagoda Ariyadasa, ed., *Pansiyapaṇas Jātaka Pot Vahansē*. 3 vols. Dehiwala, Sri Lanka: Buddhist Cultural Center, 1995.

Sheravanichkul, Arthid. "Self-Sacrifice of the Bodhisatta in the Paññāsa Jātaka," *Religion Compass*. 2/5 (2008): 769–787.

Shulman, David. *The Wisdom of Poets: Studies in Tamil, Telugu, and Sanskrit*. Oxford, UK: Oxford University Press, 2001.

Siegel, Lee. *Fires of Love—Waters of Peace: Passion and Renunciation in Indian Culture*. Honolulu: University of Hawai'i Press, 1983.

Siegel, Lee. *Sacred and Profane Dimensions of Love in Indian Traditions: As Exemplified in the Gitagovinda of Jayadeva*. Oxford, UK: Oxford University Press, 1978.

Skilling, Peter. "*Jātaka* and *Paññāsa-jātaka* in South-East Asia." *Journal of the Pali Text Society*. 28 (2006): 113–73.

Skilling, Peter. "Theravāda in History," *Pacific World*. 3rd Series, no. 11 (2009): 61–93.

Somadasa, K. D. *Catalogue of the Hugh Nevill Collection of Sinhalese Manuscripts in the British Library*, Vol. 5. London: The British Library, 1993.

Sorata, Velivitiye, ed., *Alagiyavanna Mukaveṭituman visin viracita Dahamsoňḍa Kava*. Colombo: Jinalankara Printers, 1934.

Sorata, Velivitiye, ed. *Eḷu Saňdäs Lakuṇa*. Colombo: Samayawardhana, 2005.

Sorata, Velivitiye, ed., *Kalpalatā Vyākhyā Sahita Kavsiḷumiṇa*. Galkisse, Sri Lanka: Abhaya Prakasakayo, 1966.

Sorata, Velivitiye, ed., *Śrī Sumaňgala Śabdakośaya*. 2 vols. Mount Lavinia, Sri Lanka: Abhaya Publishers, 1963, 1970.

Steele, Thomas. *Kusa Jātakaya, A Buddhistic Legend: Rendered for the First Time, into English Verse, from the Sinhalese Poem of Alagiyavanna Mohottala*. London: Trubner & Co., 1871.

Sternbach, Ludwik. "Indian Wisdom and Its Spread beyond India." *Journal of the American Oriental Society*. 101(1981): 97–131.

Sternbach, Ludwik. *Subhāṣita, Gnomic and Didactic Literature*. Wiesbaden, Germany: Otto Harrassowitz, 1974.

Stewart, Charles. "Relocating Syncretism in Social Science Discourse." In *Syncretism in Religion: A Reader*, edited by Anita Maria Leopold and Jeppe Sinding Jensen, 264–285. London: Equinox, 2004.

Strathern, Alan. *Kingship and Conversion in Sixteenth-Century Sri Lanka: Portuguese Imperialism in a Buddhist Land*. Cambridge, UK: Cambridge University Press, 2007.

Strathern, Alan. "Representations of Eastern Religion: Queyroz and Gonzaga on the first Catholic-Buddhist Disputation in Sri Lanka." *Journal of the Royal Asiatic Society of Sri Lanka*. XLIII (2000): 39–70.

Strathern, Alan. "Re-Reading Queirós: Some Neglected Aspects of the *Conquista*." *Sri Lanka Journal of the Humanities*. 26/1–2 (2000): 1–28.

Strong, John S. "'The Devil Was in That Little Bone': The Portuguese Capture and Destruction of the Buddha's Tooth Relic, Goa, 1561," *Past and Present*. 206, suppl. 5 (2010): 184–98.

Subrahmanyam, Sanjay. "Connected Histories: Notes towards a Reconfiguration of Early Modern Eurasia." *Modern Asian Studies*. 31/3 (1997): 735–62.

Subrahmanyam, Sanjay. "Hearing Voices: Vignettes of Early Modernity in South Asia, 1400–1750." *Daedalus*. 127/3 (1998): 75–104.

Subrahmanyam, Sanjay. *The Portuguese Empire in Asia 1500–1700: A Political and Economic History*. London: Longman, 1993.

Suraweera, A. V. "Alagiyavanna Mukaveṭitumā." In *Gampaha District: Socio-Cultural Studies*. Edited by A. V. Suraweera, 189–195. Battaramula, Sri Lanka: Department of Cultural Affairs, 1999.

Suraweera, A. V., trans. *Rājāvaliya*. Ratmalana, Sri Lanka: Sarvodaya Vishva Lekha, 2000.

Swearer, Donald K. "Buddhist Virtue, Voluntary Poverty, and Extensive Benevolence." *Journal of Religious Ethics* 26/1 (1998): 71–103.

Tennekoon, Rä., ed. *Sävul Sandēśaya*. Colombo: M. D. Gunasena, 1955.

Thomaz, Luís Filipe F. R. "Factions, Interests and Messianism: The Politics of Portuguese Expansion in the East, 1500–1521." *The Indian Economic and Social History Review*. 28/1 (1991): 97–109.

Trenckner, V., ed. *Majjhima-Nikāya*. Vol. I. London: Pali Text Society, 1888.

Trindade, Paulo da, *Conquista Espiritual do Oriente*. Edited by Fernando Félix Lopes. 3 vols. Lisbon: Centro de Estudos Históricos Ultramarinos, 1962–1967.

Tweed, Thomas A. "Theory and Method in the Study of Buddhism: Toward 'Translocative' Analysis." *Journal of Global Buddhism*. 12 (2011): 17–32.

Unebe, Toshiya. "Three Stories from the Thai Recension of the *Paññāsa Jātaka*: Transliteration and Preliminary Notes." *Journal of the School of Letters*. 3 (2007): 1–23.

Vacissara, Devundara, ed. *Bhāva sanna sahita Lō Väḍa Saṅgarāva*. Colombo: M. D. Gunasena, 1991.

Vijayavardhana, G. *Outlines of Sanskrit Poetics*. Varanasi, India: Chowkhamba Sanskrit Series Office, 1970.

Walshe, Maurice. *The Long Discourses of the Buddha: A Translation of the* Dīgha Nikāya. Boston: Wisdom Publications, 1995.

Warren, Henry Clarke and Dharmānanda Kosambi, eds. *Visuddhimagga of Buddhaghosācariya*. 1950. Reprint. Delhi, India: Motilal Banarsidass, 1989.

Wicki, Joseph, ed. *Documenta Indica* XVII (1595–1597). Rome: Institutum Historicum Societatis Iesu, 1988.

Wickramasinghe, K.D.P. *Haṁsa Sandēśaya*. Colombo: M. D. Gunasena, 1995.

Wickramasinghe, Martin. *Sinhalese Literature*, trans. E. R. Sarathchandra. Colombo: M. D. Gunasena, 1950.

Wickremasinghe, Nira. "La petition coloniale: objet de contrôle, objet de dissidence." *Identity, Culture & Politics*. 7/1 (2006): 1–16.

Wickramsinghe, Nira. *Sri Lanka in the Modern Age: A History of Contested Identities*. Honolulu: University of Hawai'i Press, 2006.

Wijesinghe, K.W.De A., ed. and tran. *Säḷalihiṇi Sandeśa*. New Edition. Colombo: Godage International Publishers, 2006.

Wijetunge, Edmund, trans. *Dahamsonda Jātaka Kavya: A Translation of Alagiyavanna's Dahamsonda Jataka Kavya into English Verse*. Colombo: The Colombo Apothecaries' Company, 1954.

Wimalahimi, Ambagaspitiye. *Siṅhala Haṭan (Kavi) Sāhitya Vimarśanaya.* Colombo: S. Godage and Brothers, 1998.

Wimalaratne, K.D.G. *Personalities Sri Lanka: A Biographical Study (15th-20th Century) [1490–1990 A.D.] A—Z.* Colombo: Ceylon Business Appliances, 1994.

Wittrock, Björn. "Early Modernities: Varieties and Transitions." *Daedalus.* 127/3 (1998): 19–40.

Xavier, Ângela Barreto. "Disquiet on the Island: Conversion, Conflicts and Conformity in Sixteenth-Century Goa." *The Indian Economic and Social History Review.* 44/3 (2007): 269–295.

Xavier, Ângela Barreto. *A Invenção de Goa: Poder Imperial e Conversões Culturais nos Séculos XVI e XVII.* Lisbon: Imprensa de Ciências Sociais, 2008.

Young, Robert J. C. *Colonial Desire: Hybridity in Theory, Culture and Race.* London: Routledge, 1995.

Young, Robert J. C. *Postcolonialism: A Historical Introduction.* Oxford, UK: Blackwell, 2001.

Županov, Ines G. *Disputed Mission: Jesuit Experiments and Brahmanical Knowledge in Seventeenth-Century India.* Oxford, UK: Oxford University Press, 1999.

Županov, Ines G. "Jesuit Orientalism: Correspondence between Tomás Pereira and Fernão de Querois." In *Tomás Pereira, S.J. (1646–1708): Life, Work and World,* edited by Luís Filipe Barreto, 43–73. Lisbon: Centro Científico e Cultural de Macau, 2010.

Zvelebil, K. V. *Tamil Literature.* Leiden, Netherlands: E. J. Brill, 1975.

Index

CPSIA information can be obtained
at www.ICGtesting.com
Printed in the USA
BVHW030054111221
623759BV00002B/30

9 780199 935789